CONTEMPORARY WOMEN DRAMATISTS

CONTEMPORARY LITERATURE SERIES

Contemporary American Dramatists
Contemporary British Dramatists
Contemporary Women Dramatists

CONTEMPORARY WOMEN DRAMATISTS

INTRODUCTION BY
LIZBETH GOODMAN

EDITOR
K.A. BERNEY

ASSOCIATE EDITOR
N.G. TEMPLETON

St J
St James Press

LONDON DETROIT WASHINGTON DC

Gale Research International Ltd.
PO Box 699
Cheriton House
North Way
Andover
Hants SP10 5YE
United Kingdom

or

Gale Research Inc.
835 Penobscot Bldg.
Detroit, MI 48226–4094
U.S.A.

ST. JAMES PRESS is an imprint of Gale Research International Ltd.
An Affiliated Company of Gale Research Inc.

A CIP catalogue record for this book is available from the British Library

ISBN 1–55862–212–8

Typeset by Florencetype Ltd, Kewstoke, Avon
Printed in the United Kingdom by Unwin Brothers Ltd, Woking

Published simultaneously in the United Kingdom and the United States of America

 The trade mark ITP is used under license

CONTENTS

EDITOR'S NOTE

The main part of *Contemporary Women Dramatists* contains entries on English-language writers for the stage.

The selection of writers included in this book is based on the recommendations of the advisers listed on page xvii and is intended to reflect the best and most prominent of contemporary women playwrights (those who are currently active, as well as some who have died since 1950, but whose reputations remain essentially contemporary).

The entry for each writer consists of a biography, a complete list of published and/or produced plays and all other separately published books, a selected list of bibliographies and critical studies on the writer, and a signed essay. In addition, entrants were invited to comment on their work.

We have listed plays that were produced but not published; librettos and musical plays are listed along with other plays. The dates given are those of first publication/performance.

Some of the entries in the Dramatists section are supplemented in the Works section, which provides essays on a selection of the best-known plays written by the entrants.

The book concludes with a play, radio play, television play and screenplay title index.

ACKNOWLEDGEMENTS

We would like to thank the following for their help with this project: all the advisers and contributors; Barbara Archer; Deirdre Clark; Jackie Griffin; Lesley Henderson; Jane Kellock; Daniel Kirkpatrick; Roda Morrison, Humanities Publisher, Thomas Nelson; the staff of the London Theatre Museum; the staff of the British Library and Westminster Reference Library; and our friends and colleagues at St. James.

INTRODUCTION

As the millennium approaches, the theatre is increasingly viewed as an 'industry' rather than an 'art'. The harsh economic climate demands that vital time and energy are taken up with seeking sponsorship, at the expense of concentrating on the production of plays. As a result, many theatres shy away from new plays by living authors, often resorting to the perennial revival of the 'classics' in order to ensure economic survival. In this context, it might be expected that women's theatre would die. But not so. It's true that the 'state of the arts' is not exactly conducive to the development of women's drama, but neither is it conducive to *any* work in the field of drama. However, the theatre survives, and women dramatists have proved themselves remarkably creative in finding ways not only to survive, but to thrive.

Women dramatists are on the increase, and the world is noticing. Despite the problems of the so-called industry *per se*, and the particular problems of working as women within it, women *are* making their mark: so much so that books about women's drama are now recognized as essential reading for schools and universities, rather than as optional extras. Yet this recognition has been recent, both in the theatre and in the academic and critical writing which helps to keep it alive.

Women's Drama vs. Women's Theatre

In looking at the history of women in the theatre, it is useful to begin by making a distinction between 'women dramatists' (the subject of this book) and women working in and writing for the theatre. First, the distinction between 'drama' and 'theatre' can be made: 'drama' is the body of literature written for performance, while 'theatre' is the body of performance. Drama is written, often published, and is available to be handed down to future generations. Theatre is performed; each production is ephemeral. Yet theatre is also handed down, as academic books about the theatre and journalists' reviews of individual productions serve to chronicle performances and theatre history, providing a context within which both drama and theatre can be studied.

The term 'women dramatists' refers primarily to women whose work has been published. Thus, the subject of 'women dramatists' may be approached historically, by looking to published accounts of the lives and work of women playwrights, with reference where possible to their (published) plays. But the work of women in the theatre also includes a whole range of forms, from physical theatre and devised work, to scripted plays, performance art, and solo work, none of which is published, and so not as readily available for study. All of the women included in *this* volume have published plays and each has been influenced, directly or indirectly, by the women who came before.

A Brief Historical Overview of Women's Drama

There is space here for only the most cursory overview of women's drama. To begin in ancient Greece: Sappho (7th-6th century BC), the classical lyric poet dubbed by Plato as the 'tenth muse', can be considered one of the first known women dramatists. Though most of her nine books of poems have been lost, what remains is highly valued by scholars today. While she wrote poetry rather than drama, Sappho's verse was 'dramatic' in the sense that it was intended for public presentation; some of it was performed in group choral activities for young women. Sappho is one of the earliest known woman writers in any medium. Today, both her life and her verse are often drawn upon and performed by women poets, actresses, and dramatists.

After the age of Greek classical drama, we know little of the history of theatre until the guild and church dramas (mystery and morality plays) of the Middle Ages. While women hardly feature in the recorded accounts of that period except as characters within plays, scholars have discovered recently a woman dramatist who wrote in the tenth century. Hrosvitha (also known as Hrotswitha and Roswitha), the 'nun of Gandersheim', was a Benedictine abbess who lived and worked from her cloister in Saxony. Her six verse plays in Latin were only re-discovered and translated into German in 1501. Her work dealt primarily with Christian history and morality, and some of it dramatized the lives of women saints. Thus Hrosvitha's work can be seen from a contemporary perspective as an early instance of a woman writing other women into history. Her work was probably not intended for performance, but its dramatic structure and characterization are related to the morality plays which followed, and make the plays adaptable to the stage; in fact, Edith Craig staged one of her plays, *Paphnutius*, in London in 1914.

A resounding silence from women in the theatre echoed on until the 17th century, when Aphra Behn made her mark on the English stage, soon followed by what might be seen as the first generation of English women dramatists. During the interregnum in England, only men and 'foreign' women performed in stage plays. On 21 August 1660, a Royal Warrant brought Englishwomen back to the stage. Yet even the Restoration did not immediately produce women dramatists: the return of English actresses led to an increase in parts for women and to a propensity of cross-dressing and 'breeches' parts which allowed women to show their legs, and contributed to the association of the acting profession with sexuality and promiscuity: an assumption which lingers today. The lives of women performers were made the subject of public scrutiny and in time some of these actors began to write plays for themselves (see Elizabeth Howe, *The First English Actress: Women and Drama 1660–1700*, Cambridge University Press, 1992). Theatre historians have uncovered a number of women writers, many followers of Behn, including six dramatists credited with writing over half of the total dramatic output of a period in the Queen Anne period (late seventeenth and early eighteenth centuries): Mary Pix (1666–1709), Catherine Trotter (1679–1749), Delarivier Manley (1663–1724), Susanna

Centlivre (1666–1723), Jane Wiseman (c1701), and Mary Davys (1674–1732), (see Lesley Ferris, *Acting Women*, Macmillan, 1990).

Then, to skip over the many women whose work was either not published or properly attributed ('Anonymous' *was*, quite often, a woman) in the 18th and early 19th centuries, we arrive in the late 19th century with the age of the 'New Woman' in drama. In England and in the U.S., women wrote plays, using theatre as a public platform for the artistic expression of their political views. With obvious irony—given the many female predecessors who made the suffrage movement possible—this is often referred to as the 'first wave' of women's drama (with Behn and her largely anonymous sisters classed as 'foremothers'). Names such as Elizabeth Robins and Cicely Hamilton are now familiar, and the plays of their American counterparts including Rachel Crothers, Susan Glaspell, and Sophie Treadwell have recently entered the dramatic canon as well, both in print and in performance (Treadwell's *Machinal* opened at the Royal National Theatre in London in 1993).

Contemporary Women Dramatists: 1968 to the Present

While drama was written by women in the early 20th century, it is the post-1968 period which is studied and taught in courses on modern women's drama. The quantity and the quality of women's drama produced in the past few decades is staggering, and can best be appreciated in its cultural context. It is generally agreed that the political and social unrest of the late 1960s and early 1970s was instrumental in the development of both the women's movement and alternative theatres (see, for instance, Michelene Wandor, *Carry on Understudies*, Routledge, 1981); both were necessary for the rise of women's playwriting, which developed in what had previously been a predominantly masculine domain. Theatre censorship was abolished by Act of Parliament in 1968, and the first British National Women's Liberation Conference was held in Oxford in 1969. The rise of the women's movement in this period influenced the first specifically gender-oriented political demonstrations since the suffragette movement. Such active representation of and by women in the public sphere influenced the growth of women playwrights on both sides of the Atlantic. At the same time, women's organizations emerged, from women's music companies to bookshops to magazines and political organizations, including the first women's theatre collectives.

It is difficult to discuss the rise of women dramatists without discussing the development of women's theatre groups, for such groups offered the space for trial and error which allowed women's work to develop. In the U.K., women dramatists of the 1950s and 1960s included Ann Jellicoe, Jane Arden, and Margaretta D'Arcy. Ann Jellicoe first learned the craft of playwriting with the English Stage Company at the Royal Court, where she was one woman among the much-noted 'angry young men' of her generation. Later Caryl Churchill tried out her work at the Royal Court. Churchill, now classed with Pinter as one of the most accomplished living playwrights, produced some of her greatest early work (including *Vinegar Tom, Light Shining in Buckinghamshire*, and *Cloud Nine*) with socialist and feminist theatre collectives. Similarly, many American women dramatists have worked closely with particular theatre companies; for instance, Megan Terry's work is intimately related to the development of the Omaha Magic Theater. In both England and the U.S., the growth of 'fringe' and 'alternative' theatres was influential in providing new experimental spaces where unknown playwrights, including many women, could take the stage.

In the late 1960s and 1970s, women dramatists wrote plays informed by, but not restricted to, feminist politics. Caryl Churchill, Olwen Wymark, Maureen Duffy, Pam Gems, and Louise Page were followed in the 1980s by Timberlake Wertenbaker, Sarah Daniels, Clare McIntyre, Sharman MacDonald, Winsome Pinnock, Charlotte Keatley and Deborah Levy, who began to write different kinds of feminist theatre. Many women dramatists found, unsurprisingly, that women's theatre groups were most interested in and most likely to produce their plays. The work of the playwrights named above benefited enormously from the activity of companies such as Mrs. Worthington's Daughters, Monstrous Regiment, Women's Theatre Group (now called The Sphinx), Siren and Gay Sweatshop.

In the U.S., the period immediately preceding the post-1968 'revolution' included Alice Childress, Lorraine Hansberry, and Lillian Hellman. In 1972, the Women's Theatre Council was formed in New York by six playwrights: María Irene Fornés, Rosalyn Drexler, Julie Bovasso, Adrienne Kennedy, Rochelle Owens and Megan Terry. Companies such as It's OK To Be A Women emerged, followed by At the Foot of the Mountain, the Women's Experimental Theatre, the Omaha Magic Theater, and later, Split Britches, Spiderwoman Theatre, and many others. Individual playwrights such as Marsha Norman and Wendy Kesselman followed, and were followed in turn by the current generation: Wendy Wasserstein, Tina Howe, Beth Henley, Ntozake Shange, Paula Vogel, and others. Canadian women's drama also developed, including the work of Sharon Pollock and Erika Ritter.

Of course, women's drama is not confined to (or defined by) work from the U.K. and North America. Women dramatists in Australia and Europe, and indeed from around the world, have all contributed to the body of work now known as 'women's drama'. Not much has yet made it onto any college or university reading lists, however, and this marginalization of women's drama is a subject worthy of further investigation.

Gate-Keeping: The Politics of Publication and Production

Virginia Woolf, one of the few women writers to be routinely included in the new canon of English literature, wrote about the exclusion of women from higher education and access to public power in her landmark work, *A Room of One's Own* (first published in 1929). She proposed that Shakespeare might have had a sister, who would have died unknown, her life's work hidden from history because of her sex. In a sense, all contemporary women dramatists are figurative descendants of Shakespeare's sister, helped along in their struggle for recognition by the work and words of the women who came before them. In days gone by, the lack of higher education for women imposed restrictions on many women's access to the language of dramatic writing. And of course, time for reading was a luxury which few women could afford. In previous generations as now, gender, race, and class have been used to maintain a status quo, allowing some sectors of society control of the means to education, and to the language with which to write the literature and history of each age. The system has worked to keep many potential writers locked out of 'the gate', to borrow

Virginia Woolf's metaphor for restricting women's access to education and public power.

The politics of production and publication still present obstacles to contemporary 'Shakespeare's sisters'. Even though some of these gates have been opened, there are other gate-keepers at the door: producers and commercial sponsors and publishers with everything to lose by taking a chance on unknown writers. Since real economic and political circumstances conspire to keep women dramatists on the margins, a tremendous counter-surge of energy and commitment is needed to bring them centre stage. Feminist scholars have helped tremendously on this front, not least by 'discovering' a number of important women dramatists of earlier ages, including Sappho, Hrosvitha, and Aphra Behn, whose work has now been recognized as canonical.

Firing the Canon

The dramatic 'canon' is that body of work considered to be of greatest value, and of most importance to those studying drama today. It consists of the plays most often set on secondary school and university courses: Shakespeare, Ibsen, Chekhov, Shaw et al. But in recent years, due in large part to the influence of feminist critics who have challenged the assumptions inherent to the choice of such texts, the canon has been revised and expanded, and now includes a few plays by women, a few by women of colour, and a few by lesbian women. But this process of expanding the canon has been very controversial, not only in drama but in literature as a whole. The metaphor of battle is not too extreme to represent the situation of women academics arguing for inclusion of women's work; arguing, in effect, that women have written work of great enough 'value' (a highly subjective term) to be considered worthy of the attention of readers and students today.

Because the canon traditionally has been male, and because men have been in positions of power to determine what was accepted as canonical, women's work has remained on the margins. Even successful women's theatre of recent years is often seen as 'alternative', not necessarily due to its form or politics, but because it is written by women. Yet as in all artistic and social movements, the 'alternative' eventually *becomes* the mainstream as other 'alternatives' emerge. So the 'angry young men' (the young writers thought to have transformed the nature of British theatre by their early 'radical' work, including John Osborne, John Arden, Arnold Wesker, and others) and even Ann Jellicoe are now part of the 'theatre establishment' against and in response to which younger playwrights work. Jellicoe's play *The Knack* is now part of the British theatrical canon of contemporary drama, as are a number of plays by Caryl Churchill.

Yet very few women's plays have entered the canon, except on reading lists in 'women's studies' and 'gender and performance' courses. Very few feminist plays have been produced in London's West End or New York's Broadway circuits, though there are a few notable exceptions, including Lorraine Hansberry's award-winning production of *A Raisin in the Sun* on Broadway and later in London's West End (1959), Pam Gems's *Queen Christina*, produced in Stratford by the Royal Shakespeare Company (1977), Sarah Daniels's acclaimed production of *Neaptide* at London's National Theatre (1986), Caryl Churchill's West End success with *Serious Money* (1987–8), Timberlake

Wertenbaker's success with *Our Country's Good* (1988), and Wendy Wasserstein's Broadway hit *The Heidi Chronicles* (1988). These and a few other plays excepted, it is generally the case that neither academic nor commercial values have judged women's drama, much less feminist theatre to be 'suitable' for inclusion. The few plays which are occasionally embraced are the exceptions which prove the rule. The popularity of playwrights such as Caryl Churchill and Timberlake Wertenbaker—not only in the U.K. but also in Canada and the U.S., and recently in Eastern Europe—suggests that there may be something 'mainstreamable' about the work which makes it into the canon: it is not only of a high quality, but is also acceptable to the masses. Therefore (with the very rare exception of *Neaptide*—Daniels's controversial play about the rights of a lesbian mother), it is still very rare for overtly political feminist theatre to gain widespread critical attention or acclaim, partly because theatres judge such work too risky to produce in mainstream venues, and perhaps also partly because most theatre critics are male. With this context in mind, it may seem ironic but not surprising that Agatha Christie (the phenomenally success-ful crime writer whose fiction has been frequently adapted for the stage) remains the most produced 'English woman dramatist' of our time.

Because the women included in this volume have all published plays, their work is already canonized to a much greater extent than many of their unpublished sisters. The publish or perish cycle is a very real phenomenon: plays which are produced will survive only to the extent that they are written about; hence the crucial role of the theatre critic, and the efforts made by feminist scholars to legitimize women's drama by writing and teaching about it, thereby making it a part of the literary and theatrical canon.

Themes and Issues in Women's Drama

Women have written and are writing many kinds of drama, in many styles and forms, from domestic drama to social realism to feminist issue plays to comedy to tragedy to farce. In all this work, certain themes and scenarios have emerged repeatedly in the past two decades, in work by women of very different cultures. These include: mother/daughter relationships, incest, rape, child abuse, pornography, equal pay, sexual harassment, the plight of single mothers and lesbian mothers, race relations, gender/power relations, women's com-petition and solidarity, the conflicting pressures of work and family, eating disorders, lesbian friendships and sexual relationships, the process of lesbian 'coming out', and the act of self-representation. This not only suggests that women find these themes interesting (if not necessary) to express, but also that these themes have been part of a developing feminist consciousness in the theatre. The themes, which are based on the experiences of the writers and performers as women, have informed the development of the field of drama. The theatre has in turn functioned as a public forum for representation of these issues: a framework within which women may see themselves and their own experiences, often by experimenting with the representation of self and gender in a multiplicity of ways. The operative thematic cycle of women's theatre has progressed from topics such as birth control and *Care and Control* (the title of an early play by the women of Gay Sweatshop, looking at the issue of child custody), to some of the most contentious topics of the 1990s: commercialism, political revolutions in Eastern Europe and elsewhere, the spread of AIDS, and the threat of environmental disaster. With such changes in social climates come changes in the images created by theatre makers in different cultures.

Consideration of the themes and issues raised in any playwright's work is crucial to an understanding of that writer's reception in her own context. One reason why women's work has begun to gain greater recognition is the discovery of central themes and ideas which recur in women's work from around the world. Feminist anthropologists and social scientists have assisted in a creative cross-fertilization between cultures by noting the roots of stories and myths in the folk-tales, songs, nursery rhymes and rhythms of indigenous peoples in Africa, Asia, South and North America. Today, women's work in the theatre includes 'revisions' of the classics, reworkings of Shakespeare to offer the same stories from a female perspective, plays about the lives of creative women, as well as many original plays. Contemporary women's plays can also take more experimental forms, from storytelling theatre to dance/ theatre and choropoems (choreographed poetry for performance) used in the plays of Ntozake Shange and Jackie Kay; to the performance art-inspired work of Deborah Levy to the multi-media work of Megan Terry, to traditional plays which deal with untraditional subjects. Detailed study of women's theatres shows that the work produced is wide-ranging in terms of form and content (see Lizbeth Goodman, *Contemporary Feminist Theatres: To Each Her Own*, Routledge, 1993).

Contributions of Women Dramatists Today

Publishing plays by women and biographical information about women dramatists allows scholarship to take account of women's contributions, and also has practical implications for women working in the theatre today. Women's plays tend to offer more and better parts for women, crucial to the careers of actresses, who find that parts dry up between their late twenties (when 'ingenue' parts are available) and mid forties (when offers for the 'matronly' roles may be made). But age is not the only factor affecting women's roles in the theatre. Today, women's plays offer a wide range of parts for women of all ages and physical descriptions; it seems that women drama-tists are particularly skilled at creating characters of depth and variety—not just the usual collection of feminine stereotypes. Women dramatists can— though they do not always choose to do so—write from a variety of perspec-tives, creating diverse and exciting parts for women (and men).

Plays by women also offer work for women directors, not only because some women directors find themselves particularly engaged by the themes and issues raised in women's plays—some feel they can identify, at a personal level, as well as understand at an intellectual level and interpret artistically—but also because some women playwrights prefer to work with women directors. While mainstream theatre tends still to be directed by men (with a few notable exceptions such as Annie Castledine, Deborah Warner, and Katie Mitchell), many women's plays are produced in small 'alternative' theatres, which offer space for trial and error for women directors as well as women playwrights, some of whom will eventually break into the mainstream, if they want to.

Perhaps most importantly, plays by women are popular with audiences. More than half of nearly every theatre audience is female (and some surveys suggest that the figures are much higher). Just as plays by women offer strong parts for performers and points of identification for directors, so they offer characters on stage with whom women in the audience can identify. At the same time, it must be a good thing for everyone—men as well as women, boys as well as girls—that women on stage have begun to reflect more of the diversity of 'real' women's lives. If the stage does 'hold a mirror up to life', then the mirror may finally be reflecting women as well as men, offering young people positive and plentiful role models, and lots of female characters—some good, some bad, some 'realistic' and some not—to view, interpret, and enjoy.

Despite all these benefits and contributions, however, the theatre is under threat, and women's drama along with it. Women dramatists still rely to some extent on the enthusiasm of women's theatre groups to promote and produce their work. Women's theatre groups are still formed regularly, but lack of adequate funding often forces them to close or to re-group. This lack of collective support forces women's drama into the open market, often without the initial support of collective theatre work. Individually or collectively, though, women dramatists continue to produce new work. As they write, they gain confidence in their own voices and learn to refine their styles. The public has noticed. Plays by and about women are beginning to receive more mainstream attention and awards. In general, the economic climate notwithstanding, things are looking up for contemporary women dramatists and their audiences.

In secondary schools, drama colleges, and universities in the past few years there has been a significant increase in the general awareness of the attention paid to gender in reading and studying literature and drama. This shift is evidenced in the establishment of several excellent (academic and practical) gender and performance programmes, as well as in the increasing application of gender issues to theatre studies, and of theatre and performance theory to women's studies. The playtexts of several feminist theatre companies, as well as the plays of individual women, have recently been published. It is now possible to read plays as 'drama texts', and also to consider plays in performance.

Books such as this one serve to remind us just how much work women dramatists have produced, and just how frightening that is for those who would prefer to keep their heads buried in an out-dated (and never accurate) notion that women have not been prolific dramatists. This book and others like it can help to keep women's plays alive, and to ensure that the work of women dramatists is recognized today, and remembered tomorrow.

—Lizbeth Goodman

ADVISERS

Judith E. Barlow
C.W.E. Bigsby
Michael Billington
Katharine Brisbane
Ned Chaillet
Ruby Cohn

Tish Dace
Lizbeth Goodman
Anthony Graham-White
Nick Hern
Holly Hill
Joel Schechter

CONTRIBUTORS

Addell Austin Anderson
Frances Rademacher Anderson
Roger Baker
Carol Banks
Judith E. Barlow
Joss Bennathon
Linda Ben-Zvi
Gerald M. Berkowitz
Katharine Brisbane
Constance Brissenden
Susan Carlson
Ned Chaillet
Ruby Cohn
Clare Colvin
Patricia Cooke
Karen Cronacher
Tish Dace
Elin Diamond
Tony Dunn
Jane Edwardes
Peter Fitzpatrick
Helen Gilbert
Reid Gilbert
Lizbeth Goodman
Anthony Graham-White
Frances Gray
Prabhu S. Guptara
Carole Hayman
Ronald Hayman
Morgan Y. Himelstein

Naomi Iizuka
Christopher Innes
John Istel
Kimball King
John G. Kuhn
Michael T. Leech
Frank Marcus
Howard McNaughton
Tony Mitchell
Olu Obafemi
Judy Lee Oliva
M. Elizabeth Osborn
Malcolm Page
Dorothy Parker
Sylvia Paskin
Roxana Petzold
James Roose-Evans
Arthur Sainer
Ellen Schiff
Adrienne Scullion
Elaine Shragge
Michael Sidnell
Christopher Smith
Sandra Souchotte
Carol Simpson Stern
Alan Strachan
Joanne Tompkins
Elaine Turner
Michelene Wandor
B.A. Young

LIST OF DRAMATISTS

Ama Ata Aidoo
JoAnne Akalaitis
Jane Arden

Enid Bagnold
Djuna Barnes
Bridget Boland
Carol Bolt
Julie Bovasso
Brigid Brophy

Mary Chase
Alice Childress
Agatha Christie
Caryl Churchill
Darrah Cloud
Constance S. Congdon
Rachel Crothers

Sarah Daniels
Margaretta D'Arcy
Alma De Groen
Shelagh Delaney
Rosalyn Drexler
Maureen Duffy
Andrea Dunbar
Nell Dunn

Marcella Evaristi

María Irene Fornés

Shirley Gee
Pam Gems

Lorraine Hansberry
Lillian Hellman
Beth Henley
Dorothy Hewett
Joan Holden
Margaret Hollingsworth
Debbie Horsfield
Tina Howe

Debbie Isitt

Ann Jellicoe

Charlotte Keatley
Adrienne Kennedy
Wendy Kesselman
Ruth Krauss

Bryony Lavery
Doris Lessing
Deborah Levy
Liz Lochhead
Tes Lyssiotis

Sharman MacDonald
Emily Mann
Elaine May
Clare McIntyre
Susan Miller
Rona Munro
Iris Murdoch

Marsha Norman

Mary O'Malley
Rochelle Owens

Louise Page
Suzan-Lori Parks
Winsome Pinnock
Sharon Pollock

Hannie Rayson
Christina Reid
Renée
Anne Ridler
Erika Ritter

Milcha Sánchez-Scott
Joan M. Schenkar
Ntozake Shange
Jill Shearer
Beverley Simons
Dodie Smith
Zulu Sofola
Karen Sunde
Efua Sutherland

Megan Terry
Judith Thompson
Sue Townsend

Paula Vogel

Michelene Wandor
Wendy Wasserstein
Timberlake Wertenbaker
Olwen Wymark

Susan Yankowitz

LIST OF WORKS

Alice Childress
Wedding Band

Caryl Churchill
Cloud Nine

Rachel Crothers
He and She

Sarah Daniels
Masterpieces

Alma De Groen
The Rivers of China

Shelagh Delaney
A Taste of Honey

María Irene Fornés
Fefu and Her Friends

Pam Gems
Queen Christina

Lorraine Hansberry
A Raisin in the Sun

Lillian Hellman
The Little Foxes

Beth Henley
Crimes of the Heart

Dorothy Hewett
The Chapel Perilous

Ann Jellicoe
The Knack

Adrienne Kennedy
Funnyhouse of a Negro

Wendy Kesselman
My Sister in This House

Marsha Norman
'Night, Mother

Sharon Pollock
Blood Relations

Ntozake Shange
*For Colored Girls Who Have
Considered Suicide When the
Rainbow is Enuf*

Paula Vogel
The Baltimore Waltz

Wendy Wasserstein
The Heidi Chronicles

Timberlake Wertenbaker
Three Birds Alighting on a Field

CONTEMPORARY
WOMEN DRAMATISTS

A

AIDOO, (Christina) Ama Ata.

Ghanaian. Born in Abeadzi Kyiakor in 1942. Educated at the University of Ghana, Legon (Institute of African Studies fellowship), B.A. (honours) 1964; Stanford University, California. Lecturer in English, University of Cape Coast, Ghana, 1970–82; PNDC Secretary (Minister) for Education, 1982–83; writer-in-residence, University of Richmond, Virginia, 1989. Recipient: Fulbright scholarship, 1988. Address: P.O. Box 4930, Harare, Zimbabwe.

Publications

PLAYS

The Dilemma of a Ghost (produced 1964). 1965.
Anowa (produced 1991). 1970.

NOVELS

Our Sister Killjoy; or, Reflections from a Black-eyed Squint. 1977.
Changes—A Love Story. 1991.

SHORT STORIES

No Sweetness Here. 1970.
The Eagle and the Chickens and Other Stories. 1986.

VERSE

Someone Talking to Sometime. 1985.
Birds and Other Poems. 1987.

OTHER

Dancing Out Doubts. 1982.

CRITICAL STUDIES: *Ama Ata Aidoo: The Dilemma of a Ghost* (study guide) by Jane W. Grant, 1980; *Women Writers in Black Africa* by Lloyd Brown, 1981; *Ngambika: Studies of Women in African Literature* edited by Carole Boyce Davies and Anne Adams Greaves, 1986; *Diverse Voices: Essays on Twentieth-Century Women Writers in English* edited by Harriet Devine Jump, 1991.

Ama Ata Aidoo's two plays focus upon women's relationship to traditional values; in both plays the husband—the central male character—is ineffectual and unwilling to comprehend the effect of his actions or inaction on his wife.

A stock situation in African drama is the conflict between the modern ideas of the "been-to"—the man who has been to Europe for his education—and the traditions of his community. The title of Aidoo's first play, *The Dilemma of a Ghost*, comes from a song that we hear children singing, which the university graduate Ato loved as a child and which he now sees as symbolizing his position:

> One early morning,
> When the moon was up
> Shining as the sun,
> I went to Elmina Junction
> And there and there,
> I saw a wretched ghost
> Going up and down
> Singing to himself
>   "Shall I go
>   To Cape Coast,
>   Or to Elmina
>   I don't know,
>   I can't tell.
>   I don't know,
>   I can't tell."

The title character of Aidoo's other play, *Anowa*, who has followed her own will in defiance of her community's expectations, also refers to herself as a ghost. The metaphor points to the isolation and strain felt by someone who has set himself or herself apart from the life and values of the community.

African playwrights have tended to identify with the "been-to," but in *The Dilemma of a Ghost* Ato is almost unbelievably callow. He has not told his family that while in America he married. Nor does he explain, when they are concerned about his wife's infertility—not even when they come to subject her to curative herbal massage—that he has insisted upon using contraception. Nor, it seems, has he prepared his wife Eulalie in any way for the attitudes she will encounter in his home village.

The other twist on the dramatic norm is that he has married not a white but a black woman—someone who is, to his family's horror, the descendant of slaves. She, too, is a rather unsympathetic figure, filled with false suppositions about "native" life and increasingly given to drinking too much.

Given such a central couple (and the not altogether believable Americanisms that Eulalie is given), the vitality of the play lies in the women of Ato's village, in his mother and sister and in the two neighbouring women who act as chorus. It is from their perspective that the marriage and its conflicts are seen:

> My people have a lusty desire
> To see the tender skin
> On top of a child's scalp
> Rise and fall with human life.
> Your machines, my stranger-girl,

Cannot go on an errand
They have no hands to dress you when you are dead . . .

It is the compassion of Ato's mother that in the end leads her to rebuke her son and draw his wife into the family.

In Aidoo's second play, Anowa is a beautiful but willful girl whose mother resists the vocation of priestess that others foresee for her daughter. For her part, Anowa refuses the suitors of her parents' choice, marries a man the community considers a good-for-nothing, and leaves her village forever. With her aid, her husband Kofi prospers in trade with the British, but Anowa, driven by some inner vision, refuses the perquisites and leisure that her husband and (as in her earlier play) a choral pair take for granted. Finally, after a quarrel in which Anowa guesses the priest told Kofi that she has destroyed his manhood and that he half-believes her to be a witch, he shoots himself, and she drowns herself.

Remarkably, by comparison with many other African plays, the historical events of the late 19th century are relegated to the background. The British, for example, are represented only by a picture of Queen Victoria hanging in Kofi's house. There is some suggestion that in her sensitivity to "the common pain and the general wrong," and especially in her acute discomfort with the institution of slavery, Anowa represents Africa. But more intensely felt and conveyed is the misery of her personal situation: self-exile from her community, childlessness, and profound alienation from her husband's way of life. Aidoo uses the historical setting to present freshly the call for a more liberated role for women. Anowa says, "I hear in other lands a woman is nothing. And they let her know this from the day of her birth. But here, O my spirit mother, they let a girl grow up as she pleases until she is married. And then she is like any woman anywhere: in order for her man to be a man, she must not think, she must not talk." But Aidoo avoids the overt didacticism of some other African plays on women's roles by placing her central character in another century where her attitudes appear eccentric.

Ama Ata Aidoo's plays are individual, wry, sometimes poetic, and—in the case of *The Dilemma of a Ghost*—humorous. They deal with important themes, but these are secondary to the particular characters who are comfortable in or alienated from the community at the heart of the plays.

—Anthony Graham-White

AKALAITIS, JoAnne.

American. Born in Chicago, Illinois, 29 June 1937. Educated at the University of Chicago, B.A. in philosophy 1960. Married Philip Glass (divorced); one daughter. Presented work and taught playwriting throughout North America, Europe, Australia, Nicaragua, Israel, and Japan. Co-founder of Mabou Mines, New York, 1970, and performer, designer, and director, 1970–90; playwright-in-residence, Mark Taper Forum, Los Angeles, 1984–85; artistic associate, Joseph Papp Public Theater, New York, 1990–91; artistic director, New York Shakespeare Festival, 1991–92. Recipient: Obie award, 1976, 1977, 1979, 1984; Guggenheim fellowship, 1981; Rosemund Gilder award,

1981; Drama Desk award, 1983; Rockefeller grant, 1984. Agent: Flora Roberts, 157 West 57th Street, New York, New York 10019, U.S.A.

Publications

PLAYS

Southern Exposure (produced 1979).
Dead End Kids: A History of Nuclear Power, music by David Byrne (produced 1980).
Green Card (produced 1986). 1991.
The Voyage of the Beagle, (opera), music by Jon Gibson (produced 1986).

SCREENPLAY: *Dead End Kids: A History of Nuclear Power*, 1986.

THEATRICAL ACTIVITIES

DIRECTOR: **Plays**—all her own plays; *Cascando* by Samuel Beckett, 1976; *Dressed Like an Egg*, based on the writings of Colette, 1977; *Request Concert* by Franz Xaver Kroetz, 1981; *Red and Blue* by Michael Hurson, 1982; *Through the Leaves* by Franz Xaver Kroetz, 1984; *The Photographer* by Philip Glass, 1984; *Endgame* by Samuel Beckett, 1985; *Help Wanted* by Franz Xaver Kroetz, 1986; *The Balcony* by Jean Genet;*American Notes* by Len Jenkin, 1988; *Leon & Lena (and Lenz)* by George Büchner, 1989; *The Screens* by Jean Genet, 1989; *Cymbeline* by Shakespeare, 1989; *'Tis Pity She's a Whore* by John Ford, 1990; *Henry IV, Parts One and Two* by Shakespeare, 1991; *Prisoner of Love* by Jean Genet, 1992; *Woyzeck* by Georg Büchner, 1992. **Film**—*Dead End Kids*, 1986.
ACTOR: **Plays**—Role in *Dressed Like an Egg*, 1977; *The Shaggy Dog Animation* by Lee Breuer, 1977; *Dark Ride* by Len Jenkin, 1981.

The title "avant-gardist" has stuck with JoAnne Akalaitis since she co-founded Mabou Mines. More anathema than blessing, it has prompted prejudice and a fundamental misunderstanding of her work. But Akalaitis is interested in the vicissitudes of human nature, a complex pursuit that requires her to delve deeply. Consequently, the theater of JoAnne Akalaitis has frequently been called "impenetrable," or "intimidating." Less interested in effect, she probes for cause: how does a noble quest become corrupt? (*Dead End Kids; The Voyage of the Beagle*); wherefore man's inhumanity to man? (*Green Card*). To do this, Akalaitis writes (and directs) with the focus on key links within the chain of events. Identified, the links are then viewed through a microscope. In much the same way that her physicists in *Dead End Kids* probe for the quintessence of an inanimate element, Akalaitis contemplates the cognizant animal.

    One could take such a comparison further and say that, in a sense, to experience Akalaitis's theater is to sit in at the atomic level. At first sight, it appears chaotic: it is consuming, frenetic, kinetic, volatile, and often unforgiving. She eschews plot and narrative, alternately flashing, and contrasting, theory and practice. Dubious of rhetoric, she renders dialogue almost secondary in the process. The preservation of temporal and spatial continuity does not always accurately reflect cause and effect, and when it does not, Akalaitis arranges her own chronology. Not satisfied with actors simply reading dialogue and making the occasional gesture, she synthesizes a variety of media. Thus choreographer, composer, and photographer are as integral to the play as the text. Her atomic stage is rich in both image and language, and explicitly reflects the intensity of everyday life. The result is an almost successful transmogrification of theater, forming what critics have referred to as a "gestalt"—the creation of an environment where it is impossible to distill any element from the play without radically altering the work.

Akalaitis's concern with the shortcomings of language is perhaps best reflected in *Green Card*, a rapid-fire montage of music, slides, songs, dance, words, and film. It is a caustic satire concerning superficial values, bringing face-to-face the Haves (citizens of the United States) and Have Nots (refugees seeking asylum in the States). The play demonstrates how language is a trap and how its subscribers are too easily held captive. Immigrants struggle to understand the subtleties of the English language. "Learn English! Learn English!" native speakers of Vietnamese, Yiddish, Spanish, Russian, Chinese are warned or be faced with ignorance and confusion—even death. Yet when they resolve to do so, what they learn is that they have not been adequately prepared to comprehend it. For example, when a student asks for an explanation of the "REAL difference between 'I was writing' and 'I have written',", the response is an impatient: "'I was writing' is the imperfect tense while 'I have written' is the present perfect tense." Not quite sure what to make of this answer, the student denigrates herself (acknowledging the inferiority of her race) until the evening school teacher responds grandly: "The imperfect tense refers to what WAS, while the present perfect tense refers to what HAS BEEN."

To obtain a green card, that precious document promising a life with dignity and reward to thousands of refugees, characters must compete on The Green Card Show, the "game you have to play if you want to stay." Mocking the consumer culture, Akalaitis transforms Ellis Island into a TV game show set complete with canned applause and neon lights. If they win, the prize, of course, is permission to stay in the country; to lose however, is to "get sent back to where they belong." Akalaitis pummels characters and audience with idioms, building to a frenzy: what is the difference between "burn up," "burn down," "burnt out"; how does one get "carried away" without movement; how do Zan and Rich "pull off" a joke—what is being removed and from where? Her questions are ambiguous and mischievous enough to confuse a native American-English speaker:

Q: What is the most contemporary use of the expression to TURN ONE
   ON or to TURN ONE OFF?
   a: Pretty women certainly TURN Charlie ON?
   b: Some of the Great Renaissance painters TURN me ON but some
      of the modern ones TURN me OFF.
   c. Minimalist post-modern performance art of the 1980's is a real
      TURN OFF for me.

Finally, language becomes more than just a trap—a prison and a kind of torture as an immigrant is grilled by officials to reveal his history and recent whereabouts. With search lights flashing across her stage and whistles at ear-piercing decibels, Akalaitis's immigration officials weed out the sick and undesirable and begin the examinations at break-neck speed. Struggling to keep up and misunderstanding the occasional trick question, the applicant begins blurting out responses half in English, half in Spanish.

This adroit manipulation of the traditional dramatic form is perhaps best experienced in *Dead End Kids*. Akalaitis has referred to this as an "impassioned repudiation of nuclear ineptitude." In context, it is a history of science (specifically, physics) beginning with 15th-century alchemists and ending in the present with the careless and devastating misuse of nuclear power. *Dead End Kids* is concerned with how, in spite of the best intentions, the human journey for knowledge is doomed. Released from its narrative, the play shifts into a whirling multimedia extravaganza. Switching to variety show format (circa 1962) our host and hostess primp and pose and gloss over any potentially distressing news items. Scenes change, and time shifts. Our hostess daydreams and the magic potions of an alchemist bubble forth. Another shift: suddenly, we are at a science fair where a young pupil and his perky teacher announce "This is the H bomb." Producing ingredients and parts from a bag, we are informed: "It's a question of design, not ingredients." "Be careful," our older guide counsels, "it would be such a pity to have even the tiniest explosion." Slides of Hiroshima and Nagasaki remind us just what sort of pity. "Spllllaaaaat! Nagasaki" reiterates Akalaitis. We witness explosion after explosion. Flash: a scene has changed; fragments fall and form new vignettes. She is as much an alchemist as the mysterious cloaked characters who mix potions and recite spells. The alchemist strives in vain to turn base metals into gold, while Akalaitis separates the elements of drama and recombines them to produce a strikingly original theater.

—Roxana Petzold

ARDEN, Jane.

British. Born in Wales. Has two children. Director of the women's theatre company Holocaust, since 1970. Address: c/o John Calder Ltd., 18 Brewer Street, London, W1R 4AS, England.

Publications

PLAYS

Conscience and Desire, and *Dear Liz* (produced 1954).
The Party (produced 1958). 1958.
Vagina Rex and the Gas Oven (produced 1969). 1971.
A New Communion—for Freaks, Prophets and Witches (produced 1971).

SCREENPLAYS: *The Logic Game*, 1966; *Separation* (as Jane Dewar), 1968; *The Other Side of the Underneath*, 1973; *Vibration*, 1974; *Anti-Clock*, 1979.

TELEVISION PLAY: *The Thug*, 1959.

VERSE
You Don't Know What You Want, Do You? 1978.

THEATRICAL ACTIVITIES

DIRECTOR: **Film**—*The Other Side of the Underneath*, 1973.

ACTOR: **Plays**—Betty Lewis in *Dear Liz*, and Conscience in *Conscience and Desire*, 1954; Julia Craven in *The Philanderer* by Shaw, 1966. **Films**—*A Gunman Has Escaped*, 1948; *The Logic Game*, 1966; *Separation*, 1968. **Television**—*Romeo and Juliet*, 1947; *The Logic Game*, 1965; Inez in *Huis Clos*, by Sartre.

Jane Arden comments:

Biology—physics—genetics—observation of phenomena—leading to self-discovery—opening of the inner world—books (rarely)—signpost the reader to a richer textured experience of the universe-arousing the reader from his slumber—awakening him to a more illuminating perception of 'being' in the world.

Reading can be as paralysing an act (even absorbing so-called erudite works) as Bingo, if the information does not recreate the being and radicalize the behaviour. There are no such things as creative writers—some people have better radio-sets for tuning in to the only creation.

The world needs healers, not 'artists'. Some of my signposts: Gurdjieff: *All and Everything*; *Tibetan Book of the Dead*; Wilhelm Reich's *Sexual Revolution*; C. Jung's *Psychology and Alchemy* and *Modern Man in Search of a Soul*; *I Chiang*; Rumi (12th century Sufi poet-saint); writings of Malcolm X.

Jane Arden is an astonishing, and perhaps even unique, figure in contemporary drama. She is impossible to categorize, and would almost certainly rebel against any attempt to do so for her work is notable for its very wide range of technical resources harnessed to serve her one main theme, which is the oppression of women in our society.

She is a social-political writer. There, are of course, many dramatists whose motivation is primarily political and whose dynamism is derived from an urgent need to put across a particular message. But unlike them, Jane Arden has never tried to conform to the conventional structures of the theatre; the three-walled box set, the need for careful in-depth characterization, the beginning-middle-end construction are irrelevant to her. Instead she has drawn on techniques and influences from the cinema, television, and other manifestations of contemporary media (light projection, pop music). Message and the way she puts it across are closely linked: she subverts the railway tracks of the mind and of theatrical expectations.

But this was not always so. Early in her career, as a dramatist in the most conventional manner possible, she wrote a play that is not only constructed with all the formality of conventional drama, but which was produced at a major London theatre with a major commercial cast that included Charles Laughton, Elsa Lanchester, Albert Finney, and Joyce Redman. This was *The Party*, a penetrating and often touching exploration of adolescent conflicts, providing, incidentally, some very rewarding, if wordy, roles for the actors.

It would strain the use of hindsight beyond viability to detect in this play the seeds of Jane Arden's later development. Here her concern was with the conflict between reality and the fantasy-aspirations of the teenage heroine Henrietta, who wishes to see herself as a glamorous, wealthy, perhaps even debby type of girl. Her family and circumstances deny her all of these aspirations: the father is an alcoholic just returned from a cure, the home is grim and dingy, the mother fighting a tough battle and taking in lodgers. The play shows Henrietta's cruelty in denying the reality of her existence and eventual reconciliation with a kind of truth.

It is indeed possible to see that the women in this play are oppressed, but this oppression is accepted and in the context of the play not overtly commented upon, though as a whole the play does make a strong comment on the way in which individuals are distorted, emotionally and socially, by attempting to conform to the expectations of society.

Jane Arden did not produce another stage work until more than ten years later. But in the intervening years she became well known as an actress, and also as a speaker on television programmes usually on women and politics. She also wrote screenplays. Her next stage play appeared in 1969, was in itself sensational, and revealed the radical change that had been going on. In 1966, Jane Arden had written a film called *The Logic Game* which is described as 'a surrealist puzzle attempting to locate the isolation of woman in the context of bourgeois marriage', and this was the first creative result of her increasing interest in the position of women in society. A second film came in 1968 (directed by Jack Bond). This was *Separation*, in which 'the nerve of exploitation [was] more exposed, as the woman's personal dilemma began to have a political context'. In these works, or explorations, Jane Arden is revealed as one of the first major voices of Women's Liberation which began to take on coherence in the late 1960s.

Meanwhile, practical developments within the theatre itself had been happening. Writers, directors, and actors were becoming increasingly discontented with the conventional theatrical forms; also with the financial/commercial situation of the theatre. And during the last years of the 1960s a number of experimental theatre groups came into being. The work shown in this context was at once more liberated politically and more liberated in form. In Jane Arden the two themes met with a production of her next play, *Vagina Rex and the Gas Oven*, which was given at the London Arts Laboratory, directed by Jack Bond.

This remains so far the most direct and intense expression of women's oppression in the theatre. Technically, it used one actress playing Woman (Sheila Allen) and one actor playing The Man (Victor Spinetti), plus a chorus of Furies, young actors and actresses who commented, took many parts, and became a sort of choreographed background. There was a pop group and much use of projection, lights, and varying sounds. Throughout, the techniques and images are used with a sound dramatic fluency that makes *Vagina Rex* outstanding as a political tract that is also extremely compelling theatre.

In *Vagina Rex* Jane Arden exposes every nerve related to the inferior, passive position of women. It caused considerable comment, one of the most ironic being a trendy Sunday newspaper's piece called 'Are Women oppressed?' — 'as though there was still some doubt about the matter', Jane Arden comments. In 1971, Jane Arden's next play *A New Communion—for Freaks, Prophets and Witches* was produced in Edinburgh and London. It had an all-female cast and explored the themes in more detail. *Vagina Rex* related women firmly to men and to the pre-ordained social role expected of women. *A New Communion* internalized the themes, and the expression 'women's rage' was made real.

Jane Arden's later work is excellent to read and gripping to watch when superbly performed, but it is doubtful whether it will be possible to perform *Vagina Rex* or *A New Communion* outside the context of a specialist and committed company of players. These plays are essentially products of a time and a place.

—Roger Baker

B

BAGNOLD, Enid (Algerine).

English. Born in Rochester, Kent, 27 October 1889. Educated at Prior's Field, Godalming, Surrey, in Marburg, Germany, Lausanne, Switzerland, and at the Villa Leona, Paris; studied painting with Walter Sickert. Served as a driver with the French Army and as a nurse in a London hospital during World War I. Married Sir Roderick Jones in 1920 (died 1962); three sons and one daughter. Journalist, *Hearth and Home*, London, 1912. Recipient: Arts Theatre prize, 1951; American Academy Award of Merit, 1956. C.B.E. (Commander, Order of the British Empire), 1976. *Died 31 March 1981.*

Publications

PLAYS

Lottie Dundass (produced 1942). 1941.
National Velvet, from her own novel (produced 1946). 1961.
Poor Judas (produced 1946). In *Two Plays*, 1951.
Two Plays (includes *Lottie Dundass* and *Poor Judas*). 1951; as *Theatre: Two Plays*, 1951.
Gertie (produced 1952; as *Little Idiot*, produced 1953).
The Chalk Garden (produced 1955). 1956.
The Last Joke (produced 1960). In *Four Plays*, 1970.
The Chinese Prime Minister (produced 1964). 1964.
Call Me Jacky (produced 1968). In *Four Plays*, 1970; revised version, as *A Matter of Gravity* (produced 1975). 1978.
Four Plays (includes *The Chalk Garden, The Last Joke, The Chinese Prime Minister, Call Me Jacky*). 1970.

NOVELS

The Happy Foreigner. 1920.
Serena Blandish; or, The Difficulty of Getting Married. 1924.
National Velvet. 1935.
The Squire. 1938; as *The Door of Life*, 1938.
The Loved and Envied. 1951.
The Girl's Journey: Containing The Happy Foreigner and The Squire. 1954.

VERSE

The Sailing Ships and Other Poems. 1918.
Poems. 1978.
Early Poems. 1987.

Other

A Diary Without Dates. 1918.
Alice and Thomas and Jane (for children). 1930.
Autobiography: From 1889. 1969; revised edition, 1985.
Letters to Frank Harris and Other Friends, edited by R.P. Lister. 1980.

Translator, *Alexander of Asia*, by Princess Marthe Bibesco. 1935.

Critical study: *Bagnold: The Authorized Biography* by Anne Sebba, 1986.

Enid Bagnold writes in her Foreword to *Serena Blandish*, 1946:

The Reader: This book of yours that you are now offering up again, when did you last read it?

The Author: I sent *Serena Blandish* to the publishers twenty-two years ago. On a day in November 1924 it came back to me, printed and bound. I handled it with rapture, with prayers for its success, with passionate self-pity that my father insisted on anonymity. I was too exhausted by having written it to read it.

The Reader: What happens when a book goes from its author? How soon, once more, do you receive pleasure from your work?

The Author: It left me as a wild animal leaves its mother, not again to be recognized: to be met, perhaps, as I meet it now, muzzle to stranger-muzzle, all thread of kinship snapped. For me, after that, it never freshened. The wind never blew in it. The angel never shouted in the landscape. I never read it—well I never read it for twenty-two years—not till this morning.

The Reader: Then what do you think of your work, Author?

The Author: That perhaps is a little private. But I reflect on it and how, by writing, one exorcises the devil or the angel in a stretch of life, till, the winged creature risen, the landscape which before had shaken with the bustle of his escape, is suddenly fixed, as with gum, unrevisitable. In the years preceding every book there's a hunt and a capture. But when the hunt is over the stirrup-cup is for the public. The Author cannot enjoy what he has caught. He must be off. He must shoot again. And when he shoots no more then he is old.

The Reader: But—some success—when he is old? Can't he sit back on that?

The Author: Success, to give pleasure, must be on the move. No, there's no laurel to wear that he notices is any different from his hat. And writing is like love: all that is past is ashes: and the thread snaps on every book that is done.

The Reader: The pleasure then is in the writing?

The Author (a little warm): Not at all! Writing is a condition of grinding anxiety. It is an operation in which the footwork, the balance, the knowledge of sun and shade, the alteration of slush and crust, the selection of surface at high speed is a matter of exquisite fineness. Heavens—a pleasure! when you are without judgement, and hallucinations look like the truth! When experience (which trails behind) and imagination (which runs in front) will only combine by a miracle! When the whole thing is an ambidexterity of memory and creation—of the front and back of the brain—a lethargy of inward dipping and a tiptoe of poise while the lasso is whirling for the words! (More heated.) It is a gamble, a toss-up, an unsure benevolence of God! No! It can't be called pleasure!

The Reader: One last obvious question. Why then do you write?

The Author (with a sigh): For the sake of a split second when I feel myself immortal . . .

The Reader: Yes?—And . . .

The Author: . . . and just before the impact with my want of skill.

Enid Bagnold quotes Walter Kerr's review (New York *Herald-Tribune*, 3 January 1964) of *The Chinese Prime Minister*:

I find myself touched by *The Chinese Prime Minister* . . . I am touched, I think, because I have seen one whole play in which there is not a single careless line. There are careless scenes, oh, yes. Quite a large proportion of the middle act is taken up with a crossfire of family quarrelling that has as its purpose the badgering of Miss Leighton until Miss Leighton is pushed into a vital, and mistaken, decision. The sequence is ratchety enough to badger you, too, and to make you wonder whether the silken strands of the evening can be gathered into one steady hand again. But even there 'carelessness' is not quite the right word. For playwright Enid Bagnold never does anything merely because she cannot think of anything better to do. Whatever she does, she does on impulse, inspiration, with a jump and a dagger in her hand, eyes gleaming. The gleam, the mad glint of her inspiration, may indeed flash out of the untidiest of corners. But in itself it is marvellously pure.

The obvious word for a lofty, detached, unpredictably witty play of this sort is 'civilized'. But I think we should do Miss Bagnold the justice of trying to avoid obvious words. *The Chinese Prime Minister* might more nearly, more properly be called humanely barbaric.

Its comedy is barbaric in the sense that, for all the elegance of elbow-length blue gloves and for all the urbanity of precise syntax sounded against deep chocolate drapes, the minds of the people who make the comedy are essentially brutal minds, minds capable of caring for themselves . . . All of the contestants who speak Miss Bagnold's brisk, knobby, out-of-nowhere lines somehow or other become admirable. For the lines are thoughts not echoes, not borrowings. And they are so often so very funny because they come not from the stage or from remembered literature but from a head that has no patience with twilight cant.

Miss Bagnold does not construct a play that all audiences will settle to easily. That is clear enough . . . It shimmers on the stage—and wavers there, too—like a vast, insubstantial spider's web, sprung with bits of real rain. It is not conventional, and it is not altogether secure. But it is written. And what a blessing that is.

Enid Bagnold wrote four plays before *The Chalk Garden*, her first and only big success. They are *Lottie Dundass*, *National Velvet*, *Poor Judas* and *Gertie*. Yet in her autobiography Bagnold speaks of *Lottie Dundass* as her first play and *Gertie* as her second, and as usual her discrimination is absolute. *National Velvet* is an adaptation of her successful novel; it was filmed (with the young

Elizabeth Taylor) and gave birth to soap-opera spin-offs on radio and tele-vision, but the novel is the version to remember. *Poor Judas*, a play about a writer unable to come to terms with his own lack of talent, won a prize in 1951 but has not made a mark in the current repertory. *Lottie Dundass*, an anecdotal piece, had a five-month run during the War with Sybil Thorndike and Ann Todd in the cast. *Gertie*, a comedy, opened in New York on a Wednesday and came off the following Saturday; in England it was retitled *Little Idiot* but failed. To compensate for the disappointment, Bagnold concen-trated on *The Chalk Garden*, which she worked on for the next two years. It initiated the mandarin style that characterizes her last four plays, of which only *The Chalk Garden* has had a success befitting its merit.

The most immediately perceptible quality of *The Chalk Garden* is a rich suggestion of artificiality in the dialogue—'speech of an exquisite candour', Kenneth Tynan had called it, 'building ornamental bridges of metaphor, tiptoeing across frail causeways of simile, and vaulting over gorges impassable to the rational soul'. The whole play is in fact a metaphor, comparing the development of a child starved of mother-love with the development of plants starved of compost. Bagnold claimed to have been unaware of this parallel when she was writing the play, but it must have been lurking near the surface of her mind, for it is all-pervasive; the garden, never actually seen, is almost as much a character as the old retainer lying upstairs in whose amateur advice Mrs St Maugham, the aristocratic widow at the centre of the play, has placed her mistaken trust for so long.

There is something larger than life about all the people in the play; they are not caricatured in the manner of Rowlandson but elegantly exaggerated in the manner of El Greco. Bagnold lived most of her life among exceptional people and she could draw an exceptional character with confidence and consistency, though her success lay mostly in those who can be described, in the broadest possible sense, as aristocratic. Her themes are aristocratic too, themes like breeding and courage and resolution. Oddly enough, though, *The Last Joke*, in which the principle characters are Balkan princes drawn from life, is the least aristocratic of the four late plays. Perhaps this is due to the fact that the princes, Ferdinand Cavanati and his brother Hugo, are modelled on somewhat eccentric originals whom Bagnold revealed as Prince Antoine Bibesco and his brother Emmanuel. Reproducing a live eccentric is a harder task than creating one; and the provision of a plot in *The Last Joke* that seems almost as capricious as its executants does nothing to mend matters.

Nevertheless there is something to be admired in this play. The conception of the philosopher who has worked out so much about God that he is determined to hasten their meeting is potentially a brave one. It is a pity that more is not done with it than its incorporation into a melodramatic story about the stealing of a picture; or that the story, if this is to be the one, is not more straightforwardly told. But Bagnold has had to include too much of real life in it, and the amalgam of life and romance has not worked out well. The play got poor notices when it opened in London and had only a short run. Its successor was in every way better; Bagnold herself rated *The Chinese Prime Minister* more highly than *The Chalk Garden*. But this too, for reasons not entirely attributable to the qualities of the script, had only a modest success.

The Chinese Prime Minister is a play about the pleasures of old age (and to

show that these are not available only to the wealthy the author has comple-
mented her sixty-nine-year-old protagonist with a 100-year-old butler who
dies twice during the play and finds the experience not at all unpleasant).
'She'—the only name given to the heroine—is an actress on the verge of
retiring who is suddenly reunited with the husband who left her many years
before. She has a vision of retirement with a notional Chinese Prime Minister
whose term of office is done, who writes poems to outlive his achievements,
who goes up into the mountains with no baggage but a birdcage. Her husband,
having made a fortune in oil that has kept him permanently resident in Arabia,
has other ideas; he thinks of summoning up anew all the joys of their youth.
But oil calls him back to Arabia, and She is happily resigned to being her own
Chinese Prime Minister and living her remaining years in the peaceful style she
has mapped out for them.

There is a fine serenity about the play that is marred only by what seems to
be Bagnold's uncertainty about what to do with her batch of subsidiary
characters—the heroine's children and their friends of their own generation,
who never quite get integrated into the main scheme. In New York, where She
was played by Margaret Leighton, it was a success; in London where She was
played by Edith Evans, the actress for whom it was written, it took on a
sentimental patina foreign to the writing, and was not. Bagnold was given to
blaming producers for the artistic failures of her plays; of the four last plays
The Chalk Garden is the only one (rightly or wrongly) that has acquired a
stable reputation. Her rating of *The Chinese Prime Minister* as a better play
than this was probably wrong; *The Chalk Garden* had the advantage of
formidable discussions over a long period with Irene Mayer Selznick, a producer in whom Bagnold had faith, and emerged a dramatic jewel. But *The
Chinese Prime Minister* has not deserved the neglect into which it has fallen.

Enid Bagnold's last piece, *Call Me Jacky*, won its director a grudging 'did his
best' from the author, followed by a complaint that inadequate rehearsal time
was given to it. Perhaps two years with Irene Selznick might have made
something of it; but as played, and as published, the subtleties the author
called for seemed to exist principally in her mind. Once more we have the rich
old lady at the centre of the piece, playing on the destinies of the younger
generation, represented by a cook extracted from a lunatic asylum (a reminis-
cence of *The Chalk Garden*), the lady's grandson, an Oxford student, and four
friends of his, a male homosexual pair and a female. It seems to have been
written to demonstrate how liberal this rich old lady (in which, as usual, a
certain autobiographical element is unmistakable) can be when confronted
with the problems that afflict the young.

Thus, she is undisturbed by the homosexual liaisons, or by her grandson's
marriage to a black girl and siring of a black baby, or by communist accusations of depriving the poor of the use of her grounds to live in. But the theme
appears to be that such open-mindedness is the result of the basically aristocratic nature of her character; and when, in the highly improbable conclusion, she
asks to be admitted to the paying wing of the home where her cook comes
from, and the cook asks her pathetically if she might then be called by her
Christian name, she replies coldly, 'I'll be buggered if I do'.

The combination of this attitude and this choice of words to express it in is
characteristic of the generally muddled feeling of the play. The author claimed

that the piece worked on two levels, but it is more truthful to say that it exists on two levels and works on neither of them, neither the surface frivolity nor the deeper implications. Bagnold was accustomed to taking years over the writing of her plays; that *Call Me Jacky* doesn't work suggests that the two years she worked on it and the time taken in production were neither of them enough; for the theme, a 20th-century version of *noblesse oblige*, is a characteristic one, worth developing, capable of development. In spite of Gladys Cooper's much-quoted judgement during the rehearsals for *The Chalk Garden*, Enid Bagnold was incapable of writing nonsense.

—B. A. Young

BARNES, Djuna (Chappell).

American. Born in Cornwall-on-Hudson, New York, 12 June 1892. Privately educated; studied art at the Pratt Institute, Brooklyn, New York, and the Art Students' League, New York. Journalist and illustrator, 1913–31; also an artist: exhibited at Art of This Century Gallery, New York, 1946. From 1961, trustee, New York Committee, Dag Hammarskjöld Foundation. Recipient: Merrill and Rothko grants. Member, American Academy. *Died 1982.*

Publications

PLAYS

Three from the Earth (produced 1919). In *A Book*, 1923.
Kurzy of the Sea (produced 1919).
An Irish Triangle (produced 1919).
To the Dogs, in *A Book*, 1923.
The Dove (produced 1926). In *A Book*, 1923.
She Tells Her Daughter. In *Smart Set*, November 1923.
The Antiphon (produced 1961). 1958.

NOVELS

Ryder. 1928.
Nightwood. 1936.

SHORT STORIES

A Book (includes verse and plays). 1923; augmented edition, as *A Night among the Horses*, 1929; shortened version, stories only, as *Spillway*, 1962.
Vagaries Malicieux: Two Stories. 1974.

VERSE

The Book of Repulsive Women: Eight Rhythms and Five Drawings. 1915.

OTHER

Ladies Almanack: Showing Their Signs and Their Tides; Their Moon and Their Changes; The Seasons as It Is with Them; Their Eclipses and Equinoxes; As Well as a Full Record of Diurnal and Nocturnal Distempers Written and Illustrated by a Lady of Fashion. 1928; 1972.
Selected Works. 1962.
Greenwich Village as It Is. 1978.

BIBLIOGRAPHY: *Djuna Barnes: A Bibliography* by Douglas Messerli, 1975.

MANUSCRIPT COLLECTION: University of Maryland, College Park.

CRITICAL STUDIES: *Djuna Barnes* by James B. Scott, 1976; *The Art of Djuna Barnes*; *Duality and Damnation* by Louis F. Kannenstine, 1977.

THEATRICAL ACTIVITIES

ACTOR: **Plays**—in *Power of Darkness* by Tolstoy, 1920; in *The Tidings Brought* to Mary by Paul Claudel, 1922.

Best known as the author of the novel *Nightwood*, Djuna Barnes turned to drama early and late in her career. Three one-act plays were performed by the Provincetown Players and three published in *A Book*. In 1958 she published *The Antiphon*, a play that is Jacobean in feeling and language.

Two of her three one-act plays used that stock character, a Woman with a Past. In *Three from the Earth* such a woman is confronted by three brothers who ask for the return of their father's letters to her. The curtain falls on the revelation that the youngest brother is the woman's son. In *To the Dogs* such a woman denies love to the neighbour who vaults through her window. Cowed, the neighbour retreats, but the play is ambiguous as to which of the two is going 'to the dogs'. *The Dove* focuses on a young girl living with two old maid sisters who relish their collection of knives, guns, and romantic fantasies. The young girl taunts each of the old maids to use a weapon, but she alone shoots a gun—at a painting of prostitutes. None of these plays can be taken seriously, but *The Antiphon* is an astonishing if anachronistic achievement.

The title *The Antiphon* indicates its style; one verse speech seems to call forth its verse reply, in poetic rather than dramatic structure. The language is stiff and archaic on the lips of its 20th-century characters. Set in 1939, on the eve of World War II, the play reveals sexual sin and a hint of expiation, as in Jacobean drama. To 17th-century Burley Hall in England come Miranda and her coachman companion from Paris. Her mother Augusta and her two merchant brothers have been summoned from America by a third and absent brother, Jeremy.

Act I reveals that Augusta has betrayed her aristocratic Burley lineage, marrying an American Mormon, Titus Higby Hobbs of Salem, by whom she has four children. Titus has tortured his wife, brutalized his sons, offered his daughter Miranda for rape by a middle-aged Cockney. Though he has been dead some years, his memory is stronger in Burley Hall than that of the nobles who owned it. And his immortality is the heritage of his two merchant sons, who plan to murder their mother. Daughter Miranda has a checkered past as actress, writer, and woman of the world, and there are hints that she is having an affair with her coachman, Jack Blow. Only Augusta's brother Jonathan, who never left Burley Hall, is untainted by the life of Titus Higby Hobbs.

Though diction and verse of *The Antiphon* are Jacobean, the three-act structure has the tidiness of a well-made play. After the Act I explosion, Act II develops accusations and defence, climaxed when the merchant sons don masks of pig and ass in order to taunt Augusta and Miranda, mother and daughter. A grotesque masque is interrupted by the entrance of coachman Jack Blow with a doll's house, a miniature of Hobb's Ark, the family home in America, with its memories of Titus's seven mistresses, and the rape of the 17-year-old Miranda. Obliquely, the shared family past leads to the Act III confrontation between mother and daughter. Each woman recognizes herself in the other as they slowly mount the side staircase in an antiphon of accusation. At the top Augusta realizes that her sons have abandoned her in her ancestral home, but she refuses to accept the limitation of that home, and she drives her daughter down the stairs, accusing her of conspiracy. At the bottom of the staircase Augusta Burley Hobbs rings down a giant curfew bell, killing both women. Augusta's brother Jonathan and Miranda's erstwhile coachman, actually her brother Jeremy, gaze at the two dead women, and Jeremy muses: 'But could I know/Which would be brought to child-bed of the other?' Through the rhythmed, imaged dialogue, the death of the women comes to symbolize the death of an aristocratic lineage, too easily seduced by the violence of a commoner.

—Ruby Cohn

BOLAND, Bridget.

British. Born in London, 13 March 1913. Educated at the Convent of the Sacred Heart, Roehampton, 1921–31; Oxford University, 1932–35, B.A. (honours) in politics, philosophy, and economics 1935. Served in the Auxiliary Territorial Service, 1941–46; senior commander; produced morale-orientated plays for the troops, with three companies of actors, 1943–46. Film writer from 1937. Died 19 January 1988.

Publications

PLAYS

The Arabian Nights (produced 1948).
Cockpit (produced 1948). In Plays of the Year 1, 1949.
The Damascus Blade (produced 1950).
Temple Folly (produced 1951). 1958.
The Return (as Journey to Earth, produced 1952; as The Return, produced 1953). 1954.
The Prisoner (produced 1954). In Plays of the Year 10, 1954.
Gordon (produced 1961). In Plays of the Year 25, 1962.
The Zodiac in the Establishment (produced 1963; as Time Out of Mind, produced 1970). 1963.
A Juan by Degrees, adaptation of a play by Pierre Humblot (produced 1965).

SCREENPLAYS: Spies of the Air, with A.R. Rawlinson, 1939; Laugh It Off, with Austin Melford, 1940: Old Mother Riley in Society, with others, 1940; Gaslight (Angel Street), with A.R. Rawlinson, 1940; This England, with A.R. Rawlinson and Emlyn Williams, 1941; Freedom Radio (A Voice in the Night), with others, 1941; He Found a Star, with Austin Melford, 1941: The Lost People, with Muriel Box, 1949; Prelude to Fame, 1950; The Fake, with Patrick Kirwan, 1953; The Prisoner, 1955; War and Peace, with others, 1956; Constantino il Grande (Constantine and the Cross), with others, 1961; Damon and Pythias, 1962; Anne of the Thousand Days, with John Hale, 1970.

RADIO PLAY: *Sheba*, 1954.

TELEVISION PLAY: *Forever Beautiful*, 1965.

NOVELS
The Wild Geese. 1938.
Portrait of a Lady in Love. 1942.
Caterina. 1975.

OTHER
Old Wives' Lore for Gardeners, with Maureen Boland. 1976.
Gardener's Magic and Other Old Wives' Lore. 1977.
At My Mother's Knee. 1978.

Editor, *The Lisle Letters: An Abridgement* (from 6–vol. edition, edited by
   Muriel St. Clare Byrne). 1983.

Bridget Boland writes (1987):

Although I hold a British passport I am in fact Irish, and the daughter of an
Irish politician at that, which may account for a certain contrariness in my
work. Many playwrights have become screenwriters; so I was a screenwriter
and became a playwright. Most women writers excel on human stories in
domestic settings: so I am bored by domestic problems and allergic to domestic
settings. I succeed best with heavy drama (*The Prisoner*), so I can't resist trying
to write frothy comedy (*Temple Folly*).

By the time you have written half a dozen plays or so you began to realize
you are probably still trying to write the one you started with. However
different I begin by thinking is the theme of each, I find that in the end every
play is saying: 'Belief is dangerous'—the theme of *Cockpit*. In *The Damascus
Blade*, which, produced by Laurence Olivier and with John Mills and Peter
Finch in the cast, yet contrived to fold on its short pre-London tour, I tried to
put across the theme by too complicated a paradox. An Irishman descended
from a long line of soldiers of fortune holds that you must not kill for what you
believe in, but that a man must be prepared to die for something, if only the
belief of someone else. Having offered his sword to the foreign forces of
extreme right and extreme left in turn, he ends by dying as bodyguard to the
child of a prostitute, trying to keep it for her from its father—and realizes that
in spite of all his/my theories he has come to believe in the justice of her cause:
man—alas, God—is like that.

In 1948 Bridget Boland was well ahead of her time as a playwright. *Cockpit*
was one of the early forerunners of the vogue for environmental theatre which
was to spread to England from off-Broadway in the 1960s. It was a play which
boldly turned its back on everything that was normal in the English theatre of
the time, including insularity. Its way of coming to grips with the problem
of Displaced Persons in post-war Europe was to use the whole auditorium to

create a theatrical image of a D.P. assembly centre, which itself served as an image of the chaos on the continent, with masses of bewildered hopeless people uprooted from where they belonged. Unsuspecting London theatre-goers arriving at the Playhouse found themselves faced with a curtain painted in Germanic style and with notices in various European languages forbidding them to fight or carry firearms. The dialogue begins incomprehensibly: a quarrel in Polish between two women fighting over a saucepan. Two English soldiers then take charge, appearing from the back of the stalls, shouting orders and questions, treating the whole audience like D.Ps, forcing them to feel uncomfortably involved in the action.

The discomfort becomes most acute at the climax of the play. Behind the drawn curtains of one of the boxes a man is gravely ill. A Polish Professor tells the English Captain that it may be a case of bubonic plague. The theatre has to be sealed off. Armed guards are stationed at the exits and the suspense is sustained while they wait for a doctor to arrive and then while they wait for the news that it was a false alarm. If the play ran for only 58 performances it cannot have been because it failed to make an impact.

On the face of it, the subject of *The Return*, could hardly have been more contrasted—a nun's return to the modern world after 36 years of seclusion in a convent. This is difficult material, but well dramatized it could have produced fascinating insights both into the mind of the woman and into the changes which had overtaken the world that surrounded her since she last saw it—in 1913. The play is by no means a complete failure: it has some very touching moments. But it fails to do justice to its subject because, unlike *Cockpit*, it fails to find a way of making the audience participate in the raw experience. It relies too much on dialogue which analyses and describes.

The part of the nun is quite well-written, but on leaving the convent she goes to live with a nephew and his wife, who are both sentimentally and unconvincingly characterized, while the chaplain and the man who runs a youth club where the nun does voluntary work are seen very superficially. The problem of dramatizing the impact the modern world makes on the woman's mind is largely side-stepped. What we get instead is a plot in which a series of misunderstandings are peeled off to reveal an unrealistic core of human goodness.

In spite of several forays into the past (like *Gordon*, an old-fashioned drama about Gordon and the siege of Khartoum) Boland is at her best in writing about post-war Europe, and her best play is still *The Prisoner*, which seems to have been inspired partly by the trial of the Hungarian Cardinal Mindszenty and partly perhaps by Arthur Koestler's novel *Darkness at Noon*, which presents a similar relationship between a political prisoner in a Communist country and his interrogator, though in Koestler the sympathetic interrogator is replaced half way through the action by a callous and unintelligent party-liner of peasant stock. In *The Prisoner* it is the Cardinal whose origins are proletarian, while the Interrogator is a clever aristocrat who has joined the Party. The dialogue gives clear definition to the stages in the close personal relationship that develops between the two adversaries, who like and respect each other. Most of the cut and thrust is verbal, but there are some highly theatrical climaxes, as when a coffin is brought in containing the apparently dead body of the Cardinal's mother. The revelation that she has only been anaesthetized is followed by the threat that she will be killed if he does not sign the confession his captors want.

Not only the two central parts but also that of the main warder provide excellent opportunities for actors, and the physical breakdown of the Cardinal is particularly rewarding. The main flaw in the writing is a lapse into sentimentality when the Interrogator is made to repent, revealing that in destroying his victim he has also destroyed his faith in his own work. But the damage this does to the play is almost compensated for by a fine twist at the end. The death sentence is repealed and the Cardinal, whose confession has discredited him, knows that it will be more difficult for him to live than to die.

—Ronald Hayman

BOLT, Carol (née Johnson).

Canadian. Born in Winnipeg, Manitoba, 25 August 1941. Educated at the University of British Columbia, Vancouver, 1957–61, B.A. 1961. Married David Bolt in 1969; one son. Researcher, Dominion Board of Statistics, London School of Economics, Market Facts of Canada, and Seccombe House, 1961–72; dramaturge, 1972–73, and chair of the Management Committee, 1973–74, Playwrights Co-op, Toronto; dramaturge, Toronto Free Theatre, 1973; writer-in-residence, University of Toronto, 1977–78. Recipient: Canada Council grant, 1967, 1972; Ontario Arts Council grant, 1972, 1973, 1974, 1975. Agent: Great North Artists, 345 Adelaide Street West, Toronto, Ontario M5V 1R5. Address: 76 Herbert Avenue, Toronto, Ontario, Canada.

Publications

PLAYS

I Wish (as Carol Johnson) (produced 1966). In *Upstage and Down*, edited by D.P. McGarity, 1968.

Daganawida (produced 1970).

Buffalo Jump (as *Next Year Country*, produced 1971; as *Buffalo Jump*, produced 1972). 1972.

My Best Friend Is Twelve Feet High (for children), music by Jane Vasey (produced 1972). With *Tangleflags*, 1972.

Cyclone Jack (for children; produced 1972). 1972.

Gabe (produced 1972). 1973.

Tangleflags (for children; produced 1973). With *My Best Friend Is Twelve Feet High*, 1972; published separately, 1974.

The Bluebird, adaptation of a story by Marie d'Aulnoy (produced 1973).

Pauline (produced 1973).

Maurice (for children; produced 1973). 1975.

Red Emma, Queen of the Anarchists (produced 1974). 1974.

Shelter (produced 1974). 1975.

Finding Bumble (for children; produced Toronto).

Norman Bethune: On Board the S.S. Empress of Asia (produced 1976).

Okey Doke (produced 1976).

Buffalo Jump, Gabe, Red Emma. 1976.
One Night Stand (produced 1977). 1977.
Desperadoes (produced 1977).
TV Lounge (produced 1977).
Star Quality (produced 1980). Excerpt published in *Acta Victoriana*, vol. 102, no. 2, 1978.
Deadline (produced 1979).
Escape Entertainment (produced 1981). 1982.
Love or Money (produced 1981).

RADIO PLAY: *Fast Forward*, 1976.

TELEVISION PLAYS: *A Nice Girl Like You* (*Collaborators* series), 1974; *Distance*, 1974; *Talk Him Down*, 1975.

Carol Bolt comments:

(1977) I've had a lot of opportunity to work in the theatre in the last four years, with twelve new plays commissioned. Much of this work has been inspired by the theatrical community, particularly work being done at the Toronto Free Theatre and the Théâtre Passe Muraille.

The plays often deal with "political" subjects, the characters often want to change the world, but I think my preoccupation is with the adventure, rather than the polemic, of politics. I think a play like *Red Emma* is about as political as *The Prisoner of Zenda*.

I'm interested in working in new forms of musical comedy and epic romance and in creating (or recreating) characters who are larger than life or mythic.

I'm also interested in exploring, recording, recreating, and defining Canadian concerns, characters, histories, cultures, identities. I want to create plays for this country, whether the plays are about the lost moments in Canada's past (like *Buffalo Jump*), whether they offer another view of an American mythic figure (like *Red Emma*), or whether they play at creating Canadian archetypes (*Shelter*).

I don't think this kind of cultural nationalism is parochial. I think our differences are our strengths, not our weaknesses, nationally and internationally, so I think the argument that if a Canadian play is any good the Americans or British will be happy to tell us via Broadway or the West End is specious and muddle-headed. I don't think Canadians will say anything of interest to the world until we know who Canadians are.

Through her prolific contribution to Canadian theatre Carol Bolt has shaped a unique form of social documentary using factual reference material to gain access to an imaginative Canadian mythology. Her best early plays are cohesive, rich in entertainment and dramatic values, politically inspired but romantically motivated, and imbued with a keen, sometimes riotous sense of social injustice.

Central to *Buffalo Jump*, *Gabe*, and *Red Emma* is an interest in combining theatrical styles and methods: a fluid interchange of locations loosely defined by props and emotional intensities, quick episodic scene changes, direct audience address, and the use of song to develop action or as a divertissement. This willing exhibition of the theatrical process can also be found in Bolt's approach to children's plays.

Both her adult and children's plays have a common free-form fluctuation of time, place, and space, enhanced by a strong entertainment factor which smooths abrupt or unlikely transitions with song, special lighting changes, or the emphasis of a significant prop—the train in *Buffalo Jump* or the banner of anarchy in *Red Emma*. This montage format partly results from rewriting plays in a creative collaboration with the directors and actors during the rehearsal period. *Buffalo Jump* (which originated as a revue called *Next Year Country*) and the young people's plays *Cyclone Jack* and *My Best Friend Is Twelve Feet High* were formed completely in rehearsal.

These ongoing transformations of original material also sift fiction, or rather an imaginative interpretation, into factual details aiming at a conscious redefinition of the time-blurred outlines of historical figures. Bolt has stated she would rather be interesting than accurate and rather be one-sided than give a well-rounded viewpoint honed to dullness.

The central character in *Buffalo Jump*, for example, a play about the disastrous on-to-Ottawa trek of unemployed Vancouver men during the Great Depression, combines two Canadian heroes, "Red" Walsh and "Slim" Evans, united for dramatic purposes into the single character Red Evans. A character develops not necessarily from what *is* true but from what *might* be true as the playwright understands it. The creation of myth and the reshaping of myth is more important to Bolt than the documentation of history. As she has said, "Myth is more appealing than fact. It postulates that heroism is possible, that people can be noble and effective and change things . . . what we were doing in *Buffalo Jump* was making those characters tragic heroes. It was the same with the great Native Indian runner Tom Longboat, the central character of *Cyclone Jack* and others."

Buffalo Jump, a political and social indictment of Canadian society of the 1930's, manages to be a less serious work than either *Gabe* or *Red Emma*. The play borrows from the mythology of the old west for its central metaphor, equating the workers protest march to Ottawa with a herd of buffalo about to be stampeded off a cliff. With its explicit breakdown between villains and heroes, the play might have become a modern melodrama were it not for its cut-up, cartoon style.

Gabe, based on the story of Louis Riel, the doomed Métis Indian leader of the Riel Rebellion, and his comrade in arms, Gabriel Dumont, is a constant interplay between memory images and the reality of the lives of the two modern namesakes who are the main characters of the play. The original Riel and Dumont have been refined by time into spiritual heroes who provide a constant source of romantic inspiration. Says the modern-day Louis of his historic counterpart: "Louis Riel! Was the maddest, smartest, bravest Métis bastard ever wrote his own treaty. Ever fought for the rights of his people. For their land. Fought for representation. For his people and their children." In spite of courageous poses, the figures from the past did not achieve their political ideals or their romantic fantasies. The modern-day Louis must function within the context of a failed mythology. Where there was once a battle at

Batoche there's now a sports day and a camp meeting. And Louis has just finished a jail sentence.

Red Emma is more focused, dealing with one aspect of the life of the revolutionary Emma Goldman. Although the play is the least concerned with Canadian content, its style and sensibility link it with *Buffalo Jump* and *Gabe*. Structurally, the play draws upon a fluid intermingling of scenes and juxtaposes caricature with real people. While Emma and her fellow anarchists are portrayed as full-blooded characters, Henry Clay Frick is a stereotyped capitalist oppressor, backed up by a duo of one-dimensional Pinkerton men who might have stepped from a vaudeville routine.

Set in New York in 1890, *Red Emma* glorifies the myth of freedom fighters, "the people and the things they can wish for, the beautiful radiant things." The clue to an interpretation of *Red Emma* lies in the sub-title, "Queen of the Anarchists." The Emma of this story is a young, idealistic woman given to histrionic poses and flamboyant gestures. But she is also a staunch supporter of women's emancipation, declaring "Woman's development . . . must come from and through herself . . . freeing herself from the fear of public opinion and public condemnation will set a woman free, will make her a force hitherto unknown in the world."

Bolt's first attempt to come to real terms with such assumptions began tentatively with *Shelter*, the adult play following *Red Emma*. Dealing with five women, the social rituals of a funeral, wedding, and election campaign, and one woman's decision to run for office, *Shelter* shields its concerns with comedy. Painful decisions and reactions are given an almost surrealistic stylization, absurdity tops reality, and the women tend to be representative types instead of fully developed, deeply felt human beings. *Shelter* was followed by *One Night Stand*, Bolt's most aggressively modern play to date. In this award-winning play, Daisy, a young, lonely woman, celebrates her birthday with Rafe, a charming stranger who punctuates his lies with country and western songs. The consequences of their brief encounter—murder—are chillingly realistic.

—Sandra Souchotte and Constance Brissenden

BOVASSO, Julie (Julia Anne Bovasso).

American. Born in Brooklyn, New York, 1 August 1930. Educated at City College of New York, 1948–51. Married 1) George Ortman in 1951 (divorced 1959); 2) Leonard Wayland in 1959, (divorced 1964). Founder (director, producer, actress), Tempo Playhouse, New York, 1953–56. Teacher, New School for Social Research, New York, 1965–71, Brooklyn College, New York, 1968–69, and Sarah Lawrence College, Bronxville, New York, 1969–74; playwright-in-residence, Kentucky Wesleyan University, Owensboro, 1977. President, New York Theatre Strategy. Recipient: Obie award, Best Actress, and Best Experimental Theatre, 1956; Triple Obie award, Best Playwright-Director-Actress, 1969; Rockefeller grant, 1969, 1976; New York Council on the Arts grant, 1970; Guggenheim fellowship, 1971; Public Broadcasting Corporation award, 1972; Vernon Rice award, for acting, 1972; Outer Circle award, for acting, 1972. *Died 1991.*

Publications

PLAYS

The Moon Dreamers (also director: produced 1967; revised version produced 1969). 1972.

Gloria and Esperanza (also director: produced 1968; revised version produced 1970). 1973.

Schubert's Last Serenade (produced 1971). In *Spontaneous Combustion: Eight New American Plays*, edited by Rochelle Owens, 1972.

Monday on the Way to Mercury Island (produced 1971).

Down by the River Where Waterlilies Are Disfigured Every Day (produced 1972).

The Nothing Kid, and *Standard Safety* (also director: produced 1974). *Standard Safety* published 1976.

Super Lover, Schubert's Last Serenade, and The Final Analysis (also director: produced 1975).

THEATRICAL ACTIVITIES

DIRECTOR: Plays—many of her own plays; and at Tempo Playhouse, New York: *The Maids* by Jean Genet, 1953; *The Lesson* by Eugène Ionesco, 1955; and *The Typewriter* by Jean Cocteau; *Three Sisters Who Were Not Sisters* by Gertrude Stein; *Escurial* by Michel de Ghelderode; and *Amédéé* by Eugène Ionesco, 1956; *Boom Boom Room* by David Rabe, 1973.

ACTOR: Plays—*A Maid in The Bells* by Leopold Lewis, 1943; Gwendolyn in *The Importance of Being Earnest* by Wilde, 1947; title role in *Salome* by Wilde, 1949; Belissa in *Don Perlimplin* by Garcia Lorca, 1949; Lona Hessel in *Pillars of Society* by Ibsen, 1949; title role in *Hedda Gabler* by Ibsen, 1950; Emma in *Naked* by Pirandello, 1950; Countess Geschwitz in *Earth Spirit* by Wedekind, 1950; Zanida in *He Who Gets Slapped* by Andreyev, 1950; title role in *Faustina* by Paul Goodman, 1952; Anna Petrovna in *Ivanov* by Chekhov, 1952; Margot in *The Typewriter* by Jean Cocteau, 1953; Madeleine in *Amédéé* by Eugène Ionesco, 1955; Claire, 1955, and Solange, 1956, in *The Maids* by Jean Genet, and The Student in *The Lesson* by Eugène Ionesco, 1956; Henriette in *Monique* by Dorothy and Michael Blankfort, 1957; Luella in *Dinny and the Witches* by William Gibson, 1959; The Wife in *Victims of Duty* by Eugéne Ionesco, 1960; Lucy and Martha in *Gallows Humor* by Jack Richardson, 1961; Mistress Quickly in *Henry IV*, 1963; Madame Rosepettle in *Oh Dad, Poor Dad . . .* by Arthur Kopit, 1964; Mrs Prosser in *A Minor Miracle* by Al Morgan, 1965; Fortune Teller in *The Skin of Our Teeth* by Thornton Wilder, 1966; Madame Irma in *The Balcony* by Jean Genet, 1967; Agata in *Island of Goats* by Ugo Betti, and Constance in *The Madwoman of Chaillot* by Giraudoux, 1968; Gloria in *Gloria and Esperanza*, 1970; The Mother in *The Screens* by Jean Genet, 1971. Films—*Willie and Phil*, 1980; *The Verdict*, 1982; *Daniel*, 1983; *Betsy's Wedding*, 1990. Television—Rose in *From These Roots* series, 1958–60; Pearl in *The Iceman Cometh* by O'Neill, 1960; *Just Me and You*, 1978; *The Last Tenant*, 1978; *King Crab*, 1980; *The Gentleman Bandit*, 1981; *Doubletake*, 1985; and other performances in *US Steel Hour, The Defenders*, and other series, 1958–63.

The Bovasso world is highly orchestrated; the work appears to be driven, indeed hounded, by an ideological aesthetic. Julie Bovasso, one of America's more interesting actresses, became as a playwright a kind of mad mathematician, marshalling people and events into lunatic propositions and hallucinatory equations. The work sometimes marches to a drumbeat, sometimes sidles up to you, sometimes stridently calls out to the heavens, sometimes chuckles to itself. Throughout, there is the strong sense of the child infiltrating the grown-up theatre breathlessly, stealthily while the adults are asleep, relocating the furniture, putting bells on the cat, all to see how it will come out, to see whether the cunning proposition will prove itself.

The Moon Dreamers, one of Bovasso's earlier pieces, uses as the core of its narrative a simple situation in which wife, husband, and mistress can't agree as to who is to vacate the apartment. But into the situation, Bovasso, with a sense of increasing lunacy, introduces the wife's mother (Jewish), a lawyer (specified as dark-haired) who turns out to be the wife's second cousin, a doctor who turns out to be a childhood admirer of the wife's, an Indian chief who turns out to be a Japanese Buddhist, and a chief of police who turns out to be a French midget. Doctor, Lawyer, Indian chief, as well as Jewish momma and Gallic Fuzz. All these argue and split hairs in an increasingly complicated situation that on its surface is humorous but nevertheless suggests it is going somewhere other than farce. Around this core, Bovasso adds another layer, what she designates as an 'Epic' world as opposed to the 'Personal' world. The characters of the Epic world are in shadows, there is barely dialogue for them and they seem to exist principally as witnesses. But there are dozens of them, soldiers, black stockbrokers, gangsters, belly dancers, snake dancers, Spanish royalty. The domestic squabble is thus both knotted with what we might call the presence of banal archetypes and overseen by graver archetypes until it simply ceases to be what it has been. That is, it seems to become nothing that we can intellectually comprehend—until the end when the appearance of the astronaut, a kind of deus ex machina, makes a comprehensive statement about humanity—but rather something that we must allow to wash over us if we want to continue sensing it at all. Any information seems to be taken out of our hands and we must become like children or Martians witnessing an unknown world.

Monday on the Way to Mercury Island is filled with both dialogue and silent actions that recur numerous times, sometimes repeated identically, sometimes with variations. As in The Moon Dreamers, these are sometimes banal and sometimes extraordinary. But even the banal elements usually suggest something beyond themselves. The repetition tends to ritualize these sounds and movements without providing a philosophical base. A formal, austere aesthetic seems to be at work. The ritual tends here to make the theatre more into play, a relentlessly earnest if also whimsical play. But there appears to be a political thesis at work. Servants and peasants rise at last against socialite masters. The latter are painted as corrupt and soft, the former as steadfast and hard. But even here the intellectual content seems subordinate to the flowering theatrics, to the rhythms and colours of spectacle.

Down by the River Where Waterlilies Are Disfigured Every Day is another vast landscape, another epic with vivid theatrics. The Bovasso trait of mixed, merged, or transferred identities is strong here. Phoebe and Clement, lovers for many years, exchange clothes and then sexes. Count Josef, leader of the established order, is at work on a statue of Pango, head of the revolutionary forces, breathing life and the qualities dear to him into the figure that is attempting to end his own life. Revolt is strong here. Overturned lives, overturned order. In *Monday* the peasants end by burying the aristocrat. In *Waterlilies* the children toss the old world onto the garbage heap in the town square. But again one has the sense that the playing out of the act takes precedence over the intellectual meaning of the act, that the logic of aesthetics and of forming is ultimately the prime mover.

—Arthur Sainer

BROPHY, Brigid (Antonia).

British. Born in London, 12 June, 1929. Educated at St. Paul's Girls' School, London; St Hugh's College, Oxford (Jubilee scholar), 1947–48. married Sir Michael Levey in 1954; one daughter. Co-organiser, Writers Action Group, 1972–82; executive councillor, Writers Guild of Great Britain, 1975–78; vice-chairman, British Copyright Council, 1976–80. Since 1974 vice-president, Anti-Vivisection Society of Great Britain. Since 1984 has suffered from multiple sclerosis. Recipient: Cheltenham Festival prize, 1954; *London Magazine* prize, 1962; Tony Godwin award, 1985. Fellow, Royal Society of Literature, 1973. Address: Flat 3, 185 Old Brompton Road, London SW5 0AN, England.

Publications

PLAYS

The Waste-Disposal Unit (broadcast 1964). In *London Magazine*, April 1964; in *Best Short Plays of the World Theatre 1965–67*, 1968.
The Burglar (produced 1967). 1968.

RADIO PLAY: *The Waste-Disposal Unit*, 1964.

NOVELS

Hackenfeller's Ape. 1953.
The King of a Rainy Country. 1956.
Flesh. 1962.
The Finishing Touch. 1963.
The Snow Ball. 1964.
The Snow Ball, with The Finishing Touch. 1964.
In Transit. 1969.
The Adventures of God in His Search for the Black Girl: A Novel and Some Fables. 1973.
Palace Without Chairs: A Baroque Novel. 1978.

SHORT STORIES

The Crown Princess and Other Stories. 1953.

OTHER

Black Ship to Hell. 1962.
Mozart the Dramatist: A New View of Mozart, His Operas, and His Age. 1964; revised edition, 1988.

Don't Never Forget: Collected Views and Reviews. 1966.
Religious Education in State Schools. 1967.
Fifty Works of English and American Literature We Could Do Without, with
    Michael Levey and Charles Osborne. 1967.
Black and White: A Portrait of Aubrey Beardsley. 1968.
The Longford Threat to Freedom. 1972.
*Prancing Novelist: A Defence of Fiction in the form of a Critical Biography in
    Praise of Ronald Firbank.* 1973.
Beardsley and His World. 1976.
Pussy Owl (for children). 1976.
The Prince and the Wild Geese. 1983.
A Guide to Public Lending Right. 1983.
Baroque-'n'-Roll and Other Essays. 1987.
Reads (essays). 1989.

MANUSCRIPT COLLECTION: Lilly Library, University of Indiana, Bloomington.

Brigid Brophy comments:

Between the ages of 6 and 10, I was a prolific playwright, mainly in blank
verse. An elderly widow in the London suburb where I lived, being anxious to
foster the arts, appointed herself my impresario. She assembled a cast (of local
children) and a regular audience (of their parents) and, season by season,
mounted my oeuvre in her drawing room.

This excellent arrangement was, like much else, disrupted in 1939 by the
war, and when I eventually began my public literary career it was as an author
of books. In 1961 or so I reverted to my original vocation as dramatist by
writing *The Waste-Disposal Unit*, a brief, black and I hope funny *fleur du mal*,
which I composed in two foreign languages (Italian and American), with a
touch of free verse, and through which I expressed my Baudelairean fascination with the linguistic perversion that transforms English into American.

That was first performed, to approving notices, on BBC radio and has since
been staged as a one-act play, by students and other amateurs, in London,
Cambridge, and Hong Kong. In 1967 a full-length play of mine, *The Burglar*,
was produced in the West End. It concerns the plight of a burglar who,
thinking to break into merely an empty household in order to filch material
objects, in fact irrupts into the close-woven relationships of four lovers. I
hoped to produce theatrical amusement, a pleasing formal pattern, and some
illumination of our social morality by shock confrontation of the burglar (an
economic libertarian but a sexual puritan) with the lovers, who are sexual
libertarians but conventionalists on the subject of property. The play dis-
pleased the London critics and was a moderately resounding flop. (I believe,
however, it fared more happily in Dortmund, Germany). I subsequently published it with a long preface which begins as an ephemeral defence of myself
but continues, more importantly, with a discussion of society's attitude, including its unconscious attitudes towards the behaviour it labels crime.

The play's commercial failure understandably warned impresarios against
me and brought my public career as a dramatist to an end. I have naturally
continued to pursue my vocation, enlarging and varying my expressive use of

the theatrical medium, first to create an opera in words and then to incarnate, by expressionist means, a metaphor of the unconscious wish to die. These experiments, however, remain private because of the present shortage of elderly widows anxious to foster the arts.

Brigid Brophy's *The Burglar* is a very clever piece of writing which reads far better than it plays. As Brophy points out in the long Shavian preface, she learned her stagecraft 'from thinking hard about the form of great operas and not from ASMing for ten years in provincial rep' and indeed the structure is more musical and logical than theatrical. As a piece of argument for five voices it is witty and well constructed. As a radio play it might work; in the theatre it is progressively disappointing after a highly theatrical opening—with the stage almost in darkness, a ladder heaving into view outside the bedroom window, a figure climbing stealthily into view and then into the room, a bigger man stepping out from behind a curtain to seize the intruder and then the lights coming on.

The burden of the unanimously hostile reviews was that after this promising beginning there was a lot of talk and no action. This is not, in fact, what is wrong with the play. There is the burglar's amusing feebleness when Roderick manhandles him. There is the well-phased revelation that Roderick is not Edwina's husband. The sustained anti-climax of the lovers' inability to call the police is developed when the puritanic burglar seizes the moral advantage this gives him to justify his own immorality by savaging theirs. There is a well-contrived climax to Act One when Edwina's husband is heard letting himself into the flat. Roderick and the burglar hide and William comes into the room with an attractive girlfriend. Act Two is equally full of twists and surprises. Act Three culminates in a crash which indicates the burglar's off-stage death.

If, then, the play fails to involve an audience, it is not through lack of action but because the characters and the events fail to come theatrically to life. It is a very Shavian play: moral and social attitudes are dressed up as people, and Brophy takes a Shaw-like delight in flaying the hide off sacred cows which are conventionally venerated. The burglar himself is descended from the burglar in *Heartbreak House* who makes the same point about the injustice of the equation between years of his life wasted in prison and the material value of what he steals. The four middle-class lovers are as wittily capable of stepping over the trip-wires of sexual jealousy as any Shaw hero, and as easy to make into mouthpieces for long arguments about social assumptions governing sex and property. Behind all this there is a Shavian balance in the play's moral structure which weighs the wrongness of stealing other people's property against the wrongness of sleeping with other people's marital partners. Brophy is no more guilty than Shaw of using the stage as a platform for debate, but she is less expert at creating characters to involve an audience's emotions. There is no Captain Shotover, no Ellie Dunn to be saved from marrying a middle-aged industrialist, no Mazzini Dunn to be disabused from thinking himself to be in the industrialist's debt. If the cast of *Heartbreak House* were reduced to Hector and Hesiane, Randall and Ariadne, and the Burglar, no-one would be very involved.

It becomes clear quite early on that we are not watching a naturalistic play, that we are not being asked to believe that a burglar would be more interested in delivering moral diatribes about middle-class sexual morality than in making his escape, or that four lovers would behave with as much wit and poise when trapped into such an embarrassing situation. In making her characters almost vulnerable to anything except argument, Brophy is creating a certain theatrical effect, but it is one which rules out a great many others. As the play proceeds we find that the surprises we are being given are all very much of the same quality and calibre, intellectual steps in an argument, musical modulations in a quintet. Theatrically, therefore, they are subject to a law of diminishing returns. This would matter less if it were a one-act play or even a two-act play, but to sustain an audience's interest over two intervals the play would need either to be more emotional or more farcical on a physical level to match up with Brophy's description of it as 'bedroom farce'.

On the other hand, her fifty-minute radio play, *The Waste-Disposal Unit*, is thoroughly successful as a farce within its own non-visual terms. As in her novel *In Transit*, which it prefigures, the comedy and the conflict are bedded in the language itself. The villain of the piece is the American idiom, which mangles the English language rather in the way that the waste disposal unit of the title, installed by visiting Americans in a 16th century Italian palazzo, finally crunches up the two American women, overwhelming mother and puritanic, sentimental daughter. *La donne mobile*, sing the men. *E disponibile*. But the triumph of the piece is to use both the medium and the abhorred idiom so very well, creating a bizarre farce of non-communication between Virgil Knockerbicker, the lethargic homosexual poet, Homer, his worried brother, Merry, the sweet young all-American wife, and Angelo Lumaca, the accredited agent of the Atlantic Seaboard Waste Disposal Unit Corporation. Having made the mistake of moving into three-dimensionality, Brigid Brophy should have the courage to move back to radio, a medium in which her ingenuity comes near to genius.

—Ronald Hayman

C

CHASE, Mary (née Coyle).

American. Born in Denver, Colorado, 25 February 1907. Educated in Denver public schools; Denver University, 1922–24: University of Colorado, Boulder, 1924–25. Married Robert Lamont Chase in 1928; has three sons. Reporter, *Rocky Mountain News*, Denver, 1928–31; freelance correspondent, International News Service and the United Press, 1932–36; publicity director, NYA, Denver, 1941–42, and for Teamsters Union, 1942–44. Recipient: Pulitzer prize, 1945. Litt.D.: University of Denver, 1947. *Died 20 October 1981.*

Publications

PLAYS

Me, Third (produced 1936; as *Now You've Done It*, produced 1937).
Sorority House (produced 1939). 1939.
Too Much Business. 1940.
A Slip of a Girl (produced 1941).
Harvey (produced 1944). 1944.
The Next Half Hour (produced 1945).
Mrs McThing (produced 1952). 1952.
Bernardine (produced 1952). 1953.
Lolita (produced 1954).
The Prize Play. 1961.
Midgie Purvis (produced 1961). 1963.
The Dog Sitters. 1963.
Mickey, based on *Loretta Mason Potts.* 1969.
Cocktails with Mimi (produced 1973). 1974.

OTHER

Loretta Mason Potts (juvenile). 1958; as *Colin's Naughty Sister*, 1959.
The Wicked Pigeon Ladies in the Garden (juvenile). 1968.

A comedy about a gentle alcoholic and his friend—who happens to be a six-foot-tall, invisible rabbit—made Mary Chase a significant name in the American theatre. *Harvey* won the Pulitzer prize for the 1944–45 season and had one of the longest runs ever achieved on Broadway. It was made into a successful film and it has been successfully revived on American television.

Harvey was Chase's second play to be performed in New York. Her first,

Now You've Done It, lasted only a few weeks back in 1937, giving little indication that her next comedy would be so popular. But in retrospect we can see the same setting in a western city, the same whimsy, and the same inverted morality that found fuller expression in *Harvey.* *Now You've Done It* is a comedy about a young man who seeks nomination to Congress. When he is opposed by the established party leaders, he is rescued by his mother's maid, whose former job in a brothel gives her a powerful hold on most of the male politicians in town. Mary Chase got a few good laughs out of her mischievous mixture of politics and prostitution.

In *Harvey* (originally titled *The Pooka*), Chase recounted the efforts of a widow, Veta Louise Simmons, to cure her alcoholic brother, Elwood P. Dowd, whose invisible rabbit friend has become an embarrassment to the family. She takes Elwood to Dr Chumley's Rest, a private psychiatric hospital, for shock treatment, but rescues him from the doctor because she fears that the cure will turn her harmless brother into an ogre.

The original production was a smash hit. Produced by Brock Pemberton—against the advice of his knowing Broadway friends—and staged with great fun and charm by Antoinette Perry, *Harvey* had an inspired cast. As Elwood P. Dowd, Frank Fay was making a Broadway comeback, having lost a fortune in Hollywood and having overcome—as rumour had it—his own problem with alcohol. New York audiences empathized nightly with his personal triumph as an actor almost as much as they cheered Elwood's quiet triumph over Dr Chumley. Underplaying the role, Fay projected decency and gentleness along with a warm alcoholic glow, without ever descending to vulgarity or cuteness. Josephine Hull created Veta Louise with all her scatterbrained mannerisms but with the inner compassion that made her Elwood's sister beyond any doubt. These were two of the great American performances of the 1940s.

But even after Fay was succeeded by actors such as James Stewart, who did descend to cuteness, *Harvey* remained popular. The play had substance even without the great acting.

Harvey's strength derived from its highly theatrical use of illusion and reality. Chase followed the tradition of plays like Thornton Wilder's *Our Town* that violated the laws of time and space, but she treated these dislocations of reality with a deadpan playfulness. Her comic motif of supernatural whimsy was like that of Noël Coward's *Blithe Spirit,* but she replaced his brittle sophistication with homespun compassion.

Though Harvey can hardly be regarded as a Christ symbol, Mary Chase dramatized a conflict between faith and disbelief. She suggested that the person who has faith in something invisible is mistakenly regarded as insane by 'normal' society. Amid her comedy, she suggested further that faith and illusion should triumph over reality, that the psychiatrists were crazy, and that the abnormal were really sane. The punch line of the play is delivered by the cabby who warns Veta Louise about the shock treatment that Elwood is about to receive: 'Lady, after this he'll be a perfectly normal human being, and you know what bastards they are!' Veta Louise pounds on the door of the treatment room and rescues her brother. Better a gentler alcoholic with faith in his invisible rabbit than a normal human bastard with no illusions and no ideals.

Audiences cheered Veta Louise on to her rescue of Elwood. Just as they applauded for Tinker Bell in *Peter Pan*, they gave Harvey an enthusiastic curtain call, one invisible paw held by Frank Fay and the other by Josephine Hull. The spectators may have been applauding the escape from reality to alcoholic illusion. But, on the other hand, they may have been cheering for the ideals of individualism, decency, and friendship.

Whatever audiences responded to in Harvey's invisibility gave the play much of its humour as well as its meaning. During the Boston tryout an actor in a rabbit costume played the role for one performance. So great was the loss of laughs that Harvey was rendered invisible for ever more.

A year after *Harvey*, Mary Chase tried a serious drama with a supernatural motif. In *The Next Half Hour* she wrote about an Irish immigrant woman who believed in little people and banshees. But the play failed quickly. Comedy was really her forte, she apparently decided, because her next three plays were comic treatments of illusion and reality.

In *Mrs McThing* Mary Chase told the story of the wealthy Mrs Howard V. Larue III, whose son is stolen away by a witch (Mrs McThing) and replaced by a model boy. Aided by the witch's daughter, Mrs Larue rescues her real son, who has become involved with a gang of comically incompetent gangsters. Like *Harvey*, the witch remained invisible, except for a moment in the last scene. Just as *Harvey* mixed real alcohol and whimsy, *Mrs McThing* mixed whimsy with fake gangsters and fairy-tale witchcraft. This play was written for children, but it had a moderate success with adults who went to see Helen Hayes and Brandon de Wilde as mother and son. The Jean Arthur-Boris Karloff *Peter Pan*, a mixture of pirates and whimsy, had also been fairly popular with adults a few years earlier.

Later in 1952, Mary Chase brought her whimsy back to earth with *Bernardine*, a comedy about a group of teen-age boys who search without much success for sexual experience with 'fast' women. They daydream of the accessible, but imaginary, Bernardine, who 'lives' in Sneaky Falls. But since the sexual revolution, their fantasies seem quaintly dated.

No matter how sexual mores change, nothing remains so timely as a six-foot-tall invisible rabbit. In 1961 Chase again tried the mixture of insanity and whimsy in *Midgie Purvis*, but, even with Tallulah Bankhead in the title role, the play failed. Mary Chase never succeeded in matching the comic perfection of *Harvey*. It is her classic.

—Morgan Y. Himelstein

CHILDRESS, Alice.

American. Born in Charleston, South Carolina, 12 October 1920. Educated at schools in Harlem, New York; Radcliffe Institute for Independent Study (scholar), Cambridge, Massachusetts, 1966–68, graduated 1968. Married to the musician Nathan Woodard; one daughter. Actor and director, American Negro Theatre, New York, 1941–52; columnist ("Here's Mildred"), Baltimore *Afro-American*, 1956–58. Artist-in-residence, University of Massachusetts, Amherst, 1984. Recipient: Obie award, 1956; Woodward School Book award, 1975; Paul Robeson award, for screenplay, 1977; Virgin Islands Film Festival award, 1977; Radcliffe Graduate Society medal, 1984; African Poets

Theatre award, 1985; Audelco award, 1986; Harlem School of the Arts Humanitarian award, 1987. Agent: Flora Roberts Inc., 157 West 57th Street, New York, New York 10019, U.S.A.

Publications

PLAYS

Florence (also director: produced 1949). In *Masses and Mainstream*, October, 1950.
Just a Little Simple, adaptation of stories by Langston Hughes (produced 1950).
Gold Through the Trees (produced 1952).
Trouble in Mind (produced 1955). In *Black Theatre: A Twentieth-Century Collection of the Work of Its Best Playwrights*, edited by Lindsay Patterson, 1971.
Wedding Band (produced 1966). 1974.
The World on a Hill, in *Plays to Remember*. 1968.
Young Martin Luther King (produced 1969).
String, adaptation of a story by Maupassant (produced 1969). With *Mojo*, 1971.
Wine in the Wilderness (televised 1969; produced 1976). 1970.
Mojo (produced 1970). With *String*, 1971.
When the Rattlesnake Sounds (for children). 1975.
Let's Hear It for the Queen (for children). 1976.
Sea Island Song (produced 1977).
Gullah (produced 1984).
Moms: A Praise Play for a Black Comedienne, music and lyrics by Childress and Nathan Woodard (produced 1987).

SCREENPLAY: *A Hero Ain't Nothin' But a Sandwich*, 1977.

TELEVISION PLAYS: *Wine in the Wilderness*, 1969; *Wedding Band*, 1973; *String*, 1979.

NOVEL
A Short Walk. 1979.

OTHER
Like One of the Family: Conversations from a Domestic's Life. 1956.
A Hero Ain't Nothin' But a Sandwich (for children). 1973.
Rainbow Jordan (for children). 1981.
Those Other People (for children). 1989.

Editor, *Black Scenes: Collections of Scenes from Plays Written by Black People about Black Experience*. 1971.

CRITICAL STUDIES: articles by Gayle Austin and Polly Holliday, in *Southern Quarterly*, Spring 1987; *Their Place on Stage: Black Women Playwrights in America*, by Elizabeth Brown-Guillory, 1988.

THEATRICAL ACTIVITIES
DIRECTOR: **Play**—*Florence*, 1949.
ACTOR: **Plays**—Dolly in *On Strivers Row* by Abram Hill, 1940; Polly Ann in
Natural Man by Theodore Browne, 1941; Blanche in *Anna Lucasta* by Philip
Yordan, 1944.

Most of the plays of Alice Childress are about common people. Avoiding racial
stereotypes found in much of contemporary literature and drama, her works
present deftly drawn and realistic portraits of human beings attempting to find
a sense of dignity in a world which seems rather to appreciate less noble values.
Through her dramas, Ms. Childress exposes racism in the United States and
challenges each of us to redress our racial problems. Her dynamic, poignant
plays prepared the commercial stage for the works of other African-American
playwrights, including Lorraine Hansberry, Amiri Baraka, and Ed Bullins.

Set during the rehearsal of a melodrama about lynching in the South,
Trouble in Mind concerns black and white cast members who become involved
in a real-life drama of racial tensions arising from the portrayal of black
stereotypes. The drama skillfully mirrors a world where racist and sexist
problems are initially hidden under "masks," but are forced to surface. The
play centers on Wiletta Mayer, a veteran actor. She is an attractive middle-
aged black woman, with an outgoing personality. She has made a career out of
playing stereotypical black roles, but aspires to be cast in parts more deserving
of her rich talents. Initially, she readily gives advice to a novice black actor on
how to ingratiate oneself; to stay on good terms with the management no
matter how loathsome the production may be. When rehearsals begin, however, she cannot adhere to such a strategy when the white director uses tactics
that humiliate her and the script calls for the black characters to make
statements and perform actions that offend her racial pride. Consequently, by
the play's end, Wiletta removes her "mask" and becomes an outspoken critic
of the production even though this action puts this job and, possibly, her career
in jeopardy. It is a courageous choice, but a lonely one. None of the other cast
members are willing to support her.

Wine in the Wilderness, set in Harlem in 1964, examines the arrogance of
the black middle class in their relations with lower income African-Americans.
Bill Jameson, an artist with a privileged background, seeks a model for his
painting characterizing the average African-American woman as coarse,
poorly educated, and culturally illiterate. The artist's married friends, Sonny-
man and Cynthia, bring to Bill the person they believe best represents this
ideal—Tommy, a thirty-year-old factory worker. Despite their dubious intent,
by the play's end it is Tommy who teaches the others how they are merely
dilettantes masquerading as blacks. Tommy's speech and behavior communi-
cates that being black demands a sense of unity and respect for all members of
the race, no matter how different their backgrounds and lifestyles might be.
Tommy's actions exemplify her philosophy as, unlike the others, she shows
respect to the character Oldtimer, by asking about and calling him by his birth
name. Tommy recognizes the role of black organizations in the socio-political
progress of African-Americans. Like her birth name, Tomorrow, she is
forward-looking, while the others are mired in the past. She identifies with
current black leaders, whereas Bill talks only of dead heroes. Through Tommy,

the once pretentious characters are humbled as they learn being black lies not in the way one looks, but in the way one thinks and relates to the world.

Wedding Band deals with the subject of interracial romance in an insightful, unsentimental manner unlike the usual depiction of this subject on the stage and in popular media. The drama is set in 1918 in South Carolina when it was illegal for blacks and whites to marry or cohabit. For ten years Julia, a black woman, and Herman, a white man, have nurtured a clandestine relationship held together with the promise that they will one day move to the North to marry as soon as Herman has fulfilled his financial obligations to his mother. However, Julia comes to the painful realization that marriage to Herman is nothing more than a pipe dream. She learns that Herman harbors many of the same prejudices as other whites; and he is unwilling to endure the racial taunts of others who would object to their relationship once out in the open. The recognition of the futility of their relationship also awakens a sense of racial pride within Julia. Once a passive woman, by the play's end Julia asserts her right to live the way she chooses in a country cultivated and sustained by the labors and lives of her African ancestors.

A more recent work—*Moms*—is based on the life of the famed comedienne Jackie "Moms" Mabley. A series of scenes with music and dance depict her public and private life from her performances on a early-20th century black theatre touring circuit to her death in 1975. The play pays tribute to the comedienne's impeccable comic timing and strong rapport with the audience. However, the author does not gloss over the comedienne's more ignoble traits. The play mentions her overbearing personality, miserly disposition, portrayal of degrading stereotypes, ambivalence concerning her sexual preference, and lack of personal attention to the care of her children. Still, "Moms" is a fitting, even-handed tribute and a fine tour-de-force for the appropriate black actress.

—Addell Austin Anderson

See the essay on *Wedding Band.*

CHRISTIE, (Dame) Agatha (Mary Clarissa, née Miller).

English. Born in Torquay, Devon, 15 September 1890. Studied singing and piano in Paris 1906. Married 1) Colonel Archibald Christie in 1914 (divorced 1928), one daughter; 2) the archaeologist Max Mallowan in 1930. Served as a Voluntary Aid Detachment nurse in a Red Cross Hospital in Torquay during World War I, and worked in the dispensary of University College Hospital, London, during World War II; worked with Mallowan on excavations in Iraq and Syria and on Assyrian cities. President, Detection Club. Recipient: Mystery Writers of America Grand Master award, 1954; New York Drama Critics Circle award, 1955. D.Litt.: University of Exeter, Devon, 1961. Fellow, Royal Society of Literature, 1950. C.B.E. (Commander, Order of the British Empire), 1956; D.B.E. (Dame Commander, Order of the British Empire), 1971. *Died 12 January 1976.*

Publications

PLAYS

Black Coffee (produced 1930). 1934.

Ten Little Niggers, from her own novel (produced 1943). 1944; as *Ten Little Indians* (produced 1944), 1946.

Appointment with Death, from her own novel (produced 1945). 1956.

Murder on the Nile, from her novel *Death on the Nile* (as *Little Horizon*, produced 1945; as *Murder on the Nile*, produced 1946). 1948.

The Hollow, from her own novel (produced 1951). 1952.

The Mousetrap, from her story "Three Blind Mice" (broadcast 1952; produced 1952). 1954.

Witness for the Prosecution, from her own story (produced 1953). 1954.

Spider's Web (produced 1954). 1957.

Towards Zero, with Gerald Verner, from the novel by Christie (produced 1956). 1957.

Verdict (produced 1958). 1958.

The Unexpected Guest (produced 1958). 1958.

Go Back for Murder, from her novel *Five Little Pigs* (produced 1960). 1960.

Rule of Three: Afternoon at the Seaside, The Patient, The Rats (produced 1962). 3 vols., 1963.

Fiddlers Three (produced 1971).

Akhnaton (as *Akhnaton and Nefertiti*, produced 1979; as *Akhnaton*, produced 1980). 1973.

The Mousetrap and Other Plays (includes *Witness for the Prosecution, Ten Little Indians, Appointment with Death, The Hollow, Towards Zero, Verdict, Go Back for Murder*). 1978.

RADIO PLAYS: *Behind the Screen* (serial), with others, 1930; *The Scoop* (serial), with others, 1931; *The Mousetrap*, 1952; *Personal Call*, 1960.

TELEVISION PLAY: *The Wasp's Nest*, 1937.

NOVELS

The Mysterious Affair at Styles. 1920.

The Secret Adversary. 1922.

The Murder on the Links. 1923.

The Man in the Brown Suit. 1924.

The Secret of Chimneys. 1925.

The Murder of Roger Ackroyd. 1926.

The Big Four. 1927.

The Mystery of the Blue Train. 1928.

The Seven Dials Mystery. 1929.

The Murder at the Vicarage. 1930.

Giants' Bread (as Mary Westmacott). 1930.

The Floating Admiral, with others. 1931.

The Sittaford Mystery. 1931; as *The Murder at Hazelmoor*, 1931.

Peril at End House. 1932.

Lord Edgware Dies. 1933; as *Thirteen at Dinner*, 1933.

Why Didn't They Ask Evans? 1934; as *The Boomerang Clue*, 1935.

Murder on the Orient Express. 1934; as *Murder in the Calais Coach*, 1934.

Murder in Three Acts. 1934; as *Three Act Tragedy*, 1935.

Unfinished Portrait (as Mary Westmacott). 1934.

Death in the Clouds. 1935; as *Death in the Air*, 1935.

The A.B.C. Murders. 1936; as *The Alphabet Murders*, 1966.

Cards on the Table. 1936.

Murder in Mesopotamia. 1936.

Death on the Nile. 1937.

Dumb Witness. 1937; as *Poirot Loses a Client*, 1937.

Appointment with Death. 1938.

Hercule Poirot's Christmas. 1938; as *Murder for Christmas*, 1939; as *A Holiday for Murder*, 1947.

Murder Is Easy. 1939; as *Easy to Kill*, 1939.

Ten Little Niggers. 1939; as *And Then There Were None*, 1940; as *Ten Little Indians*, 1965.

One, Two, Buckle My Shoe. 1940; as *The Patriotic Murders*, 1941; as *An Overdose of Death*, 1953.

Sad Cypress. 1940.

Evil under the Sun. 1941.

N or M? 1941.

The Body in the Library. 1942.

The Moving Finger. 1942.

Five Little Pigs. 1942; as *Murder in Retrospect*, 1942.

Death Comes as the End. 1944.

Towards Zero. 1944.

Absent in the Spring (as Mary Westmacott). 1944.

Sparkling Cyanide. 1945; as *Remembered Death*, 1945.

The Hollow. 1946; as *Murder after Hours*, 1954.

Taken at the Flood. 1948; as *There Is a Tide . . .*, 1948.

The Rose and the Yew Tree (as Mary Westmacott). 1948.

Crooked House. 1949.

A Murder Is Announced. 1950.

They Came to Baghdad. 1951.

Mrs. McGinty's Dead, 1952; as *Blood Will Tell*, 1952.

They Do It with Mirrors. 1952; as *Murder with Mirrors*, 1952.

A Daughter's a Daughter (as Mary Westmacott). 1952.

After the Funeral. 1953; as *Funerals Are Fatal*, 1953; as *Murder at the Gallop*, 1963.

A Pocket Full of Rye. 1953.

Destination Unknown. 1954; as *So Many Steps to Death*, 1955.

Hickory, Dickory, Dock. 1955; as *Hickory, Dickory, Death*, 1955.

Dead Man's Folly. 1956.

The Burden (as Mary Westmacott). 1956.

4:50 from Paddington. 1957; as *What Mrs. McGillicuddy Saw!*, 1957; as *Murder She Said*, 1961.

Ordeal by Innocence. 1958.

Cat among the Pigeons. 1959.

The Pale Horse. 1961.

The Mirror Crack'd from Side to Side. 1962; as *The Mirror Crack'd*, 1963.

The Clocks. 1963.
A Caribbean Mystery. 1964.
At Bertram's Hotel. 1965.
Third Girl. 1966.
Endless Night. 1967.
By the Pricking of My Thumbs. 1968.
Hallowe'en Party. 1969.
Passenger to Frankfurt. 1970.
Nemesis. 1971.
Elephants Can Remember. 1972.
Postern of Fate. 1973.
Curtain: Hercule Poirot's Last Case. 1975.
Sleeping Murder. 1976.
The Scoop, and Behind the Screen, with others. 1983.

SHORT STORIES

Poirot Investigates. 1924.
Partners in Crime. 1929; selection, as *The Sunningdale Mystery,* 1933.
The Underdog. 1929.
The Mysterious Mr. Quin. 1930.
The Thirteen Problems. 1932; as *The Tuesday Club Murders,* 1933; selection,
    as *The Mystery of the Blue Geranium and Other Tuesday Club Murders,*
    1940.
The Hound of Death and Other Stories. 1933.
Parker Pyne Investigates. 1934; as *Mr. Parker Pyne, Detective,* 1934.
The Listerdale Mystery and Other Stories. 1934.
Murder in the Mews and Three Other Poirot Cases. 1937; as *Dead Man's
    Mirror and Other Stories,* 1937.
The Regatta Mystery and Other Stories. 1939.
The Mystery of the Baghdad Chest. 1943.
The Mystery of the Crime in Cabin 66. 1943.
Poirot and the Regatta Mystery. 1943.
Poirot on Holiday. 1943.
Problem at Pollensa Bay, and Christmas Adventure. 1943.
The Veiled Lady, and The Mystery of the Baghdad Chest. 1944.
Poirot Knows the Murderer. 1946.
Poirot Lends a Hand. 1946.
The Labours of Hercules. 1947.
The Witness for the Prosecution and Other Stories. 1948.
The Mousetrap and Other Stories. 1949; as *Three Blind Mice and Other
    Stories,* 1950.
The Under Dog and Other Stories. 1951.
The Adventure of the Christmas Pudding, and Selection of Entrées. 1960.
Double Sin and Other Stories. 1961.
13 for Luck! A Selection of Mystery for Young Readers. 1961.
Surprise! Surprise! A Collection of Mystery Stories with Unexpected Endings,
    edited by Raymond T. Bond. 1965.
Star over Bethlehem and Other Stories (as Agatha Christie Mallowan). 1965.
13 Clues for Miss Marple. 1966.

The Golden Ball and Other Stories. 1971.
Poirot's Early Cases. 1974; as *Hercule Poirot's Early Cases,* 1974.
Miss Marple's Final Cases and Two Other Stories. 1979.
The Agatha Christie Hour. 1982.
Hercule Poirot's Casebook: Fifty Stories. 1984.
Miss Marple: Complete Short Stories. 1985.

VERSE

The Road of Dreams. 1925.
Poems. 1973.

OTHER

Come, Tell Me How You Live (travel). 1946; revised edition, 1975.
An Autobiography. 1977.

CRITICAL STUDIES: *Studies in Christie's Writings* by Frank Behre, 1967; *Christie: Mistress of Mystery* by G.C. Ramsey, 1967, revised edition, 1968; *The Mysterious World of Christie,* 1975; *A Christie Chronology* by Nancy Blue Wynne, 1976; *The Christie Mystery* by Derrick Murdoch, 1976; *Christie: First Lady of Crime* edited by H.R.F. Keating, 1977; *The Mystery of Christie* by Gwyn Robyns, 1978; *The Bedside, Bathtub, and Armchair Companion to Christie* edited by Dick Riley and Pam McAllister, 1979; *Christie and All That Mousetrap* by Hubert Gregg, 1980; *A Talent to Deceive: An Appreciation of Christie* by Robert Barnard, 1980 (includes bibliography by Louise Barnard); *The Christie Who's Who* by Randall Toye, 1980; *The Life and Crimes of Christie* by Charles Osborne, 1982; *The Christie Companion* by Dennis Sanders and Len Lovallo, 1984; *Christie: A Biography* by Janet Morgan, 1984.

Agatha Christie was a seasoned and experienced spinner of webs and yarns. Like most prolific and professional writers, the quality of her work varies considerably. A play like *Black Coffee* is contrived, an obvious juggling of plot, while in a play like *Verdict* we see Christie, with the exception of one scene, at her worst. Of all her plays this is the most one-dimensional in its characterization. The story concerns a crippled wife who whines so much it is obvious she will be murdered; Karl, her husband, who is so saintly and forbearing it is obvious he will be accused unjustly of her murder; and Helen, the daughter of a millionaire, who is out to have an affair with Karl and who is so grotesquely drawn it is obvious she will murder Lisa. The characters lurch clumsily about the stage of this creaking plot and yet, if only on the level of crude melodrama, it does work. Just as the average Victorian novelist knew how to keep the reader in suspense, how to wring an extra tear, Christie even at her lowest excels at telling a story. It is fashionable in intellectual circles to decry her as it once was fashionable to dismiss Noël Coward. Yet even in a clumsy piece of stage craft like *Verdict*, Christie is capable of surprising writing as in the final scene (marred only by a sentimental curtain) which is of an entirely different quality to the rest of the play, full of insight. It is the scene in which Lisa, the lifelong friend who has always secretly loved him, finally tells Karl the truth about himself, that he does not see people as they are but only as concepts.

'You put ideas first, not people; ideas of loyalty and friendship and pity, and because of that people who are near suffer'. Suddenly it is as though Christie were writing out of some personal experience so that the scene leaps off the page, as the characters assume an extra dimension.

Certain of her plays are destined to become minor classics, perfect examples of a particular genre. *The Mousetrap* remains an oddity, a social, perhaps even sociological phenomenon, but *Ten Little Niggers*, *Spider's Web*, and *The Unexpected Guest* are three good examples of her at her best.

In the latter play, the curtain rises on a man who that moment has been shot dead in his wheelchair. Nearby, hidden in the shadows, stands his wife. Is it she who has killed him? Through the french windows enters a motorist who has lost his way in the fog and proceeds at once to help the wife build up an alibi. Christie, with a cool assurance, leads us swiftly past this improbable beginning, introducing her characters one after the other, each sharply etched (providing just enough for an actor to fill out), building up the suspense all round and skilfully levelling out a fair share of suspicion all round, so that the audience is so engrossed it does not have time to suspect that the murderer is in fact the intruder, the outsider, the uninvited guest.

Spider's Web is a stylishly constructed thriller while at the same time a comedy of situation and of character. Clarissa, a scatty society woman, remarks how boring life is and says, jokingly, that one of these days she will surely walk into the drawing-room and find a corpse on the floor. Needless to say this is exactly what happens. The characters include a sinister figure involved with the international drug market; a small girl who is afraid of being kidnapped; a lesbian-like housekeeper; and a butler with a past. Like those recipes for old-fashioned Christmas pudding full of nuts and fruit and brandy and beer and magic charms, Christie's play is stuffed with all the right ingredients for a splendid evening out in the theatre. The essence of this particular play and its charm is perhaps best conveyed in the scene in which Clarissa's husband asks her what she has been doing all day, and when she replies, 'I fell over a body', he answers, 'Yes, darling, your stories are always enchanting, but really there isn't time now'.

Clarissa   — But Henry, it's true. That's only the beginning. The police
              came and it was just one thing after another. There was a
              narcotic ring, and Miss Peake isn't Miss Peake, she's really
              Mrs Brown, and Jeremy turned out to be the murderer and
              he was trying to steal a stamp worth £14,000.
Husband — Huh! Must have been a second Swedish yellow.
Clarissa   — That's just what it was!
Husband — The things you imagine, Clarissa!
Clarissa   — But darling. I didn't imagine it. How extraordinary it is; all
              my life nothing has really happened to me and tonight I've
              had the lot, murder, police, drug addicts, invisible ink, secret
              writing, almost arrested for manslaughter, and very nearly
              murdered. You know, in a way, it's almost *too* much all in
              one evening.
Husband — Do go and make the coffee, darling.

In that last speech of Clarissa is contained the secret of Agatha Christie's success as a writer. Her cosy, nice, middle-class audience (and they are not to be despised, fashionable though it is to decry the bourgeoisie) are able to identify with Clarissa. Their life, like that of Clarissa, is often full of boring routine and social trivia, and then after putting down the latest Agatha Christie thriller, or returning home to Forest Row after her latest play, they are able to say, Tonight I have had the lot: murder, police, drug addicts, etc—It's almost too much in one evening!

—James Roose-Evans

CHURCHILL, Caryl.

British. Born in London, 3 September 1938. Educated at Trafalgar School, Montreal, 1948–55; Lady Margaret Hall, Oxford, 1957–60, B.A. in English 1960. Married David Harter in 1961; three sons. Resident dramatist, Royal Court Theatre, London, 1974–75. Recipient: Richard Hillary memorial prize, 1961; Obie award, 1982, 1983, 1988; Susan Smith Blackburn prize, 1983, 1988; *Time Out* award, 1987; Olivier award, 1987; *Plays and Players* award, 1987; *Evening Standard* award, 1987. Agent: Casarotto Ramsay Ltd., National House, 60–66 Wardour Street, London W1V 3HP. Address: 12 Thornhill Square, London N.1., England.

Publications

PLAYS

Downstairs (produced 1958).
Having a Wonderful Time (produced 1960).
Easy Death (produced 1962).
The Ants (broadcast 1962). In *New English Dramatists 12*, 1968.
Lovesick (broadcast 1967). In *Shorts*, 1990.
Abortive (broadcast 1971). In *Shorts*, 1990.
Not, Not, Not, Not, Not Enough Oxygen (broadcast 1971). In *Shorts*, 1990.
The Judge's Wife (televised 1972). In *Shorts*, 1990.
Schreber's Nervous Illness (broadcast 1972; produced 1972). In *Shorts*, 1990.
Owners (produced 1972). 1973.
Perfect Happiness (broadcast 1973; produced 1974).
Moving Clocks Go Slow (produced 1975).
Objections to Sex and Violence (produced 1975). In *Plays by Women 4*, edited by Michelene Wandor, 1985.
Light Shining in Buckinghamshire (produced 1976). 1978.
Vinegar Tom (produced 1976). 1978.
Traps (produced 1977). 1978.
The After Dinner Joke (televised 1978). In *Shorts*, 1990.
Floorshow, with others (produced 1978).
Cloud Nine (produced 1979). 1979.
Three More Sleepless Nights (produced 1980). In *Shorts*, 1990.
Top Girls (produced 1982). 1982; revised version, 1984.
Fen (produced 1983). 1983.
Softcops (produced 1984). 1984.

Midday Sun, with Geraldine Pilgrim, Pete Brooks and John Ashford (produced 1984).
Plays 1 (includes *Owners, Vinegar Tom, Traps, Light Shining in Buckinghamshire, Cloud Nine*). 1985.
A Mouthful of Birds, with David Lan (produced 1986). 1987.
Softcops, and Fen. 1986.
Serious Money (produced 1987). 1987; revised edition, 1990.
Icecream (produced 1989). 1989.
Hot Fudge (produced 1989). In *Shorts*, 1990.
Mad Forest (produced 1990). 1990.
Shorts (includes *Lovesick; Abortive; Not, Not, Not, Not, Not Enough Oxygen; Schreber's Nervous Illness; The Hospital at the Time of the Revolution; The Judge's Wife; The After-Dinner Joke, Seagulls; Three More Sleepless Nights; Hot Fudge*). 1990.
Plays 2 (includes *Softcops, Top Girls, Fen, Serious Money*). 1990.
Lives of the Great Poisoners (produced 1991). 1993.
The Skriker (produced 1994). 1994.

RADIO PLAYS: *The Ants*, 1962; *Lovesick*, 1967; *Identical Twins*, 1968; *Abortive*, 1971; *Not, Not, Not, Not, Not Enough Oxygen*, 1971; *Schreber's Nervous Illness*, 1972; *Henry's Past*, 1972; *Perfect Happiness*, 1973.

TELEVISION PLAYS: *The Judge's Wife*, 1972; *Turkish Delight*, 1974; *The After Dinner Joke*, 1978; *The Legion Hall Bombing*, 1978; *Crimes*, 1982.

CRITICAL STUDIES: *File on Churchill* edited by Linda Fitzsimmons, 1989; *Caryl Churchill: A Casebook* edited by Phyllis R. Randall, 1989; *Churchill the Playwright* by Geraldine Cousin, 1989; *The Plays of Churchill* by Amelia Howe Kritzer, 1991.

Caryl Churchill's professional career as a playwright started in her 20's, with radio plays. These facts are important for an understanding of the unique strengths of her stage output. Her male contemporaries, such as Brenton and Hare, largely served their apprenticeship in the fringe theatre and their plays tended to articulate the romantic socialism of the late 1960's through bold theatrical effects which could be achieved with small casts and few financial resources. Radio—far easier to break into than the theatre for a young woman in an era so much less egalitarian than it looked—demanded different virtues. It works in short scenes; it has the intimacy of a story-teller's fireside; it can make ambitious leaps in time and space as long as the mind's eye of the listener is sufficiently engaged to follow them; and it can play upon that same mind's eye to create scenes of great imagined visual beauty. On the other hand, it cannot cope with clutter; redundant images can lead the imagination to give up on the job, and our closeness to the characters (they are, after all, made of pure sound, a substance which literally enters us) means that we are almost painfully alive to subtext; an attempt to spell things out too overtly will irritate. The radiophonic virtues may be summed up in a single word: concentration.

Churchill has the almost unique gift of concentrating layers of meaning in a simple, economical, and striking image. In one of her earliest plays for the

Royal Court Theatre, *Light Shining in Buckinghamshire*, an account of the upheavals of the 1640's, there is a short scene in which two women look in a mirror. On one level this is a scene about poverty and revolution: the mirror has been looted from one of the great country houses, and the woman who took it embodies the attitudes of the poor energised by Puritanism. She speaks of burning the "Norman" deeds to the land they found in the house, the symbol of an oppressive aristocracy, but of preserving the corn "because it's our corn now". She speaks of "choosing" from the array of possessions there, as if this act must be done responsibly and without greed. But this is also a scene about identity, and in particular female identity. "They must know what they look like all of the time", she says of the rich. "And now we do". To have a sense of one's own identity is to take power for oneself. The impact of the scene is increased by its juxtaposition with other scenes in which women begin to speak in church, to acquire a sense of themselves in other ways, and also by the fact that it inverts all the usual clichés of self-absorption and narcissism that adhere to the idea of a woman looking in a mirror. The woman who takes the mirror at once goes to share it with another; together they see new selves in a new world.

Churchill's economy allows her to make bold shifts in convention. Sometimes she will use the techniques of naturalism: in *Fen*, for instance, the harshness of rural East-Anglian life is seen subtextually in a scene where Val, torn between her lover Frank and her children, encounters her daughter who is living with her mother because Frank's tied cottage cannot hold them all. They swap elephant jokes. Underneath the jokes, however, we track Val's awareness that her child is slipping away from her and that she cannot hold on to her love the way things are. By the next scene she will have decided to die. But in the same play we see a ghost, casually walking in the fields and articulating her hatred of the landowner. "I live in your house", she says, "I watch television with you". She too lost her child. Nothing has changed. But the way that this surreal image integrates with the texture of everyday experience enables us to make connections and perceive Val's world in a new way.

A similar combination of the naturalistic and the surreal is employed in two plays exploring the world of the rich. *Serious Money* paints a black picture of corruption in the Stock Exchange at the time of the "big bang": it is generous with sheer information, in the style of many thrillers which use a near-documentary mode, but the slick verse spoken by the characters shifts them into the realm of the grotesque. In *Top Girls* two sisters quarrel in a realistic scene where passions are both personal and political: Marlene, who has made it as a successful executive, has left Joyce to rear her unwanted child for her, and they fight as she comes back on a visit. Their personal differences are given a political perspective by the opening scene, a banquet in which Marlene is toasted by famous women from history and hears their own stories of sexual oppression—notably that of Pope Joan, perhaps the most "successful" woman in history in terms of wielding power, albeit briefly, who was, according to legend, stoned to death for bearing a child. The play also makes leaps in time, a device explored with more complexity in her first Broadway success, *Cloud Nine*. Here the sexual and colonial oppressions of the 19th century are shown in a satirical, almost clowning spirit; but when the characters leap into the 20th century it becomes apparent that we have no right to laugh at our

Victorian legacy: the same characters struggle with their sexuality and their place in the world and only one of them, Betty, achieves any kind of personal harmony, a moment symbolised by her embrace with her Victorian self.

The multi-layered style and concentration of ideas make Churchill a difficult dramatist on the page; this has perhaps impeded or slowed up her recognition as a dramatist of major stature, but the clarity and power of her work in performance cannot be missed.

—Frances Gray

See the essay on *Cloud Nine*.

CLOUD, Darrah.

American. Born in Illinois, 11 February 1955. Educated at Goddard College, Plainfield, Vermont, B.A. 1978; University of Iowa, Iowa City, M.F.A. in creative writing 1980, M.F.A. in theater 1981. Married David Emery Owens in 1992. Recipient: University of Iowa fellowship, 1978; National Endowment for the Arts grant, 1984; Drama League award, 1991. Lives in Catskill, New York. Agent: Peregrine Whittlesey Agency, 345 East 80th Street, New York, New York 10021, U.S.A.

Publications

PLAYS

The House Across the Street (produced 1982).
The Stick Wife (produced 1987). 1987.
O, Pioneers! adaptation of the novel by Willa Cather, music by Kim D. Sherman (produced 1989).
Obscene Bird of Night (produced 1989).
The Mud Angel (produced 1990).
Braille Garden (produced 1991).
Genesis (produced 1992).
The Sirens (produced 1992).

SCREENPLAY: *The Haunted*, 1991.

MANUSCRIPT COLLECTION: New Dramatists, New York.

Darrah Cloud comments:

I am haughty enough to think that I might be able to speak for people who can't speak for themselves, so I write plays. Since I began meeting tremendous and brilliant actresses with no good parts to play, I have been obsessed with writing parts for women. And as a woman, I have found a language within my gender that is secret and which I want to reveal, so that it becomes a part of the norm. For in language is perspective, and in perspective is a whole new way of looking at things. I want women's ways of looking at things to be more prevalent in the world.

I think that I always write for my mother. I imagine her in the audience and I know what makes her laugh, what affects her, what she'll believe and what she won't. In that sense, I am always writing my mother as well. I guess I am constantly showing my mother to my mother, in order to let her see herself as not alone, as understood and appreciated, if only by me. My male characters are my mother. And so, obviously, are my female characters. If there is a dog in the play, it's always the dog my mother picked out for us when we were little. I am currently writing a musical about the life of Crazy Horse. Crazy Horse, in his struggle against an encroaching white world, and toward his own fulfill-ment as a human being, Crazy Horse is my mother.

Sometimes I put my grandmother in because she's short and funny. I have yet to write my sister. This is a goal.

I grew up in the Midwest, and there too, is a unique language based not on what is said, but on what is not said. To be midwestern is to have to intuit the subtext of conversations. If one is talking about the weather, one might actually mean something quite different; something like, "I love you," or "my wife just died and I'm lost." The weather is a very important conversational tool in the Midwest. What is not said, but felt, implied in the moment, is what I love best to write. The congress of emotions that prevent the manifestation of explanations. That creates gestures that say more than words. Open mouths with nothing coming forth from them. This strikes me as always more honest than words. I am always trying to get at the truth of a moment. And so my characters rarely say what they feel, unless they're lying, which is more honest, to me.

I believe in ghosts. I believe that animals are so much more highly evolved than people that they have gotten over language and ambition and live to live. Sometimes I think they contain the spirits of dead people.

Darrah Cloud's best work uses notable historical events as the context for her dark, satiric commentary on American domestic bliss. The result is an antic cartoonish realism that occasioned one critic to describe an early "macabre comedy" as "'Father Knows Best' as written by Joe Orton." However, Cloud's later plays, while sharing some of this loony-tune tone, tend more toward Gothic tragicomedy than farce. Fundamentally, Cloud's plays explore the means by which the violence at the heart of American society reflects itself in the dysfunction of family life—and vice versa. The plays, set in prototypical U.S. towns and cities—Birmingham, Alabama, rural Wisconsin, the suburbs of Chicago—invariably drop their sense of humor by the final fade-to-black, ending enigmatically, but ultimately questioning the poverty of American lower- and middle-class life.

Cloud's dialogue alternates passages of great lyrical beauty reminiscent of the arias Sam Shepard often wrote for his characters with scenes marked by the absurdity of a clipped, repetitious vernacular that, as David Mamet and Samuel Beckett before him discovered, creates its own powerful poeticism. All the plays contain central characters, most often female, whose struggle against their victimization tests their will, morality, and sanity. Cloud's focus on females caught in the grip of mid-American morality and restrictive social norms made her a natural choice to adapt Willa Cather's frontier fable, O, Pioneers!, for the stage. Although filmed for television, the production's success was limited. Perhaps Cloud felt her eccentric sense of humor thwarted when harnessed to the slow-burn emotionalism of Cather's novel.

The Mud Angel explores Cloud's feminist themes allegorically. In this bizarre play a rural Wisconsin farm family, symbolically named Malvetz, owns a horse named Shadow whose part is written as a speaking role to be portrayed by a female actor. The action centers around the tensions derived from the mother's threat to sell the valued yet victimized family pet. (*Braille Garden* seems a departure, focusing on a recently married couple and the consequences of the bridegroom's mysterious incapacitation that leaves him in bed, weak and frightened.)

Cloud offers her most fully developed investigation of society's subjugation of women in *The Stick Wife*. The title refers to Jessie, a woman struggling against her domesticated, dominated (identity-less) status as spouse of the Ku Klux Klan member responsible for the bombing of a Birmingham church in 1963 that resulted in the murder of four young black girls. Cloud's parallel between sexism and racism is a conscious one; she once noted in an interview how women in a patriarchical society must deny their true feelings much like slaves once did, forced to hide "their vibrant, inner life behind the 'Yes, Master' pose." The play begins with Ed leaving home to commit his despicable deed. Jessie prefers to ignore her husband's actions; when her neighbor tries to tell her that someone has bombed "a colored church," Jessie responds by pulling her dress up over her head. Jessie pays a high price for her existence: she has lost all contact with her two grown children. When alone, she experiences delusions of self-importance, playing a movie star relating her life story to an imaginary Hollywood interviewer; and she hallucinates "white ghosts" (perhaps fleeting images of her husband's evil alternate identity). The action takes place exclusively in Jessie's backyard, dominated by the clothes-line on which she hangs the white sheets that double as Ed's KKK costume and as symbols of her complicity in his crimes by virtue of their marriage bed. In this play based on a true incident, Jessie tries to free herself neither by divorcing her husband nor running away, but by secretly informing on him.

Cloud sets the action of the second act on the day of President Kennedy's assassination, two months after Ed has been indicted and imprisoned for murder. However, the independence Jessie has gained from her surreptitious action dissipates—Ed is acquitted and returns home. The ending mirrors the beginning: Ed says, "Here we go again," and although he senses something about Jessie has changed, he stalks out of the house as the lights fade on her repeatedly asking him, "Where are you going?" Jessie's helpless question mirrors the uncertainty felt by many Americans during a period marked by the violent murder of its moral and political leaders.

Cloud's earlier exploration of the violence of American life, *The House Across the Street*, contains the seeds of many of these themes. The title refers to the home in which a mass-murderer, very loosely based on John Wayne Gacy, lived. The farcical black comedy focuses on the ironically named Fortune family who never noticed anything amiss in their sedate suburban community, even though their front window looked out on the murderer's house. Donald, a thirteen-year-old budding amateur scientist (he performs experiments on his comatose Grandma), and his kid sister Donna resemble characters from a

Charles Addams cartoon. Impertinent, hip, and wizened choristers, they watch the police unearth more and more bodies across the street from their front window. For Donald, this ghoulish activity is "like watchin' a movie." Donald's gleeful shouts accompanying each discovery of a body punctuate the play, much to his mother's frustration. For like Jessie in *The Stick Wife*, Lillian, the matriarch of the family, tries to shut out ugliness by insisting on shutting the front window's blinds, as if such willed ignorance offers protection from the terrors of contemporary reality.

Cloud humorously shows such efforts to be futile. The coroner Norman Bird (a nod here to Hitchcock's Norman Bates), enters late in the first act and to Lillian's horror tracks mud from the murder site all over the carpets. Unfortunately, Cloud's dramatic energy soon spins out of control: as body-bags sprout in the living room and the catatonic grandmother returns to consciousness, a heavy-handed Freudian family feud ensues that reads like a second-rate Albee one-act. Yet within this morass Cloud still manages to summon powerful imagery to state her themes—at the point Grandma crawls into a body-bag, a succinct metaphor for American's willingness to view its elders as disposable. Although occurring in an early and uneven play, such hilarious and heartbreaking moments help mark Cloud as a playwright of original and incisive vision.

—John Istel

CONGDON, Constance S.

American. Born in Rock Rapids, Iowa, 26 November 1944. Educated at Garden City High School, Kansas, 1963; University of Colorado, Colorado Springs, B.A. 1969; University of Massachusetts, Amherst, M.A., M.F.A. 1981. Married Glenn H. Johnson, Jr. in 1971; one son. Car hop, Bob's A & W Root Beer, 1960–63, columnist, Garden City *Telegram*, 1962–3, and grocery checker, Wall's IGA, 1963–65, all in Garden City; library clerk, Pikes Peak Regional District Library, 1965–66; library clerk, University of Colorado, 1966–69, and leather worker, What Rough Beast, 1969–70, all Colorado Springs; instructor in remedial writing, St. Mary's College of Maryland, St. Mary's City, 1974–76; instructor in rhetorical writing, University of Massachusetts, Amherst, 1977–81; instructor in English composition and theatre, Western New England College, Springfield, Massachusetts, 1981–83; literary manager, 1981–88, and playwright-in-residence, 1984–88, Hartford Stage Company, Connecticut, 1984–88. Recipient: American College Theatre Festival National Playwriting award, 1981; Great American Play Contest prize, 1985; National Endowment for the Arts fellowship, 1986–87; Rockefeller award, 1988; Arnold Weissberger award, 1988; Dramalogue award, 1990; Oppenheimer award, 1990; Guggenheim fellowship, 1991. Agent: Peter Franklin, William Morris Agency, 1350 Avenue of the Americas, New York, New York 10019, U.S.A.

Publications

PLAYS

Gilgamesh (produced 1977).
Fourteen Brilliant Colors (produced 1977).

The Bride (produced 1980).
Native American (produced 1984).
No Mercy (produced 1986). 1985; in *Seven Different Plays*; edited by Mac Wellman, 1988.
The Gilded Age, adaptation of the novel by Mark Twain (produced 1986).
Raggedy Ann and Andy (for children), adaptation of the books by Johnny Gruelle, music by Hiram Titus (produced 1987).
A Conversation with Georgia O'Keeffe (produced 1987).
Tales of the Lost Formicans (produced 1988). 1990.
Rembrandt Takes a Walk (for children), adaptation of the book by Mark Strand and Red Grooms (produced 1989). In *Plays in Process 4: Plays for Young Audiences*, vol.10 no.12, 1989.
Casanova (produced 1989).
Time Out of Time (produced 1990).
Mother Goose (for children), music by Hiram Titus (produced 1990).
The Miser, adaptation of the play by Molière (produced 1990).
Madeline's Rescue (for children), adaptation of the book by Ludwig Bemelmans, music by Mel Marvin (produced 1990).
Beauty and the Beast (for children; produced 1992).

CRITICAL STUDIES: "An Interview with Constance Congdon" by Nancy Klementowski and Sonja Kuftinec, in *Studies in American Drama*, vol.4, 1989; "Constance Congdon: A Playwright Whose Time Has Come" by Susan Hussey, in *Organica*, Winter 1990; "Trying to Find a Culture: An Interview with Connie Congdon" by Lisa Wilde, in *Yale/Theatre*, vol.22 no.1, Winter 1990; article by Craig Gholson, in *Bomb*, Fall 1991; "Connie's *Casanova*" by M. Elizabeth Osborn, in *Theatre Week*, June 3–9, 1991.

Constance Congdon comments:

I have an eclectic taste in theatre, although I usually hate everything I see on Broadway. My main influences are Thornton Wilder, The Wooster Group, Caryl Churchill, also rhythm and blues and country western music, Richard Wilbur, Joni Mitchell. The American critical scene is still culturally embarrassed and defensive and trying to be something it's not—cold, cynical, politically strident, trying to out-European the changing Europeans. The American art scene is still dominated by too many people from "good" schools who have intellectual agendas that have nothing to do with what I go to theatre for. I go to have an experience that taps the mystery of living, one that comes from great passion on the part of the artist, one that has something to do with awakening or calling up the spirit that is in every theatre.

I come from about as far away from the Ivy League as is possible and am proud of it. I see myself more as an "outside artist"—one of those people who makes sculpture out of car parts in their backyard. I don't live in New York although I enjoy going in to see the work of my friends which is very good and usually found in small theatres painted flat black with bad seats and great risk or big fun (or both) going on onstage.

When I start to write a play, I imagine an empty theatre space and see who or what turns up—this is my opening image and, if I mess with it, I always pay for it and lose my way in the play. I feel that the first things I create in a new play are like coded messages for the rest of the play, and I just return to them for clues about the rest of the play. The code is in metaphor, image, and given circumstances and I just need to see it. In *Native American*—the only naturalistic play I ever wrote—I saw, very clearly, the image of a cowboy lying face down on a couch with a sheet covering him. I also saw that the couch was outside on a porch. Then I saw an old Hudson automobile up on blocks. Some of these images were memories, I realize now, but at the time, they seemed all new and rich. Why the cowboy was on the couch, face down, gave me, bit by bit, the story and then the theme. I also knew that the play had to take place in consecutive real time. I trust these early strong impulses.

I need to entertain myself and surprise myself, so my plays are usually different from each other in style—I don't like to repeat myself. I make my living doing adaptations, and I don't recommend it to young playwrights, but it's better, for me, than teaching or trying to get media work.

Constance Congdon was a published poet before she was a playwright. Her plays come to her as a series of images; they are made up of many small scenes, sometimes comic, often emotionally direct, with dialogue that goes straight to the heart of the matter. When these scenes are linked together, the result reflects the world's true complexity.

Though the lives of ordinary decent people, the pleasure and pain of sexuality, the damaging effects of gender stereotypes are primary Congdon concerns, her central subject is loss. Her very first play was a dramatization of *The Epic of Gilgamesh*, at its heart the inconsolable grief of the hero at the death of his beloved friend Enkidu. The award-winning drama *No Mercy* deals with the testing of the first atomic bomb and its after-effects, but it is fundamentally about faith, and the loss of faith—in science, in religion, in life itself. Watching the scientist J. Robert Oppenheimer cross and recross the stage—the play takes place in 1945 and 1985 simultaneously, and he is lost in time— we wonder if he is dreaming this world, whose other inhabitants are the kind of undistinguished Americans this writer lovingly brings to life. Our uncertainty about who rules the play's universe is part of the point: we are watching characters lose *their* certainty, then pick themselves up and go on.

By far the most successful of Congdon's plays to date is *Tales of the Lost Formicans*, which looks at the life of contemporary suburbia through the eyes of aliens, a perspective which shows this taken-for-granted world to be complicated, mysterious, and absurd. Behind this tragicomedy lies the death of Congdon's father, many years ago, from what we now call Alzheimer's disease, but the play is really about *America's* Alzheimer's. The father in *Formicans* is far from the only character who's confused. His recently divorced daughter has moved back home with her teenaged son, who expresses in pure form the anger and distress everyone in the play feels. By donning sunglasses the play's actors become the aliens who are trying to make sense of this disoriented civilization; *Formicans* suggests that we ourselves are the aliens, attempting to distance ourselves from our own feeling. Finally we're not sure whether "real" aliens are "really" telling the story; as in *No Mercy*, this not knowing reflects our actual position in the actual world.

The opening words of Congdon's *Casanova* are the scream of a young woman in labor: "What—is—LOVE!" The playwright's answer to this most fundamental of questions is characteristically complex. An epic play not quite under control at its first showing, *Casanova* is Congdon's richest text, and may one day be seen as a revelation of the way of our own world.

Casanova's focus on sexuality and gender was presaged by an early play, *The Bride*, which brings to mind both *Our Town* and *Spring Awakening* in its depiction of the sexual awakening of four teenagers during the 1950's. In *Casanova* Congdon uses more than 60 years of her central character's life to present the full range of sexuality in men, women, and children. The famous lover is played by two actors: during the first act the old man who is writing his memoirs watches the irresistible boy he once was; after intermission Young Casanova is horrified to witness what he has become.

Congdon's *Casanova* is a feminist corrective to those one-sided memoirs; the author's deepest sympathy goes to the very young girls this man loves and leaves. Yet Young Casanova is almost wholly appealing; Congdon sees that his society gives him permission to behave as he does, that he is not so different from other men. She shows us the complicity of women: having no other power, mothers pimp their daughters, using their beauty and virginity for their own ends. The older Casanova commits monstrous acts, including rape and child seduction, but at the same time we see that he is aging, frightened, as trapped in his sexual role as any female.

In *Casanova* bedrock biological difference makes women inevitably vulnerable. Yet there is hope in the play, and it lies in those characters who transcend the usual limits of gender. The two women who come through their encounters with Casanova unscathed are bisexual, and the play's exemplar of lasting devotion is Bobo, an aging transvestite. Once tutor to Casanova's daughter, Bobo is still taking care of her 30 years later. He is Casanova's equal and opposite force, and the most memorable incarnation yet of Congdon's special feeling for gay men.

Congdon's talent flows in many directions. Her poetic gift lends itself to opera librettos; her comic sense has enlivened a series of delightful plays for the Children's Theatre of Minneapolis. Her one-woman piece about painter Georgia O'Keeffe lets her speak of her own love of the West and her complicated feeling about the position of women artists. What knowledgeable theatre people across the country have said for years is becoming more widely known: Constance Congdon is one of the most original and revelatory writers in the American theatre today.

—M. Elizabeth Osborn

CROTHERS, Rachel.

American. Born in Bloomington, Illinois, 12 December 1878. Educated at Illinois State University Normal High School, Bloomington, graduated 1891; New England School of Dramatic Instruction, certificate 1892; Stanhope-Wheatcroft School of Acting, New York, 1897. Elocution teacher, Bloomington, 1892–96; teacher, Stanhope-Wheatcroft School, 1897–1901; founder, Stage Women's War Relief Fund, 1917; president, Stage Relief Fund, 1932–51; founder and first president, American Theatre Wing, and organized

American Theatre Wing for War Relief, 1940. Recipient: Megrue prize, 1933; Chi Omega award, 1939. *Died 5 July 1958.*

Publications

PLAYS

Elizabeth (produced 1899).
Criss-Cross (produced 1899). 1904.
Mrs. John Hobbs (produced 1899).
The *Rector* (produced 1902). 1905.
Nora (produced 1903).
The Point of View (produced 1904).
The Three of Us (produced 1906). 1916.
The Coming of Mrs. Patrick (produced 1907).
Myself, Bettina (produced 1908).
Kiddie. 1909.
A Man's World (produced 1910). 1915.
He and She (produced 1911; as *The Herfords*, produced 1912). In *Representative American Plays*, 1917; revised edition, 1925.
Young Wisdom (produced 1914). 1913.
Ourselves (produced 1913).
The Heart of Paddy Whack (produced 1914). 1925.
Old Lady 31, from the novel by Louise Forsslund (produced 1916). In *Mary the Third*, 1923.
Mother Carey's Chickens, with Kate Douglas Wiggin, from the novel by Wiggin (produced 1917). 1925.
Once upon a Time (produced 1917). 1925.
A Little Journey (produced 1918). In *Mary the Third*, 1923.
39 East (produced 1919). In *Expressing Willie*, 1924.
Everyday (produced 1921). 1930.
Nice People (produced 1921). In *Expressing Willie*, 1924.
Mary the Third (produced 1923). In *Mary the Third*, 1923.
Mary the Third; Old Lady 31; A Little Journey: Three Plays. 1923.
Expressing Willie (produced 1924). In *Expressing Willie*, 1924.
Expressing Willie; Nice People; 39 East: Three Plays. 1924.
Six One-Act Plays (includes *The Importance of Being Clothed; The Importance of Being Nice; The Importance of Being Married; The Importance of Being a Woman; What They Think; Peggy*). 1925.
A Lady's Virtue (produced 1925). 1925.
Venus (produced 1927). 1927.
Let Us Be Gay (produced 1929). 1929.
As Husbands Go (produced 1931). 1931.
Caught Wet (produced 1931). 1932.
When Ladies Meet (produced 1932). 1932.
The Valiant One. 1937.
Susan and God (produced 1937). 1938.

SCREENPLAY: *Splendor*, 1935.

CRITICAL STUDY: *Rachel Crothers* by Lois C. Gottlieb, 1979.

Theatrical activities
Directed and staged her own plays.

Rachel Crothers was America's most successful woman playwright during the early decades of the 20th century. From the turn of the century until the late 1930's her plays were a staple of the New York stage, with productions of two dozen full-length works. Her career was made still more astonishing by the fact that she usually directed her own plays and sometimes produced, designed, and (in the case of the 1920 revival of *He and She*) starred in them. In an era when women directors were even rarer on Broadway than women playwrights, Brooks Atkinson of the *New York Times* called Crothers "one of the best directors we have".

Crothers was among the first American dramatists to attempt the problem play, already popular in Europe. These dramas comprise her most important early works and, in fact, may be her most enduring legacy to American drama. *A Man's World* is a perceptive look at the double standard of morality—an issue Crothers would continue to explore throughout her career. The heroine of the play is Frank Ware, an independent 'New Woman', who is a writer, social activist, and single mother of an adopted son. When Frank eventually renounces her suitor, she does so not because he had impregnated a young single woman but because he fails to acknowledge that he, a man, shares equal responsibility for the consequences of their affair. Critics compared her rejection of him to Nora's slamming the door of her 'doll's house' in Ibsen's play.

Also powerful, in different ways, is *He and She*, which presents the dilemma of a talented woman artist caught between her desires for a career and the needs of her teenage daughter. Although Crothers resolves the play along conventional lines—family taking priority over career—she is sensitive enough to present the difficulty of the choice involved, a choice being faced by more and more women of the period.

After a spate of cloyingly sentimental comedies like *Old Lady 31* (based on Louise Forsslund's novel) and *39 East*, Crothers turned to the form that would dominate the last two decades of her career and earn her great commercial success: social comedies about women of the upper and upper-middle classes. The action is typically set in an opulent house, and the dialogue—particularly toward the end of Crothers' career—is the witty repartee of high comedy. Although the works of the early 1920's tend to focus on flappers at odds with their parents, while the later ones center on more experienced women, they share a concern with the choices and challenges facing women in a world of shifting moral values.

Among the most effective of the plays of the 1920's is a dark comedy entitled *Mary the Third*. While Crothers' comedies usually end with that most conventional of conclusions, the uniting of hero and heroine, her picture of marriage is often so bleak that the traditional ending scarcely qualifies as a happy one. Young Mary has seen the flaws in her grandmother's marriage, a union based on wheedling and deception, as well as her parents' marriage, an angry clash of disparate personalities that her mother says went sour after only five years. Mary is an articulate spokeswoman for what Crothers believed was wrong with the American marriage: young people wed before they had a chance to know their prospective mates, and women's economic dependence kept them hostages to their husbands. When Mary finally accepts the proposal of her conservative suitor, responding to much the same urges that her mother and grandmother did, her decision can only be viewed with deep irony.

Numerous characters in Crothers' later plays comment on the prevalence of sexual affairs and divorce, reflecting the changing social climate in post-World-War-I America, but none of Crothers' heroines seems to find a satisfying alternative to the flawed institution of marriage. Kitty Brown, in *Let Us Be Gay,* divorces her unfaithful husband and then tries a life of sexual adventure herself, only to discover that neither free love nor a budding business career can replace the husband she still misses.

Crothers' last produced play was also her most successful: *Susan and God,* a satirical portrait of a woman infected by a European religious enthusiasm much like the Oxford Movement. A better effort—both more substantial and wittier—is *When Ladies Meet.* Ringing still one more change on the love triangle that is a virtual constant throughout her canon, the playwright presents talented, self-sufficient Mary Howard, a novelist in love with her married publisher, Rogers Woodruff. When Mary meets his wife, the two discover empathy for each other and a realization of how badly he has treated all women. Instead of forgiving him one more time, as conventional comedy would demand, Claire Woodruff abandons her husband because of his cruelty to Mary.

Rachel Crothers was very much a Broadway playwright: she considered the art theaters of the 1910's and 1920's a 'very grave menace' to the New York stage, and her plays of the 1930's largely ignored the economic disaster that had struck the nation and the theatrical world. The author of well-crafted plays that are rarely structurally innovative, she proclaimed that 'realism at its best . . . is the highest form of dramatic writing'. Crothers' critique of a society that treats women unfairly comes from an often traditional point of view likely to alienate many late 20th-century audiences. Her 'answer' to the question of the double standard is to hold both sexes to a rigid code of morality and, along with most of her generation, Crothers seems unable to imagine women successfully synthesizing career and family.

But if Crothers is scarcely the daring artist and feminist some defenders would claim her to be, neither is she simply a prolific crafter of conventional comedies. Like her character Mary Howard, who hoped in her writing to 'say something *new* and *honest*—from a woman's standpoint', Crothers saw her work as a '*Comédie Humaine de la Femme*' that traces women's 'evolution' in modern society. The best of her problem plays and comedies combine a genuine sense of what works on stage with a thoughtful investigation of such serious issues as the double standard, the conflict between career and domestic responsibility, the challenges of the new sexual freedom, the loneliness of the career woman, and the hollowness of many marriages—problems that time and the slow currents of social change have still not resolved.

—Judith E. Barlow

See the essay on *He and She*.

D

DANIELS, Sarah.

British. Born in London in 1957. Writer-in-residence, Royal Court Theatre, London, 1984. Recipient: George Devine award, 1983. Agent: Judy Daish Associates, 83 Eastbourne Mews, London W2 6LQ, England.

Publications

PLAYS

Penumbra (produced 1981).
Ripen Our Darkness (produced 1981). With *The Devil's Gateway*, 1986.
Ma's Flesh Is Grass (produced 1981).
The Devil's Gateway (produced 1983). With *Ripen Our Darkness*, 1986.
Masterpieces (produced 1983). 1984; revised version (produced 1984), 1984, revised version, 1986.
Neaptide (produced 1986). 1986.
Byrthrite (produced 1986). 1987.
The Gut Girls (produced 1988). 1989.
Beside Herself (produced 1990). 1990.
Head-Rot Holiday (produced 1992).

Sarah Daniels has been accused of many things, but never of writing boring plays. There are some critics who find her work alarming in its representations of strong, confused, complicated, or angry women. Daniels's plays rarely portray strong men, unless we count men who abuse their positions of power. In this, she has been accused of misconstruing reality, of allowing her "feminist anger" to stand in the way of writing "good theatre." But Daniels's work is not purposefully angry or intentionally controversial in critical terms.

One suspects that a good deal of the critical alarm with which some of Daniels's work has been received is a reaction to the centrality of women in the plays and to Daniels's style, which tends to be informed by street-smart rather than academic ideas about aesthetic standards. Yet Daniels's plays need no apology, for her work is highly innovative in its self-consciously radical approach to the representation of social issues of relevance to her audiences. Daniels's work is powerful: sometimes raw, sometimes unpleasantly close to reality. Her writing is fuelled by her awareness of the complexity of life in the modern world, of different forms of sexual and racial discrimination, and of class difference. But most importantly, her writing is fuelled by two qualities rare in contemporary playwriting: a penchant for black humour, and a strength and depth of vision—unacademic, straightforward, biased, and determined—which allows Daniels to touch on subjects which others tend to gloss over or avoid altogether.

Daniels's work is often controversial, centering on themes such as pornography and violence (*Masterpieces*), rewriting of myth and reviewing of archetypal images of women (*Ripen Our Darkness*), male appropriation of women's bodies in the birthing process (*Byrthrite*), and the rights of lesbian mothers (*Neaptide*).

The best known and most controversial of her plays is *Masterpieces*, a play which deals with the issue of pornography. The central character is Rowena, a woman who watches a snuff film and who is so upset by it that she cannot separate the brutal sexual murder she has witnessed on the screen and the threat of real violence outside the cinema. When a stranger accosts her in the station, she reacts in automatic defense and shoves him; he dies on the subway line. The play shifts back and forth between exchanges with Rowena, her partner, and friends. All have different experiences of pornography, and all have difficulty seeing the issue objectively. Finally, Rowena is taken to trial for the murder of the stranger. She does not deny shoving him, but cites legal precedents of men found guilty of murder being let off with excuses such as "nagging wives." At the end of the play, Rowena describes the snuff film in graphic detail to the policewoman who waits with her for the verdict. Her final words are chilling:

> Rowena: I don't want anything to do with men who have knives or whips or men who look at photos of women tied and bound, or men who say relax and enjoy it. Or men who tell misogynist jokes.
> *Blackout.*

Masterpieces is unsettling, not only because it deals with the issue of pornography but because it challenges the distinction between soft and hard porn, and—in Rowena's final words—it suggests that the continuum from sexist jokes to real sexual violence against women is a real and dangerous one. In this way, the play depicts and challenges aspects of contemporary controversy over the pornography issue. Years after its first production *Masterpieces* is frequently produced, particularly by student and community theatre groups using it as an impetus to academic debate and social action.

Neaptide is, after *Masterpieces*, Daniels's best known and most important play, not least because it is the only play dealing with the subject of lesbianism to be produced at Britain's National Theatre. But more important is the play itself. In *Neaptide*, Daniels tells the story of Claire, a woman who finds it necessary to hide her sexual identity in order to protect her job and thereby support her young daughter. Claire is a teacher in a small secondary school, torn between defending the rights of a few lesbian pupils and remaining silent, thereby keeping the secret of her own sexuality from her peers. While she is involved in a potential child custody case, the pressure to "appear normal" is great. Meanwhile, she reads the myth of Persephone. The ending of the play is optimistic, but not overly so. Only individual women transcend such limitations: the lesbian pupils are saved when the principal of the school is embarrassed into a confession of her own homosexuality, the mother comes out of the proverbial closet and decides to fight for her child. The myth functions as a convenient analogue to contemporary problems, but not as an over-simplified model of a social corrective, nor as an all-encompassing statement about the function of roles.

Sarah Daniels often conducts research for her plays: for *Masterpieces*, she read feminist literature on the subject of pornography; for *Byrthrite* she investigated the role of midwives in the 17th century; for *The Gut Girls* she did local research into the history of women's work in the Deptford slaughterhouses. Before writing *Beside Herself*, Daniels contacted survivors of child sexual abuse, which is the play's underlying theme. *Beside Herself* is Daniels's latest full-length stage play, and her least realistic. It extends the earlier experimentation with myth and history into a complicated weaving of time frames, fiction, and "reality" in the world of one play. Her writing has taken another turn, however, in her most recent project, *Head-Rot Holiday*, a play for Clean Break Theatre Company involving the stories of women ex-prisoners and their children.

In all her plays, as in *Masterpieces*, Sarah Daniels takes issues of real importance to women's lives and puts them centre stage. Her plays are not easily pigeonholed: they don't quite fit the canon of great drama, and are difficult to argue for as replacements for any of the so-called classics on university reading lists. But they teach more about the power of the theatre and of the written word than do many of the texts found in the average classroom. Her work is difficult and controversial in the most positive, change-oriented sense. She is a playwright of courage and considerable talent.

—Lizbeth Goodman

See the essay on *Masterpieces*.

D'ARCY, Margaretta Ruth.

Irish. Born in London, England, 14 June 1934. Educated at eight different schools in and around Dublin. Left school at age 15. Trained as an actress. Married the writer John Arden in 1957; five sons (one deceased). Founding member, Kirkby Moorside Entertainment, Yorkshire, and Norman Productions, Dublin, 1963. Regents' professor, University of California, Davis, 1973; co-founder, Corrandulla Arts and Entertainment, County Galway, Ireland, 1973–75; founding member, Galway Theatre Workshop, 1976–77, Women in Media and Entertainment, from 1982, and Women's Sceal Radio and Radio Pirate Women, 1987, and from 1989, all County Galway, Ireland. Visiting lecturer, University of Bologna, Italy, 1986, and visiting examiner, University of Oran, Algeria, 1991. Recipient: Arts Council of Great Britain Playwright's award, 1972. Member, Aosdana, 1981, Time Off For Women, 1989, and honorary member, Trinidad and Tobago Domestic Workers' Union, 1989. Lives in Galway. Agent: Casarotto Ramsay Ltd., National House, 60–66 Wardour Street, London W1V 3HP, England.

Publications

PLAYS

The Happy Haven, with John Arden (produced 1960). In *New English Dramatists 4*, 1962; in *Three Plays*, 1964.

The Business of Good Government: A Christmas Play, with John Arden (also
   co-director: as *A Christmas Play*, produced 1960; as *The Business of Good
   Government*, produced 1978). 1963.
Ars Longa, Vita Brevis (for children), with John Arden (produced 1964). In
   Eight Plays 1, edited by Malcolm Stuart Fellows, 1965.
The Royal Pardon; or, The Soldier Who Became an Actor (for children), with
   John Arden (also co-director: produced 1966). 1967.
Friday's Hiding, with John Arden (produced 1966). In *Soldier, Soldier and
   Other Plays*, 1967.
The Vietnam War Game (produced 1967).
The Hero Rises Up: A Romantic Melodrama, with John Arden (also co-
   director: produced 1968). 1969.
Harold Muggins Is a Martyr, with John Arden and the Cartoon Archetypical
   Slogan Theatre (produced 1968).
Two Hundred Years of Labour History, with John Arden (produced 1971).
Granny Welfare and the Wolf, with John Arden and Roger Smith (produced
   1971).
My Old Man's a Tory, with John Arden (produced 1971).
Rudi Dutschke Must Stay, with John Arden (produced 1971).
The Ballygombeen Bequest, with John Arden (produced 1972). In *Scripts 9*,
   September 1972; revised version, as *The Little Gray Home in the West: An
   Anglo-Irish Melodrama* (produced 1982), 1982.
The Island of the Mighty: A Play on a Traditional British Theme, with John
   Arden (produced 1972; section produced, as *Handful of Watercress*, 1976)
   1974; in *Performance*, 1974.
The Henry Dubb Show (produced 1973).
The Devil and the Parish Pump, with John Arden and Corrandulla Arts and
   Entertainment (produced 1974).
The Crown Strike Play, with John Arden and the Galway Theatre Workshop
   (produced 1974).
*The Non-Stop Connolly Show: A Dramatic Cycle of Continuous Struggle in
   Six Parts*, with John Arden (also co-director; produced 1975). 5 vols.,
   1977–78; 1 vol. edition, 1986.
Sean O'Scrudu, with John Arden and the Galway Theatre Workshop (pro-
   duced 1976).
The Mongrel Fox, with John Arden and the Galway Theatre Workshop
   (produced 1976).
No Room at the Inn, with John Arden (produced 1976).
A Pinprick of History (produced 1977).
Silence, with John Arden and the Galway Theatre Workshop (produced 1977).
Mary's Name, with John Arden and the Galway Theatre Workshop (produced
   1977).
Blow-in Chorus for Liam Cosgrave, with John Arden and the Galway Theatre
   Workshop (produced 1977).
Voices of Rural Women (produced 1978).
Countess Markevicz' Incarceration (produced 1978).
The Poisoned Stream (produced 1979).
Vandaleur's Folly: An Anglo-Irish Melodrama, with John Arden (also co-
   director, produced 1978). 1981.

The Mother, with John Arden, adaptation of a play by Brecht (produced 1984).
The Making of Muswell Hill, with John Arden (produced 1984).
Opera Ag Obair (produced 1987).
Whose Is the Kingdom?, with John Arden (broadcast 1988). 1988.
Ducas Na Saoirse (produced annually, 1987–92). In *Theatre-Ireland*, 1993.
The Eleanor Mary Show (produced 1991).
Arden/D'Arcy, Plays One (includes *The Business of Good Government*; *The Royal Pardon*; *The Little Gray Home in the West*; *Ars Longa, Vita Brevis*; *Friday's Hiding*; *Vandaleur's Folley*; *Immediate Rough Theatre*). 1991.

RADIO PLAYS: *Keep Those People Moving!* (for children), with John Arden, 1972; *The Manchester Enthusiasts*, (in two parts) with John Arden, 1984, (in three parts), as *The Ralahine Experiment*, 1985; *Whose Is the Kingdom?*, with John Arden, 1988.

DOCUMENTARIES: *The Kirkbymoorside Film*, 1963; *The Unfulfilled Dream*, 1969; *Galway Rent and Rate Strike*, 1972; *Sean O'Casey: Portrait of a Rebel*, with John Arden, 1973; *The St. Bridget's Place Lower Film*, 1990.

VIDEO: *The Corrandulla Film*, 1974; *Ireland for Nicaragua*, 1985; *Greenham for Libya*, 1987; *Circus Exposé*, 1988.

OTHER

Tell Them Everything (autobiographical). 1981.
Awkward Corners: Essays, Papers, Fragments, with John Arden. 1988.

BIBLIOGRAPHY: *Arden on File* edited by Malcolm Page (for listing of collaborative work with John Arden), 1985.

THEATRICAL ACTIVITIES

DIRECTOR: **Plays**—with John Arden: several of their own plays.
Documentary and Video—*The Kirkbymoorside Film*, 1963; *The Unfulfilled Dream*, 1969; *Galway Rent and Rate Strike*, 1972; *The Corrandulla Film*, 1974; *Ireland for Nicaragua*, 1985; *Greenham for Libya*, 1987; *Circus Exposé* , 1988; *The St. Bridget's Place Lower Film*, 1990.

Margaretta D'Arcy comments:

I was struck all of a heap a few years back, when I was invited to take part in an international theatre conference—upon looking through all the bumph outlining the sessions, I discovered that the word "play" had been dropped from the vocabulary of every item. Instead, there was "text", "performers", "plastic arts", "venues", "workshops", "symposia", "practitioners", etc., etc. I decided to use the occasion to query the disappearance of "play".

From *Webster's Dictionary*: "Brisk, lively, or light activity involving change". From *Amazons, Bluestockings and Crones* (a feminist dictionary): "Play is something women are encouraged to give up at puberty in exchange for dedication to the needs of others".

And yet I remember, when I was young, going to see "plays" by the "Garryowen Players"; although by that time the word "playhouse" had already been removed and we went to see them in a "theatre". I am not sure whether there is a connection between the loss of the concept of "play" and our present-day mechanistic bums-on-seats "task-profit" syndrome where the finished commodity off the cultural production-line is all that matters and to hell with the personal growth and vision of the workers.

But on the cover of the brochure for that international conference was a quote from Mayakovsky: "Today these are only stage prop doors but tomorrow reality will replace this theatrical trash."

He wrote that in 1921, and at the same period someone else was also exploring ways of breaking down the hierachic conventions of theatrical artificiality which mirror our society, ways to put human beings in the centre. She was Neva L. Boyd, a pioneer in the field of creative group play in Chicago. Her techniques were taken up by Viola Spolin, "to stimulate expression in both children and adults through self-discovery and personal experiencing". In Spolin's book, *Improvisation for the Theatre* (1963), summing up her 30 years' work, she states: "The game is a natural group form providing the involvement and personal freedom necessary for experiencing. There must be group agreement on the rules of the game, and group-interaction moving towards the objective if the game is to be played. The first step towards playing is personal freedom. Before we can play (and then experience) we must be free to do so. Our simplest move out into the environment is interrupted by our need for favourable comment, or interpretation by established authority. We either fear we will not get approval, or we accept outside comment and interpretation unquestionably. In a culture where approval/disapproval has become the predominant regulator of effort and position, and often the substitute for love, our personal freedoms are dissipated."

It is no accident that this was written by a woman. We women are the most conditioned of the species to accept, from birth, the culture of approval/disapproval, which automatically deprives us of play. So how to reclaim play ? Monitoring my own feelings and my own feelings of stress and contradiction throughout my career in the regular non-commercial theatre (whether community theatre, political theatre, street theatre, agitprop)—feelings caused by the tension of having to organise myself between child-rearing in the home and putting together my theatre outside the home—I finally resolved the contradictions in 1981 at a women's conference in Dublin where it became apparent that women's most enjoyable activity is neither to go to a theatre, nor to act in a theatre, but to talk and listen with women, telling each other stories, making fools of ourselves and laughing at ourselves.

In consequence I came also to realise that radio is the one medium that really fulfills these requirements for women: listening to it does not interrupt the natural rhythm of one's own life, one can still get on with one's work and yet receive everything that the radio is putting out to us.

A short step from this understanding: radio as potentially the cheapest and most flexible form for women's expression.

In 1987 I set up a short-range women's radio in my own home in Galway in the west of Ireland. Not a public service for people to consume, but a radio where women can be freely on the airwaves not caring whether anyone is listening or not. In other words we play on the airwaves.

Recently in the *Irish Times* I read an economic affairs article called "New Interest in Concept of Self-reliance". It said: "A new interactive emphasis between global and indigenous forces may be discerned in recent thinking. This can lay the intellectual groundwork for policies through which small, poor or weak states may find windows of opportunity to participate more equally in the world economy. Marginalisation and how to escape from it are increasingly urgent issues. The effort must be made to ensure that an international system in which the poor transfer money to the rich can be brought to an end."

In our radio/theatre this is exactly what happens. We combine tapes of women's expression from all over the world with our own indigenous impromptus of a small corner of a provincial city—the intellect and imagination coming together, the global and the local, all intermingled with trivial gossip from one or two neighbouring streets—as someone said to me, "It has all the fascination of overhearing women chat over a garden wall, you never know where it's going to take you."

No set programmes, no profit-directed tasks for the "service of others" or the "approval of others", no hidden agenda whereby such service and such approval must always assist the patriarchal military/industrial culture which envelops us—but simply play.

And of course our greatest problem—when women are trying to do something new in contradiction of the demands of the military/industrial culture, how can we have that work recognised, valued and counted? First we must understand how to count it for ourselves; and only through the freedom of PLAY can we do so, only through the freedom of PLAY can we pass our understanding on to others.

Margaretta D'Arcy is the wife of, and collaborator with John Arden. It is customary for D'Arcy to be included as little more than a footnote in critical works on Arden. However, the plays they have written in collaboration are distinguishable in content, form, and intent from those that John Arden has written alone.

Born in Ireland, D'Arcy began acting in the fringe theatres in Dublin. Her active political commitment has been seen to stem from her Irish roots, struggling against the double bind between either being paternally absorbed by the British establishment or being marginalised. D'Arcy is too clear-minded, however, not to associate the relevance of Irish issues with other similar political structures and struggles. Her work confronts not only the patriarchal arrogance of the established hierarchy but also exposes the connections between capitalism, patriotism, and patriarchy, and the resulting misogyny.

For D'Arcy, "politics starts with the personal", describing the necessity to live with her political and social commitment in everyday life : "Had John Arden and I sorted out our values, in relation to one another, in relation to the way we thought theatre ought to be made, in relation to the relation between theatre and life?" (from *Arden/D'Arcy, Plays One*, London, Methuen, 1991).

Wherever they lived, Arden and D'Arcy became active members of the community. In the winter of 1960, when D'Arcy herself was pregnant, they created a nativity play, *The Business of Good Government*, for and with the villagers of Brent Knol, where they were living. The nativity is placed in a familiar everyday context. By clearly offering the social, personal, and political perspectives of all the characters, the play retains the quality of a traditional nativity play while simultaneously opening the socio-political context for discussion.

This active commitment to community—creating theatrical events with the community about issues central to that community—is the hallmark of the D'Arcy-Arden collaboration. D'Arcy's contribution lies arguably in the firm link between the political and the personal, in finding political implications in personal experiences and exposing the personal consequences of political issues.

The plays are boisterous expressions of popular theatre with songs, verses, mime, and larger-than-life caricatures.

D'Arcy and Arden's denials of the rigid separation between performance and audience is a political expression in itself; a blow against established conventions and the "Arts" as the province of the elite.

The Royal Pardon deals openly with the workings of the theatrical world and how it reflects the social hierarchy. A bit player and a stage hand save a theatre company's performance, but the reward for their enterprise is to be fired before the company's Royal Command Performance.

The Little Gray Home in the West tells the story of a wealthy British businessman's unscrupulous handling of the property he has inherited in Ireland. The play spans the period from 1945, when Baker-Forescue inherits the property, to 1971 when internment and the British army prompt active resistance. The property includes a ramshackle small-holding inhabited by the impoverished Seamus, his wife Teresa, and their increasing family. The play opens with Padraic, son of Seamus and Teresa, aged 26, and dead. We later discover that he was murdered at a road block where he was tortured by British soldiers who describe themselves as "mercenaries". The ghosts of the dead haunt the British in Ireland.

The characters are drawn broadly, defined by their economic and social status which, in turn, forms their motives and desires. The play's Marxist position is unabashed, dividing its world between the haves and have-nots, even denoting a no man's land where a few have-nots, in this case Hagan, are willing to betray to get more. However, typical of all the Arden-D'Arcy plays, despite its clear though complex political analysis and critical perspective, the play is neither didactic nor sentimental. Each character is given ample opportunity to voice his/her reasons and explain his/her motives. In the end it is these motives, along with their practical implications for both personal experience and social morality, that are at stake. One empathises with the landlord's disappointment and anger when his friends holiday at his "chalet" and find it filthy and full of chickens, or when the high winds cause rack and ruin. But the greed and callousness that drive his feelings and form the guile with which he cheats his tenants turn our sympathies against him.

Seamus is forced to sign a document that gives Baker-Forescue ownership of the humble cottage when Seamus dies. As Seamus signs, he and Baker-Forescue take on the roles of Michael Collins and Lloyd George, clearly exposing the contract as an encapsulation of Anglo-Irish relations, a symbol of the greed and deceit practiced by the powerful on the powerless.

Caricature, song, verse, and music-hall asides give the performance a vibrant energy which gives the complex moral and political analysis emotional power by setting it in relief. *The Little Gray Home in the West* ends perversely with a custard pie fight, the climax of a Laurel and Hardy type antagonism between Hagan and Baker-Forescue initiated by the dead Padraic. The property is summarily blown up by the I.R.A., and Baker-Forescue takes his business methods to Europe.

It has been suggested that the fundamental antagonism between the West End theatre and D'Arcy-Arden plays (they have not had a play produced in the West End since 1972) lies in the form of the plays rather than directly with the content. This is a salient argument. If the theatre is "the world", a microcosm of the social context, then the structure of each play implies social structure. The formal, highly-structured conventional theatre with its audience firmly separated from the performance and the controlled, enclosed structure of the realistic play can be seen to reflect an image of a highly-structured hierachical society. Inevitably, the anarchic, varied structure of a D'Arcy-Arden play with its myriad of scenes, its songs and poems, its open stage where anything can happen, its cartoon characters and broad sweeps of time and space, and its direct relationship with the audience suggests an energetic rejection, if not ridicule, of the established hierarchies and offers a viable alternative.

In 1972 the *The Island of the Mighty* was produced by the Royal Shakespeare Company. The play presents the problems of the lame King Arthur against the poverty and suffering of his subjects. The text requires equal weight be given to Arthur's struggling subjects and his personal crisis, opening discussions regarding historical perspectives, national myth, patriotism, and storytelling. Without this balance the issues are aborted and the story becomes a shallow depiction of the romantic pathos of a failing hero.

D'Arcy and Arden expressed their commitment both to the macrocosm of socio-politics and the microcosm of theatre by literally picketing the Aldwych Theatre where the play was rehearsing. The RSC insisted the quarrel was personal rather than political or moral; ironically reflecting the onstage reduction of complex discussion of the political implications of national mythologising to a sentimental illustration of personal pathos. D'Arcy who had not been allowed to visit rehearsals until the run-throughs was dismissed as a "difficult woman".

Nothing could more explicitly illustrate the necessity and urgency in this talented, tireless woman's energetic fight against the patriarchal hierarchy.

— Elaine Turner

DE GROEN, Alma (née Mathers).

New Zealander. Born in Foxton, 5 September 1941. Educated at Mangakino District High School, Waikato, 1954–57. Married Geoffrey De Groen in 1965; one daughter. Library assistant, New Zealand National Library Service, Wellington and Hamilton, 1958–64, and Sydney University library, Australia, 1964–65; librarian, New Zealand Trade Commission, Sydney, 1965; writer-in-residence, West Australian Institute of Technology, Perth, 1986; dramaturg,

Griffin Theatre Company, Sydney, 1987; writer-in-residence, University of Queensland, St. Lucia, 1989, and Rollins College, Florida, 1989. Recipient: Canada Council grant, 1970; Australian Writers Guild award, 1985; New South Wales Premier's award, 1988; Victorian Premier's award, 1988. Agent: Hilary Linstead & Associates, Suite 302, Easts Tower, 9–13 Bronte Road, Bondi Junction, New South Wales 2022, Australia.

Publications

PLAYS

The Joss Adams Show (produced 1970). In *Going Home and Other Plays*, 1977.
The Sweatproof Boy (produced 1972).
Perfectly All Right (produced 1973). In *Going Home and Other Plays*, 1977.
The After-Life of Arthur Cravan (produced 1973).
Going Home (produced 1976). In *Going Home and Other Plays*, 1977.
Chidley (produced 1977). In *Theatre Australia*, January/February, 1977.
Going Home and Other Plays. 1977.
Vocations (produced 1981). 1983.
The Rivers of China (produced 1987). 1988.
The Girl Who Saw Everything (produced 1991).

RADIO PLAY: *Available Light* (two monologues for women), 1991.

TELEVISION PLAYS: *Man of Letters*, adaptation of the novel by Glen Tomasatti, 1985; *Chris* (episode) in *Singles* series, 1986; *After Marcuse*, 1986; *The Women* (episode) in *Rafferty's Rules* series, 1987.

Swathed in bandages, the figure of a hospital patient, featuring in Alma De Groen's most acclaimed play, *The Rivers of China*, provides an appropriate icon for much of her work which focuses on the more painful moments of human existence while generally rejecting nihilism or despair. Always interested in relationships between the sexes, De Groen frequently foregrounds art as the contested ideological space on and through which male/female conflicts are enacted. She is deeply concerned with the role of the female artist in patriarchal society, exploring this issue not only through dialogue but also in structure which she aims to make exactly parallel to the audience's experience of a particular play. Although she has experimented with naturalism and episodic realism, De Groen's best works achieve a fluidity of form that characterises the feminist aesthetic in its ability to break down boundaries and challenge conventional expectations.

The *Joss Adams Show*, an early but very accomplished one-act play, exhibits precisely this fluid movement between time and place, reality and the surreal, as it presents the biting story of a young woman who beats her baby to death while those around her fail to notice how unhappy, trapped, and desperate she feels. Framed by its introduction as a television show, Joss's story positions her husband and relatives, as well as the audience, as voyeuristic accomplices to the baby's beatings. Understated, and at times even funny, the narrative clearly lays much of the blame for Joss's actions on the shoulders of an uncaring patriarchal society which provides women with few real economic and social options to cope with neglect and violence.

Going Home and *Vocations* also explore contemporary woman's search for a meaningful "home," a position or reference point from which to act without being overwhelmed by the demands of a male-dominated society. *Going Home*, which focuses on the relationships between a group of Australians living in Canada, uses the physical exile of its antagonists to stress their alienation from each other and their lack of a sense of identity rooted in place. While the men are caught up in bombast and petty rivalries over their successes and failures as expatriate artists, the women show their dislocation more elliptically through compulsive spending and eating. These symptoms point not only to general unhappiness but also to deeply felt pain that can be linked to emotional trauma, and, in Molly's case, even rape. Although most of the characters idealise the environments they left behind, the play suggests that "going home" is clearly a problematic process which involves not just physical relocation but some kind of resolution to the enacted gender conflicts. *Vocations* extends some of these themes in its representation of two couples struggling to maintain meaningful relationships with each other while they develop their individual careers. Though the four find some kind of "home" in artistic expression, the struggle for recognition and independence is clearly much harder for the women. For them, "home" remains an elusive place best posited as a feeling of connectedness with the universe and the self, a space fiercely defended but always vulnerable. In particular, Vicki's profession as an actor is not only compromised by her pregnancy but also by her partner Ross who is bent on managing the pregnancy, the baby, and everything else. Her friend Joy, a writer, faces similar usurpation when her husband uses her as the subject of his feminist novel, "packag[ing] all her pain" without first feeling it. Much of the dramatic energy of the play results from the women's efforts to resist this appropriation of their space, their vocations, and indeed their bodies. Though richly comic in its depictions of the battle of the sexes, *Vocations* nonetheless poses some complex questions about what men, as well as women, should be allowed to be.

The Rivers of China marks an important point in De Groen's development as a dramatist. It brings together many of her earlier themes, dealing even more incisively with contemporary sexual politics while merging content with form to create a visually exciting and intellectually provocative play. Indulging her interest in "walking around in other times," here De Groen follows two earlier pieces on historical figures, *Chidley* and *The After-Life of Arthur Cravan*, with an account of the last few months in the life of Katherine Mansfield. Although its major thrust is undoubtedly feminist, *The Rivers of China* also offers powerful moments for post-colonial readings through Mansfield's efforts to delineate a position for the nascent colonial woman artist immured in the territorialised spaces of the imperial patriarchal canon. To recuperate Mansfield as an historical figure is only one aim of the play. Her story is interwoven with, and indeed transformed by, a contemporary narrative set in a feminist dystopia in present-day Sydney. In this "brave new world," women have physical, economic and cultural power, while the men continually struggle for recognition and freedom of expression. But the play never suggests that this dystopia is preferable to patriachal society; rather it problematises simple inversions of the current power structures by recreating Mansfield's mind and spirit in the body of a young man who wakes up in hospital after trying to commit suicide. Structurally, the narrative disrupts chronology, taking the audience on a difficult journey that emphasises slippages between past and present, between masculine and feminine, and between sickness and health. Above all, this play is about ways of seeing.

De Groen's most recent play, *The Girl Who Saw Everything*, similarly focuses on ways of interpreting the world but its characters are more question-ing of the aesthetic refractions of reality that art provides, especially when they are faced with marital breakdown and mid-life crises. Witty as always but less complex and challenging than *The Rivers of China*, this latest critique of patriarchy also avoids polemic and demonstrates a great deal of sympathy for the position of men as well as women in our society.

—Helen Gilbert

See the essay on *The Rivers of China*.

DELANEY, Shelagh.

British. Born in Salford, Lancashire, 25 November 1939. Educated at Broughton Secondary School. Has one daughter. Worked as salesgirl, usher-ette, and photographer's laboratory assistant. Recipient: Foyle New Play award, 1959; Arts Council bursary, 1959; New York Drama Critics Circle award, 1961; BAFTA award, 1962; Robert Flaherty award, for screenplay, 1962; Encyclopaedia Britannica award, 1963; Writers Guild award, for screenplay, 1969; Cannes Film Festival award, 1985. Fellow, Royal Society of Literature, 1985. Agent: Tessa Sayle, 11 Jubilee Place, London SW3 3TE, England.

Publications

PLAYS

A Taste of Honey (produced 1958). 1959.
The Lion in Love (produced 1960). 1961.
The House That Jack Built (televised 1977; produced 1979). 1977.
Don't Worry about Matilda (broadcast 1983; produced 1987).

SCREENPLAYS: *A Taste of Honey*, with Tony Richardson, 1961; *The White Bus*, 1966; *Charlie Bubbles*, 1968; *Dance with a Stranger*, 1985.

RADIO PLAYS: *So Does the Nightingale*, 1981; *Don't Worry about Matilda*, 1983.

TELEVISION PLAYS: *Did Your Nanny Come from Bergen?*, 1970; *St. Martin's Summer*, 1974; *The House That Jack Built* series, 1977; *Find Me First*, 1981.

OTHER

Sweetly Sings the Donkey. 1963.

CRITICAL STUDIES: *Anger and After* by John Russell Taylor, 1969; *Feminist Theatre* by Helene Keyssar, 1984; *Look Back in Gender* by Michelene Wandor, 1987.

Judged solely on the plots, Shelagh Delaney's first two plays would seem to place her with her hands firmly in the kitchen-sink world of working-class life: all penny-in-the-slot and gasworks-in-view, Northern grime and vowel sounds. *A Taste of Honey* takes place in a seedy bedsit. Helen, a "semi-whore", leaves with her latest fancy man, abandoning her teenage daughter. The girl, Jo, is an embarrassment: old enough to undermine Helen's perpetual youth, and pregnant by a black sailor. Jo and Geoffrey (a homosexual art student) care for each other, but he leaves when Helen returns, her latest romance in ruins. The two women are left alone, together. There is no suggestion that life will be much different for the unborn child.

Less well known, *The Lion in Love* features a larger cast coping with the same lack of choices. Frank is forever about to leave Kit who, typically, has been arrested for drunk and disorderly behaviour just as the play opens. Both their children dream of a better life. One is set to emigrate, the other is falling in love. Not much hope is suggested for either. A street corner prophet appears from time to time, predicting change. The action demonstrates the unlikeliness of this. Social determinism reigns.

Obviously Delaney was influenced by what came before, but it is a mistake to regard her plays as part of any continuum of social realism.

John Osborne's *Look Back in Anger* is popularly held to have hurled stones through the drawing-room windows of British theatre in the mid-1950's, and a comparison of the depiction of female characters in that play with the protagonists of *A Taste of Honey* and *The Lion in Love* is revealing. Constantly Delaney presents women toughened by circumstance. Frustrated, trapped, and dissatisfied, they are offered only momentary sweetness in a bleak world. Economic dependency is stressed, whether in marriage or prostitution, which Delaney depicts without sentiment or moral judgements. The unsatisfactory nature of sexual relationships is revealed again and again. Peg's careless rapture in *The Lion in Love* is undercut by her mother and father's tormented marriage and the life of Nell, the local street-corner tart. Sex results in unwanted pregnancy. The only tenderness displayed between men and women (other than siblings) is between the pregnant Jo and the homosexual Geoffrey. Even that relationship is doomed; unfortunately, Delaney is of her time in her stereotypical depiction of the feminised and unhappy gay outsider.

Delaney's women's lives and actions are responsive to male behaviour. (Ruth Ellis, the heroine of Delaney's notable screenplay for *Dance with a Stranger*, is perhaps the ultimate example of this.) Nevertheless the very act of representing such lives, of celebrating the strength and endurance of these women, of declaring that such things are an appropriate subject to place centre-stage, is a proto-feminist gesture.

In the same way that Delaney began the reclamation of women's domain that is seen in the work of later, feminist playwrights, her plays anticipate the concern with how a story is told, as much as with what is told. On both sides of the Atlantic, writers such as Megan Terry, Caryl Churchill, and Pam Gems have abandoned traditional (male) theatrical structures in the belief that form *and* content must change to reflect different concerns. Joan Littlewood, who was attempting to establish a new, populist form of theatre saw the potential and significance of the expressionistic, non-naturalistic style of *A Taste of Honey*. The play—first staged by Littlewood's Theatre Workshop—has no fourth wall. A jazz trio accompany and heighten the action. Characters turn from each other mid-sentence, and address the audience directly. In *The Lion in Love*, music is again integral. The structure is episodic, following the various related but separate stories, while the location shifts accordingly between home and street market. (All in all, the play is probably unstageable. Certainly, it met nowhere near the acclaim of *A Taste of Honey* nor has it been revived in the same way.)

It is beyond the brief of this piece to speculate why, after only two plays for the stage and just turned 20 years old, Delaney gave up writing for the theatre in favour of other media. It is tempting to imagine that she was already weary of the patronising amazement of much contemporaneous criticism, which constantly marvelled that a teenage, Northern shop girl could produce art. With hindsight, it is easy to dismiss Delaney's plays as minor period pieces. Like most work which resolutely addresses and reflects the social mores of its time, the plays have not worn well. But Delaney's plays were unique, not to say isolated at the time. Her concern with form and the emphasis she places on working-class women's experience means that Delaney's true significance lies beyond her plays, in her influence.

—Joss Bennathon

See the essay on *A Taste of Honey*.

DREXLER, Rosalyn.

American. Born in New York City, 25 November 1926. Self-educated. Married Sherman Drexler in 1946; one daughter and one son. Painter, sculptor, singer, and wrestler; taught at the University of Iowa, Iowa City, 1976–77. Recipient: Obie award, 1965, 1979, 1985; Rockefeller grant, 1965 (2 grants), 1968, 1974; *Paris Review* fiction prize, 1966; Guggenheim fellowship, 1970; Emmy award, 1974. Agent: (drama) Helen Harvey Associates, 410 West 24th Street, New York, New York 10011; (literary) Georges Borchardt Inc., 136 East 57th Street, New York, New York 10022, U.S.A.

Publications

PLAYS

Home Movies; and Softly, and Consider the Nearness, music by Al Carmines (produced 1964). In *The Line of Least Existence and Other Plays*, 1967.
Hot Buttered Roll (produced 1966). In *The Line of Least Existence and Other Plays*, 1967; with *The Investigation*, 1969.
The Investigation (produced 1966). In *The Line of Least Existence and Other Plays*, 1967; with *Hot Buttered Roll*, 1969.
The Line of Least Existence (produced 1967). In *The Line of Least Existence and Other Plays*, 1967.
The Line of Least Existence and Other Plays. 1967.

The Bed Was Full (produced 1972). In *The Line of Least Existence and Other Plays*, 1967.
Skywriting, in *Collision Course* (produced 1968). 1968.
Was I Good? (produced 1972).
She Who Was He (produced 1973).
The Ice Queen (produced 1973).
Travesty Parade (produced 1974).
Vulgar Lives (produced 1979).
The Writers' Opera, music by John Braden (produced 1979).
Graven Image (produced 1980).
Starburn, music by Michael Meadows (produced 1983).
Room 17–C (produced 1983).
Delicate Feelings (produced 1984).
Transients Welcome (includes *Room 17–C, Lobby, Utopia Parkway*) (produced 1984). 1984.
A Matter of Life and Death (produced 1986).
What Do You Call It? (produced 1986).
The Heart That Eats Itself (produced 1987).
The Flood (produced 1992).

NOVELS

I Am the Beautiful Stranger. 1965.
One or Another. 1970.
To Smithereens. 1972; as *Submissions of a Lady Wrestler*, 1976.
The Cosmopolitan Girl. 1975.
Dawn: Portrait of a Teenage Runaway (as Julia Sorel). 1976.
Alex: Portrait of a Teenage Prostitute (as Julia Sorel). 1977.
Rocky (novelization of screenplay; as Julia Sorel). 1977.
See How She Runs (novelization of screenplay; as Julia Sorel). 1978.
Starburn: The Story of Jenni Love. 1979.
Forever Is Sometimes Temporary When Tomorrow Rolls Around. 1979.
Bad Guy. 1982.

OTHER

Rosalyn Drexler: Intimate Emotions. 1986.

Rosalyn Drexler comments:

I try to write with vitality, joy, and honesty. My plays may be called absurd. I write to amuse myself. I often amuse others.

Almost all my reviews have been excellent, but I am not produced much. It seems that every theatre wants to premiere a play. (That's how they get grants.) Therefore, if a play is done once, good or bad, that's it for the playwright— unless she is Ibsen, Shaw . . . etc.

Playwriting is my first love, I'm considered established, but I have just begun.

Rosalyn Drexler came to prominence as a novelist and playwright at a time when the absurdist symbolism of Albee was very much in vogue. Her own work of the 1960's has sometimes been called "pop art," and it has also been billed as "An Evening of Bad Taste"; whichever, it seems very much a reaction against the intellectualism and pretentiousness which surrounded the theatre of the absurd. She has remained true to her early style in the 1980's, and has found sympathetic—and still emphatically "alternative"—production milieus with groups like the Omaha Magic Theater.

Bad taste is often both the subject and the style of Drexler's plays, manipulating the audience into compromising corners. *The Investigation* presents itself as a simple if not naïve parable about a police interrogation of an adolescent murder suspect, a timid, puritanical boy who is eventually bullied by the police into suicide. Some critics found it a fashionable tract against police brutality, and hence a very slight work. The characters are, as usual in Drexler, two-dimensional, but the boy is so colourless that he is unengaging as an object of sympathy. The detective, on the other hand, is so resourceful that his techniques of sadistic attrition become the main theatrical dynamic. Much of the detective's imaginative energy is invested in verbal reconstruction of the grotesque rape and murder, putting the boy in the central role. As the audience receives no evidence from any external source, there remains the possibility that the facts which the detective narrates may be correct, and that what appears to be his sadism is in fact nausea at an outrageous crime. In the second scene there is a surprising technical twist when the murder victim's twin sister introduces herself to the audience and volunteers to re-enact the crime, using a boyfriend of hers as the accused boy. That this is parodic is obvious—they congratulate each other on their performances and show no sadness that a girl has been killed—but the mechanics of the parody are obscure. Does the scene represent the detective's hypothesis? or the boy's nightmare? or public assumptions about what happens when repression meets precociousness? The only possibility to be eliminated is that the scene shows what really happened. When questions like these are left open at the end of a play, the author can hardly be accused of triteness.

If questions are generated prodigally, Drexler also seems to have many techniques for ensuring that her plays do not become too meaningful; the title-piece for her collection, *The Line of Least Existence*, may consist of profundity or malapropism. Verbal vandalism certainly does exist in that play, but so also does an utterly unpretentious playfulness, in which words are discovered and traded just for their phatic values. Because Drexler's dramatic world is never remotely naturalistic, the reference of words is often totally unclear; one wonders whether "least existence" actually defines the dramatic cosmos as a sort of limbo, especially when at the end the central character, with a heroic irresponsibility, commits his wife and himself to a mental asylum. In *Hot Buttered Roll*, Mr Corrupt Savage, a senile bedridden billionaire, exercises his waning appetites with the assistance of a call girl and an amazonian bodyguard who from time to time throws him back into bed. The cast also includes two pimps, a "purveyor of girly girls" and a "purveyor of burly girls," but the essential action seems to be in a bunker, where all connections and relationships have been severed and the use of appetite is tentative and vicarious. As with the detective in *The Investigation*, the more scabrous parts of the dialogue sometimes have a vatic quality, so that the impact is often in its vagueness or suggestiveness. Thus the play's central image is never clearly stated, but seems to be that of (gendered) man as a sort of transplant patient, his facilities being monitored externally, his needs being canvassed through a huge mail-order system, and his responses being tested by the bizarre performances by the call girl at the foot of the bed. Very similar in rationale is *Softly, and Consider the Nearness*, in which a woman uses a television set as a surrogate world of experience.

In a later play, *Skywriting*, there are only two characters, and their referential functions are trimmed back even further: the unnamed Man and Woman seem to be archetypes, and as such make this an important work, a transition from the pop plays of the 1960's towards the mythical work of the 1970's. Beyond the fact that the diction seems closer to Drexler's Bronx than to Eden, the play is not located in any time or place. The two characters, segregated on either side of the stage, argue about the possession of a huge (projected) picture postcard of clouds. As in Shepard, the sky is perceived as a fantasy arena, and the characters instinctively take a territorial attitude to it, invading each other's minds as they defend their sexuality. This is a very clever and economical play, in which the primordial merges with the futuristic before dissolving in a throw-away ending. *She Who Was He* investigates the world of myth and ritual in an exotic, distant past; the style is lavish and operatic, but the attempt at transcendence has been problematic for audiences. In her Obie-winning *The Writers' Opera*, Drexler returns to her more familiar mode, the perversely illogical associative collage of stereotypical items. The pretentiousness and fickleness of the art world is the satirical target in this play, and this world is reflected in the domestic behaviour of the central characters, where a transsexual finds himself in an Oedipal relationship with his son. Such events differ only in degree from the ingredients of her first stage success, *Home Movies*, where outrageous farcical grotesquerie revolves round the prodigal and inventive sexuality of the characters. There, as throughout Drexler's large output of plays, novels, and novelizations, her most characteristic trait, the ridiculous pun, typifies an author who defies critical assessment while at the same time—in her own inimitable phrasing—she "shoots the vapids."

—Howard McNaughton

DUFFY, Maureen (Patricia).

British. Born in Worthing, Sussex, 21 October 1933. Educated at Trowbridge High School for Girls, Wiltshire; Sarah Bonnell High School for Girls; King's College, London, 1953–56, B.A. (honours) in English 1956. Schoolteacher for five years. Co-founder, Writers Action Group, 1972; joint chair, 1977–78, and president, 1985–89, Writers Guild of Great Britain; chair, Greater London Arts Literature Panel, 1979–81; vice-chair, 1981–86, and since 1989 chair, British Copyright Council; since 1982 chair, Authors Lending and Copyright Society; vice-president, Beauty Without Cruelty; fiction editor *Critical Quarterly*, Manchester, 1987. Recipient: City of London Festival Playwright's prize, 1962; Arts Council bursary, 1963, 1966, 1975; Society of Authors travelling scholarship, 1976. Fellow, Royal Society of Literature, 1985. Agent: Jonathan Clowes Ltd., Ironbridge House, Bridge Approach, London NW1 8BD. Address: 18 Fabian Road, London SW6 7TZ, England.

Publications

PLAYS

The Lay-Off (produced 1962).
The Silk Room (produced 1966).
Rites (produced 1969). In *New Short Plays 2*, 1969.
Solo, Old Thyme (produced 1970).
A Nightingale in Bloomsbury Square (produced 1973). In *Factions*, edited by
    Giles Gordon and Alex Hamilton, 1974.

RADIO PLAY: *Only Goodnight*, 1981.

TELEVISION PLAY: *Josie*, 1961.

NOVELS

That's How It Was. 1962.
The Single Eye. 1964.
The Microcosm. 1966.
The Paradox Players. 1967.
Wounds. 1969.
Love Child. 1971.
I Want to Go to Moscow: A Lay. 1973; as *All Heaven in a Rage*, 1973.
Capital. 1975.
Housespy. 1978.
Gor Saga. 1981.
Scarborough Fear (as D.M. Cayer). 1982.
Londoners: An Elegy. 1983.
Change. 1987.
Illuminations. 1991.
Occam's Razor. 1993.

VERSE

Lyrics for the Dog Hour. 1968.
The Venus Touch. 1971.
Actaeon. 1973.
Evesong. 1975.
Memorials of the Quick and the Dead. 1979.
Collected Poems. 1985.

OTHER

The Erotic World of Faery. 1972.
The Passionate Shepherdess: Aphra Behn 1640–1689. 1977.
Inherit the Earth: A Social History. 1980.
Men and Beasts: An Animal Rights Handbook. 1984.
A Thousand Capricious Chances: A History of the Methuen List 1889–1989.
    1989.

Editor, with Alan Brownjohn, *New Poetry 3*. 1977.
Editor, *Oroonoko and Other Stories*, by Aphra Behn. 1986.

Editor, *Love Letters Between a Nobleman and His Sister*, by Aphra Behn. 1987.
Editor, *Five Plays*, by Aphra Behn. 1990.

Translator, *A Blush of Shame*, by Domenico Rea. 1968.

MANUSCRIPT COLLECTION: King's College, University of London.

CRITICAL STUDIES: by Dulan Barber, in *Transatlantic Review 45* Spring 1973; *Guide to Modern World Literature* by Martin Seymour-Smith, 1973, as *Funk and Wagnalls Guide to Modern World Literature*, 1973; *A Female Vision of the City* by Christine Sizemore, 1989.

Maureen Duffy comments:

(1973) I began my first play in my third year at university, finishing it the next year and submitting it for the *Observer* playwriting competition of 1957–58. I had done a great deal of acting and producing at school and at this stage my aim was to be a playwright as I was already a poet. I wrote several more plays and became one of the Royal Court Writers Group which met in the late 1950's to do improvisations and discuss problems. I have continued to write plays alternately with novels and every time I am involved in a production I swear I will never write anything else. From early attempts to write a kind of poetic social realism I have become increasingly expressionist. *Solo, Olde Tyme* and *Rites* are all on themes from Greek mythology. *Megrim*, the play I am working on at present, is a futurist study of racialism and the making of a society. I believe in theatrical theatre including all the pantomime elements of song, dance, mask and fantasy and in the power of imagery.

Maureen Duffy is firmly established as one of the foremost novelists of her generation. During the past 30 years she has also written plays; the fact that these, with the possible exception of *Rites*, have not yet received the recognition they deserve is due quite as much to an absence of a fortuitous conjunction of circumstance typical of the theatre and necessary for the achievement of success, as to the demands made on the audience by the author.

Duffy's plays are not "easy." They are densely written, pitched between fantasy and realism, and have allegorical undertones. At the centre of her work lie three short plays derived from Greek myths: The Bacchae (*Rites*), Narcissus (*Solo*), and Uranus (*Olde Tyme*).

Rites, which first appeared in an experimental programme of plays presented by the National Theatre, is set in a ladies' public lavatory, presided over by the monstrous Ada (*Agave*). Duffy describes it as a black farce. She use a chorus of modern prototypes—three office girls, a cleaner, an old tramp—and involves them in situations both modern (a girl's attempted suicide in a cubicle) and parallel to the myth. Her Dionysus is a boy doll, brought in by two women and examined with gloating curiosity; her Pentheus a transvestite lesbian, dressed like a man. She is brutally murdered as a consequence of entering this exclusive women's domain, and disposed of in the incinerator for sanitary towels. It helps to know *The Bacchae*, but it is by no means essential. The strength of the play resides in the power of the writing, the violence of its situations, and the deliberate "Peeping Tom" element.

In *Solo* her Narcissus is a man, reflecting on his image in a bathroom mirror: again a deft blending of the modern and the ancient mythical.

Olde Tyme, which deals with the castration of Uranus, is in many ways her most interesting and original play, but dramatically the least convincingly realized. It is studded with brilliant, Pirandellian ideas. Her hero is a television tycoon, keeping his employees in slavish dependence. He sustains his confidence with the help of cherished memories of his mother, a queen of the Music Halls. The slaves get their chance to revolt when he hires a derelict theatre and forces them to recreate an old Music Hall evening, with his mother as the star. This he plans to film and preserve for posterity.

Sexual fantasies are enacted, and at last his "mother" appears and punctures with her revelations the whole basis of the tycoon's life. He is destroyed ("castrated") and his minions take over. There are echoes here of Jean Genet's *The Balcony*, but the play's effectiveness is undermined by the lack of credibility of the characters. To dehumanize a three-dimensional character and make him two-dimensional will engage an audience's emotions, but you cannot flatten caricatures.

Among Duffy's other works for the stage are *The Silk Room*, which chronicles the gradual disintegration of a pop group, and a play about François Villon. The unproduced *Megrim* is an expressionist, futuristic fantasy about a secluded society. It combines the nightmarish quality of Fritz Lang's film *Metropolis* with the intellectual daring of the discussions contained in Shaw's late extravaganzas. To these Duffy has added a human, mainly sexual dimension of her own. It makes a rich but probably undigestible concoction.

More modestly, and entirely successfully, *A Nightingale in Bloomsbury Square* shows us Virginia Woolf going though a lengthy creative stocktaking prior to suicide before a spectral audience consisting of Sigmund Freud and Vita Sackville-West. It is an interrupted monologue, written with great sympathy and power.

Duffy is a writer of fierce originality and imaginative depth; hopefully, she will take the opportunity at some point to prove herself to a wider public as a dramatist, too.

—Frank Marcus

DUNBAR, Andrea.

British. Born in Bradford, Yorkshire, 22 May 1961. Educated at Buttershaw Comprehensive School, Bradford. Has two daughters and one son. Recipient: George Devine award, 1981. Died 1991.

Publications

PLAYS

The Arbor (produced 1980). 1980.
Rita, Sue, and Bob Too (produced 1982). 1982; screen version, 1988.

Shirley (produced 1986). 1988.
Rita, Sue, and Bob Too; The Arbor; Shirley. 1988.

SCREENPLAY: *Rita, Sue, and Bob Too*, 1987.

Andrea Dunbar was unique: an original voice, not waving but shouting from the underclass of the North of England, a class that is jobless, school-less, and money-less. Her plays, not so much slices as hacksaw chunks, expose rough life on a Bradford council estate, where family violence is the norm, drinking and fighting the main entertainments, and you're odd one out if you haven't been sexually abused by the time you are 12. Dunbar wrote, not as a middle-class voyeur, but as an active protagonist, and it is this which gives her plays a bleak truthfulness and rich vein of humour. Dunbar's characters, particularly the women, have a resilience and wit that make their actions funny and moving, as well as shocking.

Her first and still most famous play describes family life on a breezeblock estate, inappropriately named The Arbor by some town planner with a sense of humour. A young girl becomes pregnant and her family react in various ways. Her father, a drunken bully, beats her up; her mother, a put-upon but still spirited woman, tries ineptly to help. Her brothers, sisters, and neighbours join in the family battles, which eventually rage up and down the entire street. The girl is sent away to a mother-and-baby home where she learns sums in the morning and nappy changing in the afternoon and comes up against a very different class of people. Figures of authority punctuate this play, as in all Dunbar's others. Social workers, teachers, policemen all attempt to interfere and alter the course of the girl's life. Dunbar sees them as through the small end of the telescope, not necessarily with hostility but with curiosity. They inhabit another world, strange and distant from the lives of the main protagonists. Some of Dunbar's wittiest scenes lie in the addressing of authority across a major gap in life experience.

In *Rita, Sue, and Bob Too* a married man has sex with two under-aged girls, who then compete with each other and with his wife for his favours. Again, violence is never far (a couple of lagers, usually) from the surface, and often quickly erupts. The men visit it upon the women, the women upon each other. It's a fact of life, no better or worse than any other. A black eye or broken tooth is proof of love. Or at least of possession. Thrills in this environment consist of what comes cheap—beer, glue, and sex, with a preference for the last as it comes cheapest of all. But if a girl falls pregnant, she's on her own and she's a sissy if she can't cope.

In *Shirley* Dunbar examines for the first time the relationship between two women. Shirley and her mother, at violent odds with each other at the start of the play, screaming abuse in the presence of their respective alarmed and embarrassed lovers, end by arriving at a tacit understanding of and agreement with each other. Throughout their desperate rows, fuelled by jealousy and the struggle for power over poor and barren territory, the bond between them is evident. They hate and love each other, and have a whole range of explicit curses to demonstrate their passion.

Passion is the keynote of all Dunbar's plays. There's nothing tame or reasoned about them. The major passions are rage, envy, spite, jealousy, and sexual desire. The action proceeds through emotion in a culture which revolves around grabbing what you can, before you are toothless and hairless and old before your time. The plays rarely move outside the boundaries of the estate with its pubs, chippies, bedrooms, and streets. All of life, for its inhabitants, is contained in this isolated cube. They have little apparent curiosity for the outside world and scorn the ways of those not of their kind. Their life may be brutal but it has its mores and niceties like any other, and strangers ignore them at their peril.

Dunbar was not a prolific writer. She remained devoted to the world which created her, the fights and feuds of which charge her work. Women have no rights in her work other than those they kick and bite for. Above all they respect, no, revere, the power of the male, although it be the power to bruise, impregnate, and terrify them. This was not Ripper country for nothing. Nevertheless, these women rise to challenge the terms of their existence and express their anarchy. They cheek policemen, flout the education officer, spit at the social worker. Andrea Dunbar created a band of bloodied but unbowed women whose raw existence is supported, not by the men in their lives, but by the offer of survival techniques from other women: their friends and mothers who've been there before.

—Carole Hayman

See the essay on *Rita, Sue, and Bob Too.*

DUNN, Nell (Mary).

British. Born in London in 1936. Educated at a convent school. Married the writer Jeremy Sandford in 1956 (marriage dissolved); three sons. Recipient: Rhys Memorial prize, 1964; Susan Smith Blackburn prize, for play, 1981; *Evening Standard* award, for play, 1982; Society of West End Theatre award, 1982. Agent: Curtis Brown, 162–168 Regent Street, London W1R 5TB. Address: 10 Bell Lane, Twickenham, Middlesex, England.

Publications

PLAYS

Steaming (produced 1981). 1981.
Sketches in *Variety Night* (produced 1982).
I Want, with Adrian Henri, adaptation of their own novel (produced 1983).
The Little Heroine (produced 1988).

SCREENPLAY: *Poor Cow*, with Ken Loach, 1967.

TELEVISION PLAYS: *Up the Junction*, from her own stories, 1965; *Every Breath You Take*, 1988.

NOVELS

Poor Cow. 1967.
The Incurable. 1971.
I Want, with Adrian Henri. 1972.
Tear His Head Off His Shoulders. 1974.
The Only Child: A Simple Story of Heaven and Hell. 1978.

SHORT STORIES
Up the Junction. 1963.

OTHER
Talking to Women. 1965.
Freddy Gets Married (for children). 1969.
Grandmothers. 1991.

Editor, *Living Like I Do.* 1977; as *Different Drummers*, 1977.

Nell Dunn was best known in the 1960's and 1970's as a chronicler of the lives of working-class women. The child of a securely middle-class background, with a convent school education, she became fascinated by the haphazard lives of women who existed without the safety net of money or education to sustain them. In 1963 she published a collection of short stories, *Up the Junction*, which consisted of vignettes of life as she had observed it among the young in Clapham. The book, which she later adapted for television, emphasised the vitality and sharpness of perception of the women, together with their accept-ance of the fate life had mapped out for them—a few short butterfly days, followed by a hopeless and unrewarding existence.

In her first novel, *Poor Cow*, Dunn centred on one woman, Joy, whose life from early on is set on a downward spiral. At 22 she has gone through one broken marriage and has a young son, Jonny. As her own life deteriorates, she transfers her hopes onto her son, trusting that his life, at least, will be better. Her epitaph on her own is: "To think when I was a kid I planned to conquer the world and if anyone saw me now they'd say, 'She's had a rough night, poor cow.'" A film was made of the book by director Ken Loach.

Dunn's stage play, *Steaming*, continues her fascination with working-class women and with the character on whom Joy was based in particular: the woman who lives for freedom and fun, but in reality remains a prisoner of her lack of self-confidence and the hard brutalities of life. Josie, the "Joy" figure, is lively, earthy, enjoys leading her men a dance, but invariably ends up the worse for it. "How come I always get hit on the left side?" she asks, after yet another beating up.

Steaming is set in a London Turkish bath, which provides Dunn with the background for what she is best at—women talking among themselves, with-out the constraints of a male presence. The only male, the caretaker of the Baths, is dimly glimpsed through a glass door, unable to enter the female domain. The six characters are a mixture of age and class. Apart from Josie, there is Mrs. Meadow, a repressive mother, who will not let her retarded, overweight daughter take her "plastics" off, even in the shower. There are two middle-class women—Jane, a mature student with a bohemian past, and Nancy, who shops at Peter Jones and whose husband has just left her after 22 years of marriage. The Baths are presided over by Violet, in her forties, who has worked there as attendant for 18 years and who is threatened with early retirement if the Council goes ahead with its intention to close the building.

Not a great deal happens in the play, but the humour and conversation sustain the evening. Without their clothes, and in the steamy companionship of the Baths, the women develop a sisterhood that transcends class barriers. The new entrant, Nancy, at first nervous of the milieu, is drawn in and at one point breaks down and talks about her broken marriage and the pressures that have kept her dependent on a man. Josie reveals that her seeming sexual freedom is also tied to dependence on a man's finances. Their campaign against the closure of the Baths gives them a new lease of life, and by the end Josie, after making a brilliant, if disregarded, speech at a public meeting, says she is going to get an education; Nancy, the rejected wife, announces she is "going to get fucked"; and Dawn asserts herself against her over-protective mother.

Whether this ending is anything more than a way of giving an upbeat finale to the play is a matter for debate, and Dunn's characters will probably find they are not able to change their lives greatly after their temporary euphoria. The dialogue of the working-class women has far more of a ring of truth about it than the dialogue of the middle-class women, but the author has always found a richness and rhythm in working-class speech that she fails to find in the more educated voice. *Steaming* can be regarded as a gentle piece of female consciousness-raising. It must also be one of the few feminist plays to have brought large numbers of male chauvinists in, attracted by the fact that the cast members are nude for much of the time.

I Want, written in 1972 in collaboration with Adrian Henri, is about a love affair between a well-bred, convent-educated girl but "with the devil in her" and a scholarship boy from a Liverpool terrace home. They meet in the 1920's and the play charts the course of their relationship over the next 60 years. It has moments of humour, but lacks the strength of *Steaming*. Dunn also wrote a book of interviews, *Talking to Women*, published in 1965. It is of interest for its recording of the stirrings of "female consciousness" among divergent women. In 1991 she published a sequel in *Grandmothers*. Dunn, herself a grandmother, drew on her own experiences as well as those of her friends to investigate the pleasures and pains of being a grandmother. Based on conversations with 14 of her female friends, it is particularly interesting because of the variety of backgrounds from which her subjects come, and because of the contrast between the traditional image of a grandmother and present-day reality.

Dunn's play *The Little Heroine*, which deals with a young woman's addiction to heroin, was produced during the same year as Granada Television produced her *Every Breath You Take*. This play deals with the effect on a newly divorced woman, Imogen, of finding her 13–year-old son diagnosed as diabetic. Obsessed with Tom's diet and insulin injection, she is unable to concentrate on anything else. In the end it is Tom, mature and sensible for his age, who restores her sense of proportion and helps her rebuild the life and career which she had seemed ready to abandon.

—Clare Colvin

E

EVARISTI, Marcella.

British. Born in Glasgow, 19 July 1953. Educated at Notre Dame High School for Girls, Glasgow, to 1970; University of Glasgow, 1970–74, B.A. (honours) in English and drama. Married Michael Boyd in 1982; one son and one daughter. Playwright-in-residence, University of St. Andrews, Fife, 1979–80; creative writing fellow, University of Sheffield, Yorkshire, 1979–80; writer-in-residence, universities of Glasgow and Strathclyde, 1984–85. Recipient: BBC Student Verse Competition prize, 1971; Arts Council bursary, 1975–76; Pye award, 1982. Agent: Andrew Hewson, John Johnson Authors' Agent, 45/47 Clerkenwell House, Clerkenwell Green, London EC1R 0HT, England.

Publications

PLAYS

Dorothy and the Bitch (produced 1976).
Scotia's Darlings (produced 1978).
Sugar and Spite (revue), with Liz Lochhead (produced 1978).
Mouthpieces (revue; produced 1980).
Hard to Get (produced 1980).
Commedia (produced 1982). 1983.
Thank You For Not in *Breach of the Peace* (revue; produced 1982).
Checking Out (produced 1984).
The Works (produced 1984). In *Plays Without Wires*, 1989.
Terrestrial Extras (produced 1985).
Trio for Strings in 3 (sketch; produced 1987).
Visiting Company (produced 1988).
The Offski Variations (produced 1990).

RADIO PLAYS: *Hard to Get*, 1981; *Wedding Belles and Green Grasses*, 1983; *The Hat*, 1988; *The Theory and Practice of Rings*, 1992; *Troilus and Cressida and La-di-da-di-da*, 1992.

TELEVISION PLAYS: *Eva Set the Balls of Corruption Rolling*, 1982; *Hard to Get*, 1983.

THEATRICAL ACTIVITIES

ACTOR: **Plays**—roles in *Dorothy and the Bitch*, 1976; *Twelfth Night*, 1979; *Sugar and Spite*, 1981; *Mystery Bouffe*, 1982; *The Works*, 1985; *Terrestrial*

Extras, 1985; Rhona Andrews in *Visiting Company*, 1988; *The Offski Variations*, 1990. **Radio** — roles in *The Works*, 1985; *The Hat*, 1988.

A rare but consistently recognizable sensibility marks the work of Marcella Evaristi. To explain it, she has frequently remarked on her heritage; part Italian Catholic, part Jewish, altogether Glaswegian. It is a blend that has kept her a significant part of the Scottish theatre scene since her first play, *Dorothy and the Bitch*, in 1976, although her most important plays have had life south of the border in England as well.

Her qualities are seen at their most harmonious in her emotionally powerful play, *Commedia*. Set partly in Evaristi's native Glasgow and partly in Bologna, the drama marries the passionate domesticity of an Italian home in Scotland to the volatile politics of Italy in 1980. As in all her work, she reveals the most intimate details of her characters' private lives with a coroner's attention to opening up wounds, but her concerns in *Commedia* are also the ways in which the broader world determines the fate of the individual.

The play begins with edgy comedy as the adult sons of the widowed Elena bring their wives to Elena's house for their usual Chianti Hogmanay, a Scottish New Year's Eve full of "pasta, pollo alla cacciatore and wine" and seemingly lacking in the traditional whisky and tall, dark stranger "first-footing it" through the door at midnight. But there is a handsome stranger, Davide, a young teacher from Bologna working in Glasgow schools, and working on Elena's heart.

An affair between Davide and Elena, for all its uncertainties caused by a 20-year age gap, brings up less generational conflict than might be expected: the lovers are prepared to work at their differences. Typically for Evaristi, conflict erupts from within the family, from the jealousy of one of Elena's own sons. The men in Evaristi's plays regularly cling to boyhood, while the women accept whatever responsibility is required.

There are fairy-tale elements that promise a happy ending: Elena is entertainingly eccentric from the first and engages the audience's sympathy. She receives the support of an "outsider": Lucy, the American wife of the jealous son, Stefano. Davide's radical left politics provide a philosophy and a circle of friends that accommodate his relationship with Elena. But there is a bitterness in the writing; when Elena and Davide take a holiday in Bologna, it provokes a family showdown which inadvertently leads to the death of her gentler son, Cesare, one of the innocent people killed in the fascist bombing of Bologna's railway station.

The relationship subsequently fails, Lucy leaves Stefano, Elena's late-life freedom is curtailed when Cesare's widow and her daughter move in and, in effect, all the women return to a world without men. A happy ending will remain a fairy-tale until male and female relationships can survive without illusion.

There is a poetic grace and imagination in the best of Evaristi's writing that elevates the most domestic of themes. In *Commedia* Elena's conflicts are encapsulated in a song, "Tin Mags the Kitchen Witch," which divides her character into disciplinarian mother and libertarian witch, a kind of lady of misrule. In a play such as *Wedding Belles and Green Grasses* she follows two sisters and their half-sister through childhood to puberty and first boyfriends;

to jobs, marriage, and divorce, lyrically raising the familiar material into ironic understanding through musical repetition of themes with subtle variations for each character.

In her major radio play, *The Hat*, her poetic imagination makes even greater leaps. The world is full of objects which are given voice; an elegant olde worlde mirror observes the troubled relationship of Marianne and her artist lover, Crispin, and comments on it to Marianne's dismay. Other inanimate characters develop conversational relationships with her, including her compact mirror and most importantly her cloche hat. The hat, despised by Crispin, can be seen symbolically as Marianne's sexuality, but the imagery of the play transcends Freud. Crispin's great achievement as an artist is a collage representing Marianne's free spirit. As Marianne establishes her own independence, the collage in its gallery deteriorates and Crispin's only hope of retaining his artistic reputation is to sexually subjugate her once again.

Women remain at the mercy of men in another of her radio plays, a potent reworking of the Troilus and Cressida story, *Troilus and Cressida and La-di-da-di-da*. Fine elevated sentiments from the two lovers begin the play, beautifully stating a bodily and spiritual commitment from each partner. When war intervenes, Troilus reluctantly becomes a soldier and continually restates his love, but Cressida is deprived of his words by other men who prostitute her. Corruption of ideals is again the natural product of male society.

Evaristi also writes well for herself as a performer, appearing in one-woman shows such as *The Offski Variations* where she further investigates the seemingly endless separations of people, from abandoned child to divorcing parents and departing partners, but her best work transcends the strong persona of her own character. She is a lyric dramatist of intense subjectivity, constantly observing the impact of society on the individual.

—Ned Chaillet

F

FORNÉS, María Irene.

American. Born in Havana, Cuba, 14 May 1930; emigrated to the United States, 1945; became citizen, 1951. Educated in Havana public schools. Lived in Europe, 1954–57; painter and textile designer; costume designer, Judson Poets Theatre and New Dramatists Committee productions, 1965–70; teacher at the Teachers and Writers Collaborative, New York, privately, and at numerous drama festivals and workshops, from 1965. President, New York Theatre Strategy, 1973–80. Recipient: Whitney fellowship, 1961; Centro Mexicano de Escritores fellowship, 1962; Office for Advanced Drama Research grant, 1965; Obie award, 1965, 1977, 1979, 1982, 1984, 1985, 1988; Cintas Foundation fellowship, 1967; Yale University fellowship, 1967, 1968; Rockefeller fellowship, 1971, 1985; Guggenheim fellowship, 1972; Creative Artists Public Service grant, 1972, 1975; National Endowment for the Arts grant, 1974; American Academy award, 1985; Home Box Office award, 1986. Agent: Helen Merrill Ltd., 435 West 23rd Street, 1A, New York, New York 10011. Address: 1 Sheridan Square, New York, New York 10014, U.S.A.

Publications

PLAYS

The Widow (produced 1961). As *La Viuda*, in *Teatro Cubano*, 1961.

Tango Palace (as *There! You Died*, produced 1963; as *Tango Palace*, produced 1964; revised version produced 1965). In *Promenade and Other Plays*, 1971.

The Successful Life of Three: A Skit for Vaudeville (produced 1965). In *Promenade and Other Plays*, 1971.

Promenade, music by Al Carmines (produced 1965; revised version produced 1969). In *Promenade and Other Plays*, 1971.

The Office (produced 1966).

A Vietnamese Wedding (produced 1967). In *Promenade and Other Plays*, 1971.

The Annunciation (also director: produced 1967).

Dr. Kheal (produced 1968). In *Promenade and Other Plays*, 1971.

The Red Burning Light; or, Mission XQ3 (produced 1968). In *Promenade and Other Plays*, 1971.

Molly's Dream, music by Cosmos Savage (also director:produced 1968). In *Promenade and Other Plays*, 1971.

81

Promenade and Other Plays. 1971; revised edition, 1987.
The Curse of the Langston House, in *Baboon!!!* (produced 1972).
Dance, with Remy Charlip (also co-director: produced 1972).
Aurora, music by John FitzGibbon (also director: produced 1974).
Cap-a-Pie, music by José Raúl Bernardo (also director: produced 1975).
Lines of Vision (lyrics only), book by Richard Foreman, music by George Quincy (produced 1976).
Washing (produced 1976).
Fefu and Her Friends (also director: produced 1977). In *Wordplays 1,* 1980.
Lolita in the Garden, music by Richard Weinstock (also director: produced 1977).
In Service (also director: produced 1978).
Eyes on the Harem (also director: produced 1979).
Blood Wedding, adaptation of a play by García Lorca (produced 1980).
Evelyn Brown: A Diary (also director: produced 1980).
Life Is Dream, adaptation of a play by Calderón, music by George Quincy (also director: produced 1981).
A Visit, music by George Quincy (also director: produced 1981).
The Danube (also director: produced 1982). In *Plays,* 1986.
Mud (also director: produced 1983; revised version, also director: produced 1985). In *Plays,* 1986.
Sarita, music by Leon Odenz (also director: produced 1984). In *Plays,* 1986.
Abingdon Square (produced 1984).
The Conduct of Life (also director: produced 1985). In *Plays,* 1986.
Cold Air, adaptation of a play by Virgilio Piñera (also director: produced 1985). 1985.
Drowning, adaptation of a story by Chekhov, in *Orchards* (produced 1985). 1986.
The Trial of Joan of Arc on a Matter of Faith (also director: produced 1986).
Lovers and Keepers, music by Tito Puente and Ferrando Rivas, lyrics by Fornés (also director: produced 1986). 1987.
Art, in *Box Plays* (produced 1986).
The Mothers (also director: produced 1986).
Plays. 1986.
A Matter of Faith (produced 1986).
Uncle Vanya, adaptation of the play by Anton Chekhov (also director: produced 1987).
Hunger (also director: produced 1988).
And What of the Night? (includes *Hunger; Springtime; Lust; Charlie*) (also director: produced 1989).
Oscar and Bertha (produced 1991).

MANUSCRIPT COLLECTION: Lincoln Center Library of the Performing Arts, New York.

CRITICAL STUDIES: "The Real Life of María Irene Fornés," in *Theatre Writings* by Bonnie Marranca, 1984; "Creative Danger" by Fornés, in *American Theatre,* September 1985; preface by Susan Sontag to *Plays,* 1986; 'The Madwoman in the Spotlight: The Plays of María Irene Fornés', in *Making a Spectacle: Feminist Essays on Contemporary Women's Theatre.* 1989.

DIRECTOR: **Plays**—several of her own plays; *Exiles* by Ana Maria Simo, 1982; *Uncle Vanya* by Anton Chekhov, 1987; *Going to New England* by Ana Maria Simo, 1990.

María Irene Fornés is one of the most prolific and bold playwrights in contemporary American theatre, with a voice that expresses uniquely her Caribbean roots and her experimental aesthetic. In a career that spans nearly 30 years, Fornés has created a large and multi-textured body of work. A self-taught emigrée from Cuba who lives and writes in the United States, she is committed to a theatre in which modernist experiments in form and language are inextricably intertwined with questions of politics and philosophy: in short those central questions "about . . . the conduct of life" (Susan Sontag, Preface to *María Irene Fornés: Plays*). The issues she grapples with are political in the broadest sense of the word. The questions animating her plays are nothing less than the origin of evil and the site of salvation, the nature of societies and of the individual soul.

From Isidore's bullfight with Leopold in *Tango Palace* to Mae's murder in *Mud*, Fornés' plays locate themselves at that place where the mystery of the human condition and the enigma of human relationships reveal themselves in sudden, elusive, and often violent spasms. Desire and fear form the poles of the complex universe she recreates in her work. It is a world where lovers and cripples, convicts and dictators struggle to articulate themselves. It is a world where the threat of torture, rape, and nuclear war are palpable constants. And yet it is also a world of slapstick, dancing, and song.

Fornés' 1965 play *Promenade* embodies many of the functional paradoxes of her work. From the plaintive cries of the Mother who has lost her babies to the Ionesco-inspired hilarity of Miss I, O, U and Mr., R, S, T, tragedy mingles with comedy, and fear rubs up against desire. At that point where these oppositions meet and bleed into one another is that moment of instant, inexplicable revelation. Whether it be that moment when the gunshot sounds and Julia falls in *Fefu and Her Friends* or the sudden bright light of a nuclear holocaust at the close of *The Danube*, Fornés' plays find meaning in that moment when the disparate and seemingly irreconcilable collide and fuse in an unexpected marriage. The union is at once beautiful and horrific, like a Goya painting where ivory-skinned maidens and bug-eyed devils dance side by side.

Fornés' theatre borrows from traditions and conventions outside of theatre, weaving them together with dramatic forms to create works that are vibrant and multi-faceted responses to a contemporary world. She began her career not as a playwright, but as a painter. Over and over again, this early training in painting is evident in her written work. Her conception of time and space alludes to both cubist and surrealist traditions. Modernist experiments from Braque and Picasso onwards shaped her conception of fractured narrative as well as shifting character. Like the room in *Tango Palace* with its whip, toy parrot, and "two masks in the form of beetles' faces", where "an androgynous clown" and "an earnest youth" engage in mortal combat, the dramatic situations of most of Fornés' work are warped and dream-like, peppered with vivid, mysterious images. Like the instantaneous jump cuts across years and locations in *The Successful Life of Three*, the transitions and movements across time are disjunctive, subject to conflation, expansion and unexpected upheaval, echoing not only cubism and surrealism, but also the neo-expressionist experiments in representing a lived reality on canvas. From her beginnings in the Judson Poet Theatre in the early 1960's to her recent work at INTAR where she writes, directs, and teaches a new generation of Hispanic-American playwrights, Fornés is engaged in the constant stretching of dramatic form. Whether it be the freeze frames of *Mud* or the musical interludes of *Sarita*, the result is a dramatic synthesis of genres ranging from poetry and painting to music and film.

Despite their varied influences from other art forms, Fornés' plays are very much of and about theatre. Indeed, her work is informed by an acute aware-ness of the context and constraints of theatre—the frame of the black box, the fact of live performers, the effect of light and sound within a confined space and within a delimited period of time. In almost all of her work there is an aspect of ritual as though Fornés were trying to get at some essential underpin-ning in the theatrical experience. In some instances, the component of ritual is explicit, as in *A Vietnamese Wedding*, an actual re-enactment of the marriage ceremony involving audience and actors alike. Yet even when ritual plays a less explicit role, primal relationships and essential conflicts animate Fornés', drama. The struggle between dominant and submissive, male and female, teacher and student—these are the operative power dynamics that fuel the action of her plays.

Whether the play is a dissection of a love triangle, as in *Mud* and *The Successful Life of Three*, or the examination of women's lives, as in *Sarita* and *Fefu and Her Friends*, Fornés' gift is to strip away the surface peculiarities layer by layer until she reaches the bedrock conflicts structuring individual human lives. Her work detects and dramatizes these universals. Beneath the specifics of gender, race, and social class, Fornés' characters are archetypes fated to act the way they do with an almost primitive, unwavering, unavoidable necessity. Whether it is the mad savant in *Dr. Kheal* who is compelled to articulate, with compulsive detail, his theory of the universe to an audience of strangers and skeptics, or the tragic Fefu who shoots and kills her weaker friend, Julia, a casualty of years of misogyny and abuse as much as of a single bullet, Fornés' characters move with the fatalism of characters from a classical Greek drama. Their expressions of love, their violent explosions aimed at one another and at circumstance, and the sudden silence following their extinction, represent the rituals of living where struggle and loss are necessary trials in some mysterious initiation.

—Naomi Iizuka

See the essay on *Fefu and Her Friends*.

G

GEE, Shirley (née Thieman).

British. Born in London, 25 April 1932. Educated at Frensham Heights, Farnham, Surrey; Webber-Douglas Academy of Dramatic Art, London. Married Donald Gee in 1965; two sons. Stage and television actress, 1952–66. Member of the Radio Committee, Society of Authors, 1980–82. Since 1986 member of the Women's Committee, Writers Guild. Recipient: *Radio Times* award, 1974; Pye award, for radio play, 1979; Sony award, for radio play, 1983; Susan Smith Blackburn prize, 1984; Samuel Beckett award, 1984. Agent: John Rush, David Higham Associates, 5–8 Lower John Street, London W1R 4HA. Address: 28 Fernshaw Road, London SW10 0TF, England.

Publications

PLAYS

Typhoid Mary (broadcast 1979; produced 1983). In *Best Radio Plays of 1979*, 1980.
Never in My Lifetime (broadcast 1983; produced 1984). In *Best Radio Plays of 1983*, 1984.
Ask for the Moon (produced 1986). 1987.
Warrior (produced 1989). 1991.

RADIO PLAYS: *Stones*, 1974; *The Vet's Daughter*, from the novel by Barbara Comyns, 1976; *Moonshine*, 1977; *Typhoid Mary*, 1979; *Bedrock*, 1979; *Men on White Horses*, from the novel by Pamela Haines, 1981; *Our Regiment* (documentary), 1982; *Never in My Lifetime*, 1983; *Against the Wind*, 1988; *The Forsyte Chronicles*, co-adaptation of *The Forsyte Saga* by John Galsworthy, 1990.

TELEVISION PLAYS: *Long Live the Babe*, 1984; *Flights*, 1985.

CRITICAL STUDIES: *British Radio Drama* edited by John Drakakis, 1981; *The Way to Write Radio Drama* by William Ash, 1985; *The Feminist Companion to Literature in English*, edited by Virginia Blain, Patricia Clements, and Isobel Grundy, 1990.

THEATRICAL ACTIVITIES

ACTOR: roles with Worthing, Hull, Malvern, and other repertory companies, and in more than 100 television plays and series episodes, 1952–66.

Shirley Gee comments:

I really don't like to make statements about my work; I hope those who see or hear the plays will have the freedom to draw their own conclusions. However, I'll try. I suppose I write to try to understand. To make sense out of chaos. To confront some terrors. I wonder what particular individuals might do trapped in a particular public event or social context. I watch them grapple, try to come to terms, fight to find the meaning of their lives. Often they are in a besieged landscape: the dead in *Stones*; Mary the typhoid carrier, imprisoned, in *Typhoid Mary*; British soldiers and Irish nationals in Belfast in *Never in My Lifetime*; the Victorian laceworkers and present-day sweatshop workers in *Ask for the Moon*. They are tyrannised by fear or poverty or loneliness or war. Their individual needs and desires run counter to the needs and desires of society, and must be sacrificed to that society. Still, they behave with love and courage. They save one another despite themselves. They beam a little light into a dark world. I wonder what I would have done, had I been in their place.

The list of women playwrights who have won major awards is, although increasing daily, not long, and one might expect Shirley Gee's name to be better known. Sadly, it is easy to account for her comparative lack of fame: most of her work has been written for radio, the most critically neglected medium of the past few decades. In Gee's case this is doubly unfortunate, for her radio experience is what gives her work for the stage its special vitality.

The radio playwright enjoys virtually unlimited freedom of approach; as long as he or she can unlock the listener's imagination anything is possible. Radio allows all kinds of spatial and temporal jumps; it is possible to create and instantly change the scenery, flash backwards or forwards in time, simply by the use of a few words or a snatch of song. Gee has always been one of the most technically authoritative of radio writers, and it was perhaps the triple accolade given to her radio play *Typhoid Mary*—a Giles Cooper award, a Pye award, a Special Commendation in the Italia prize—that prompted the Royal Shakespeare Company to stage the play and discover that its darting, fragmented structure worked onstage with verve and power.

Typhoid Mary is Mary Mallon, the tragic Irish immigrant who unwittingly spread the disease around New York at the beginning of the century. Instead of narrating her story straightforwardly, Gee creates a kaleidoscope of fragments: in one brief scene, for example, disembodied voices chant sensationalist newspaper headlines ("Calamity Cook Kills Wholesale"), a lawyer pronounces on her status in dry legal prose, a chorus sings "Molly Malone" to the accompaniment of spoons, and Mary in the midst speaks of her pain and grief as if she was in her own living room.

This lively variety of styles (from naturalism to the surreal) provides an analysis of her plight from several simultaneous angles. The spoon music stresses her background as struggling immigrant desperate to make good in a new world, and the humming of "Molly Malone" counterpoints this; Mary is already enshrined in popular song and in the popular imagination as a killer. The crude unthinking bias against her is fed by the press and allowed by the law. In fact Gee allows us in a few seconds to see Mary with the whole of American society ranged against her, with a vividness and compression naturalistic techniques would never permit.

For all its liveliness *Typhoid Mary* remained a study of a tragic individual without wider resonance. Gee's next ambitious work, also originating in radio, showed her wrestling with political drama. *Never in My Lifetime* opens shatteringly with the shooting of two British soldiers in a Belfast disco, then flashes backwards and forwards in time to explain the motives behind the shooting and its consequences. We follow the lives of the soldiers—Charlie, badly wounded, with a pregnant wife, and Tom, who dies—and the girls who lured them into ambush—the terrorist Maire, and Tess who is sleeping with Tom and joins Maire to save her own life when this becomes known to the IRA. By juxtaposing past and present, snatches of song, and snippets of Belfast life, Gee creates their lives and evokes unforgettably the grief of their loved ones. On a less personal level, however, the play is not so satisfying. The breadth and daring of the structure give the misleading impression that the play is presenting the fullest possible spectrum of Belfast politics. In fact, the cards are stacked. The only voice to speak for the Republican cause, for instance, is the voice of terrorism. Through the violent and twisted Maire, not just this killing but the whole concept of Irish nationhood is associated with a chain of ugly and sexually perverse imagery, contrasting with the wholesome lyricism of the naive Tess. The soldiers are described taking part in a brutal attack, but it is not shown, whereas the disco incident is terrifyingly realised. Essentially the play takes a pro-British stance while presenting itself as a slice of life; it seems that Gee is not fully in control of her material.

Ask for the Moon, however, shows a clearer political direction, and also translates the techniques of radio into striking visual terms. It shows simultaneously two generations of workers, Victorian lacemakers and women in a modern sweat shop. Gee's talent for conveying the texture of working life does more than lament their exploitation; she also shows how working conditions are structured to prevent unionisation. A lacemaker is forced to provide her child with opium so that the group will not slow up production; an old sweatshop hand steals another's piece-work to escape the sack. Gee makes it clear that this is forced on them despite real comradeship and caring and pride in their work. There is a touching moment when time barriers are broken and both groups join in wonder to admire a wedding veil that has cost one woman her eyesight. The women have no illusions about why they betray one another, and in the final anger of one of them, at first blind rage and then quiet planning for her own future, there is a hint that they are learning at last how to change.

—Frances Gray

GEMS, (Iris) Pam(ela, née Price).

British. Born in Bransgore, Dorset, 1 August 1925. Educated at Brockenhurst County High School, 1936–41; Manchester University, 1946–49, B.A. (honours) in psychology 1949. Served in the Women's Royal Naval Service, 1944–46. Married Keith Gems in 1949; two sons, including the writer Jonathan Gems, and two daughters. Research assistant, BBC, London, 1950–53. Agent: ACTAC, 16 Cadogan Lane, London S.W.1, England.

Publications

PLAYS

Betty's Wonderful Christmas (for children; produced 1972).
My Warren, and After Birthday (produced 1973).
The Amiable Courtship of Miz Venus and Wild Bill (produced 1973).
Sarah B. Divine! (additional material), by Tom Eyen, music by Jonathan Kramer (produced 1973).
Go West Young Woman (produced 1974).
Up in Sweden (produced 1975).
Dusa, Fish, Stas, and Vi (as *Dead Fish*, produced 1976; as *Dusa, Fish, Stas, and Vi*, produced 1976). 1977.
The Project (produced 1976).
Guinevere (produced 1976).
The Rivers and Forests, adaptation of a play by Marguerite Duras (produced 1976).
My Name Is Rosa Luxemburg, adaptation of a play by Marianne Auricoste (produced 1976).
Franz into April (produced 1977).
Queen Christina (produced 1977; revised version produced 1982). 1982.
Piaf (produced 1978). 1979.
Ladybird, Ladybird (produced 1979).
Sandra (produced 1979).
Uncle Vanya, adaptation of a play by Chekhov (produced 1979). 1979.
A Doll's House, adaptation of a play by Ibsen (produced 1980).
Sketches in *Variety Night* (produced 1982).
The Treat (produced 1982).
Aunt Mary (produced 1982). In *Plays by Women 3*, edited by Michelene Wandor, 1984.
The Cherry Orchard, adaptation of a play by Chekhov (produced 1984).
Loving Women (produced 1984). In *Three Plays*, 1985.
Camille, adaptation of a play by Dumas fils (produced 1984). In *Three Plays*, 1985.
Pasionaria, music by Paul Sand, lyrics by Gems and Sand (produced 1985).
Three Plays (includes *Piaf, Camille, Loving Women*). 1985.
The Danton Affair, adaptation of a work by Stanislawa Przybyszewska (produced 1986).
The Blue Angel, adaptation of a novel by Heinrich Mann (produced 1991).
Yerma, adaptation of the play by Federico García Lorca (produced 1993).

TELEVISION PLAYS: *A Builder by Trade*, 1961; *We Never Do What They Want*, 1979.

NOVELS

Mrs. Frampton. 1989.
Bon Voyage, Mrs. Frampton. 1990.

THEATRICAL ACTIVITIES

ACTOR: Film—*Nineteen Eighty-Four*, 1984.

Contemporary women playwrights explore areas of experience that the stage has traditionally ignored, and are developing styles designed as a radical contrast to the standard dramatic forms. Indeed, from a feminist viewpoint the category of "woman-writer" defines "a species of creativity that challenges the dominant image," since "the very concept of the 'writer' implies *maleness*." However, like Caryl Churchill, Pam Gems rejected this extreme position, declaring that "the phrase 'feminist writer' is absolutely meaningless because it implies polemic, and polemic is about changing things in a direct political way. Drama is subversive."

Like Churchill too, Gems developed her vision and theatrical techniques through dealing with historical subjects; and their example has been influential, making the history play characteristic of women's drama over the last decade. The tension between received ideas of the past—reinforcing the subservient status of women by relegating them to invisibility—and the very different feminist perspective, contributes to the thematic complexity of such plays.

Like many women dramatists, Pam Gems came to the theatre late, after 20 years of marriage and child-raising. Starting on the fringe, her early work for feminist theatre groups included an autobiographical piece, together with two monologues about female isolation and abortion, and a satiric pantomime. *Queen Christina*, her first major play, struck a new note and established all her central themes.

As in this play, Gems's most characteristic work dramatizes the human reality of women who have been transformed into cultural symbols. These range from the 17th-century Swedish Queen who renounced her crown, and a 19th-century courtesan, to a modern nightclub singer, or most recently *The Blue Angel* image of Marlene Dietrich as vampire sexuality. In each case the character is set against a familiar and highly romanticized picture. The counter-source for the earliest of Gems's historical dramas was the classic Garbo film of an ethereal and intellectual beauty, who abdicates for love, then finds consolation in religion when the man for whom she has sacrificed everything is killed in a duel. *Piaf* turns from Hollywood myth to the sanitized commercial image of a vulnerable street-sparrow, a purely emotional being whose songs are the direct expression "of unhappiness . . . of being made helpless by love . . . of being alone." *Camille* is a reversal of both Dumas's sentimentally tragic *La Dame aux camélias* and Verdi's operatic idealization in *La Traviata*.

The deforming pressures of society are most fully explored in *Queen Christina*, who provides a test-case for issues of sexual definition, biological determinism and social programming. As the sole heir to a kingdom at war, this historical figure has been "reared as a man . . . And then, on her accession, told to marry and breed, that is to be a woman. By which time, of course, like males of her era, she despised women as weak, hysterical, silly creatures." For Gems "It is a confusion which seems as apposite as ever." Forced to abdicate, she searches Europe for a way of life in which she can be herself. She is hailed as "an inspiration" to man-hating feminists (in the shape of 18th-century French "blue-stockings") in their campaign for control over their bodies through abortion. However, she finds herself repulsed by their life-denying warfare against the opposite sex, which she recognizes as the mirror image of male domination. She seeks spiritual emancipation in the Catholic Church, but finding that the Pope is interested only in exploiting her celibacy as religious propaganda, she asserts that "We won't deny the body." Offered the kingdom of Naples, she attempts to return to her masculine role. But when it forces her to kill her lover for betraying her invading armies, she rejects the whole male ethos, setting herself against domination in all its forms, master/servant as well as man/woman. Finally—when too old to bear children—she discovers the value of maternal instincts and affirms her biological nature.

For Gems, "Whichever way we look at it, the old norms won't do any more." The play asks what it means to be "female"; and Christina's example implies that a valid definition can only be reached through "the creation of a society more suited to both sexes"—which Gems has described as her aim in writing. Her concept of drama as subversive, rather than confrontational, means working on public consciousness indirectly. In line with this, her protagonist comes to realize that positive change can only be achieved through the specifically female, undervalued qualities of "weakness," non-violent resilience, and maternal nurture: "Half the world rapes and destroys—must women, the other half, join in?"

Typically, Gems creates an opposition between what is depicted on the stage and the audience's expectations. This is most obvious in *Piaf*, where incidents from the Parisian singer's life are interpolated with renditions of her popular lyrics. The gutter milieu, her prostitution and involvement in murder, drunkenness, and drugs contrast with the glittering public persona. Piaf disintegrates under the contradiction; and when the gap between idol and real woman can no longer be disguised, society preserves the false image by divorcing musical soul from female body.

At the same time, the way the songs rise out of the scenes emphasizes that Piaf's unconventional art and her physical crudity are inseparable. Her rise to stardom is a process of continual exploitation by the men who manage or marry her, and by her public (by extension the audience for Gems's play) who project their desires onto her. Yet it is also her status as a star that enables her to assert a personal autonomy, however provisional. This is expressed through her sexual freedom, which overturns all the moral codes. And the same reversal of conventional values is reflected in the play itself, which shows Piaf not only copulating but ostentatiously pissing on stage. Physicality at its most basic (a stock way of representing reality) demolishes the socially acceptable female stereotype, promoted and imposed by men, and thus provides an example of alternative values.

—Christopher Innes

See the essay on *Queen Christina*.

H

HANSBERRY, Lorraine (Vivian).

American. Born in Chicago, Illinois, 19 May 1930. Educated at the Art
Institute, Chicago; University of Wisconsin, Madison, 1948–50. Married
Robert Nemiroff in 1953 (divorced 1964). Journalist, 1950–51, and associate
editor after 1952, *Freedom*. Recipient: New York Drama Critics Circle award,
1959. Died 12 January 1965.

Publications

PLAYS

A Raisin in the Sun (produced 1959). 1959.
The Sign in Sidney Brustein's Window (produced 1964). 1965.
To Be Young, Gifted, and Black: A Portrait of Hansberry in Her Own Words,
    adapted by Robert Nemiroff (produced 1969). 1971.
Les Blancs, edited by Robert Nemiroff (produced 1970). In *Les Blancs: The
    Collected Last Plays*, 1972.
The Drinking Gourd. In *Les Blancs: The Collected Last Plays*, 1972.
What Use Are Flowers? In *Les Blancs: The Collected Last Plays*, 1972.
Les Blancs: The Collected Last Plays (includes *Les Blancs; The Drinking
    Gourd; What Use Are Flowers?*), edited by Robert Nemiroff. 1972.

SCREENPLAY: *A Raisin in the Sun*, 1961.

OTHER

The Movement: Documentary of a Struggle for Equality. 1964; as *A Matter of
    Colour*, 1965.
To Be Young, Gifted, and Black: A Portrait of Hansberry in Her Own Words,
    edited by Robert Nemiroff. 1969.

CRITICAL STUDIES: *Lorraine Hansberry* by Anne Cheney, 1984; "Diverse Angles
of Vision: Two Black Women Playwrights"by Margaret B. Wilkerson in
Theatre Annual, 40, 1985.

In her short life, Lorraine Hansberry completed two plays and left three others
uncompleted; a sixth theatre piece was assembled by others out of excerpts
from her dramatic and nondramatic writing. But her reputation must rest on
her first produced play, *A Raisin in the Sun*, the first play by a black woman to
be staged on Broadway, and one of the very few plays by black authors to be
mainstream successes before the 1960's.

A Raisin in the Sun is the story of the Younger family: matriarch Lena, her adult son and daughter, Walter Lee and Beneatha, and Walter Lee's wife Ruth and son Travis, all living in a Chicago slum apartment. The father's death has left the family with $10,000 in insurance money, and much of the first act is devoted to a debate on what to do with the windfall, Walter Lee wanting to invest it in a liquor store and Lena holding out for buying a house in a better part of town. As the head of the family, Lena wins, and uses some of the money as a down payment on a house in a white neighborhood, only to be visited by a representative of the neighbors offering to buy back the house, to prevent the black family from moving in. He is sent away, but called back when Walter Lee impulsively loses the rest of the money in a swindle. In the play's climax, Walter Lee finds the strength to send the man away again, and the family prepares for the move.

There are two plot lines to *A Raisin in the Sun*. The more obvious one concerns the family's attempt to raise itself, and its encounter with one more example of racial prejudice. Curiously, while that plot is built on the fact that the Youngers are black, it does not really *depend* on it. It would take very little rewriting to make the play one about Jews, the Irish, Italians, or any working-class group unwelcome in a restricted neighborhood; and probably much of the play's power and success comes from white audiences' recognition of an experience not very foreign to their own.

The second, more subtle, story line of the play is built on the conflicts within the family, particularly between Lena and Walter Lee, which expose one of the tragic paradoxes of black family life in America: generations of prejudice have limited the potential and weakened the will of black men, forcing the women (who, for various reasons, have not been quite as broken in spirit) to be strong; yet the women know that every step they take to help their men is an addition to their emasculation. The argument between Walter Lee and his mother over how to spend the insurance money is not just monetary; it is a contest for the role as head of the family. By all objective considerations Lena's plan is far superior; but her insisting on it is also a slap in the face for her son, and she knows it. When Walter Lee loses his share, he is clearly in the wrong, and yet too much of his manhood is at stake to allow the women to condemn him too harshly.

The play dramatizes the delicate balance and subtle adjustments the women must constantly make in the very real and vital struggle to protect their men from further indignities. Having won the first-act battle, Lena makes a point of giving Walter Lee the rest of the money, to make use of (implicitly, to make foolish use of) as he sees fit, because the act of respect in giving him this authority is worth more than the money. When Walter Lee calls the white man back to sell him the house, the women see that this is not just a financial setback, but a final capitulation to failure, and unite to save his soul. And when Walter Lee finds in himself the strength to reject the racists a second time, and the white man turns to Lena for help, she can reply, "My son said we was going to move and there ain't nothing left for me to say", as a joyous abdication of power. It is in these, and similar, quiet insights into the dynamics of family life, more than in the conflict with racism, that *A Raisin in the Sun* offers its greatest insights into the American black experience.

The Sign in Sidney Brustein's Window, Hansberry's only other completed play, was a commercial and critical failure, though it did attract some passionate supporters. It is a sympathetic study of the plight of the white liberal. The title character, a right-thinking but apolitical man, is slowly drawn into action, working to support a reform candidate in a city election; the titular sign is a banner declaring his political commitment. But dedication, and even victory, does not change the world, and Sidney discovers that people who believe the right things can be personally corrupt or weak in ways that invalidate their theoretical commitment: the candidate sells out, a black friend proves to be prejudiced, a homosexual friend is sexually manipulative. Driven to the point of despair, Sidney regains his determination to fight for the good in spite of all the obstacles and defections along the way.

The play is excessively talky, and secondary characters are either underwritten (such as the politician) or overwritten (as with Sidney's conservative sister-in-law, too complexly developed for the minor role she plays). A character on whom the plot turns does not even appear until Act III, while the important subplot of Sidney's marital problems is never integrated with the other action or themes. Still, it is a failure of accomplishment rather than of conception, and one can see the core of a play that might have been stronger had Hansberry (who was terminally ill at the time of production) been able to work on it more.

—Gerald M. Berkowitz

See the essay on *A Raisin in the Sun*.

HELLMAN, Lillian (Florence).

American. Born in New Orleans, Louisiana, 20 June 1905 (some sources give 1906). Educated at New York University, 1924–25; Columbia University, New York, 1925. Married the writer Arthur Kober in 1925 (divorced 1932). Reader, Horace Liveright publishers, New York, 1924–25; reviewer, New York *Herald-Tribune*, 1925–28; theatrical play reader, 1927–30; reader, Metro-Goldwyn-Mayer, 1930–32; began long relationship with Dashiell Hammett in 1930; teacher at Yale University, New Haven, Connecticut, 1966, and at Harvard University, Cambridge, Massachusetts, Massachusetts Institute of Technology, Cambridge, and University of California, Berkeley. Recipient: New York Drama Critics Circle award, 1941, 1960; American Academy gold medal, 1964; Paul Robeson award, 1976; MacDowell medal, 1976. MA: Tufts College, Medford, Massachusetts, 1940; Litt.D: Wheaton College, Norton, Massachusetts, 1961; Rutgers University, New Brunswick, New Jersey, 1963; Brandeis University, Waltham, Massachusetts, 1965; Yale University, New Haven, Connecticut, 1974; Smith College, Northampton, Massachusetts, 1974; New York University, 1974; Franklin and Marshall College, Lancaster, Pennsylvania, 1975; Columbia University, 1976. Vice-president, National Institute of Arts and Letters, 1962; Member, American Academy of Arts and Sciences, 1960, and American Academy, 1963. *Died 30 June 1984.*

Publications

PLAYS

The Children's Hour (produced 1934). 1934.

Days to Come (produced 1936). 1936.

The Little Foxes (produced 1939). 1939.

Watch on the Rhine (produced 1941). 1941.

Four Plays (includes *The Children's Hour; Days to Come; The Little Foxes; Watch on the Rhine*). 1942.

The North Star: A Motion Picture about Some Russian People. 1943.

The Searching Wind (produced 1944). 1944.

Watch on the Rhine, with Dashiell Hammett. In *Best Film Plays of 1943–44*, edited by John Gassner and Dudley Nichols, 1945.

Another Part of the Forest (also director: produced 1946). 1947.

Montserrat, from a play by Emmanuel Roblès (also director: produced 1949). 1950.

Regina, music by Marc Blitzstein (produced 1949).

The Autumn Garden (produced 1951). 1951.

The Lark, from a play by Jean Anouilh (produced 1955). 1956.

Candide, music by Leonard Bernstein, lyrics by Richard Wilbur, John LaTouche, and Dorothy Parker, from the novel by Voltaire (produced 1956). 1957.

Toys in the Attic (produced 1960). 1960.

Six Plays. 1960.

My Mother, My Father and Me, from the novel *How Much?* by Burt Blechman (produced 1963). 1963.

The Collected Plays (includes *The Children's Hour; Days to Come; The Little Foxes; Watch on the Rhine; The Searching Wind; Another Part of the Forest; Montserrat; The Autumn Garden; The Lark; Candide; Toys in the Attic; My Mother, My Father and Me*). 1972.

SCREENPLAYS: *The Dark Angel*, with Mordaunt Shairp, 1935; *These Three*, 1936; *Dead End*, 1937; *The Little Foxes*, with others, 1941; *Watch on the Rhine*, with Dashiell Hammett, 1943; *The North Star*, 1943; *The Searching Wind*, 1946; *The Children's Hour* (*The Loudest Whisper*), with John Michael Hayes, 1961; *The Chase*, 1966.

OTHER

Three. 1979; contents separately published as:
  An Unfinished Woman: A Memoir. 1969.
  Pentimento: A Book of Portraits. 1973.
  Scoundrel Time. 1976.

Maybe: A Story. 1980.

Eating Together: Recollections and Recipes, with Peter Feibleman. 1984.

Conversations with Hellman (interviews), edited by Jackson R. Bryer. 1986.

Editor, *Selected Letters*, by Chekhov, translated by Sidonie K. Lederer. 1955.

Editor, *The Big Knockover: Selected Stories and Short Novels,* by Dashiell Hammett. 1966; as *The Hammett Story Omnibus,* 1966; as *The Big Knockover* and *The Continental Op* (2 vols.), 1967.

BIBLIOGRAPHY: *Lillian Hellman: An Annotated Bibliography*by Steven H. Bills, 1979; *Lillian Hellman: A Bibliography 1926–1978* by Mary M. Riordan, 1980.

CRITICAL STUDIES: *Lillian Hellman* by Jacob H. Adler, 1969; *Lillian Hellman: Playwright* by Richard Moody, 1972; *The Dramatic Works of Lillian Hellman* by Lorena Ross Holmin, 1973; *Lillian Hellman* by Doris V. Falk, 1978; *Lillian Hellman* by Katherine Lederer, 1979; *Lillian Hellman: Plays, Films, Memoirs: A Reference Guide* by Mark W. Estrin, 1980; *Stage Left: The Development of the American Social Drama in the Thirties* by R.C. Reynolds, 1986; *Lillian Hellman: The Image, the Woman* by William Wright, 1986; *Lilly: Reminiscences of Lillian Hellman* by Peter Feibleman, 1988; *Lillian Hellman: Her Legend and Her Legacy* by Carl Rollyson, 1988.

THEATRICAL ACTIVITIES

DIRECTOR: **Plays**—*Another Part of the Forest,* 1946; *Montserrat,* 1949. Narrator—*Marc Blitzstein Memorial Concert,* 1964.

Lillian Hellman is one of America's major dramatists. She entered a male-dominated field when she was nearly thirty and wrote some dozen plays in three decades. Her early model was Ibsen, and she shared his love of tightly knit plots and emphasis on sociological and psychological forces. Her best plays, like Ibsen's, are those in which a powerful character cuts loose and transcends the limitations of the play's rigid symmetry and plot contrivance. Along with Clifford Odets, the other significant writing talent of the 1930's, Hellman showed a keen interest in Marxist theory and explored the relationship between the nuclear family and capitalism. Hellman, more than Odets, held ambiguous views of man and society. Her antagonists are not wholly the products of environment but seem at times innately malicious. The quest for power fascinated the author and her characters became famous for their ruthlessness and cunning. Most of her plays verge on melodrama but are admired for their energetic protagonists and swift-moving plots.

In her first play, *The Children's Hour,* Hellman showed how the capricious wielding of power could ruin innocent people. Two young women at a girl's school are falsely accused of having a lesbian relationship by a disturbed child. They are brought to trial by outraged parents and eventually lose their case—and their school. One of the teachers commits suicide and, too late, the child's treachery is discovered. The homosexual motif, though discreetly handled, accounted for the play's notoriety in 1934; but the abuse of power by an arrogant elite is its enduring theme.

Usurping power is also the motivating force in Hellman's best-known play, *The Little Foxes,* at once a political statement and a complex study of family dynamics. The rapacious Hubbard family represents a new brand of Southern capitalist who subordinates all traditions and human values to the goal of acquiring wealth and property. The strength of the play lies in Hellman's implicit comparison of the Hubbard siblings' rivalries with the competitiveness of Americans in the free enterprise system. The role of Regina Hubbard, who withholds her dying husband's heart medicine and who outwits her equally greedy brothers in a major business coup, has become a favorite vehicle for American actresses.

At the beginning of World War II Hellman wrote *Watch on the Rhine* and *The Searching Wind*, both of which dealt with the fascist menace. The former play contains some witty repartee and suspenseful moments; but its solutions to the international crisis are simplistic, and it is better described as an adventure story than a thesis play.

When the War ended, Hellman returned to the easy-to-hate Hubbard family in *Another Part of the Forest*. Unfortunately the exaggerated spitefulness and hysteria of the characters and the unrelieved high-tension atmosphere of this play become nearly ludicrous. The concept of personal manipulation had become an obsession with the author, and a correlation seemed to have developed between her studies of social and societal exploitation and her own excessive control over plot characterization and stage effects. Perhaps the playwright realized this, because in her last plays she turned from Ibsen to Chekhov for inspiration. Both *The Autumn Garden* and *Toys in the Attic* recall the mood and ambiguous moral judgments of Chekhov. Neither of these plays has a truly pernicious villain, and most of the characters seem to be suffering from a Chekhovian paralysis of will. The atmosphere is deterministic and the plots are truer to life. What has changed is that all bids for personal power prove self-defeating—the predatory are caught in traps of their own making and hardly struggle before acknowledging defeat. Nevertheless these plays also include sharp, amusing verbal exchanges and the famous blackmail scenes associated with Hellman. Blackmail, present in all of her plays, is Hellman's favorite metaphor for personal manipulation; but in the later works she uses blackmail and other devices with greater subtlety, and presents a somewhat blurred but more convincing vision of stumbling modern man and his society.

Hellman's dramatic mode, based on her adherence to continental models, was bound to an earlier era. Most of her experiments with screenwriting proved frustrating. Her best later works were autobiographical sketches: in *An Unfinished Woman*, *Pentimento*, and *Scoundrel Time* she revealed her penetrating intelligence but tacitly acknowledged that her insights and talents were better suited to the historical memoir.

—Kimball King

See the essay on *The Little Foxes*.

HENLEY, Beth (Elizabeth Becker Henley).

American. Born in Jackson, Mississippi, 8 May 1952. Educated at Southern Methodist University, Dallas, B.F.A. 1974; University of Illinois, Urbana, 1975–76. Actress, Theatre Three, Dallas, 1972–73, with Southern Methodist University Directors Colloquium, 1973, and with the Great American People Show, New Salem, 1976; teacher, Dallas Minority Repertory Theatre, 1974–75. Recipient: Pulitzer prize, 1981; New York Drama Critics Circle

award, 1981; Oppenheimer award, 1981. Lives in Los Angeles. Agent: Gilbert
Parker, William Morris Agency, 1350 Avenue of the Americas, New York,
New York 10019, U.S.A.

Publications

PLAYS

Am I Blue? (produced 1973; revised version produced 1981). 1982.
Crimes of the Heart (produced 1979). 1982.
The Miss Firecracker Contest (produced 1980). 1985.
The Wake of Jamey Foster (produced 1982). 1983.
The Debutante Ball (produced 1985). 1991.
The Lucky Spot (produced 1987). 1987.
Abundance (produced 1989). 1991.
Control Freaks (also director: produced 1992).

SCREENPLAYS: *The Moon Watcher*, 1983; *True Stories*, with Stephen
Tobolowsky, 1986; *Crimes of the Heart*, 1987; *Nobody's Fool*, 1987; *Miss
Firecracker*, 1990.

Portraying women who seek to define themselves outside of their relationships
with men and beyond their family environment is a unifying factor in all of
Beth Henley's plays.

Surprisingly, her first play to be produced in New York, *Crimes of the
Heart*, won the Pulitzer prize and most of her work continues to be compared
to it. There are strong similarities between her plays, not only in theme but also
in plot; but it is Henley's characters who provide unique contributions to the
dramaturgy. The McGrath sisters in *Crimes of the Heart* are probably the most
traditionally well-developed characters in that each has a strong connection to
the plot; each grows from her experience; and each comes to understand
others better. However, in *The Debutante Ball*, *The Wake of Jamey Foster*,
and the more recent *Abundance*, Henley masterfully creates characters who
explore their identities within a complex plot and who transcend their experience with uncertain and unexpected results.

The Debutante Ball is a quirky play filled with Henley's typical southern
humor and Chekhovian characters. The play includes action that is not often
dramatized, such as women cutting themselves shaving, and an unsympathetic
treatment of a deaf girl. The ball serves as a structural device for all the
characters to come together in hopes of re-establishing their place in society.
However Teddy the debutante cannot go through with the façade and in the
end she is left bleeding all over her ball gown, having aborted a child. Pregnant
by a one-armed man with a scarred face, whom Teddy had called ugly, she
explains that: "I kinda just did it to be polite. I couldn't take on any more, ah,
bad feelings, guilt."

In *The Wake of Jamey Foster* the occasion is the burial of Marshael's
husband, Jamey. The unhappy and bitter widow eventually resolves her feelings and, like the debutante, is actually empowered by the difficulties and
troubled feelings that the death has brought to light. In *Abundance* two
pioneer women, Macon Hill and Bess Johnson, are also empowered by the

unexpected twists of fate which in the end leave them both looking like freaks, a powerful physical representation of disfigured dreams.

Death, disaster, and freakish accidents play a major role in all of Henley's plays. However, Henley's treatment of this recurring motif is often humorous. Most of her southern characters accept such events matter-of-factly, so that when Babe shoots her husband in *Crimes of the Heart*, or when Bess is kidnapped by the Indians in *Abundance*, or when orphan Carnelle in *The Miss Firecracker Contest* speaks nonchalantly about people dying— "It seems like people've been dying practically all my life, in one way or another"—it is never maudlin.

Structurally Henley relies on storytelling, especially those stories in which female characters can turn to other female characters for help. She often employs one or two female characters to center her story around, usually an occasion of some sort and then adds dimension to the plot with minor characters who are bleakly comic or mildly eccentric. Leon, the slow-witted brother in *The Wake of Jamey Foster*, Cassidy, the pathetic tom-boy teenager in Henley's least successfuly play *The Lucky Spot*, or Delmount, the mentally unstable cousin in *The Miss Firecracker Contest*, are all good examples. These secondary characters reinforce a comic pathos established by the central characters. The cruelties of life befall all Henley's characters and the playwright is adept in dramatizing their sadness with a rare duality of expression that creates laughter and tears. One of the most memorable examples is that of Cassidy who clings to a dream in which a "furry animal" pledged his love for her.

Male characters often serve as plot devices and are rarely fully developed, especially problematic in *Abundance* with the character of Elmore, an opportunist who shows up late in the play to help Bess write about her ordeal of being kidnapped and living with the Indians for five years. Brighton in *The Debutante Ball* and Doc in *Crimes of the Heart* are necessary to advance the plot but remain one-dimensional. Male characters rarely take any definite positive action, but rather serve as the impetus for action by the female characters. Will in *Abundance* and, to a lesser degree, Brocker in *The Wake of Jamey Foster*, are exceptions.

Linguistically, Henley's style couples witty dialogue with poetic colloquial speech that at its best produces a powerful personal voice for her characters, especially when the playwright trusts the simplicity and honesty of her southern characters. Language becomes forced when Henley moves beyond descriptions of experience. When characters reveal how they feel, Henley makes good use of her own strong feelings and observations. However, she is less successful in descriptive metaphors, which are especially clumsy in the opening scenes of *Abundance*, an epic play that spans 25 years beginning in the late 1860's. The dialogue creates a forced rhythm unnatural and uncharacteristic of Henley. For example, in the early moments of the play Bess says: "Thanks kindly. I'm near pined t'death with famine." Later in the play Henley overuses metaphor as when Bess says: "I try not to show my hurt. I hide it in different parts of the house. I bury jars of it in the cellar; throw buckets of it down the well; iron streaks of it into the starched clothes and hang them in the closet."

Crimes of the Heart is Henley's most fully integrated play in terms of dramatic elements, but *Abundance* is her most ambitious. The latter contains many elements of earlier plays including freak accidents, female bonding, and the exploration of identity. It also shares one of the less successful dramaturgical strategies seen in other plays where too much happens between scenes; character transformations happen in mental space so that it is difficult to believe the changes that occur, especially in the character of Bess. The problem is more pervasive in *Abundance* because of the epic nature of the play. Still, the play is Henley's most sober and explicit work, filled with a strong sense of irony and uncompromising in its depiction of the evils that befall women who sell out their identities to men.

—Judy Lee Oliva

See the essay on *Crimes of the Heart*.

HEWETT, Dorothy (Coade).

Australian. Born in Perth, Western Australia, 21 May 1923. Educated at Perth College; University of Western Australia, Perth, 1941–42, 1959–63, B.A. 1961, M.A. 1963. Married Lloyd Davies in 1944 (marriage dissolved 1949), one son (deceased); lived with Les Flood, 1950–59, three sons; married Merv Lilley in 1960, two daughters. Millworker, 1950–52; advertising copywriter, Sydney, 1956–58; senior tutor in English, University of Western Australia, 1964–73. Writer-in-residence, Monash University, Melbourne, 1975, University of Newcastle, New South Wales, 1977, Griffith University, Nathan, Queensland, 1980, La Trobe University, Bundoora, Victoria, 1981, and Magpie Theatre Company, Adelaide, 1982. Poetry editor, *Westerly* magazine, Nedlands, Western Australia, 1972–73. Member of the editorial board, *Overland* magazine, Melbourne, since 1970, and *Sisters* magazine, Melbourne, since 1979; since 1979 editor and director, Big Smoke Books, and review editor, *New Poetry*, both Sydney. Member of the Communist Party, 1943–68. Recipient: Australian Broadcasting Corporation prize, for poetry, 1945, 1965; Australia Council grant, 1973, 1976, 1979, 1981, 1984, lifetime emeritus fellowship, 1988; Australian Writers Guild award, 1974, 1982, 1986; International Women's Year grant, 1976, Australian prize, for poetry, 1986; Grace Levin prize, for poetry, 1988; Mattara Butterfly Books prize, for poetry, 1991; Nettie Palmer prize, for non-fiction, 1991; Victorian Premier's award, 1991. A.O. (Member, Order of Australia), 1986. Agent: Hilary Linstead and Associates, 302 Easts Towers, 9–13 Bronte Road, Bondi Junction, New South Wales 2022. Address: 496 Great Western Highway, Faulconbridge, New South Wales 2776, Australia.

Publications

PLAYS

Time Flits Away, Lady (produced 1941).
This Old Man Comes Rolling Home (produced 1966; revised version produced 1968). 1976.
Mrs. Porter and the Angel (produced 1969). In *Collected Plays 1*, 1992.
The Chapel Perilous; or, The Perilous Adventures of Sally Banner, music by Frank Arndt and Michael Leyden (produced 1971). 1972.

Bon-Bons and Roses for Dolly (produced 1972). With *The Tatty Hollow Story*, 1976.
Catspaw (produced 1974).
Miss Hewett's Shenanigans (produced 1975).
Joan, music by Patrick Flynn (produced 1975). 1984.
The Tatty Hollow Story (produced 1976). With *Bon-Bons and Roses for Dolly*, 1976; in *Collected Plays 1*, 1992.
The Beautiful Miss Portland, in *Theatre Australia*,   November-December and Christmas 1976.
The Golden Oldies (produced 1976). With *Susannah's Dreaming*, 1981.
Pandora's Cross (produced 1978). In *Theatre Australia*, September-October 1978.
The Man from Mukinupin (produced 1979). 1980.
Susannah's Dreaming (broadcast 1980). With *The Golden Oldies*, 1981.
Golden Valley (for children; produced 1981). With *Song of the Seals*, 1985.
The Fields of Heaven (produced 1982).
Song of the Seals (for children), music by Jim Cotter (produced 1983). With *Golden Valley*, 1985.
Christina's World (opera libretto; produced 1983).
The Rising of Peter Marsh (produced 1988).
Zoo with Robert Adamson (produced 1991).
Collected Plays 1 (includes *This Old Man Comes Rolling Home*, *Mrs. Porter and the Angel*, *The Chapel Perilous*, *The Tatty Hollow Story*). 1992.

SCREENPLAYS: *For the First Time*, with others, 1976; *Journey among Women*, with others, 1977; *The Planter of Malata*, with Cecil Holmes, 1983; *Song of the Seals*, 1984; *Catch the Wild Fish*, with Robert Adamson, 1985.

RADIO PLAYS: *Frost at Midnight*, 1973; *He Used to Notice Such Things*, 1974; *Susannah's Dreaming*, 1980.

NOVEL
Bobbin Up. 1959; revised edition, 1985.

SHORT STORIES
The Australians Have a Word for It. 1964.

VERSE
What about the People, with Merv Lilley. 1962.
Windmill Country. 1968.
The Hidden Journey. 1969.
Late Night Bulletin. 1970.
Rapunzel in Suburbia. 1975.
Greenhouse. 1979.
Journeys, with others, edited by Fay Zwicky. 1982.
Alice in Wormland. 1987.
A Tremendous World in Her Head. 1989.
The Upside Down Sonnets. 1991.

OTHER
Wild Card (autobiography). 1990.

Editor, *Sandgropers: A Western Australian Anthology.* 1973.

MANUSCRIPT COLLECTIONS: Australian National Library, Canberra; Fisher Library, University of Sydney; Flinders University, Adelaide, South Australia.

CRITICAL STUDIES: "Quest or Question? Perilous Journey to the Chapel" by Reba Gostand, in *Bards, Bohemians, and Bookmen* edited by Leon Cantrell, 1976; *After "The Doll"* by Peter Fitzpatrick, 1979; *Contemporary Australian Playwrights* edited by Jennifer Palmer, 1979; articles by Brian Kiernan and Carole Ferrier, in *Contemporary Australian Drama* edited by Peter Holloway, 1981, revised edition, 1986; *Dorothy Hewett: The Feminine as Subversion* by Margaret Williams, 1992.

It is hard to be indifferent to the work of Dorothy Hewett. Everything she has goes into it, provoking in the observer anger, distaste, admiration, extravagant praise and partisanship, and, on two occasions, threat of court action. First a poet, author of one important novel and much left-wing journalism, she turned to playwriting in 1965. Her materials are the female psyche and the burden that men and society lay on the romantic imagination and the artistic soul. She disclaims any autobiographical intention, bending her mind as she does to the universal experience of the artist as woman through her own painful experience of the role; but it is nevertheless true that most of her characters can be identified by a style of language and imagery that refers noticeably to her own life and literary experience.

The progress of her work shows a steady motion from dramatic narrative to ritual poetry; and much of the discomfort she causes stems from her defiant intrusion of the private nature of the poetic experience into the naked public arena of the theatre.

Her first play, *This Old Man Comes Rolling Home*, remains her most immediately accessible and contains some of her best dramatic writing. It is the story of a household of communist activists in Redfern, an inner Sydney suburb, in the early 1950's, the fierce time of the unsuccessful attempt by Sir Robert Menzies to ban the Communist Party. The play was a response to her own time in Redfern and is an acknowledgement of what she calls her "love affair with the working class."

Two early dramatic influences were Patrick White and Tennessee Williams, both of them moving out of realism towards a poetic interpretation of the ordinary man and woman. Like them but in her own way she has since progressed into a landscape not "real" in the accepted sense but born of and reflecting the mind and sensibilities of Hewett and her characters. She made a leap into this landscape with *Mrs. Porter and the Angel*, a play in which a deranged woman teacher wanders through the gathering dark to the houses of her colleagues in search of an imaginary dog. The play is replete with black dog images of impotence and closet sexuality, of men and women destroying each other out of their own fantasies. And yet the play adds up to a kind of celebration of the good and evil in them all: it shares the optimism of *This Old Man*, a comedy of poverty which pays tribute to the force of life and laughter.

Journeys are endemic to Hewett's writing. The major journey to date is that taken by Sally Banner in *The Chapel Perilous*, her most widely performed play. In it she audaciously compares to the questing of Malory's heroes a woman's search for spiritual truth through literary striving, sexual adventures, marriage, communism, and public recognition. In *Bon-Bons and Roses for Dolly* her heroine is a teenager of the 1940's, indulged by her emotionally starved parents and grandparents and fed on the fairy floss of the Hollywood movie. In Act 2 Dolly returns, middle-aged, to the now crumbling Crystal Palace—a meeting of two empty and neglected monuments to second-hand dreams.

Hewett's rock opera *Catspaw* in different style offers a drop-out guitar player in search of the real Australia. In a ribald grand parade of legendary characters the author postulates that most of these enlightened minds were stick-in-the-mud conservatives.

The Tatty Hollow Story and *Joan* return to the theme of the female predicament and demonstrate how women rise to the roles men create for them. The former ritually brings together the five lovers of the mysterious Tatty Hollow, whom each remembers in a different fantasy. At last, in retaliation for what she sums up as a wasted life, Tatty takes revenge on them and dissolves—and the play with her—into a poetic madness. *Joan* is the Joan of Arc story as a rock opera with four eponymous heroines—Joan the peasant, Joan the soldier, Joan the witch, and Joan the saint.

The Golden Oldies, a savage mood piece on the round of domestic duty and mutual exploitation which is the lot of many women, emerges in retrospect as a turning point for Hewett's imagination, an exorcism of the past. Leaving us with the image of an old woman's death and her daughter sifting through the flotsam of a lifetime, Hewett moves away from her exploration of isolation towards unifying the elements of life. In the work which follows she begins to live down the old defiance and absorb the destructive forces, which had hitherto preoccupied her, into a total creative vision.

Pandora's Cross is a nostalgic attempt to rally the old creative forces of the once bohemian Kings Cross, today a haunt of drug addicts and racketeers. The play contains some of her best poetry but suffers, like other work from this middle period, from unresolved dramatic action. In 1979, however, the challenge of writing a festive work for the Western Australian sequicentennial celebrations, drew from her a play which changed her fortunes and reconciled her with the State of her birth. *The Man from Mukinupin* mingles childhood memories of the wheat-farming district in which she grew up with a dense education in Shakespeare and the English and Australian Romantics. The play is set during World War I, and she brings to the story of a grocer's daughter and her sweetheart, and of their darker siblings, a half-Aboriginal whore and her outcast lover, a world view of the good and evil forces over which the mad water diviner Zeek Perkins presides, Prospero-like, in a parched but magical land.

This was the beginning of what has come to be known as Hewett's pastoral period, which produced in close succession *Susannah's Dreaming*, a radio play about the tragic intrusion of adult brutality into the magical sea-world of a retarded innocent; *The Fields of Heaven*, about the takeover of a farming community by an ambitious escapee from Mussolini's Italy; and two children's plays, *Golden Valley*, set in the wheatfields, and *Song of the Seals*, set in a mystical sub-Antarctic bay, which use the forces of nature, in the form of people transmuted into birds and fish, to fight the intrusion of acquisitive outsiders into their rural harmony.

Hewett's work is informed by a strongly literary background and an incorrigible romanticism which contrasts oddly with her critical armoury. Part of the romanticism is an attention-getting daring and a determination to prove that life can be beautiful—a desire so strong in some plays that the energy consumes an often shaky structure. The source of her romanticism can be traced to the artistic isolation of her girlhood in Western Australia and her private schooling which together encouraged poetry and idealism. Her long allegiance to the Communist Party was an emotional, even a religious commitment, which, after her expulsion in 1968, left her isolated, bereft of beliefs, and newly aware of her mortality—a sense confirmed by the senility and death of her mother. These factors are strongly represented in the work of her middle period and come to an end with the sudden force of *The Man from Mukinupin*. Hewett's subsequent works still take the same journey through idealism to understanding but they carry a new optimism and a new acceptance of the follies of life; a new recognition of the splendour and the resilience of the human spirit.

—Katharine Brisbane

See the essay on *The Chapel Perilous*.

HOLDEN, Joan.

American. Born in Berkeley, California, 18 January 1939. Educated at Reed College, Portland, Oregon, B.A. 1960; University of California, Berkeley, M.A. 1964. Married 1) Arthur Holden in 1958 (divorced); 2) Daniel Chumley in 1968, three daughters. Waitress, Claremont Hotel, Berkeley, 1960–62; copywriter, Librairie Larousse, Paris, 1964–66; research assistant, University of California, Berkeley, 1966–67. Since 1967 playwright, publicist, 1967–69, and business manager, 1978–79, San Francisco Mime Troupe. Editor, Pacific News Service, 1973–75; instructor in playwriting, University of California, Davis, 1975, 1977, 1979, 1983, 1985, 1987. Recipient: Obie award, 1973; Rockefeller grant, 1985. Address: San Francisco Mime Troupe, 855 Treat Street, San Francisco, California 94110, U.S.A.

Publications

PLAYS

L'Amant Militaire, adaptation of a play by Carlo Goldoni, translated by Betty Schwimmer (produced 1967). In *The San Francisco Mime Troupe: The First Ten Years*, by R. G. Davis, 1975.

Ruzzante; or, The Veteran, adaptation of a play by Angelo Beolco, translated by Suzanne Pollard (produced 1968).

The Independent Female; or, A Man Has His Pride (produced 1970). In *By Popular Demand*, 1980.

Seize the Time, with Steve Friedman (produced 1970).

The Dragon Lady's Revenge, with others (produced 1971). In *By Popular Demand*, 1980.

Frozen Wages, with Richard Benetar and Daniel Chumley (produced 1972). In *By Popular Demand*, 1980.

San Fran Scandals, with others (produced 1973). In *By Popular Demand*, 1980.

The Great Air Robbery (produced 1974).

Frijoles; or, Beans to You, with others (produced 1975). In *By Popular Demand*, 1980.

Power Play (produced 1975).

False Promises/Nos Engañaron (produced 1976). In *By Popular Demand*, 1980.

The Loon's Rage, with Steve Most and Jael Weisman (produced 1977). In *West Coast Plays 10*, Fall 1981.

The Hotel Universe, music by Bruce Barthol (produced 1977). In *West Coast Plays 10*, Fall 1981.

By Popular Demand: Plays and Other Works by The San Francisco Mime Troupe (includes *False Promises/Nos Engañaron*; *San Fran Scandals*; *The Dragon Lady's Revenge*; *The Independent Female*; *Frijoles*; *Frozen Wages* by Holden, and *Los Siete* and *Evo-Man*). 1980.

Factperson, with others (produced 1980). In *West Coast Plays 15–16*, Spring 1983.

Americans; or, Last Tango in Huahuatenango, with Daniel Chumley (produced 1981).

Factwino Meets the Moral Majority, with others (produced 1981). In *West Coast Plays 15–16*, Spring 1983.

Factwino vs. Armaggedonman (produced 1982). In *West Coast Plays 15–16*, Spring 1983.

Steeltown, music by Bruce Barthol (produced 1984).

1985, with others (produced 1985).

Spain/36, music by Bruce Barthol (produced 1986).

The Mozamgola Caper, with others (produced 1986). In *Theater*, Winter 1986.

Ripped van Winkle, with Ellen Callas (produced 1988).

Seeing Double, with others (produced 1989).

Back to Normal, with others (produced 1990).

The Marriage of Figaro, adaptation of a play by Beaumarchais (produced 1990).

MANUSCRIPT COLLECTION: University of California, Davis.

CRITICAL STUDIES: "*Hotel Universe*: Playwriting and the San Francisco Mime Troupe" by William Kleb, in *Theater*, Spring 1978; "Joan Holden and the San Francisco Mime Troupe," in *Drama Review*), Spring 1980, and *New American Dramatists 1960–1980*, 1982, both by Ruby Cohn.

Joan Holden comments:

I write political cartoons. For years, I was ashamed of this. I agreed meekly with those critics who said, "*mere* political cartoons." To please them, and led astray by well-wishers who'd say, "You can do more—you could write *serious* plays," I've tried my hand, from time to time, at realism. Each time I've been extremely impressed, at first, with the solemnity of what I've written. Rereading those passages, I always find I've written melodrama. The fact is, I'm only inspired when I'm being funny. Writing comedy is not really a choice: it's a quirk. On a certain level, making things funny is a coward's way of keeping pain at arm's length. But that same distance allows you to show certain things clearly: notably, characters' social roles, their functions in history. These generalities, not the specifics which soften them, interest caricaturists—who have serious reasons for being funny, and in whose ranks I now aspire to be counted.

For 20 years, I've written for a permanent company, for particular actors, directors, and composers, and in collaboration with them. This has put conditions on my writing; it has also supplied a nearly constant source of ideas, and a wonderful opportunity to learn from mistakes.

Joan Holden has been the principal playwright of the San Francisco Mime Troupe, which has always performed with words as well as gesture. Although chance led to this association, a 30-year career was launched.

The Holden/Goldoni *Military Lover/L'Amant Militaire* drew large audiences to nearly 50 park performances, and Holden wrote: "Comedy, which in its basic action always measures an unsatisfactory reality against its corresponding ideal, may be the revolutionary art form *par excellence*." It became Holden's art form *par excellence*, pitting satirized Establishment figures of unsatisfactory reality against the satisfactory dream of working-class harmony and celebration.

After the Mime Troupe went collective in 1970, *The Independent Female* expressed the new spirit. *Commedia* characters gave way to those of soap opera with satiric telltale names—Pennybank for a business tycoon, Heartright for a junior executive, Bullitt for a militant feminist. A pair of lovers is faced with an obstacle to their marriage, as in soap opera. But subverting the genre, Holden identifies the obstacle as the young ingénue's growing independence. Instead of dissolving the obstacle for a happy curtain clinch, Holden sees a happy ending in sustained feminist revolt which the audience is asked to link to working class revolt.

The Dragon Lady's Revenge is grounded in another popular form, the comic strip, with assists from Grade B movies, and its intricate plot involves the corrupt American ambassador in Long Penh, his soldier son, a CIA agent Drooley, and the titular Dragon Lady, as well as the honest native revolutionary Blossom. Holden shifted from global to local politics with *San Fran Scandals* blending housing problems into vaudeville. Science fiction and detective story were then exploited for *The Great Air Robbery*.

In the mid-1970s the San Francisco Mime Troupe reached out beyond the white middle class, actively recruiting Third World members, and Holden's scripts reflect their new constituency. *Frijoles* (Spanish for beans) zigzags from a Latin American couple to a North American couple, joining them at a food conference in Europe, and joining them in identical class interests. As *Frijoles* travels through space, *Power Play* travels through time in order to indict the anti-ecological monopoly of the Pacific Gas and Electric Company.

By 1976, America's bicentennial year, Holden was in firm command of her style: a specific issue attacked through a popular art form; simple language and clean story line; swift scenes often culminating in a song. The group wished to present a play on the uncelebrated aspects of American history—the role of workers, minorities, women. Based on collective research, Holden scripted *False Promises*, which deviated from her usual satiric formula in presenting heightened realism of working-class characters. They continue to appear in such subsequent plays as *Steeltown* and the final play of the Factwino trilogy. In *Factperson* the person of the title is an old black baglady with the power to cite facts that contradict the lies of the media. In *Factwino vs. Armaggedonman* "the double-headed dealer of doom" or the military-industrial powers subjugate an old black wino with alcohol, but in the most recent Factwino play he emerges triumphant through his own research beneath lies: "Everybody has to find their own power." *Ripped van Winkle* is a hilarious reversion to satire, when a 1960s hippy awakens from a 20-year acid trip, adrift in Reaganomics. Local or global, probing character, or tickling caricature, Holden theatricalizes current events with theatrical verve.

—Ruby Cohn

HOLLINGSWORTH, Margaret.

Canadian. Born in Sheffield, England, in 1940; emigrated to Canada, 1968; became citizen, 1974. Educated at Hornsey High School, London; Loughborough School of Librarianship, Leicestershire, A.L.A.; Lakehead University, Thunder Bay, Ontario (gold medal), B.A. 1972; University of British Columbia, Vancouver, M.F.A. in theatre and creative writing 1974. Journalist, editor, librarian, and teacher in England, 1960–68; chief librarian, Fort William Public Library, Ontario, 1968–72. Since 1972 freelance writer. Assistant professor, David Thompson Centre, University of Victoria, Nelson, British Columbia, 1981–83; writer-in-residence, Concordia University, Montreal, 1985–86, Stratford Festival Theatre, Ontario, 1987, and University of Western Ontario, London, Ontario, 1989–90; since 1992 assistant professor of creative writing, University of Victoria, British Columbia. Recipient: Association of Canadian Television and Radio Artists award, 1979; Chalmers award, 1985; Dora Mavor Moore award, 1986, 1987. Lives in Victoria. Address: c/o Playwrights Union of Canada, 8 York Street, 6th Floor, Toronto, Ontario M5J 1R2, Canada.

Publications

PLAYS

Bushed (produced 1974). With *Operators*, 1981.

Operators (produced 1975; revised version produced 1981). With *Bushed*, 1981.

Dance for My Father. 1976.
Alli Alli Oh (produced 1977). 1979.
The Apple in the Eye (broadcast 1977; produced 1983). In *Willful Acts*, 1985.
The Writers Show (revue), with others (produced 1978).
Mother Country (produced 1980). 1980.
Ever Loving (produced 1980). 1981.
Islands (produced 1983). 1983.
Diving (produced 1983). In *Willful Acts*, 1985.
War Babies (produced 1984). In *Willful Acts*, 1985.
It's Only Hot for Two Months in Kapuskasing (produced 1985). In *Endangered Species*, 1989.
Willful Acts (includes *The Apple in the Eye, Ever Loving, Diving, Islands, War Babies*). 1985.
The Green Line (produced 1986).
Endangered Species (includes *The House That Jack Built, It's Only Hot for Two Months in Kapuskasing, Prim and Duck, Mama and Frank*). 1989.
Prim and Duck, Mama and Frank (produced 1991). In *Endangered Species*, 1989.
Alma Victoria (produced 1990).
There's a Few Things I Want to Tell You (produced 1992).
Making Greenpeace (produced 1992).

RADIO PLAYS: *Join Me in Mandalay, Prairie Drive, As I Was Saying to Mr. Dideron, Wayley's Children*, and *War Games*, from 1973; *The Apple in the Eye*, 1977; *Webster's Revenge*, 1977; *Operators*, 1986; *Alli Alli Oh*, 1986; *Responsible Party*, 1986; *Woman on the Wire*, 1986; *Surreal Landscape, The Cloud Sculptors of Coral D, Sailing Under Water, A Mother in India*, from 1986; *Mussomeli-Dusseldorf*, adaptation of the radio play by Dacia Maraini, 1991.

TELEVISION PLAYS: *Ole and All That*, 1968 (UK); *Sleepwalking* (*AirWaves* series), 1986; *Scene from a Balcony*, 1987; *The Last Demise of Julian Whittaker*, 1989.

SHORT STORIES
Smiling Under Water. 1989.

CRITICAL STUDIES: "Margaret Hollingsworth," in *The Work: Conversations with English Canadian Playwrights*, edited by Cynthia Zimmerman, 1982; introduction by Ann Saddlemyer to *Willful Acts*, 1985; "Margaret Hollingsworth," in *Fair Play: 12 Women Speak/Conversations with Canadian Playwrights*, edited by Judith Rudakoff and Rita Much, 1990.

Margaret Hollingsworth comments:

(1988) My work is very wide-ranging in style and subject. Constantly recurring themes are the search for a home, sex roles and sexual stereotypes, and war. My latest plays are *The Green Line* which is set on the green line in Beirut, and *Marked for Marriage*, a 3–act farce set against the background of the survival games which are an extremely popular pseudo-military outdoor activity among Canadian men.

Some of my more experimental work, such as *Prim and Duck, Mama and Frank*, has yet to get beyond the workshop production stage, since there are very few outlets for experimental work in Canada at this time.

Margaret Hollingsworth, born in England, emigrated to Canada at the age of 28. Now she insists: "Canada is what I write about. Canada is where I come from; it's what feeds me. My plays always, in some way, come out of Canada." She believes, as she said in a 1982 interview, that her distinctive style accounts for the infrequent staging of her work: "It tends to read flat but it isn't flat in production. Often directors are very tentative about how to handle it because it doesn't fall into any category. It isn't like what anyone else is doing. My work has got a surreal level to it. That's the way I see life. I see it in a very surreal way but rooted in practical realism." The broad trend of Hollingsworth's work ranges from relatively conventional drama (perhaps shaped by the assumptions of the New Play Centre in Vancouver) to more obscure styles and technique, linked with her gradual evolution of her own female aesthetic.

Bushed and *Operators*, early one-acts, are set in northern Ontario. *Bushed* depicts tired immigrant men in a laundromat and *Operators* features two women nightshift workers whose long-term friendship is disrupted by a newcomer. These are pieces of mood, of place, and of displacement.

Ever Loving (an ironic title) is her most accessible drama. In 38 scenes, starting in 1970 and going back as far as 1938, we see three war marriages between near-strangers: a Dundee fishergirl with an Ontario millworker of Irish descent; a posh Englishwoman with a Ukrainian Prairie farmer; and an Italian aristocrat with a would-be musician in Nova Scotia. Hollingsworth includes pre-war life, first meetings, courtship, crossing the Atlantic, and the ups and downs of 25 years. "Canada's roots," writes Helen Thomson, are shown as in "other and older cultures," while "Canadian nationalism excludes its women, and is only a spurious emotion in men." *Ever Loving* explores an important aspect of recent Canadian experience; it is about romance though it avoids all the clichés; and it is unobtrusively adventurous structurally (with two or three separate actions onstage at the same time; inter-weaving date and comment with 29 popular songs; and juxtaposing different accents and speech rhythms).

The murder of Francis Rattenbury by his wife's toy boy, perhaps aided by the wife, was a sensation in England in 1935. Rattenbury, an architect, worked mostly in British Columbia. The story prompted two plays, *Cause Célèbre*, by Terence Rattigan, and—distantly—*Molly*, by Simon Gray. Hollingsworth's treatment, *Alma Victoria*, commissioned for the 1990 Nanaimo Festival, occurs largely before the murder, with the first half in the 1920's, promisingly sketching the English-style middle-class way of life in Victoria, British Columbia. Rattenbury, at 58, abandons his wife for young Alma, a successful New York pianist and already twice married. The more routine conclusion in Bournemouth has Rattenbury drinking and in decline while his wife composes songs. The focus becomes a troubled woman circumscribed by her times.

Though Hollingsworth was active in the Campaign for Nuclear Disarmament in Britain, her political principles become overt only in *Woman on the Wire*. She explained that she lacked the confidence to write politically explicitly for a long time as "part of being a woman. You don't feel that your voice is important enough to matter. It takes a lot of writing to be able to get to the point where I feel confident enough to do that." In *Woman on the Wire*, Kate, a Canadian wife and mother, is drawn to the peace camp at the missile base at Greenham Common. The tension of night beside the barbed-wire is created, with a lonely male sentry on one side and a female look-out on the other. Both are tired, jumpy, afraid. In snippets, we learn how Kate had to accompany her manager husband to London and how an English friend first takes her to the Common, then how the commitment becomes more vital than the marriage. Another camper is a teacher who found she could teach war because it was history, but not peace, because it was politics. Kate proclaims polemically: "Just being here can make a difference to life on this planet." *Woman on the Wire* shows the usual enterprise in structure, as when song, the husband's "I love you," and the trial judge's "How do you plead?" are intercut and overlapped.

Mother Country shows Hollingsworth attempting to create on both a literal and a super-realist level. The characters are an English emigré family, three daughters returning to celebrate their dominating mother's 65th birthday, on an island off the British Columbia coast. The themes were stated succinctly by Cynthia Zimmerman: it is a play "about country and culture, about belonging and home."

Hollingsworth believes, as she told the Vancouver *Sun* in 1984, that womens' drama is "unlinear, concerned with getting inside people's heads, into the thought process. There's an earthy rhythmic sense to a lot of female writing, an effort to be more universal, to find a wholeness, a diffusing quality." Later she explains that she seeks "a poetic drama that isn't self-conscious." In a 1985 article she probed further into the problems of the woman dramatist: the domination of men as decision-makers in the theatre; the tendency for women to write for ensembles, "always a stumbling block to smooth production"; but also the way that a true woman's way defies the rules of playwriting; "The concept of a hero is perhaps a male invention, a male need." Women prefer to write of "inner states and tensions," which often do not "fit neatly into an accepted dramatic form."

An early piece such as *The Apple in the Eye* shows concern with the differences between a woman's public and private voice, together with puzzles about precisely what the apple represents. The four self-published short scripts collected as *Endangered Species* reveal Hollingsworth clearly pushing in new directions, ignoring the expectations of mainstream theatre. To select two of these, *Poppycock* develops from work with masks and clowning. Here time is "scrambled" and three well-researched relationships are brought together; H.D. and Ezra Pound, Dora Maar and Picasso, and Winifred Wagner and Hitler, with the same actor playing the three men. The semi-absurdist *Prim and Duck, Mama and Frank* has its four characters in four different rooms, with the movements of the play entitled Feet, Hands, Body, and Head.

While commentators have examined Hollingsworth's work in the light of her degree in psychology and through the influence of Pinter, neither provides the key; nor is she precisely "absurd" or "surrealist." Using short forms and evolving her own kind of non-realism, her work is increasingly individualistic, even idiosyncratic. Her writing is characterized by care for language, by focus on women in a man's world, and by a continuing restless search for something new, the perfect form of self-expression. But will these plays be produced— preferably without the restrictions of low budgets and short rehearsal periods —before she is discouraged?

—Malcolm Page

HORSFIELD, Debbie.

British. Born in Manchester, 14 February 1955. Educated at Eccles Grammar School, Manchester, 1966–73; Newcastle University, B.A. (honours) in English literature 1977. Assistant administrator, Gulbenkian Studio Theatre, Newcastle-upon-Tyne, 1978–80; assistant to the artistic director, Royal Shakespeare Company, London, 1980–83; writer-in-residence, Liverpool Playhouse, Liverpool, 1983–84. Recipient: Thames Television award, 1983. Agent: Sheila Lemon, Lemon, Unna, and Durbridge, 24 Pottery Lane, Holland Park, London W11 4LZ, England.

Publications

PLAYS

Out on the Floor (produced 1981).
Away from It All (produced 1982).
The Next Four Years, Parts 1–2 (produced 1983).
All You Deserve (produced 1983).
Red Devils (produced 1983). In *Red Devils Trilogy*, 1986.
True Dare Kiss (produced 1983). In *Red Devils Trilogy*, 1986.
Command or Promise (produced 1983). In *Red Devils Trilogy*, 1986.
Touch and Go (produced 1984).
Revelations (produced 1985).
Red Devils Trilogy. 1986.
Royal Borough (produced 1987).
In Touch (produced 1988).
Making Out (televised 1989). 1989.

RADIO PLAY: *Arrangements*, 1981.

TELEVISION PLAYS: *Face Value*, in *Crown Court* series, 1982; *Out on the Floor*, 1983; *Making Out* series, 1989–91.

Debbie Horsfield is among the most successful of Britain's young women playwrights, primarily due to the popularity of her television drama writing. Her original idea for *Making Out* was to focus on working-class women's issues. Horsfield sets the series in a factory; thus, rather than putting one woman at the centre of a largely male world, she has created a community of women who live and work with men, yet who are not primarily identified through their relationships (social or sexual) with those men. *Making Out* reached a wide audience eager to see reflections of real women on the screen. Significantly, the series is not only written by a woman (Horsfield) but has tended to be directed and produced by women as well.

The same focus on strong, realistic women is what fuels Horsfield's writing for the theatre. Her best-known theatre work is the *Red Devils Trilogy*. All three plays in the trilogy focus on the same four characters: Alice, Nita, Phil, and Beth. These four young women grow up together and their relationships, careers, hopes, and fears develop as they share their experiences and their love of football (Manchester United, to be precise). Of course, Manchester United is not only the name of a football team, but is also an accurate phrase to describe the relationship between the four central female characters, all from Manchester, all united as friends whose lives develop in different ways but stem from common roots and shared experiences.

In this trilogy of comic plays, the same idea which gives energy to *Making Out* likewise fuels the power of the theatre performance: women working and playing together, women who share interests (non-stereotypically "feminine" interests at that), women who like each other and enjoy each other's company, women who know how to make each other laugh, just as Horsfield clearly knows how to make her audiences laugh. The power of Horsfield's writing is her combination of unusual scenarios and settings for women with a frank, unsentimental, yet playful style. The working-class settings invite men as well as women into the worlds of the plays. Working-class situations are rarely portrayed as well in the theatre. Thus, the *Red Devils Trilogy* has a certain interest, even for those with no interest in football.

In the first play, *Red Devils*, the four central characters are Manchester schoolgirls on their way to the 1979 Cup Final at Wembley Stadium. The action takes place in Manchester before the game, in London during the game, and at a motorway service station between the two cities after the game. The cast of characters is laid out on the page of the published version in the shape of a football formation, with Horsfield's name (as author) in the goal box. This playful presentation of the "facts" of the performance is in keeping with the mood of the play: like much of Horsfield's work (including several of her earlier plays), it emphasizes female friendship and the enjoyment which women, like men, find in each other's company. Petty differences are presented in a humorous rather than a "catty" way.

The same positive spirit enlivens the remaining two plays in the trilogy: *True Dare Kiss* and *Command or Promise*, both staged in London's Cottesloe Theatre (The Royal National Theatre) in 1985. In both of these plays, the same four characters have grown up and remain friends, sharing different aspects of their adult lives, as well as their continued love of football. The plays have been criticized for being "too much like soap opera," a criticism which says as much about our cultural expectations as it does about the plays. It is true that the depiction of the young women's lives in these later plays is channeled through multiple storylines, familiar from televised soap operas and serials (and very effectively utilized in Horsfield's own television success, *Making Out*). But to identify the form of the plays as a fault is misleading: they are episodic and weighted with the conflicting and overlapping stories of four different women's lives. Relationships are represented between women and men, women and work, women and higher education, women and cultural trends (punk culture and football). Yet the uniting thread of the four stories, as they develop and grow in the three plays of the *Red Devil's Trilogy*, is the relationship between the four women. That focus on women's friendship is still uncommon on the stage. Debbie Horsfield has begun to make it more acceptable, and has thereby opened the way for other playwrights to experiment with a wide range of common but little-represented experiences in contemporary theatre.

—Lizbeth Goodman

HOWE, Tina.

American. Born in New York City, 21 November 1937. Educated at Sarah Lawrence College, Bronxville, New York, B.A. 1959; Chicago Teachers College, 1963–64. Married Norman Levy in 1961; one son and one daughter. Since 1983 adjunct professor, New York University; since 1990 visiting professor, Hunter College, City University of New York. Recipient: Rosamond Gilder award, 1983; Rockefeller grant, 1983; Obie award, 1983; Outer Critics Circle award, 1983, 1984; John Gassner award, 1984; National Endowment for the Arts grant, 1984; Guggenheim fellowship, 1990. Honorary degree: Bowdoin College, Brunswick, Maine, 1988. Agent: Flora Roberts Inc., 157 West 57th Street, New York, New York 10019, U.S.A.

Publications

PLAYS

Closing Time (produced 1959).
The Nest (produced 1969).
Museum (produced 1976). 1979.
Birth and After Birth, in *The New Women's Theatre*, edited by Honor Moore. 1977.
The Art of Dining (produced 1979). 1980.
Appearances (produced 1982).
Painting Churches (produced 1983). 1984.
Three Plays (includes *Museum*, *The Art of Dining*, *Painting Churches*). 1984.
Coastal Disturbances (produced 1986). 1987.
Approaching Zanzibar (produced 1989). 1989.
Coastal Disturbances: Four Plays (includes *Painting Churches*, *The Art of Dining*, *Museum*). 1989.
Teeth. In *Antaeus*, no.66, Spring 1991.
Swimming (produced 1991).

CRITICAL STUDIES: *Creating Theater: The Professionals' Approach to New Plays* by Lee Alan Morrow and Frank Pike, 1986; *Interviews with Contemporary Women Playwrights* edited by Kathleen Betsko and Rachel Koenig, 1987; *A Search for Postmodern Theater: Interviews with Contemporary Playwrights* by John L. DiGaetani, 1991.

Tina Howe is a marvelously perceptive observer of contemporary mores, and much of the pleasure one receives from her plays comes from her comic skewering of pretentious amateur art critics, couples moaning orgasmically over the yuppie menu of their dreams, and thoroughly enlightened parents thoroughly unable to cope with their monstrous four-year-old. At their best, however, her comedies probe beneath the surface to reveal the inextricable mixture of the humorous and horrific to which modern culture—including art, ritual, and table manners—is a barely adequate response.

Although it already hints of better things to come, *The Nest* is the least satisfying of Howe's full-length plays. The influence of Ionesco and Beckett, whose work Howe admires, is evident here in the use of repeated scenes as well as in the heavy reliance on verbal and physical farce. Still, this play about a trio of female roommates lacks the satirical and emotional bite of her subsequent creations even as it offers glimpses of her prodigious imagination.

"Family life has been over-romanticized; the savagery has not been seen enough in the theatre and in movies," Howe once complained. She attempts to fill this gap with *Birth and After Birth*, a sometimes hilarious, often frightening portrait of the Apples. As their name implies, the Apples (including a four-year-old son played by an adult actor) are a parody of the TV-fare all-American family, continually declaring how happy they are and continually belying this claim. What keeps *Birth and After Birth* from being simply another satire on Ozzie and Harriet is not only Howe's accurate portrait of the physical and emotional brutality inherent in family life but her disturbingly negative exploration of why women choose to have—or not to have—children. Despite the often broad slapstick, *Birth and After Birth* is one of Howe's darkest comedies.

Museum is less a plotted play than a wonderful series of comic turns as visitors—singly and in groups—wander through an exhibit entitled "The Broken Silence." As Howe has acknowledged in interviews, all of her plays are about art, and *Museum* examines the complex interrelationships among creator, creation, and viewers. On one level, *Museum* reveals what fools art makes of us (witness the young woman painstakingly copying an all-white canvas); on another level, however, it shows that artworks cannot fully exist except in the presence of an audience, foolish or not. Finally, in one of the comically horrific monologues that seem an essential part of the Howe landscape, a museum-goer recounts a foraging expedition she took with Agnes Vaag, a young artist represented in the show but never seen on stage. The story reveals the frightening, non-rational roots of art. Vaag, at once a mysterious being who makes "menacing constructions" out of animal carcasses and a ludicrous figure who lugs suitcases through state parks, may well be Howe's archetypal artist.

Another loosely knit comedy, *The Art of Dining* combines Howe's obsession with food (first manifest in *The Nest*) and her concern with art and its consumption. Because the fragility of art is a repeated motif throughout Howe's canon, in a sense food is for her the ultimate artistic medium: it must be destroyed to be appreciated. Set in a restaurant, *The Art of Dining* contains one of Howe's most brilliant creations, Elizabeth Barrow Colt, a wonderfully comic and pathetic figure who embodies every cliché about writers; comfortable only in the world of the imagination, she's a genius with a pen but a total failure with a soup spoon. In *The Art of Dining*'s spectacular conclusion—all the restaurant guests gathered around a flaming platter of crepes tended by the female chef—Howe uses Elizabeth to point out the connection between art and ritual as well as the redemptive power of artistic creation, a theme that runs through several of Howe's works.

Howe's biggest critical success to date is *Painting Churches*, in some ways her most conventional play as well as one of her most lyrical. Returning to the favorite subject of the American playwright—the nuclear family—Howe gives us a comedy about the necessity of acceptance: a daughter accepting the inevitable decline of her aging parents, parents accepting their daughter as a capable adult (and artist). Howe's quirky sense of humor and her distinctive verbal and visual idiom mark the work as uniquely her own, however familiar her starting point. Although Howe denies that she is an autobiographical writer, there is obviously a kinship between the playwright and Mags Church, the young artist who learns that the portrait she is painting of her parents reveals her as well as them. In a moving final tour-de-force that erases the line between Mags' painting and Howe's play, the stripped-bare stage becomes the portrait, the aging characters rescued from decline for the space of a magical moment.

Howe favors unusual settings—a museum, a restaurant kitchen—and the beach locale of *Coastal Disturbances* is as much metaphor as place: like human beings and their relationships, the sand and ocean remain essentially the same over millennia yet change from moment to moment. The main character is a young woman photographer; appropriately, the play is divided into numerous short scenes that rely heavily on visual effects—resembling, in other words, a sequence of snapshots. Although the central situation, a love triangle, is not Howe's most original, her verbal and especially her visual wit are amply in evidence.

Swimming shares the beach location and largely affirmative vision of *Coastal Disturbances*, while *Teeth* is a serio-comic meditation on fear set, appropriately, in a dentist's office. These two add to the small but growing canon of Howe's one-act plays, which also includes *Appearances*, an encounter between a dressing room attendant and a painfully awkward customer. *Approaching Zanzibar*, Howe's latest major work, is a "road play" that follows a family of four on a cross-country trip to visit a dying relative (an elderly artist reminiscent of Georgia O'Keeffe). The Blossoms' journey is both physical and metaphysical as they engage in hilarious—and sometimes nasty— travel games while wrestling with anxieties about change, loss, and death. Not only is this the first of Howe's plays to exploit multiple settings, but its relatively large cast also represents a deliberate attempt on the playwright's part to include a wider range of characters in terms of ethnicity as well as age. Despite being one of Howe's most complex and ambitious works, however, *Zanzibar* received mixed reviews and enjoyed only a brief New York run.

Howe has acknowledged her debt to Absurdist writers, a debt more apparent in her earlier work than in her most recent plays. Like many other American playwrights, Howe doesn't quite share the nihilistic vision of her European counterparts; although salvation is transitory and more likely to be aesthetic than religious or social, there are moments of redemption in most of her plays. Her work has grown in emotional depth over the years and her focus on art and the artist has become stronger. Women artists are her favored protagonists: she writes from a clearly female perspective even if not from a consistently feminist one. Howe's comedies reveal a playwright with a fine sensitivity to the terrors of existence, a splendidly anarchic sense of humor, and a willingness to take risks on the stage.

—Judith E. Barlow

I

ISITT, Debbie.

British. Born in Birmingham, 7 February 1966. Educated at Lordswood Girls' School, Birmingham, 1977–82; Coventry Centre for the Performing Arts, 1983–85. Dancer, Unique, Birmingham, 1978–82; receptionist, Hendon Business Association, Birmingham, 1982–83; actor, Cambridge Experimental Theatre Company, European tour, 1985–86; co-founder and since 1986, artistic director, Snarling Beasties Theatre Company, Longford, Coventry; guest director, Coventry Centre for Performing Arts, 1991, Other Theatre of Comedy Trust, London, 1992, and Repertory Theatre, Heilbronn, Germany, 1992. Recipient: *Scottish Daily Express* award, 1988; Independent Theatre award, 1989; Perrier Pick of the Fringe award, 1989, 1990; *Time Out* Theatre award, 1990/91; Edinburgh Fringe Festival first, 1992. Agent: Nick Marston, A. P. Watt Ltd., 20 John Street, London WC1N 2DR. Address: c/o Snarling Beasties Coventry Touring Theatre Co-op Ltd., 36 Sydnall Road, Longford, Coventry CV6 6BW, England.

Publications

PLAYS

Gangsters (produced 1988).
Punch and Judy: The Real Story (also director: produced 1989).
Valentino (also director: produced 1990).
Femme Fatale (also director: produced 1990).
The Woman Who Cooked Her Husband (produced 1991).
You Never Know Who's Out There (produced 1992).
Out of the Ordinary (produced 1993).

TELEVISION PLAY: *The Lodger*, 1992.

THEATRICAL ACTIVITIES

DIRECTOR: **Plays**—all her own plays; *East* by Steven Berkoff, 1986.
ACTOR: **Plays**—all her own plays; *A Midsummer Night's Dream*, 1985–86.

Debbie Isitt comments:

Writing for me has to have a purpose and that purpose is usually to reach people and hopefully make them feel something, see something, hear something, think something, and maybe even do something. In my experience

116

writing for the theatre is vitally important; I am not reliant very often on producers, publicists, marketing machines, sponsors, donors, editors, censors, men in suits and women in shoulder pads to be able to create and get my work seen. Part of this freedom comes from directing and appearing in my own work; I only have to find a willing person to let me have a space, find others willing to push themselves and take a few risks and put it on. This is the most important bit—to put it on and say—this is what I wanted to say and it's how I wanted to say it—it is a truthful interpretation of what I intended and let people take from it what they wish. I could not stand to be part of a system that compromised my plays, that shaped them and bent them and formed them into someone else's. If a writer is not herself behind the words then she is not a writer. She should put herself on the line and create dramas that draw people into her world just for the duration of the play; even if the world is one from her imagination it is HER imagination and no one else's that we should be sharing. So much emphasis is put on criteria for funding, fitting in, opting out. I would like to think I can maintain control of my writing, although as I move some way into film I begin to see that things are very difficult, there seems to be little room for guts, imagination, and risk.

I tend to choose themes that are at once personal and close to home while smacking of larger social issues. Heterosexual relationships and the dark forces seething behind contemporary marriage is a theme that I am drawn to time and again. Social myths and secrets that we hide and disguise and twist to fit in and conform. Domestic violence, tranvestism, betrayal, phobias, lies are the stuff my plays are made of. They are real and surreal fusing together. Music is a massive influence, especially the great works of contemporary heros like Frank Sinatra, Ella Fitzgerald, Patsy Cline. The woman's psyche being put centre stage is another of my interests; I like to put women into certain situations to see how they react and then make them do things and think things and say things that we're not supposed to and see how the men react. It's really a very interesting process. I also like to leave room for movement and mime and visual techniques often influenced by films and incorporate it on the stage. Above all I think I like to be truthful to the characters, the situation, and myself. The plays are usually funny even though they are often dark. I cannot stand to get depressed—we need to recognize the funny side of pain and guilt and grief. We also need fight and spirit and punch and my plays must be performed with pace and vitality. I am not the sentimental type—just the mental type.

Debbie Isitt's plays are inextricably linked to her productions in which she usually also acts. The company was formed in 1986 and called Snarling Beasties (Steven Berkoff's creative slang for testicles) because Isitt fancied the idea of strait-laced bureaucrats unwittingly referring to male genitalia in the course of deciding whether or not to give the company money. After their inaugural production of Berkoff's *East* at Edinburgh, it fell upon Isitt to come up with some follow-up material. Not for her the luxury of dwelling on every syllable; her best work has been produced under the pressure of the deadline of the Edinburgh Festival. *Punch and Judy*, *Femme Fatale*, and *The Woman Who Cooked Her Husband* are a trio of plays exploring the underbelly of heterosexual relationships on the themes of wife-battering, transvestism, and adultery respectively. In production her words are supported by an expressionistic, mimetic presentation of character, loud popular music, and a set that hits you between the eyes. The effect is intensely theatrical and reminiscent of Berkoff in the aggressive use of rhyming couplets. Such an upfront presentation is exhilarating to watch, although sometimes one wonders whether it is the raucous music that is providing the uplift rather than Isitt's words.

Judging from Isitt's work, she is not a woman in need of courses in assertiveness. Her approach is unashamedly partisan: men appear as boorish, unimaginative wimps with little or nothing to recommend them. *The Woman Who Cooked Her Husband* was inspired by the real-life case of Nicholas Boyce in 1985 in which Boyce chopped his wife up and distributed the pieces because he could no longer stand her nagging. The Judge, summing up, said that Boyce was sorely provoked and he only served six years for manslaughter. In contrast, Sara Thornton is serving life for killing her husband after being abused for years. Such an imbalance of justice fuels Isitt's anger. *The Woman Who Cooked Her Husband* depicts a triangular relationship between Kenneth, his wife Hilary, and Laura, his mistress. Kenneth is torn between Laura's skills in bed and Hilary's in the kitchen. Hilary has devoted her life to serving up tempting delicacies in the belief that a well-fed man will never leave her. Through flashback, we see Kenneth's first encounters with the sulky Laura who can hardly summon up enough energy to open a packet of fish fingers. Cringing, shifty, and a poor liar, Kenneth continues to meander between the two until Laura takes matters into her own hands and spills the beans to Hilary, forcing Kenneth to leave her. At a strange reunion, Kenneth salivates as he anticipates his first good meal for a long time, but Hilary, finally supported by Laura, has other ideas for the menu.

There is no doubt that Kenneth is the most unpleasant character on stage and there can be few audiences who wouldn't cheer Hilary on in her grisly deed. But Isitt also criticises the wife's tendency to blame "the other woman" instead of her spouse. The woman, it seems, is seen as inadequate if she is left and criticised as a homewrecker if she does the leaving. Isitt doesn't see that marriage has much to offer a woman. So one-sided and dogmatic is the approach that it can inspire resistance in an audience. It is the black humour that transforms the bile into something more memorable.

Femme Fatale, the second play in the trilogy, is more complex because for once Isitt doesn't have all the answers. Georgia and Jimmy could be a model couple, with lots of disposable income and a good sex life, only Jimmy is drawn irresistibly towards a black cubicle at the back of the stage where he is transformed into Jessica. Apart from the shock and distaste, what enrages Georgia is that Jessica should be such a paragon of femininity, lying on the sofa painting her nails and eager to do all she can to make their domestic life run smoothly. Her perfection challenges Georgia's refusal to be a slave to the sink or her husband. Jimmy likes to dress up because he says it makes him feel "free from pressure." But being a woman is far from being free of pressure. Isitt tentatively explores why transvestites are drawn to such stereotypical images of femininity, tottering around on high heels and crowned with their beehive hairdos—everything that feminists are trying to escape. As Georgia gets more aggressive, so Jimmy becomes more passive. Beneath the feminist rhetoric, there is some sympathy for the man who feels he has to adopt the clothes of a woman in order to explore the more feminine side of his nature. But Isitt never loses sight of the fact that discovering one's husband dressed in a pair of one's knickers does have a funny side.

Since the trilogy the Other Theatre of Comedy Trust commissioned *You Never Know Who's Out There*, which explores the seedy, racist and misogynist world of the Northern club and is reminiscent of Trevor Griffiths's *Comedians*. A power struggle amongst the performers results in much spilling of blood but little illumination. Snarling is Isitt's hallmark. Now that we know that she is not afraid to show her teeth, it would make a change if she occasionally concealed them.

—Jane Edwardes

J

JELLICOE, (Patricia) Ann.

British. Born in Middlesbrough, Yorkshire, 15 July 1927. Educated at Polam Hall, Darlington, County Durham; Queen Margaret's, Castle Howard, Yorkshire; Central School of Speech and Drama, London (Elsie Fogarty prize, 1947), 1944–47. Married 1) C. E. Knight-Clarke in 1950 (marriage dissolved 1961); 2) Roger Mayne in 1962, one son and one daughter. Actress, stage manager, and director, in London and the provinces, 1947–51; founding director, Cockpit Theatre Club, London, 1952–54; lecturer and director, Central School of Speech and Drama, 1954–56; literary manager, Royal Court Theatre, London, 1973–75; founding director, 1979–85, and president, 1986, Colway Theatre Trust. O.B.E. (Officer, Order of the British Empire), 1984. Agent: Casarotto Ramsay Ltd., National House, 60–66 Wardour Street, London W1V 3HP, England.

Publications

PLAYS

Rosmersholm, adaptation of the play by Ibsen (also director: produced 1952; revised version produced 1959). 1960.

The Sport of My Mad Mother (also co-director: produced 1958). In *The Observer Plays*, 1958; revised version, 1964; with *The Knack*, 1964.

The Lady from the Sea, adaptation of a play by Ibsen (produced 1961).

The Knack (produced 1961; also co-director, 1962). 1962.

The Seagull, with Adriadne Nicolaeff, adaptation of a play by Chekhov (produced 1964).

Der Freischütz, translation of the libretto by Friedrich Kind, music by Weber (produced 1964).

Shelley; or, The Idealist (also director: produced 1965). 1966.

The Rising Generation (produced 1967). In *Playbill 2*, edited by Alan Durband, 1969.

The Giveaway (produced 1968). 1970.

You'll Never Guess (also director: produced 1973). In *3 Jelliplays*, 1975.

Two Jelliplays: Clever Elsie, Smiling John, Silent Peter, and A Good Thing or a Bad Thing (also director: produced 1974). In *3 Jelliplays*, 1975.

3 Jelliplays (for children; includes *You'll Never Guess; Clever Elsie, Smiling John, Silent Peter; A Good Thing or a Bad Thing*). 1975.

Flora and the Bandits (also director: produced 1976).

The Reckoning (also director: produced 1978).

The Bargain (also director: produced 1979).
The Tide (also director: produced 1980).
The Western Women, music by Nick Brace, adaptation of a story by Fay
   Weldon (also co-director: produced 1984).
Changing Places (produced 1992).

OTHER

Some Unconscious Influences in the Theatre. 1967.
Devon: A Shell Guide, with Roger Mayne. 1975.
Community Plays: How to Put Them On. 1987.

THEATRICAL ACTIVITIES

DIRECTOR: **Plays**—*The Confederacy* by Vanbrugh, London, 1952; *The Frogs*
by Aristophanes, 1952; *Miss Julie* by Strindberg, 1952; *Rosmersholm* by
Ibsen, 1952; *Saint's Day* by John Whiting, 1953; *The Comedy of Errors*,
1953; *Olympia* by Ferenč Molnár, 1953; *The Sport of My Mad Mother* (co-
director, with George Devine), 1958; *For Children* by Keith Johnstone, 1958;
The Knack (co-director, with Keith Johnstone), 1962; *Skyvers* by Barry
Reckord, 1963; *Shelley*, 1965; *You'll Never Guess*, 1973; *Two Jelliplays*,
1974; *A Worthy Guest* by Paul Bailey, 1974; *Six of the Best*, 1974; *Flora and
the Bandits*, 1976; *The Reckoning*, 1978; *The Bargain*, 1979; *The Tide*, 1980;
The Poor Man's Friend by Howard Barker, 1981; *The Garden* by Charles
Wood, 1982; *The Western Women* (co-director, with Chris Fog and Sally-Ann
Lomax), 1984; *Entertaining Strangers* by David Edgar, 1985.

The major plays by new young writers in London between 1956 and 1959
included *Look Back in Anger*, *The Birthday Party*, *Roots*, *Serjeant Musgrave's
Dance*, *A Resounding Tinkle*, *The Long and the Short and the Tall*, *Flowering
Cherry*, *Five Finger Exercise*, *The Hostage*, *A Taste of Honey*—and Ann
Jellicoe's *The Sport of My Mad Mother* at the Royal Court, the heart of this
activity.

   Since this impressive debut, Jellicoe has written only three other full-length
stage plays, two of them slight. The 16 brief scenes of *Shelley* take the poet
from his Oxford years, through two marriages, to Harriet Westbrook and
Mary Godwin, to his drowning in Italy. *Shelley*, subtitled "the Idealist," is
written as though for a 19th-century touring company of twelve: heavy,
walking gentleman, juvenile, and so on. Jellicoe remarks that as a writer she is
tackling a new set of problems here, working "within a set narrative
framework—partly for the sheer technical discipline involved." Shelley interests her because he is very young, and trying to be good: "the problems of
goodness which are so much more interesting than those of evil." He is tragic
because of "his blindness to the frailty of human nature." *Shelley* is a flat work,
with conspicuous explanatory sections in which the poet talks like a letter or
tract.

   The Giveaway turns on a suburban housewife who wins a competition prize
of ten years' supply of cornflakes (which are conspicuously on stage); she has
had to pretend to be under 14. While the only production may not have done it
justice, *The Giveaway* seems to be a clumsy attempt to write a farce, with a

hint of satire on consumerism and a touch of the kind of non-verbal comedy Jellicoe had written earlier.

Jellicoe's best play, *The Knack*, is an exuberant, liberating, youthful comedy. Three young men share a flat: Tolen (he has only this one curious name), who has "the knack" of success with women; likeable Colin, who lacks it and envies Tolen; and the garrulous Tom, half outside the sex war. Enter Nancy, a lost, gawky, 17–year-old Northerner, looking for the YWCA, who will give Tolen a chance to demonstrate his knack. The staccato, repetitive dialogue skims along like jazz, and is sometimes hard to follow on the page. A bed provides comic business (they pretend it is a piano), as do entries through the window. An undercurrent is Tolen's Nazi characteristics, and whether negotiation is possible with such people. (The film, scripted by Charles Wood and directed by Richard Lester, is substantially changed, and also great fun.)

Jellicoe's *succès d'estime*, *The Sport of My Mad Mother*, is much more unusual and demanding. This is about four London teenagers and three people they come across, a liberal American, a retarded girl of 13, and Greta, an Australian who comes to represent also the Hindu goddess of destruction and creation, Kali. Yet character, plot, dialogue hardly matter. This is a piece to be brought to life by a director, and, to make reading really difficult, stage-directions are few. The form is non-linear; Jellicoe writes in the Preface to the revised text of 1964 that the play "was not written intellectually according to a prearranged plan. It was shaped bit by bit until the bits felt right in relation to each other and to the whole. It is an anti-intellect play not only because it is about irrational forces and urges but because one hopes it will reach the audience directly through rhythm, noise and music. . . . Very often the words counterpoint the action or intensify the action by conflicting with it." *The Sport of My Mad Mother* is highly original (especially for Britain and for the 1950's) in its Artaudian use of ritual, in its stress on physical expressiveness, in its use of speech and drums for rhythms, in its audacious non-literary form and apparent shapelessness, and in its search for the roots of arbitrary violence. Proper recognition and appreciation will require a readily available film version, as yet unmade.

In 1972 Jellicoe told Carol Dix in the *Guardian*: "Directing, as I see it, is an interpretative art, and writing is a creative art, and it's a bloody relief not to have to be creative any longer. The impulse to create is linked with the aggressive instinct."

A ten-year silence ended when in 1978 Jellicoe moved to Lyme Regis, Dorset; she has since staged numerous community plays in the southwest. These ambitious works involve many local people (up to 180 onstage), use the town as the setting and have a promenade production. Jellicoe wrote the first, *The Reckoning*, about the Monmouth Rebellion of 1685. Allen Saddler described it in *Plays and Players*: "It is all action. The mayor and his cronies scramble about in a frenzy, people rush by in terror, beg for mercy or confide strange secrets in your ear. A girl who is pregnant by a Catholic finds herself in a strange dilemma, proclamations are read from various parts of the hall. Soldiers burst in. Bands play. Prisoners are dragged off screaming. Brawls break out just where you are standing. Events proceed so quickly that there is no time to examine the Catholic or the Protestant case." *The Western Women*, about the part played by women in the siege of Lyme in the Civil War, was rewritten by Jellicoe from a script by Fay Weldon. Another local history piece, *The Bargain*, concerned Judge Jeffreys and was commissioned by the Southwest Music Theatre. Jellicoe in her essay in *Women and Theatre* writes of the satisfaction of this community activity: "It was extraordinary, the people of Lyme, in rehearsal and in performance, watching a play about themselves. There is a unique atmosphere. It's partly the promenade style of performance, partly that the play is specially written for the town, but it has never failed, that excitement, they just go wild. . . . What I love about it is slowly building something in the community."

In May 1992 Jellicoe took up the challenge of devising a community play for Woking, Surrey, a place lacking much history or sense of identity. Her *Changing Places* focused on women, on Ethel Smythe, composer and militant suffragette, contrasting her with a working-class woman—outside the middle-class movement for votes-for-women—who achieves self-realisation as a nurse in World War I. Jellicoe appears unlikely to return to the Royal Court, or to the West End, as her fulfilment now comes from her community work in the West Country.

—Malcolm Page

See the essay on *The Knack*.

K

KEATLEY, Charlotte.

British. Born in London in 1960. Educated at Manchester University, B.A. in drama 1982; University of Leeds, M.A. in theatre arts 1983. Theatre critic for the Yorkshire *Post*, *Times Educational Supplement*, *Plays and Players*, Glasgow *Herald*, 1980–86, and for the *Financial Times*; writer, actor, and director in performance art and community theatre in Leeds and Manchester, 1982–84; teacher in drama in primary and secondary schools around Britain, 1985–86; Judith E. Wilson visiting fellow in English, Cambridge University, 1988–89; lecturer in playwriting and theatre skills, University of London, Royal Court Young People's Theatre and Women's National Touring Theatre, London, University of Birmingham, and Vassar College, Poughkeepsie, New York, 1988–92. Recipient: *Sunday Times* award, for acting, 1980; Manchester *Evening News* award, 1987; George Devine award, 1987; *Plays and Players* award, 1989; Edinburgh Fringe first, for direction, 1991. Agents: Peregrine Whittlesey Agency, 345 East 80th Street, New York, New York 10021, U.S.A.; and Rod Hall, A.P. Watt, 20 John Street, London WC1N 2DR, England.

Publications

PLAYS

Underneath the Arndale (produced 1982).
Dressing for Dinner (produced 1982).
An Armenian Childhood, with Pete Brooks and Steve Schill (produced 1983).
The Legend of Padgate, music by Mark Vibrans (also director: produced 1986).
Waiting for Martin (produced 1987).
My Mother Said I Never Should (produced 1987). 1988; revised version, 1989.
You're a Nuisance Aren't You, in *Fears and Miseries of the Third Term*, with others (produced 1989).
The Singing Ringing Tree (for children), music by Errollyn Wallen (produced 1991).

RADIO PLAYS: *My Mother Said I Never Should*, 1989; *Citizens* series, with others, 1989–90.

TELEVISION PLAY: *Badger* (for children), 1989.

THEATRICAL ACTIVITIES
DIRECTOR: **Plays**—*The Legend of Padgate*, 1986; *Autogeddon* by Heathcote Williams, 1991.

Charlotte Keatley is one of the youngest playwrights to have a main stage performance at the Royal Court. Her play *My Mother Said I Never Should* received wide-spread acclaim after its run at that theatre. It was compared by reviewers to the work of Sharman MacDonald in its depiction of generations of women learning about themselves and each other. This play is Keatley's primary claim to fame in the theatre, though she has also written *Underneath the Arndale* and *Dressing for Dinner*. In addition, she is known as one of the writers of the television serial *Citizens*. She is currently at work on another full-length play.

In interview in 1989, Charlotte Keatley compared her work to that of the early feminist and alternative theatres. She said: "When you start making plays about your own experiences and in your own language, there is so much to say that the temptation is to say it all quickly and crudely, and so you throw up big signs. After that, you can become more sophisticated and more subtle in the way you say things, which I would say started happening in the late seventies." Keatley's work has developed in a similar way, from the dark humour of *Dressing for Dinner* to the more sophisticated balance of humour and drama which is explored in *My Mother Said I Never Should*.

Keatley performed in her play *Dressing for Dinner*, a visual theatre piece devised and produced by Keatley's own company, The Royale Ballé. The (unpublished) play centred on the image of the feminine woman and her essential item of apparel: the obligatory "little black number." It experimented with images and ideas, movement and gesture, in a form which borrowed both from 1980's feminist thought and the theatrical styles of visual and performance theatre artists such as Clare MacDonald. Visual tricks such as comparing —through innuendo and layered symbolism—the dressing of a woman and the dressing of a fish in aspic were utilized as "shock techniques" which first made the audience laugh, and then made them question the source of their laughter.

Keatley continued to experiment with "shock techniques" in her later work, and most notably in *My Mother Said I Never Should*. But in the latter, the "shock" is primarily directed at audience empathy rather than such radical questioning of audience values and motives. Both *Dressing for Dinner* and *My Mother Said* explore the relations between generations of women and their shared experiences and memories. Yet *My Mother Said I Never Should* is a much more sophisticated piece of writing, and of theatre. It can be studied as a script or literary text, chronicling the lives of four generations of women in war-torn and post-war Britain. It can also be studied in larger terms as a performance of self in society, that is, it can be analyzed as a play informed by feminist politics and theories, played out in the differences between generations of woman.

Keatley, of course, belongs to one of those generations. But her skill as a playwright has transcended the limitations of the author's own perspective, offering instead a play which can be—and often is—seen to be filtered through the perspective of different generations. In fact, as Keatley herself has observed when sitting in the audience of her own play, members of the audience tend to identify with a particular character, and with her generation. The critical conception of "the gaze" is manipulated in terms of generational difference rather than gender difference.

Gender is, though, also a crucial consideration in the play. No male characters appear on stage. Yet unlike many women's plays which are criticized for the lack of men or for "cardboard depictions of men," Keatley seems somehow to have sidestepped that kind of red-herring criticism, partly through humour and partly through a skillful manipulation of audience expectation in regard to the invisible male characters. While no men appear on stage in *My Mother Said I Never Should*, Keatley has incorporated references to male characters in the script: husbands and partners are referred to and seem at times to be present in the wings as the women on stage shout questions and comments to them. This manipulation of audience expectation is used to comic effect, but also has a more serious purpose. In Keatley's words: "I finally decided to do the play without men at all because I wanted to present whole ways of being for women which only happen when the men have gone out of the room."

That introduction to female characters as they appear when no men are present is one of Keatley's greatest contributions. That men seemed to enjoy the plays as well is a tribute to the quality of the writing. With or without male characters, the creation of plays which deal intelligently and evocatively with the performance of gender roles on stage makes Keatley a playwright whose work should be read and seen.

—Lizbeth Goodman

KENNEDY, Adrienne (Lita, née Hawkins).

American. Born in Pittsburgh, Pennsylvania, 13 September 1931; grew up in Cleveland, Ohio. Educated in Cleveland public schools; Ohio State University, Columbus, B.A. in education 1953; Columbia University, New York, 1954–56. Married Joseph C. Kennedy in 1953 (divorced 1966); two sons. Joined Edward Albee's workshop in 1962. Lecturer in play-writing, Yale University, New Haven, Connecticut, 1972–74, Princeton University, New Jersey, 1977, and Brown University, Providence, Rhode Island, 1979–80; chancellor's distinguished lecturer, University of California, Berkeley, 1986. Member of the Board of Directors, PEN, 1976–77. Recipient: Obie award, 1965; Guggenheim fellowship, 1967; Rockefeller grant, 1967, 1969, 1973; New England Theatre Conference grant; National Endowment for the Arts grant, 1972; CBS-Yale University fellowship, 1973; Creative Artists Public Service grant, 1974. Agent: Bridget Aschenberg, 40 West 57th Street, New York, New York 10019. Address: 325 West 89th Street, New York, New York 10024, U.S.A.

Publications

PLAYS

Funnyhouse of a Negro (produced 1964). 1969.
The Owl Answers (produced 1965). In *Cities in Bezique*, 1969.
A Beast's Story (produced 1965). In *Cities in Bezique*, 1969.

A Rat's Mass (produced 1966). In *New Black Playwrights*, edited by William Couch, Jr., 1968.

The Lennon Play: In His Own Write, with John Lennon and Victor Spinetti, adaptation of works by Lennon (produced 1967; revised version produced 1968). 1968.

A Lesson in Dead Language (produced 1968). In *Collision Course*, 1968.

Boats (produced 1969).

Sun: A Poem for Malcolm X Inspired by His Murder (produced 1969). In *Scripts 1*, November 1971.

Cities in Bezique: 2 One-Act Plays: The Owl Answers and A Beast's Story. 1969.

An Evening with Dead Essex (produced 1973).

A Movie Star Has to Star in Black and White (produced 1976). In *Wordplays 3*, 1984.

Orestes and *Electra* (produced 1980). In *In One Act*, 1988.

Black Children's Day (produced 1980).

A Lancashire Lad (for children; produced 1980).

Solo Voyages (includes excerpts from her previous plays; produced 1985).

In One Act (includes *Funnyhouse of a Negro, The Owl Answers, A Lesson in Dead Language, A Rat's Mass, Sun, A Movie Star Has to Star in Black and White, Electra, Orestes*). 1988.

The Ohio State Murders (produced 1990).

She Talks and Beethoven: 2 One-Act Plays. In *Antaeus*, no.66, Spring 1991.

OTHER

People Who Led to My Plays (memoirs). 1987.

Deadly Triplets: A Theatre Mystery and Journal. 1990.

The Alexander Plays. 1992.

Adrienne Kennedy comments:

My plays are meant to be states of mind.

As black power gathered strength in America in the 1960's, the dramatist Adrienne Kennedy, who is black, was discovering more uses for the word Negro. She marks the beginnings of celebratory blackness with *Funnyhouse of a Negro* in which a woman's personal history of miscegenation, rape, and madness inscribes the larger history of black experience in white America, a history that Americans now sanitize and democratize under the rubric "race relations." Kennedy makes no totalizing claims to represent anyone, but the play's motifs resonate sharply in collective history.

In her New York apartment, Kennedy's "Negro-Sarah" enshrines an enormous statue of Queen Victoria and, in the course of the play, splits into a hunchbacked Jesus, the Duchess of Hapsburg, the African liberation leader Patrice Lumumba, and even Queen Victoria—each denoted as "One of Herselves." This is history and identity in a funnyhouse of distorted mirrors whose reflections are as unthinkable in racist America emerging from the 1950's as Sarah herself, child of a light-skinned black woman supposedly raped by her missionary black husband in Africa. Slowly Sarah's incarnations emerge from darkness to narrate bits of the original trauma: the missionary zeal of the father who "wanted the black man to rise from colonialism," the mother who "didn't want him to save the black race and spent her days combing her hair . . . and would not let him touch her in their wedding bed and called him black," the daughter conceived in violence, who rejects the father but resembles him and watches her mother lapse into madness, then death, the remembered sign for which is hair falling out.

Throughout the play, shining hairless skulls appear in dialogue and enacted fantasy until Sarah tries to stifle her father's (and her race's) claim on her by bludgeoning him with an ebony mask. Yet he returns: "He keeps returning forever, coming back ever and keeps coming back forever." Sarah's white friends whose (Victorian) culture "keep [her] from reflecting too much upon the fact that [she is] a Negro" cannot protect her from this returning and recurring repressed racial memory, signified by the repeated sound of knocking and the obsessively repeated images of fallen hair, kinky and straight, on a white pillow; of yellowness, the sickly white color of Sarah's skin; of swarming ravens and of death's-heads. The expressionistic funnyhouse of Sarah's memory defies linear logic. Her father hangs himself—or does not—in two versions of the story, but the last play image shows Sarah herself hanged, reclaimed by the jungle that engulfs the stage. Sarah's split subjectivity bears the scars of Afro-American history; her identification with her mother and murderous repression of her father's culture engage the discourses of feminism and psychoanalysis, and reveal the desire and exclusion embodied in Kennedy's "Negro."

The Owl Answers brilliantly extends these issues through the laminated identities of Kennedy's protagonist, She who is Clara Passmore who is the Virgin Mary who is the Bastard who is the Owl, whose history generates another violently skewed family romance, this time with a poor black mother and the "Richest White Man in the Town." Gradually a story emerges of a bastard daughter of miscegenous union, adopted by the Reverend Passmore, renamed Clara, but who carries her black mother's color and a passion for her white father's culture, "the England of dear Chaucer, Dickens and dearest Shakespeare," whose works she reads as a child in the Passmore library, and later disseminates as a "plain, pallid" schoolteacher in Savannah, Georgia. The glorious fathers of literary history merge with those of Christian myth as God's white dove (associated with Reverend Passmore's preaching) replaces the jungle father's black ravens in *Funnyhouse*. Her black mother called a whore, the adopted Clara identifies with the Virgin Mary, but in a fantasy visit to England the white fathers who have colonized her desire refuse Clara access to St. Paul's where she imagines burying her own white father, and lock her in the Tower of London. Rejected by her father, but unable to bury or repress him, Clara is imprisoned in her own history. In the play's associative logic the Tower is also a New York subway car in which the adult Clara, lost in guilt and rage, picks up a Negro man, introduces herself as Mary, addresses him as God, and tries to stab him.

The surrealistic Tower (dominant white culture) and the High Altar (sacrificial Christianity) are the phallic edifices against which Clara Passmore measures her being. Ultimately she transforms into the screeching Owl, symbol

of her black mother and her criminal origins: "The Owl was [my] beginning."
Although her adopted status allows her to "pass more," Clara belongs to the
owls as she cannot belong to the world of "Buckingham Palace, . . . the
Thames at dusk, and Big Ben" or the "Holy Baptist Church . . . on the top of
the Holy Hill." Near the end of the Play, Clara kneels to pray: "I call God and
the Owl answers."

This summary conveys nothing of Kennedy's surrealistic spectacle: "There is
the noise of the train, the sound of moving steel on the track." "The WHITE
BIRD's wings should flutter loudly"—a cacophony that should evoke, says
Kennedy, "a sense of exploding imprisonment."

Two shorter works, *A Lesson in Dead Language* and *A Rat's Mass*, add new
elements of Kennedy's bestiary. In the first Western culture in the form of a
Latin lesson and a schoolteacher, costumed from waist up as a White Dog, and
Christian doctrine in the form of enormous statues of Jesus, Joseph, Mary, two
Wise Men, and a shepherd, instruct and overwhelm seven little girls, whose
initiation into menstruation marks them (and their white dresses) as guilty. In
A Rat's Mass redemptive authority resides in a schoolmate, Rosemary, who
refuses to expiate the incestuous crime of Brother and Sister Rat; and the sister
goes mad. In this as in all of Kennedy's beautifully crafted plays, cultural
exclusion translates into sexual terror and guilt, the signs of "Negro"
womanhood.

Funnyhouse of a Negro won an Obie, but Kennedy's work is rarely discussed or performed in the United States.

—Elin Diamond

See the essay on *Funnyhouse of a Negro*.

KESSELMAN, Wendy (Ann)

American. Teaching fellow, Bryn Mawr College, Pennsylvania, 1987. Also a
composer and songwriter. Recipient: Meet the Composer grant, 1978, 1982;
National Endowment for the Arts fellowship, 1979; Sharfman award, 1980;
Susan Smith Blackburn prize, 1980; Playbill award, 1980; Guggenheim
fellowship, 1982; Ford Foundation grant, 1982; McKnight fellowship, 1985;
ASCAP Popular award, for musical theatre, 1992. Agent: George Lane,
William Morris Agency, 1350 Avenue of the Americas, New York, New York
10019; and, Jane Annakin, William Morris Agency Ltd., 31–32 Soho Square,
London W1V 6AP, England. Address: P.O. Box 680, Wellfleet, Massachusetts
02667, U.S.A.

Publications

PLAYS

Becca (for children), music and lyrics by Kesselman (produced 1977).
    1988.
Maggie Magalita (produced 1980). 1987.
My Sister in This House, music by Kesselman (produced 1981; revised version
    produced 1987). 1982.
Merry-Go-Round (produced 1981).

I Love You, I Love You Not (one-act version produced 1982; full-length version produced 1986). 1988.
The Juniper Tree: A Tragic Household Tale, music and lyrics by Kesselman (produced 1982). 1985.
Cinderella in a Mirror (produced 1987).
The Griffin and the Minor Cannon, music by Mary Rodgers, lyrics by Ellen Fitzhugh (produced 1988).
A Tale of Two Cities, adaptation of the novel by Dickens (produced 1992).
The Butcher's Daughter (produced 1993).

FICTION (FOR CHILDREN)
Franz Tovey and the Rare Animals. 1968.
Angelita. 1970.
Slash: An Alligator's Story. 1971.
Joey. 1972.
Little Salt. 1975.
Time for Jody. 1975.
Maine Is a Million Miles Away. 1976.
Emma. 1980.
There's a Train Going by My Window. 1982.
Flick. 1983.
Sand in My Shoes. 1993.

CRITICAL STUDY: "Wendy Kesselman: Transcendence and Transformation" by Jay Dickson, in *Harvard Advocate*, 1986.

THEATRICAL ACTIVITIES
ACTOR: **Play**—role in *The Juniper Tree*, New York, 1983.

Already an author of children's books, Wendy Kesselman began her play-writing career with *Becca*, a play ostensibly for a young audience, though older spectators responded to the implicit subtext of parental neglect and a brother's abuse of his sister. Kesselman charms tiny tots with her book, lyrics, and music, particularly the songs for caged animals (parrot, sala-mander, grasshopper, and bullfrog) and the creatures (rats, Ida the Spider, escaped snake, and witches) who terrify Becca when her bullying brother Jonathan, as a means of controlling her, locks her in the closet. Yet Kesselman teaches as well as entertains: relegated to his room by parents who never appear but by implication both ignore him and dictate his every move, Jonathan mirrors that behavior by neglecting to provide his pets with food and water and tyrannizing his sister, treating her like a toy doll, not a person. He eventually learns to respect others, relinquishes his pets (after Becca tells them they can free themselves), and stops hitting and threatening his sister. Jonathan changes because Becca changes first, finding the courage to put a stop to his dehumanizing treatment, to take control of her own life, and to toss onto the closet floor the long white dress which reduced her to a mere object. The most amazing moment in this startling feminist parable occurs when Becca rebels against her tormentor and it finally dawns on us that she is not a doll.

Becca prefigures Kesselman's later dramas in its use of her own music, its parallels (Becca and the pets) and contrasts (the pets versus the creatures, Becca versus Jonathan), and its themes of loneliness, maturation, violence to soul and body, fear, family relations, control, and courage. Kesselman continues to write about children and adolescents and about gender inequities, while expanding this exploration to include conflicts fueled by disparities of class, age, and culture. Further, she imbues her plays with a feminist sensibility to the ways patriarchal, social, and economic structures stunt women's minds and stifle their souls.

Kesselman's early masterpiece *My Sister in This House* exemplifies the way in which she keeps her viewpoint implicit, never preaching, always dramatizing. She constructs the play in a dazzling series of parallels and contrasts, satirizing life in the drawing room and dining room, while portraying with compassion life in the kitchen and garret. Conversations between the maids and between the mother and daughter for whom they slave frequently intersect, the concerns of each economic class reflecting those of the other. But so great is the social stratification separating them that not until the play's bloody climax do the two sets of women converse across class lines. Instead the Danzards beckon or point or nod or, when the white glove detects dust, scowl. Yet the sisters and the two women who employ them share a common obstacle to their humanity and self-actualization: female existence in a time and place (France in the early 1930's) which permit their sex only a domestic function. Conservative arbiters of conduct require women without men to repress their sexuality as well as their needs for personal and professional fulfillment. While the women in both social strata lead empty lives, at least the sisters provide each other with the tender love and sex missing from their vacuous employers' existence. Yet the young women's inability to control their own economic destinies dooms both them and their bourgeois nemeses, as the impulse towards aggression, though stifled, on both sides builds and builds.

When Jean Genet based *The Maids* on the same horrendous Le Mans double murder committed by incestuous sisters, he wasn't attempting to create sympathetic portraits of the killers, but Kesselman accepts that challenge. She succeeds by depicting impoverished innocents trapped in a claustrophobic world devoid of stimulation, affection, or purpose except for each other's solace. After the mutual enthusiasm of the Danzards and the sisters gives way to suspicion and fear, Madame explodes with a venomous denunciation which guarantees that the sisters will be thrown on the street without references, food, or shelter; this tragedy can end only in the destruction of all four bleak lives.

A prize-winning composer as well as a dramatist, Kesselman has supplied music for most of her texts. By the end of *My Sister*, we're already deeply affected by the play's action, but Kesselman enhances its impact by the recurrence of the musical refrain "Sleep my little sister, sleep." In *The Juniper Tree: A Tragic Household Tale* Kesselman renders the drama's macabre murder, dismemberment, cannibalism, revenge, and resurrection both funnier and more horrifying by describing and enacting events with lovely solos and eerie duets. As usual, Kesselman takes a child's perspective in dramatizing this Grimm's fairy-tale about parental abuse. Both narrating and acting out the plot in the style of story theatre, *The Juniper Tree* portrays the irrational but compulsive murder of a child by (as in her *Cinderella in a Mirror*) a wicked stepmother, who compounds the crime by blaming her own daughter for the boy's death, then cooking him and serving him as soup for supper. Among Kesselman's funny, folksy touches are the men's descriptions of their personal activities, the father's ravenous appetite—gruesomely comic—and the daughter's disgust at her father's gross table manners while he unknowingly devours his son.

Merry-Go-Round, using as music only a title song, considers childhood largely by depicting its outcome in young adults: we see a similar child within each quite different grown-up. The play's structure jumps from present to past, not with flashbacks, but with the adults re-enacting the earlier scenes. After they reconnect with their past selves, their roots, their early powerful bond broken by their parents, and their loneliness after Michael moved away, Daisy and Michael consummate sexually their earlier relationship, coming full circle —as the title suggests. Kesselman keeps all this understated, implicit, subtle, but authentically evokes the feelings engendered by a reunion of former soul mates.

In *Maggie Magalita* Kesselman depicts an immigrant adolescent struggling to win acceptance from her classmates in New York City while responding with embarrassment to her Spanish-speaking grandmother. Eventually their culture clash educates them both, after screaming arguments, sullen rejection, and cruelties to the aging Abuela which correspond to what her tormentors inflicted upon little Magalita before she became Americanized into Maggie. In addition to her characteristic theme of loneliness—Magalita's as well as Abuela's—Kesselman dramatizes such values as respect for those who are different, self-acceptance, and courage when confronting pressures to conform. Although set largely in the family apartment, the episodes shift freely from present to past and among such other locales as the zoo, the seashore, and Maggie's high-school. The playwright visually expresses her protagonist's transformation from Latin American to North American when the teenager dons flashy sunglasses and earrings and a baggy T-shirt bearing a photo of a rock group.

In *I Love You, I Love You Not* the dramatist narrows this confrontation of cultures and generations to its essentials: wilful adolescent Daisy (a favorite name?) and Nana, her grandmother from the Old World. Jewish rather than Hispanic, Daisy (the flower used in playing the ambivalent petal-plucking game of the play's title) actually wants to learn the language of her heritage (in this case German) so as to deprive her parents of the capacity to speak privately in her presence, whereas Nana, a Holocaust survivor, hates the tongue of her persecutors, who killed Nana's sisters and parents. As in *Becca*, Kesselman keeps Daisy's parents off-stage, but employs them as a formidable hostile presence. Like this playwright's other domestic dramas, this one also compels our attention to the love/hate relations within a family. While the high-strung teenager spends this weekend in her rites of passage to maturity skirmishing with her grandmother, her parents intrude by telephone as they attempt to remove her from her grandmother's nurturing care. "Care" proves the operative word. Never maudlin—indeed, Daisy proves spoiled, narcissistic, self-indulgent, childish—*I Love You, I Love You Not* dramatizes the volatile but nurturing relationship between an emotionally needy, insecure youngster and the woman who can develop her fragile "Daisy" into hardier stock with survival skills, capable of overcoming her intolerance, guilt, and especially fears.

In the late 1980's Kesselman began work on two more musical plays, each set in France during the Revolution. Both again in some part concern young people, contrast classes, and dramatize events in brief episodes, and each ends with execution by guillotine. In *A Tale of Two Cities* she adapts Dickens' novel, whereas *The Butcher's Daughter* breaks audacious new ground. *A Tale of Two Cities* employs the parallels of Charles and Sydney, young Thérèse and young Lucie, the burning of shoemaking tools and burning the Bastille, Lucie's imprisoned father and then little Lucie's imprisoned father. Kesselman also utilizes flashbacks, building suspense about events we can't fully comprehend when we first observe them, until we grasp how Thérèse Defarge's sister was raped on her wedding day by the Évremondes, who killed her husband, father, and brother. The latter's moving song "Quieting the Frogs" proves one of the best among Kesselman's extraordinary compositions for musical theatre.

The Butcher's Daughter's parallels constitute the play's whole structure, as we follow the destinies of two young women, one adopted by a butcher, the other the daughter of the executioner who decapitates the butcher's daughter at the end, when the executioner's daughter hangs herself. A grandmother lives in each household; images of blood permeate the play, which indicts such male-driven acts as capital punishment and incest. Once more, the world proves pernicious to women of any talent or spirit, so utterly denying them autonomy and equity they cannot survive. Kesselman selects as one of her central figures the pioneer playwright and feminist Olympe de Gouges, and both women's spirits soar. The women interact only twice, for a few wordless but indelible moments. Linking the two protagonists, the street singer Pierrot knows, loves, and celebrates them both—just as Kesselman sings of women young and old, timid and bold, some of the most memorable female characters in contemporary drama.

—Tish Dace

See the essay on *My Sister in This House.*

KRAUSS, Ruth (Ida).

American. Born in Baltimore, Maryland, 25 July 1911. Educated in public elementary schools; at Peabody Institute of Music, Baltimore; New School for Social Research, New York; Maryland Institute of Art, Baltimore; Parsons School of Art, New York, graduate. Married David Johnson Leisk (i.e., the writer Crockett Johnson) in 1940 (died 1975). Address: c/o Scholastic Books, 730 Broadway, New York, New York 10003, U.S.A.

Publications

POEM—PLAYS

The Cantilever Rainbow. 1965.
There's a Little Ambiguity Over There among the Bluebells and Other Theatre Poems. 1968.

If Only. 1969.
Under Twenty. 1970.
Love and the Invention of Punctuation. 1973.
This Breast Gothic. 1973.
If I Were Freedom (produced 1976).
Re-examination of Freedom (produced 1976). 1981.
Under 13. 1976.
When I Walk I Change the Earth. 1978.
Small Black Lambs Wandering in the Red Poppies (produced 1982).
Ambiguity 2nd (produced 1985).

PRODUCTIONS INCLUDE: *A Beautiful Day, There's a Little Ambiguity Over There among the Bluebells, Re-Examination of Freedom, Newsletter, The Cantilever Rainbow, In a Bull's Eye, Pineapple Play, Quartet, A Show, A Play—It's a Girl!, Onward, Duet* (or *Yellow Umbrella*), *Drunk Boat, If Only, This Breast,* many with music by Al Carmines, Bill Dixon, and Don Heckman, produced since 1964.

FICTION (FOR CHILDREN)

A Good Man and His Good Wife. 1944; revised edition, 1962.
The Carrot Seed. 1945.
The Great Duffy. 1946.
The Growing Story. 1947.
Bears. 1948.
The Happy Day. 1949.
The Big World and the Little House. 1949.
The Backward Day. 1950.
The Bundle Book. 1951.
A Hole Is to Dig: A First Book of First Definitions. 1952; 1963.
A Very Special House. 1953.
I'll Be You and You Be Me. 1954.
How to Make an Earthquake. 1954.
Charlotte and the White Horse. 1955.
Is This You? 1955.
I Want to Paint My Bathroom Blue. 1956.
The Birthday Party. 1957.
Monkey Day. 1957.
Somebody Else's Nut Tree and Other Tales from Children. 1958.
A Moon or a Button. 1959.
Open House for Butterflies. 1960.
"Mama, I Wish I Was Snow" "Child, You'd Be Very Cold." 1962.
Eye Nose Fingers Toes. 1964.
The Little King, The Little Queen, The Little Monster, and Other Stories You Can Make Up Yourself, illustrated by the author. 1966.
This Thumbprint: Words and Thumbprints, illustrated by the author. 1967.
Little Boat Lighter Than a Cork. 1976.
Minestrone: A Ruth Krauss Selection, illustrated by the author. 1981.
Big and Little. 1987.

VERSE (FOR CHILDREN)
I Can Fly. 1950.
A Bouquet of Littles. 1963.
What a Fine Day for . . ., music by Al Carmines. 1967.
I Write It. 1970.
Everything under a Mushroom. 1974.
Somebody Spilled the Sky. 1979.

MANUSCRIPT COLLECTION: Dupont School, Wilmington, Delaware.

Ruth Krauss comments:

All the "works"—or "plays"—are essentially poems—with an approach from the words themselves, rather than ideas, plot, etc. (This division cannot be made in so cut-and-dried a fashion.) The interpretation is *mostly* left completely to the director—i.e., one line can be made to take dozens of forms in actual presentation.

Part of the philosophy behind this is: say *anything*—and leave it to the director to see what happens. This does not always work out for the best— depending on the director.

The nature of Ruth Krauss's work is that it is bursting with health, bursting with greenery, with fresh promise. This nutritional assault, this vitality asserts itself beyond all the emotions of the day, all of which, sadness, wistfulness, and hilarity, appear ephemeral beside the steady residue of glowing good health.

But health seems to issue from a steadying optimism and a kind of bravery, an ability to look the universe in the eye. Nothing cannot be looked at, nothing is so awful that it cannot be faced, perhaps mended, always accepted.

But the world that she sees appears to be without serious menace, without horror; it appears to be essentially benign, so that in effect what Krauss faces is what she perhaps nearsightedly envisions. The bursting sense to her work is matched by a quieter sense, one of comic wistfulness. And one of whimsy. The world viewed in comic tranquility.

I recall a series of Krauss whimsies. A number of years ago the Hardware Poets, long since gone not only from Manhattan but from the planet, presented an evening of her works which, if memory doesn't betray me, had the generic term of seven-second plays. I may be inventing this name but they certainly *felt* like seven-second plays. They were little, exploding, comic pellets which appeared, exploded and disappeared in dazzling succession for many long minutes. Or what appeared to be many long minutes. They were delightful charmers, about nothing that I can now possibly recall, except the essential sense of them—comic energy organisms, dramatic meteorites which lasted long enough to be retained forever in the spirit.

My sense of Krauss's work is that it consists of fragmented interruptions in the more sombre concourse of human events, healthy winks from over the fence. The fragments give off the sense also of interrupting shards of sunlight in a universe grown perceptibly greyer as the years go on. Here are excerpts from a Krauss fragment, a monologue called *If Only* which Florence Tarlow, a performer with an especially dry wit, delivered with comic gravity at the Judson Poets Theatre in New York:

If only I was a nightingale singing
If only I was on my second don't-live-like-a-pig week
If only the sun wasn't always rising behind the next hill
If only I was the flavor of tarragon
If only I was phosphorescence and a night phenomena at sea
If only Old Drainpipe Rensaleer as we used to call him hadn't hit bottom in Detroit the time he made a fancy dive and got absentminded and forget to turn and all his shortribs got stove in he got sucked down the drain-pipe because the grate wasn't on
If only I didn't have to get up and let our dog out now
If only the glorious day in April because it has no beginning or end that all Flatbush had awaited impatiently between creation and construction had come
If only I was Joyce and had written Finnegans Wake only then I'd be gone
If only somebody would kiss me on the back of the neck right now
If only those degraded bastards hadn't monkeyed around with the Oreo Sandwich pattern

Krauss is a playwright to turn to when both the flesh and spirit grow weak.

—Arthur Sainer

L

LAVERY, Bryony.

British. Born in Wakefield, Yorkshire, 21 December 1947. Educated at the University of London, 1966–69, B.A. (honours) in English 1969. Artistic director, Les Oeufs Malades, 1976–78, Extraordinary Productions, 1979–80, and Female Trouble, 1981–83, all London. Resident dramatist, Unicorn Theatre for Young People, London, 1986–88; artistic director, Gay Sweatshop, London, 1989–91. Agent: Andrew Hewson, John Johnson Ltd., Clerkenwell House, 45–47 Clerkenwell Green, London EC1R 0HT. Address: 17 Maitland Road, London E15 4EL, England.

Publications

PLAYS

Of All Living (produced 1967).
Days at Court (produced 1968).
Warbeck (produced 1969).
I Was Too Young at the Time to Understand Why My Mother Was Crying (also director: produced 1976).
Sharing (also director: produced 1976).
Germany Calling, with Peter Leabourne (produced 1976).
Grandmother's Footsteps (also director: produced 1977).
Snakes (produced 1977).
The Catering Service (also director: produced 1977).
Floorshow, with others (produced 1978).
Helen and Her Friends (also director: produced 1978).
Bag (also director, produced 1979).
Time Gentlemen Please (cabaret; produced 1979).
The Wild Bunch (for children; produced 1979). In *Responses*, edited by Don Shiach, 1990.
Sugar and Spice (for children; produced 1979).
Unemployment: An Occupational Hazard? (for children; also director: produced 1979).
Gentlemen Prefer Blondes, adaptation of the novel by Anita Loos (produced 1980).
The Joker (for children; also director: produced 1980).
The Family Album (also director: produced 1980).
Pamela Stephenson One Woman Show (cabaret; produced 1981).
Missing (also director: produced 1981).

Zulu, with Patrick Barlow (produced 1981).
Female Trouble (cabaret; produced 1981).
The Black Hole of Calcutta, with Patrick Barlow (produced 1982).
Götterdämmerung; or, Twilight of the Gods, with Patrick Barlow and Susan Todd (produced 1982).
For Maggie, Betty and Ida, music by Paul Sand (produced 1982).
More Female Trouble (cabaret), music by Caroline Noh (produced 1982).
Uniform and Uniformed, and Numerical Man (broadcast 1983). In *Masks and Faces*, edited by Dan Garrett, 1984.
Hot Time (produced 1984).
Calamity (produced 1984).
Origin of the Species (produced 1984). In*Plays by Women: Six*, edited by Mary Remnant, 1987.
The Wandsworth Warmers (cabaret; also director: produced 1984).
The Zulu Hut Club (for children; produced 1984).
The Wandsworth Warmers Christmas Carol Concert (cabaret; also director: produced 1985).
Over and Out (also director: produced 1985).
Witchcraze (produced 1985). In*Herstory*, edited by Gabrial Griffin and Elaine Aston, 1991.
Getting Through (additional lyrics only), by Nona Shepphard, music by Helen Glavin (produced 1985).
The Wandsworth Warmers in Unbridled Passions (cabaret; also director: produced 1986).
Sore Points (for children; produced 1986).
Mummy, with Sally Owen and L. Ortolja (produced 1987).
Madagascar (for children; also director: produced 1987).
The Headless Body, music by Stephanie Nunn (produced 1987).
The Dragon Wakes (for children; produced 1988).
Puppet States (produced 1988).
The Drury Lane Ghost, with Nona Shepphard (produced 1989).
Two Marias (produced 1989). In *Her Aching Heart, Two Marias, Wicked*, 1991.
Wicked (produced 1990). In *Her Aching Heart, Two Marias, Wicked*, 1991.
Her Aching Heart (produced 1990). In *Her Aching Heart, Two Marias, Wicked*, 1991.
Kitchen Matters (produced 1990).
Her Aching Heart, Two Marias, Wicked. 1991.
Flight (produced 1991).
Peter Pan, with Nona Shepphard (produced 1991).
The Sleeping Beauty, with Nona Shepphard (produced 1992).
The Way to Cook a Wolf (produced 1993).

RADIO PLAYS: *Fire the Life-Giver*, 1979; *Changes at Work* series, 1980; *Let's Get Dressed*, 1982; *Uniform and Uniformed*, 1983; *Numerical Man*, 1983; *Magical Beasts*, 1987; *Cliffhanger* series, 1990; *Laying Ghosts*, 1992.

TELEVISION PLAYS: *Revolting Women* series, with others, 1981; *Rita of the Rovers*, 1989; *The Cab Wars*, 1989.

VIDEO: *The Lift*, 1988; *Twelve Dancing Princesses*, 1989.

CRITICAL STUDY: "But Will Men Like It; or, Living as a Feminist Writer Without Committing Murder" by Lavery, in *Women and Theatre* edited by Susan Todd, 1984.

THEATRICAL ACTIVITIES

DIRECTOR: **Plays**—most of her own plays; *More Female Trouble* (revival), 1983; *Homelands: Under Exposure* by Lisa Evans, and *The Mrs. Docherties* by Nona Shepphard (co-director, with Shepphard), 1985; *Hotel Destiny* by Tasha Fairbanks, 1987.

Bryony Lavery's plays are comic in the best sense of the term, funny, and engaging at a popular level. As Lavery's work tends to deal with controversial issues, including the representation of lesbian and gay sexuality and the funding of the theatre itself, its popularity is all the more significant. Lavery has worked in British alternative theatre for many years; she was, for instance, one of the early contributors to the work of both Gay Sweatshop and Monstrous Regiment. In the 1970's, Lavery collaborated with Caryl Churchill and Michelene Wandor on *Floorshow*, the Monstrous Regiment's cabaret. She also worked on the Regiment's cabaret *Gentlemen Prefer Blondes* and on comic shows such as *Female Trouble* and *More Female Trouble*, as well as in writing full-length plays. More recently, she has worked in children's theatre, theatre in education, and in teaching playwriting.

By drawing on this wide range of experience, Lavery has developed a voice which is quite unique in British theatre. Her style is intelligent and comic without being too sarcastic or snide; her writing reveals a certain jolly approach to important topical issues. In this way, Lavery has succeeded in developing a style which reaches beyond the typical middle-class forms of farce and drawing-room humour. Her work is self-consciously aware of those forms, but has found a balance between parody and celebration which is politically effective because it makes the plays so engaging, so enjoyable to read and watch.

Origin of the Species and *Her Aching Heart* are probably Lavery's best-known plays. Both illustrate Lavery's skill for combining humour with serious social commentary.

Origin of the Species was first produced by Monstrous Regiment in 1984, with Gillian Hanna as Molly, the anthropologist looking for said origins, who finds them in Victoria, the living creature-woman she unearths, played by Mary McCusker. Directed by Nona Shepphard, this play was ambitious in its scope (all of history) but remarkably unambitious in its use of resources: two actors, minimal sets and props, a small playing space. The power of the play is in its language and its use of humour. Similarly, *Her Aching Heart* is a sophisticated piece of writing, another two-hander which combines wit and parodies of courtly and poetic language with the representation of social issues in entertaining form.

Her Aching Heart was first produced in 1990 at the Oval House, London, directed by Claire Grove and performed by Nicola Kathrens and Sarah Kevney. The play is a "lesbian historical romance" which casts two modern-day women as the readers of bodice-ripping fiction, and concurrently as the heroines and heroes of that fiction. Modern-day characters Molly and Harriet engage in a budding romance in "real life" which parallels the stories of Molly, the servant girl, and Lady Harriet of Helstone Hall, the fiery aristocrat of the novel. Molly and Harriet read the novel and engage in the fictional romance, while they begin to know each other through telephone conversations. The audience gets to know the story, the highs and lows and misunderstandings of their romance, through the narratives and songs of these two central characters. They sing of love and of longing, and the songs are enriched by their references to stereotyped images of romance lifted from fiction and fairytales. That the two lovers are both women is important, but is not the key to the play's politics. Rather, the interweaving of the modern and the "historical," the real and the fictional, the serious and the silly, results in a complicated play which is a delight to read and to watch.

Her Aching Heart toured twice with the Women's Theatre Group in 1990 and 1991, both times with great success. That the play is so accessible and so amusing, as well as so beautifully constructed, makes the choice of a lesbian story-line all the more significant. Similarly, the play engages with gender, class, and power as issues intrinsic to an informed examination of bodice-ripper as a popular form, and to the expectations involved in reading romantic fiction. Yet all these important considerations are represented as parts of the larger fabric of the play rather than as "politically correct" issues to be evaluated in and of themselves.

Of course, not all Lavery's work is written for two actors. Some of the work has been much larger in scale, and some has been immediately linked to contemporary social issues. In 1990, for instance, Lavery wrote *Kitchen Matters*, a play for Gay Sweatshop. As a mixed group with feminist politics, Sweatshop has promoted women's work since its founding in 1974. Sweatshop's struggle with viability in the current economic climate of the arts inspired Bryony Lavery to write the play as an "epic comedy." In a humorously self-referential scene. *Kitchen Matters* opens with a narrator (a woman at a typewriter) discussing her decision to write a (the) play:

> . . . There were some kids in a touring theatre company.
> They were Gay they were Poor they were Minority
> but they wanted a show.
> I had to help them out.
> I'm a writer with a Large Soul and Big Bills.
> My brain met up with my heart and they took a walk
> down into my guts to see what was there.
> The place was full of undigested matter.
> I chewed it over.
> A heavenly light shone on my blank A4 paper.
> I lit my two hundred and thirty-fourth cigarette.
> I started to write.

Lavery's enjoyment of and facility with language is evident even in this short extract. So is her dedication to the theatre. The narrator of this scene, like Lavery, wrote for the benefit of the theatre company. The play was highly successful, and reached many people from different communities, of different classes and sexual orientations. It was a political play with a point to make. But the comedy made the point, and the self-conscious nature of the humour made it all the more powerful as a play.

Lavery's current work is even larger in scale. In early 1992, she was at work on another "epic", but one which involves "a cast of 17" and which is "set in the tomb of an 11th-century Chinese Emperor." Whether or not such an ambitious play will find sufficient financial backing in Britain is a large question, and no doubt one which Lavery will weave into the humour of the play itself.

One thing is certain: if there is a contemporary playwright whose work deserves more attention—on theatrical and social grounds—it is Bryony Lavery.

—Lizbeth Goodman

LESSING, Doris (May, née Tayler).

British. Born in Kermansha, Persia, 22 October 1919; moved with her family to England, then to Banket, Southern Rhodesia, 1924. Educated at Dominican Convent School, Salisbury, Southern Rhodesia, 1926–34. Married 1) Frank Charles Wisdom in 1939 (divorced 1943), one son and one daughter; 2) Gottfried Lessing in 1945 (divorced 1949), one son. Au pair, Salisbury, 1934–35; telephone operator and clerk, Salisbury, 1937–39; typist, 1946–48; journalist, Cape Town *Guardian*, 1949; moved to London, 1950; secretary, 1950; member of the Editorial Board, *New Reasoner* (later, *New Left Review*), 1956. Recipient: Maugham award, for fiction, 1954; Médicis prize (France), 1976; Austrian State prize, 1981; Shakespeare prize (Hamburg), 1982; W.H. Smith Literary award, 1986; Palermo prize (Italy), 1987; Mondello prize (Italy), 1987; Cavour award (Italy), 1989. Honorary doctorate: Princeton University, New Jersey, 1989, University of Durham, 1990. Associate member, American Academy, 1974; honorary fellow, Modern Language Association (U.S.A.), 1974; distinguished fellow in literature, University of East Anglia, Norwich, 1991. Agent: Jonathan Clowes Ltd., Iron Bridge House, Bridge Approach, London, NW1 8BD, England.

Publications

PLAYS

Before the Deluge (produced 1953).
Mr. Dollinger (produced 1958).
Each His Own Wilderness (produced 1958). In *New English Dramatists*, 1959.
The Truth about Billy Newton (produced 1960).
Play with a Tiger (produced 1962). 1962; in *Plays by and about Women*, edited by Victoria Sullivan and James V. Hatch, 1973.
The Storm, adaptation of a play by Alexander Ostrovsky (produced 1966).
The Singing Door (for children), in *Second Playbill 2*, edited by Alan Durband. 1973.
The Making of the Representative for Planet 8 (opera libretto), music by Philip Glass, adaptation of the novel by Lessing (produced 1988).

TELEVISION PLAYS: *The Grass Is Singing,* from her own novel, 1962; *Care and Protection* and *Do Not Disturb* (both in *Blackmail* series), 1966; *Between Men,* 1967.

NOVELS

The Grass Is Singing. 1950.
Children of Violence:
   Martha Quest. 1952; with *A Proper Marriage,* 1964.
   A Proper Marriage. 1954; with *Martha Quest,* 1964.
   A Ripple from the Storm, 1958; with *Landlocked,*1966.
   Landlocked. 1965; with *A Ripple from the Storm.* 1966.
   The Four-Gated City. 1969.
Retreat to Innocence. 1956.
The Golden Notebook. 1962.
Briefing for a Descent into Hell. 1971.
The Summer Before the Dark. 1973.
The Memoirs of a Survivor. 1974.
Canopus in Argos: Archives:
Shikasta. 1979.
   The Marriages Between Zones Three, Four, and Five. 1980.
   The Sirian Experiments. 1981.
   The Making of the Representative for Planet 8. 1982.
   The Sentimental Agents. 1983.
The Diaries of Jane Somers. 1984.
   The Diary of a Good Neighbour (as Jane Somers). 1983.
   If the Old Could—(as Jane Somers). 1984.
The Good Terrorist. 1985.
The Fifth Child. 1988.

SHORT STORIES

This Was the Old Chief's Country. 1951.
Five: Short Novels. 1953.
No Witchcraft for Sale: Stories and Short Novels. 1956.
The Habit of Loving. 1957.
A Man and Two Women. 1963.
African Stories. 1964.
Winter in July. 1966.
The Black Madonna. 1966.
Nine African Stories, edited by Michael Marland. 1968.
The Story of a Non-Marrying Man and Other Stories. 1972; as *The Temptation of Jack Orkney and Other Stories,* 1972.
Collected African Stories. 1981.
   1. *This Was the Old Chief's Country.* 1973.
   2. *The Sun Between Their Feet.* 1973.
(Stories), edited by Alan Cattell. 1976.
Collected Stories: To Room Nineteen and *The Temptation of Jack Orkney.* 2 vols., 1978; as *Stories,* 1 vol., 1978.
London Observed. 1991.
The Real Thing. 1991.

VERSE
Fourteen Poems. 1959.

OTHER
Going Home. 1957; revised edition, 1968.
In Pursuit of the English: A Documentary. 1960.
Particularly Cats. 1967.
A Small Personal Voice: Essays, Reviews, Interviews, edited by Paul Schlueter.
   1974.
Prisons We Choose to Live Inside. 1986.
*The Wind Blows Away Our Words, and Other Documents Relating to
   Afghanistan.* 1987.
The Doris Lessing Reader. 1989.
African Laughter: Four Visits to Zimbabwe. 1992.

BIBLIOGRAPHY: *Doris Lessing: A Bibliography* by Catharina Ipp, 1967; *Doris Lessing: A Checklist of Primary and Secondary Sources* by Selma R. Burkom and Margaret Williams, 1973; *Doris Lessing: An Annotated Bibliography of Criticism* by Dee Seligman, 1981; *Doris Lessing: A Descriptive Bibliography of Her First Editions* by Eric T. Brueck, 1984.

CRITICAL STUDIES (SELECTION): *Doris Lessing* by Dorothy Brewster, 1965; *Doris Lessing,* 1973, and *Doris Lessing's Africa,* 1978, both by Michael Thorpe; *Doris Lessing: Critical Studies* edited by Annis Pratt and L.S. Dembo, 1974; *Notebooks/Memoirs/Archives: Reading and Re-reading Doris Lessing* edited by Jenny Taylor, 1982; *Doris Lessing* by Lorna Sage, 1983; *Doris Lessing* by Mona Knapp, 1984; *Doris Lessing* edited by Eve Bertelsen, 1985; *Critical Essays on Doris Lessing* edited by Claire Sprague and Virginia Tiger, 1986; *Doris Lessing: The Alchemy of Survival* edited by Carey Kaplan and Ellen Cronan Rose, 1988; *Doris Lessing* by Ruth Whittaker, 1988; *Doris Lessing* by Jeannette King, 1989; *Understanding Doris Lessing* by Jean Pickering, 1990.

In any theatre, a deal of talent must go to waste, especially among playwrights, but it is a great pity that Doris Lessing's career as a playwright should have been abortive. One of the failures of George Devine's successful regime at the Royal Court was its failure to help her to go on from *Each His Own Wilderness,* which was given a Sunday night production in 1958. Though it was dismissed by many of the critics as a novelist's play can so readily be dismissed, simply by describing it as "a novelist's play," in fact it was remarkably free from the flaws that might have been expected—flat characters, over-leisurely development, verbal analysis written out as dialogue, lack of dramatic drive. Lessing had, on the contrary, a very keen instinct for how to ignite a situation theatrically.

By building the play around a mother–son conflict and empathizing success-fully with the son, she steered clear of the pitfall of subordinating all the other characters to the woman she could most easily identify with. Myra Bolton is an attractive, middle-aged campaigner for left-wing causes, warm, well-meaning, but gauche in human relationships, liable to inflict unintended pain not only on her son but on the three men in the play she has had relationships with—two of her own generation, one of her son's. The muddles and misunderstandings of these involvements are all developed in a way that contributes richly to the play's dramatic texture, and the untidiness we see on the set—the hall of her London house—contributes visually to the impression of an inability to keep things under control.

The men are all well characterized—the sad, ageing, lonely politician, the architect trying to embark on a new marriage with a young girl, the opportunistic 22–year-old son of a woman friend, and above all Tony, the son, who returns from National Service to find Myra did not know which day to expect him. His pained anger at his own inability to commit himself to any outside reality and at the lack of understanding between them mounts effectively through the play, reaching a climax when he discovers that Myra has sold the house he loves more than anything, intending to help him by raising money to set him up on his own in a flat. It may be a well-made play but it is made remarkably well, with an unusual talent for keeping a number of relationships simultaneously on the boil, and it catches the flavour of the life of left-wing intellectuals in the 1950's. Showing private people devoting their lives to protesting about public issues, Lessing successfully merges personal and political themes. Like the characters in John McGrath's play, these people are all "plugged-in to history."

Lessing had started writing for the theatre five years earlier, in 1953, and of the three plays she turned out *Mr. Dollinger* was also produced in 1958, earlier in the year, at the Oxford Playhouse, and *The Truth about Billy Newton* was produced in 1960 at Salisbury. But the only play of hers to receive a full-scale London production was *Play with a Tiger* which was written in 1958 and had a seven-and-a-half week run at the Comedy in 1962 with Siobhan McKenna as the central character, who is, unfortunately, very much more central than any of the characters in *Each His Own Wilderness*.

Lessing was determined to turn her back on both naturalism and realism. "It is my intention," she wrote in a 1963 note on the play,

> that when the curtain comes down at the end, the audience will think: Of course! In this play no one lit cigarettes, drank tea or coffee, read newspapers, squirted soda into Scotch, or indulged in little bits of "business" which indicated "character." They will realize, I hope, that they have been seeing a play which relies upon its style and its language for its effect.

But it starts off naturalistically in an underfurnished room with a litter of books and cushions, paraffin heaters, a record player, and a telephone. There are also sound effects of traffic noises. Anna Freeman is a woman of "35 or so" who lives as a literary freelance, has a son by a broken marriage and has recently decided not to marry an Englishman who is about to settle for a safe job on a woman's magazine. She is in love with an American Jew who would never settle and if she had been entertaining ideas of marrying him, these would be killed off in Act 1 by the visit of a nice young American girl who announces that she is going to have Dave's baby.

The play's starting points, in other words, are all naturalistic and there is even a naturalistic cliché neighbour who fusses about an invisible cat. But towards the end of Act 1 the walls disappear, and though the neighbour is going to reappear and the play is still going to make gestures towards satisfying the audience expectations that its first half-hour has aroused, its centre has been shifted. With only a few interruptions from other characters, about 62 pages of the 92-page script are taken up with a dialogue between Anna and Dave. But the language and the style cannot depart completely from those of the naturalistic beginning. Some of the writing in it is very good, some of it bad and embarrassing, especially when they play games reminiscent of the psycho-analytical situation.

Even the best sections of the dialogue, which make a defiant and articulate declaration of rights on behalf of the woman against the male predator, tend to generalize the play away from its roots in the specific predicament of a specific woman. In reacting against naturalism, Lessing is renouncing all its disciplines, some of which were very useful to her in *Each His Own Wilderness*. *Play with a Tiger* may look more like a public statement and it was seized on by feminist groups, whose performances unbalanced the central relationship by failing to give Dave equal weight with Anna. Lessing complained about this in a 1972 postscript, but the fault is basically in the play, which is really more private than *Each His Own Wilderness*, and more self-indulgent, in that the dialogue is spun too directly out of personal preoccupations.

—Ronald Hayman

LEVY, Deborah.

British. Born in South Africa in 1959. Educated at Dartington College of Arts, Devon, 1978–81, B.A. (hons.) in theatre language 1981; fellow in creative arts, Trinity College, Cambridge, 1989–91. Since 1992 writer and director for MANACT Theatre Company, Cardiff and London. Agent: Leah Schmidt, Curtis Brown, 162–168 Regent Street, London W1R 5TB, England.

Publications

PLAYS

Pax (produced 1984). 1985.
Clam (produced 1985). 1985.
Our Lady (produced 1986).
Heresies (produced 1987). With *Eva and Moses*, 1987.
Eva and Moses. With *Heresies*, 1987.
Blood Wedding, (libretto) adaptation of the play by Federico García Lorca (produced 1992). 1992.
The B File (also director: produced 1992). 1992.
Call Blue Jane (produced 1992).

TELEVISION PLAYS: *Celebrating Quietly*, 1988; *Lickin' Bones*, 1990; *The Open Mouth*, 1991.

NOVEL

Beautiful Mutants. 1987.

SHORT STORIES
Ophelia and the Great Idea. 1986.

VERSE
An Amorous Discourse in the Suburbs of Hell. 1990.

OTHER
Editor, *Walks on Water: Five Performance Texts.* 1992.

Deborah Levy comments:

I now mostly direct my own texts for the theatre, working with ensemble companies who come from diverse arts backgrounds and cultures. I hope to create with them as writer and director, work that is visual, visceral, kinetic, and physical.

A female world without patriarchy can be deduced from Deborah Levy's dramatic work. Its primary substances are bread, fruit, and eggs, its primary symbols are fish, the sea, and the moon, and its religion is a combination of Goddess-worship and the ritual aspects of Catholicism and Judaism. Children (female) are parented by the whole community, which is itself inter-generational and the collective guardian of a herstory of revolutionary élan as well as domestic drudgery. The wisest women are witches and eccentrics like The Keeper in *Pax* and Leah in *Heresies*. Money-making is the most abhorred activity, art-making the best. Even the betrayers can be redeemed, such as Mayonnaise (*Heresies*) who is the beautiful wife and mistress respectively of a securities-dealer (Edward) and a commercial architect (Pimm), and who forces her lover's ex-wife and child to return to Budapest. Her hair falls out and, it is implied, she loses Pimm, but she is welcomed into the circle of women at the end who gather to hear Leah's final composition. The Domesticated Woman's presence in *Pax* is intensely resented by the fiercely independent and autocratic Keeper, but she is accepted by the other younger women, The Mourner (a geologist), and H.D., the hidden daughter of The Keeper, but also a reference, presumably, to the great American Modernist writer Hilda Doolittle. When The Mourner leaves at the end she gives an egg to the Domesticated Woman, a symbol not just of fertility but also of professional expertise. The Mourner specialises in the egg fossils of dinosaurs. The two older women come to look on the younger generation with a wry affection. "We have," observes The Keeper, "two young women between us. Mad as nettles in a storm." In an end-note to the play Levy admits she began by detesting what the Domesticated Woman represented and finished with respect and even liking for her. Perhaps Mary, the devout Catholic servant of Pimm, best sums up the ideal existence: "I'd like a house with a garden and a tree." Active, mobile women are respected in the plays but the settings are all interiors and rapid movements of flight or travel are either in retrospect or prospect.

These, along with emotionally numb men and distracted hunts for fathers and mothers, are the commonplaces of second-wave feminist Utopias; indeed, there are distinct echoes of the first, Edwardian wave. The posed eccentricity of Leah playing the piano in a hat rimmed with lighted candles, and of her

companion, Violet, trampling a tub of grapes, recalls the desperate bohemia-
nism of Gudrun and Ursula in *Women in Love*. Mayonnaise's staccato statements of inconsequent desires ("I want to be a Catholic") echo the disjointed
utterances of Evelyn Waugh's Agatha Runcible, and H.D., with her fishing-rod
and her cigars, can trace her ancestry back to Una Troubridge and Vita
Sackville-West. But Levy defamiliarises these themes by a persistent preoccupation with Eastern Europe, as site both of terrible history and of a more
humane community. In *Clam* Alice and Harry, a domestic couple, who double
as Lenin and Krupskaya, another domestic couple, play out a history of the
defeat of revolution. A fishtank, as in *Heresies*, is a key prop. It is a cornucopia
of objects to provoke fantasies. Alice imagines the sea bringing in Poland and
Latvia and other Eastern bloc countries like fish so that "a little boy kissed the
Ukraine . . . a woman in a bikini put Poland on her belly." For Cholla,
domestic cleaner and mother of Pimm's child, Hungary is her lost homeland of
song and fecundity, a culture she rejected for that of the frozen English and to
which she now wishes to return. Leah remembers the Russians as beautiful in
their revolution and The Keeper counterpoints a refrain of "I want to go back
to Vienna/Prague etc." with horrific recollections of the Holocaust. Cholla fled
from Hungary at the age of 17 because of the claustrophobia of family life, but
now she dreams of her mother standing on Liberty Bridge "in her red shoes . . .
calling me." Cholla sums up East/West relations in a prescient line: "The West
only likes Eastern Europe when she cries."

Levy is both of and not of the performance art movement of the 1980's. She
has an interest in visual theatre and her symbol for the imagined funeral of
H.D.'s father, one bright light on a polished marble column, effectively con-
denses a multiplicity of signs. Music strains to become a language in its own
right under Leah's promptings and the abrupt emotional shifts of Mayonnaise
and Krupskaya are typical of the distrust of continuous narrative in much
performance art. But Levy also has a traditional interest in plot and character-
conflict. The many histories that are recounted indicate a concern for verbal
language that many performance artists would consider quite outmoded. One
suspects that Levy is still struggling to reconcile her commitment to a distinctive female voice in theatre with her determination to find her own voice. Too
often her characters, particularly male, mouth attitudes rather than dramatise
situations. With the decline of feminism and the collapse of communism she
will be forced back onto her own linguistic resources, although, in true
postmodernist fashion, she may find her way to them through the words of
others, as her libretto-version of Lorca's *Blood Wedding* for The Women's
Theatre Trust would seem to indicate.

—Tony Dunn

LOCHHEAD, Liz.

Scottish. Born in Motherwell, Lanarkshire, 26 December 1947. Educated at
Dalziel High School, Motherwell, 1960–65; Glasgow School of Art, 1965–70,
diploma in art. Art teacher at Bishopbriggs High School, Glasgow, and other
schools in Glasgow and Bristol. Recipient: BBC Scotland prize, 1971; Scottish
Arts Council award, 1973, and fellowship, 1978. Address: 11 Kersland Street,
Glasgow G12 8BW, Scotland.

Publications

PLAYS

Blood and Ice (produced 1982; revised version, produced 1984). 1982.
Tickly Mince (revue), with Tom Leonard and Alasdair Gray (produced 1982).
The Pie of Damocles (revue), with others (produced 1983).
A Bunch of Fives, with Tom Leonard and Sean Hardie (produced 1983).
Silver Service. 1984.
Dracula, adaptation of the novel by Bram Stoker (produced 1985). With *Mary
   Queen of Scots Got Her Head Chopped Off*, 1989.
Tartuffe, adaptation of the play by Molière (produced 1985). 1985.
Mary Queen of Scots Got Her Head Chopped Off (produced 1987). With
   Dracula, 1989.
The Big Picture (produced 1988).
Patter Merchant (produced 1989).
Jock Tamson's Bairns, with Gerry Mulgrew (produced 1990).
Quelques Fleurs (produced 1991).
The Magic Island, adaptation of Shakespeare's *The Tempest* (for children;
   produced 1993).

SCREENPLAY: *Now and Then*, 1972.

RADIO PLAY: *Blood and Ice*, 1990.

TELEVISION PLAY: *Sweet Nothings* in *End of the Line* series, 1984.

VERSE

Memo for Spring. 1972.
The Grimm Sisters. 1981.
Dreaming Frankenstein, and Collected Poems. 1984.
True Confessions and New Clichés. 1985.
Three Scottish Poets: MacCaig, Morgen, Lochhead. 1992.

CRITICAL STUDY: "Feminist Nationalism in Scotland: *Mary Queen of Scots Got
Her Head Chopped Off*" by Ilona S. Koren-Deutsch, in *Modern Drama*,
September 1992.

THEATRICAL ACTIVITIES

ACTOR: **Play**—*The Complete Alternative History of the World, Part 1*, 1986.

> Once upon a time there were *twa queens* on the wan green island, and the
> wan green island was split inty two kingdoms. But no equal kingdoms,
> naebody in their richt mind would insist on that.
> —La Corbie, *Mary Queen of Scots Got Her Head Chopped Off*

Liz Lochhead is a teller of tales, the author of strongly narrative plays,
dramatic monologues, and poetry. The stories she recounts are often drawn
from popular memory and folk culture but are retold with a distinctively
female voice. History, myth, and memory interconnect and are analysed and
deconstructed in a body of work that finds reference in both literary and

popular culture. In common with other contemporary women writers Lochhead has been attracted to the images and the conventions of the Gothic and has discovered in fairytales and in childhood rhymes a new set of meta- phors for the role of women in society. Like Angela Carter, Lochhead twists the familiar to find a dark and bloody unconscious with new perspectives on the assumed truths of our society.

Lochhead's plays retell the stories of Mary Shelley and Frankenstein, Mary Queen of Scots and Elizabeth I, Tartuffe, and Dracula with a compelling mix of traditional Scots, contemporary vernacular dialogue, and a subtle lyricism that contemporary theatre writing often effaces in favour of bald realism. Lochhead is not afraid to mix the prosaic and the poetic in one play, one scene, one speech. This combination brings to her already credible and recognisable characters new heights of tragedy or pathos. In *Quelques Fleurs* the extended monologues of Verena and her oilrig-worker husband, Derek (characters as recognisable in a Scottish context as Mike Leigh's characters are within English culture), are written in a mordantly idiomatic and scathingly witty prose to blackly comic effect.

Across a range of genres and subjects Lochhead writes about women and about monsters. Rarely, however, does she write about monstrous women. Focusing on the experiences of women in history, in literature, and in our contemporary world, Lochhead's writing uncovers society's fears of the *unheimlich* aspects of the feminine. Her plays foreground the social and domestic, sexual and creative roles of women within societies which politically and culturally marginalise and devalue their work and their lives. Lochhead takes the common view of these women—Mary as *femme fatale* and Elizabeth as scheming politician in *Mary Queen of Scots Got Her Head Chopped Off*, Mary Shelley as daughter of Mary Wollstonecraft and William Godwin and lover and wife of Percy Bysshe Shelley, with Elise as mere downtrodden maid, in *Blood and Ice*—and peels back the mythology, drawing out the essential humanity of the person. She strives to find in each of her creations a more empowering identity than has traditionally been projected.

Lochhead's plays reset the role of women within both historical and contem- porary society with a ubiquity of language that draws on her skills as poet and performer. The subjects of her plays may be historically diverse but they are united by an energetic, vibrant, and precise use of language.

Blood and Ice, her first full-length play, achieved after several revisions, is essentially a memory play with characters and spirits emerging from the life and imagination of Mary Shelley. Time, place, and degree of "reality" are all signalled in the prose and the verse of the text. In a play dealing with Mary Shelley's creativity and the writing process, with commentary on the lives of both Shelley and Byron, there is a deliberate overemphasis on the importance of words. Language is used to mark shifts in time and space, memory and imagination. Variations in tone suggest in turn the lyricism of the idyll of Lake Geneva, the artificiality of the conversation and society of Mary's Romantic companions, the prosaic language of domestic duties and responsibilities, and the obsessive and violent nature of her imagination and her creativity.

The nature and value of creativity is also examined by presenting alternative visions of Mary Shelley as mother and author. The process of writing the novel is mirrored in her role as mother (to her children and in her increasingly maternal relationships with Shelley and her half-sister Claire) and as creator of the fiction of *Frankenstein*. This is further compared to the character of Frankenstein bringing life to his monster. Society's restricting expectations of roles of wife/lover and mother are described as problematic—particularly to the creative and powerful woman. *Blood and Ice* shows that society demands a heavy price from the woman who steps outside the framework of family and wants to be more than muse to another's imagination. At the end of the play Mary Shelley may be left isolated and alone but Lochhead has recovered her and her life from a distraction of myths and received ideas to posit an impression of her heroine as a person, as a mother, and as a writer in her own right.

As with *Blood and Ice*, the demands of society upon woman to be wife and mother is a central theme of *Mary Queen of Scots Got Her Head Chopped Off*. In this play, however, the dramatic conflict is not played out in private places or in the psyche of one woman but in the public sphere and the political conflicts of two nations. The play's narrator, chorus, and sometime conscience La Corbie poses the central riddle of the play: ". . . I ask you, when's a queen a queen/And when's a queen juist a wummin?"

Plays like *Blood and Ice*, *Mary Queen of Scots Got Her Head Chopped Off*, and *Dracula*, although written with a strongly narrative spine, are structurally dense—with complex layerings of temporal, geographic, and psychological spaces. Lochhead uses doubling with psychological intent, actors being required to play two, three, or even four different but fundamentally linked characters. Mary and Elizabeth are matched at each step by parallel and complimentary characters, each time played by the same actors. The pairings of the maids Marian and Bessie, the beggars Mairn and Leezie, and the children Marie and Wee Betty each reveal another facet of Lochhead's project to show the similarities in the problems faced by Mary and Elizabeth in particular, but also by other women both in the time-frame of the drama and in our own age.

Scottish theatre writing is often criticised for its essential nostalgia and preoccupation with the nation's history, and certainly *Mary Queen of Scots Got Her Head Chopped Off* is a play about a privileged moment in Scotland's political development. Typically of Lochhead, however, the play energises the discourse of nostalgia through the use of rhymes and games. Using *Doppelgänger* for all the main players in the drama and an omnipresent narrator who speaks in an eclectic version of 16th-century Scots, and introducing parallel scenes within contemporary culture, her use of the past is very much more precise and focused than is the case with plays that offer a more straightforward version of historical drama. Lochhead sets out to reinterpret the past and to draw out a new and political agenda for the contemporary audience. She mixes the introspection of much of Scottish culture with a desire to develop a new set of images and a new system of metaphors for the depiction of domestic and psychological drama. The activation of memory as well as history is again reflected in her use of language. The play ends with the characters of the drama transformed into children playing a demonic game in which Mary/Marie is again the victim of prejudice and group hysteria.

Just as the received images society holds of Mary Shelley are dissected in *Blood and Ice*, so in *Mary Queen of Scots Got Her Head Chopped Off*

Lochhead re-examines the mythology associated with both Mary and Elizabeth and again finds disturbing parallels between the demands made of the women in the play and the prejudices that still limit their expectations and ambitions. The play functions as an explicit metaphor for contemporary society.

Lochhead's plays re-examine the deeply rooted prejudices and assumptions held by our culture. Using the conventions of historical drama in *Mary Queen of Scots Got Her Head Chopped Off*, restoring the real horror and tragedy of *Dracula*, and revealing the isolation of women as different as Mary Shelley and Verena, Lochhead rewrites the myths of our culture to reinstate the experiences and the voices of women.

—Adrienne Scullion

LYSSIOTIS, Tes.

Australian. Educated at Rusden State College, Melbourne, degree in teaching. Married in 1974; two children. Secondary school teacher, from 1975–81, and 1983; drama consultant for the Knox Region, 1980; playwright-in-residence, La Mama, 1984, and LaTrobe University, 1991, both Melbourne. Address: 33 Lorraine Drive, East Melbourne, Victoria 3151, Australia.

Publications

PLAYS

I'll Go to Australia and Wear a Hat (produced 1982).
Come to Australia They Said (produced 1982).
Hotel Bonegilla (produced 1983).
On the Line (produced 1984).
The Journey (produced 1985).
Café Misto (produced 1986).
A White Sports Coat (produced 1988).
The Forty Lounge Café (produced 1990). 1990.
The Past Is Here (produced 1991).
Zac's Place (for children; produced 1991).

RADIO PLAY: *A Small Piece of Earth*, 1990.

Biculturalism is at the heart of the multilingual plays of Greek-Australian writer-director Tes Lyssiotis: "I grew up aware that I wasn't just Greek and I wasn't just Australian—I'm both." The daughter of a proxy bride who came to Australia in 1949 from the island of Cythera, she draws on her own background in exploring the historical experiences of southern European migrant women. *I'll Go to Australia and Wear a Hat* contrasts the bleak and barren reality of low-paid menial work which awaited migrant women in the 1950's with their expectations of Australia as "a paradise, a place where men made money and women got to be ladies with fine jewellery and sophisticated hats." Workshopped with an all-woman cast, this semi-documentary play incorporated extracts from parliamentary debates, editorials, and letters from newspapers of the period expressing prevalent, often openly racist,

Anglo-Australian attitudes towards migrants of non-English-speaking back-ground (NESB). It also showed the value of migrant oral history as dramatic material: "It dawned on me that my mother had so many stories to tell. I believe the most ordinary people have the most extraordinary stories to tell if you talk to them."

Come to Australia They Said examined the experiences of Italian migrants in Australia during World War II, and their internment as enemy aliens, as well as the widening generation gap within Italo-Australian families. Lyssiotis drew on the experiences of the Italian actors in her cast, and although she does not speak Italian herself, she stresses the importance of workshopping material with NESB actors in their native languages. *Hotel Bonegilla* was developed with actors of Greek, Italian, and German backgrounds, and dealt with the infamous eponymous migrant camp formed from temporary army huts in 1947. As many as 10,000 migrants of 32 different nationalities lived at Bonegilla until more permanent housing and employment could be found for them elsewhere. The play opens with a slow-motion imagistic sequence inspired by Theodoros Angelopoulos's film *The Travelling Players*—a strong influence on Lyssiotis's work—in which a group of migrants carrying suitcases enter through the audience and form a tableau. The alienation of the different language groups becomes a vehicle for comedy: Italian, Greek, and German families forced to share cramped adjacent cubicles attempt with disastrous results to discuss the misfortunes of communal living, while a Greek girl looking for the place where her brother sleeps is misunderstood as wanting to sleep with her brother, and a camp official asks if anyone can speak "Euro-pean" to interpret for her. *Hotel Bonegilla* also re-enacts the riots which occurred in the camp when poor food, lack of work and money, the remote and alienating environment, and racist attitudes became too much to bear, and tanks were sent in to quell the violence.

In 1984 Lyssiotis formed the Filiki Players with actors Nikos Zarkadas and Lu Beranek, and as writer-in-residence at La Mama Theatre in Melbourne she was commissioned to write *On the Line* about migrant factory workers. She had spent a year working with a group of women suffering from repetitive strain injuries from working on production lines, and built their experiences at home and at work into the play. The following year she devised *The Journey*, a "collage of events" selected from her four previous plays, which transferred to the larger Universal Theatre in Melbourne and later toured other states of Australia, bringing national attention to her work for the first time, although critical response to the play's inevitable discontinuities was not always posi-tive. It was not until the German periodical *Theater Heute* described the play as "a synthesis, by minimal means, of history and individual fates, of stage play and reality, as it is seldom seen in Germany" that the importance of her work began to be fully recognised. Playbox Theatre in Melbourne commissioned her to write *The Forty Lounge Café*, her only published play to date. Using songs and sections of dialogue in Greek, it draws on Lyssiotis's mother's sometimes comic experiences working in her brother-in-law's family fish and chip shop in rural Australia as a basis for flashbacks to the protagonist Elefteria's childhood and adolescence in Greece. As she states to her sister when she returns to Greece for her mother's funeral in the play's final scene, Elefteria's whole life has been a sacrifice:

"I was working in the orphanage, so Irini could have some kind of dowry. I worked so my younger sister could marry . . . She sent me away, I didn't ask to be married to a stranger. Did anyone ever ask me what I wanted? Why did she send me away? I curse the day I set foot on that plane. For years I was a servant to this family."

Elefteria's forced subjugation to the welfare of others makes her determined to provide an upbringing for her daughter Toula which makes the most of her cultural heritage. She counters Toula's dismissal of Greece as "just a bunch of old rocks" and her adoption of Anglo-Australian attitudes by insisting on passing on to her Greek skills and traditions. In a play dominated by mourning, sadness, and deprivation the briskness of the café scenes provide welcome moments of levity. In the monologue *A White Sports Coat* a pregnant playwright reminisces about her mother, her Greek family home, and her Australian childhood while desperately trying to finish her play before she gives birth to her child. *Zac's Place* focuses on the dilemmas of a young Greek-Australian torn between the romanticised notions of Greece, of his father, who wants to close down the family milk bar and go back to their homeland, and the peer pressure of his Australian friends. Lyssiotis presents Greek-Australian migrant experience "from the inside out," but avoids the "ghetto" of much non-Anglophonic Australian community theatre, and rejects the tokenism of multiculturalism: "I don't want to be labelled as 'multicultural'. I want to be regarded as an artist, and the fact that I am working on things to do with migrants is irrelevant. It could just as well be elephants or disabled people."

—Tony Mitchell

M

MacDONALD, Sharman.

British. Born in Glasgow, Scotland in 1951. Educated at Edinburgh University. Married to Will Knightley; two children. Thames Television writer-in-residence, The Bush Theatre, London, 1984–85. Recipient: *Evening Standard* award, 1984. Agent: Patricia MacNaughton, MacNaughton Lowe Representation, 200 Fulham Road, London SW10 9PN, England.

Publications

PLAYS

When I Was a Girl, I Used to Scream and Shout . . . (produced 1984). 1985.
The Brave (produced 1988). In *When I Was a Girl, I Used to Scream and Shout . . ., When We Were Women*, 1990.
When We Were Women (produced 1988). In *The Brave, When I Was a Girl, I Used to Scream and Shout . . .*, 1990.
When I Was a Girl, I Used to Scream and Shout . . ., The Brave, When We Were Women: Three Plays. 1990.
All Things Nice (produced 1991). 1991.
Shades (produced 1992).
Winter Guest (produced 1993).

TELEVISION PLAY: *Wild Flowers*, 1990.

NOVELS
The Beast. 1986.
Night, Night. 1988.

Familial bonds, the confusions of adolescence, a Celtic heritage—all are powerfully recurrent themes in Sharman MacDonald's work, which deals with mother/child relationships with an emotional charge and engaging comedy that mark her as a distinctive voice in the British theatre. Celtic writers seem especially strong on this territory—many of the scenes between MacDonald's adolescent girls Fiona and Vari in *When I Was A Girl, I Used To Scream and Shout . . .* recall the Edna O'Brien of *A Pagan Place*. But MacDonald's landscape of small Scottish towns where the climate seems to be predominantly grey and rainy is very much her own.

She made an electrifying debut with *When I Was A Girl, I Used To Scream and Shout . . .*, which transferred from the tiny Bush Theatre to enjoy a long

West End run with Julie Walters initially starring. MacDonald was an actress for some years before becoming a full-time writer, and this play—like the work of many actor-dramatists—had refreshingly lively dialogue which at once stamped her as an original. The play may have relatively little plot, but as it swings across time (it moves between 1983, when it was written, 1955, and 1960), a complex web of family tensions and bonds is built up.

It opens on a rocky beach on the east coast of Scotland in 1983, with the 32-year-old Fiona, unmarried and childless, revisiting a childhood haunt with her mother Morag, one of MacDonald's outstanding creations—a garrulous, warm, but often sharp-tongued woman, much given to commenting on the lack of a grandchild ("A woman's body is a clock that runs down very rapidly," she is prone to remark). Later in the play it transpires that Fiona was pregnant at 15—the scenes in flashback involving the 17-year-old Ewan who fathers the child are superbly written—a deliberate move on Fiona's part, in the complicated emotional relationship between Fiona and Morag, to prevent her mother going abroad with a new man, ending in an abortion with Morag remaining at home. All the 1983 scenes between Morag and Fiona beautifully convey the loving but acerbic relationship between them, and equally assured are the time-shifts to 1955, with Fiona and her friend Vari giggling through their first sexual fumblings and comparing notes on boys, and to 1960 with Fiona's decision, made with the devastating candour of adolescence, to use Ewan to father her child. Tough and tender as well as funny, it was a remarkable first play.

There was a cooler reaction to MacDonald's subsequent work; it is not an uncommon pattern for British critics to moderate their enthusiasm for dramatists to whose early work they awarded high praise. But it must be admitted that *The Brave* and *When We Were Women*, both produced in 1988, were somewhat disappointing. *The Brave* was an admirable effort to break away from a Scottish setting; set in Morocco, it had a startling opening sequence by an hotel poolside with Ferlie, a Scottish woman in her mid-thirties, lumbered with what transpires to be the dead body of a Moroccan whom she has killed in self-defence. She and her sister Susan, a political terrorist who has jumped bail and fled to Morocco where Ferlie has been visiting her, spend most of the play trying to get rid of the body, finally burying it in the desert on the site of the crumbling movie-set for *Samson and Delilah*, with the help of two engineers working in Morocco and taking a brief vacation at the hotel. This pair—the spaced-out Robert, endlessly strumming his guitar, and his friend Jamie, a Scottish exile with false teeth and an abrasive wit—provide much of the vitality in a play which only fitfully sparks into life. There are some splendid scenes, specially Susan's efforts to steal a spade from the poolside with which to bury the body while her sister distracts the barman, and Jamie gives the play energy whenever he is on stage, his raw Scottish vigour reminding both the sisters and the audience that geography cannot fundamentally alter cultural heritage, but too often the play remains obstinately arid.

When We Were Women, which came out of work at the National Theatre Studio, may bear some of the hallmarks of laboratory conditions, but it was a significant technical experiment for MacDonald too. Again, the background is Scotland—this time during World War II—and centres round another of MacDonald's young heroines. Isla lives with her mother, the indomitable

Maggie, and her common-law husband Alec. Written in a series of short scenes, alternating between Isla's life at home and her encounters with a serviceman, Mackenzie, the play subtly evokes the sense of time suspended during war. Isla becomes pregnant by Mackenzie, who marries her only for the marriage to be revealed as bigamous. At the close the family is left turned in on itself.

All Things Nice also covered familiar MacDonald terrain while she continued to experiment technically. The play inhabits two worlds. Scotland again provides one, with another adolescent heroine in 15-year-old Moira, staying with her Gran and her "paying guest," the Captain, and becoming aware of life in the company of her best friend Linda. Parallel with these scenes, earthy and funny, we also focus on the isolated figure of Rose, Moira's mother, absent with Moira's father who is working for a Middle-Eastern oil company. Rose's increasingly revealing letters disclose a woman trapped in an unhappy marriage and beginning to seek refuge in drink and affairs. MacDonald traces the tension between the two worlds with delicate precision, and the scenes between Moira and Linda have all the insight into the closed world of adolescence that distinguished *When I was a Girl . . .*, whilst the figure of the bedridden Captain, cajoling and frightening, reveals again her ability to create rich male roles as well as female ones.

MacDonald returned to the embrace of the commercial theatre with *Shades*, with Pauline Collins starring in what is perhaps the richest role MacDonald has yet written. Once again, a mother/child relationship is at the heart of the play, which begins with a widowed mother in her forties dressing to go out to a dance with a new man friend and which, for virtually the entire first act, consists of a dialogue between the woman, Pearl, and her 10-year-old son. This act delicately probes the unusual relationship—flirtatious as well as possessive —between a single parent and a sensitive child, while the second act contains a beautifully-handled scene with Pearl's new man backing off from further commitment once he realises how strong her love remains for her husband, who died young. The play is fundamentally a chamber piece and suffered to a degree from the commercial pressures of playing in a large West End theatre. The experience of the production seems to have been tricky for MacDonald, who announced shortly before the play's opening that she would not be writing for the theatre again. It is to be hoped she will change her mind.

—Alan Strachan

MANN, Emily.

American. Born in Boston, Massachusetts, 12 April 1952. Educated at Radcliffe College, Cambridge, Massachusetts, B.A. in English 1974 (Phi Beta Kappa); University of Minnesota, Minneapolis (Bush Fellow), 1974–76, M.F.A. in theater arts 1976. Married Gerry Bamman in 1981 (divorced), one son. Associate director, Guthrie Theatre, Minneapolis, 1978–79; resident director, BAM Theater Company, Brooklyn, New York, 1981–82; member of the board, 1983–87, and vice-president of the board, 1984–86, Theatre Communications Group, and director, New Dramatists workshop for play development, 1984–91, both New York. Since 1989 artistic director,

McCarter Theatre Center for the Performing Arts, Princeton, New Jersey; artistic associate, Crossroads Theatre, New Brunswick, New Jersey, 1990; lecturer, Council of the Humanities and Theatre and Dance program, Princeton University, New Jersey, 1990. Recipient: Obie award, 1981 (for writing and directing); Guggenheim fellowship, 1983; Rosamond Gilder award, 1983; National Endowment for the Arts grant, 1984, 1986; Creative Artists Public Service grant, 1985; Edinburgh Festival Fringe first award, 1985; McKnight fellowship, 1985; Dramatists Guild award, 1986; Playwrights USA award, 1986; Helen Hayes award, 1986; Home Box Office U.S.A. award, 1986. Lives in Princeton, New Jersey. Agent: George Lane, William Morris Agency, 1350 Avenue of the Americas, New York, New York 10019, U.S.A.

Publications

PLAYS

Annulla, An Autobiography (as *Annulla Allen: The Autobiography of a Survivor*, also director: produced 1977; revised version, as *Annulla, An Autobiography*, produced 1985). 1985.
Still Life (also director: produced 1980). 1982; in *Coming to Terms: American Plays and the Vietnam War*, edited by James Reston, Jr., 1985.
Execution of Justice (produced 1984; also director: produced 1986). In *New Playwrights 3*, edited by James Leverett and Elizabeth Osborn, 1986.
Nights and Days, adaptation of a play by Pierre Laville, in *Avant-Scène*, July 1984.
Betsey Brown, adaptation of the novel by Ntozake Shange, book by Shange and Mann, music by Baikida Carroll, lyrics by Shange, Mann, and Carroll (also director: produced 1989).

THEATRICAL ACTIVITIES

DIRECTOR: **Plays**—*Cold* by Michael Casale, 1976; *Ashes* by David Rudkin, 1977; *Annulla Allen*, 1977; *Surprise, Surprise* by Michel Tremblay, 1978; *On Mount Chimborazo* by Tankred Dorst, 1978; *Reunion* and *Dark Pony*, by David Mamet, 1978; *The Glass Menagerie* by Tennessee Williams, 1979, and 1990; *He and She* by Rachel Crothers, 1980; *Still Life*, 1980 and 1986; *Oedipus the King* by Sophocles, 1981; *A Tantalizing* by William Mastrosimone, 1982; *The Value of Names* by Jeffrey Sweet, 1982 and 1984; *A Weekend near Madison* by Kathleen Tolan, 1983; *Execution of Justice*, 1985 and 1986; *A Doll's House* by Ibsen, 1986; *Hedda Gabler* by Ibsen, 1987; *Betsey Brown*, 1989 and 1990; *The Three Sisters* by Chekhov, 1991.

Emily Mann has referred to her work as "theatre of testimony." Documentary drama is her métier, and recent history has provided her subjects ranging from the horrors of war, to peacetime violence, to the revolution in gender roles and sexual politics. Her first three stage plays are based wholly or in part on interviews with the people whose stories she tells.

   Annulla, An Autobiography is the prototype. Mann visited the protagonist, a survivor of Nazism, in 1974, and the work hews so closely to what the playwright heard in Annulla Allen's London kitchen that she credits her as co-author. The short play turns Annulla's own words into an uninterrupted monologue. Annulla's privileged girlhood in Galicia is a distant memory, eclipsed by the Nazi terror. Her self-assurance and unsemitic good looks helped her escape the camps and rescue her Jewish husband from Dachau. Now widowed, she cares for a demanding invalid sister. However compelling her harrowing story, Annulla insists, "It is not me who is interesting, it is my play." An enormous manuscript covers her kitchen table, stage center. Annulla's play argues for global matriarchy as the solution to evil and barbarism. "If women would only start thinking, we could change the world," she observes, declaring women incapable of the monstrous acts of Hitler or Stalin.

Still, Annulla is unable to read out representative passages from her work in progress. The manuscript is so disorganized and the need to get dinner for her ailing sister so pressing that she loses patience sifting through the jumbled pages. Therein lies Mann's point. However reasoned Annulla's thesis or promising her creativity, she is chronically distracted by more traditional female roles and by the anxieties and guilt which stem from her terrible past. Annulla can no more impose order on her play than she can on her life. Mann does not try to do that for her. In setting down the unmediated monologue of this scarred but plucky woman, Mann makes a statement about her own role. *Annulla* testifies to the freedom for creativity exercised by the playwright who recognizes that, by sheer accident of time and place, she was spared the life of her co-author and subject.

In *Still Life* Mann again draws on interviews with real people who become the *dramatis personae*. She calls this work a documentary, specifying that it be produced with that genre's characteristic objectivity. That tone is the first of the ironies that mark this work about the virulent psychic and emotional conditioning suffered by a Vietnam veteran and about the troubled society to which he returns. As a Marine, Mark learned that he could kill civilians as easily as enemy soldiers. After the war, he cannot get rid of the memory of having wielded power over life and death. His obsession is alternately the source of rage, guilt, and physical pleasure. Incapable of talking either to those who were not in Vietnam, or to those who were, Mark turns to drugs, crime, and domestic violence. He is not too self-centered to appreciate that his wife, Cheryl, whom he abuses, is as much of a casualty of the war years as he. Cheryl wants to return to the securities of a traditionalism more alive in her memories than in post-1960's America. She longs to play the roles her mother did, noting that, except in wartime, it is women who protect men—a point of view strikingly antithetical to that of Annulla Allen. Mark's mistress Nadine has done battle with all manner of "naughtiness." "A woman with many jobs and many lives," in Mann's words, Nadine describes herself as being so busy that she sleeps with her shoes on. The observation is metaphoric. Nadine steps over troubled waters, never feeling the cold or agitation, and never plunging beneath the surface. Mark can tell Nadine his ugly truths, for absolutely nothing offends, disturbs, or even touches her.

Still Life is staged so as to make palpable the lack of genuine communication between Mark, who lives in the past, Cheryl, who yearns for an unrealizable future, and Nadine, who hovers above an unexamined present. The three characters sit side by side behind a table, like members of a panel discussion — or witnesses at a trial. They talk about, but rarely to, one another, their intersecting speeches often juxtaposed ironically. So, for example, Nadine's innocence about her near fatal pregnancies overlaps the ingenuous Cheryl's shock in coming upon Mark's pictures of war casualties. Projections on a screen behind the actors underscore the hopelessness of anyone's enjoying the full understanding of others. Gruesome pictures of horribly mutilated war injured, for instance, illustrate Mark's inability to talk to his parents who supported the war. Indeed, this seething play whose self-possessed characters never touch one another on stage ironically reflects a society where people, however uncommunicating, are continually in violent and destructive collision.

The notion of the audience as jury, implicit in *Still Life*, is central to *Execution of Justice*. Significantly, the work was commissioned by the Eureka Theatre of San Francisco. Its subject is the 1978 murder of George Moscone, Mayor of San Francisco, and Harvey Milk, a City Supervisor and the first avowed homosexual voted into high public office. The play brings to the stage the case of the People against Dan White, the assassin. It demonstrates the instability of White, who had been elected a City Supervisor, resigned, changed his mind and, when Moscone refused to reappoint him to his former post, vented his rage by shooting him and Milk. Mann bases her script on the transcript of the trial, reportage, extensive interviews with some of the principals, as well as what she calls in a prefatory note "the street." The play neatly synthesizes background pertinent to the case, such as the evolution in the social and political spheres caused by the migration to San Francisco of a large homosexual population. It recreates the climate of fear provoked by the mass deaths in Jonestown, Guyana, and the reputed connections between James Jones and liberal elements in San Francisco. The play captures effectively the unprecedented violence that stalked American political life in the 1970's.

As the testimony piles up, one appreciates the implausible defense arguments (e.g., the famous "Twinkies defense," which attributed criminal behavior to the accused's junk food diet) and its unlikely claim that the murders were purely politically and not homophobically motivated. *Execution of Justice* shows that what was really on trial was conservative values, outraged and threatened by the growing power of the gay community. The use of video projections and film clips from documentaries intensify the passions of the trial; the inclusion of reporters and photographers heightens its immediacy. Though Mann treats this explosive material with an even hand, there is no question that she wants the audience as jury to find that Dan White's conviction and light jail sentence for the lesser charges of voluntary manslaughter amount to the miscarriage of justice referred to in the play's title.

Mann's penchant for transforming life to the stage takes a new turn with *Betsey Brown*, a rhythm and blues musical. She came to the project at the invitation of Ntozake Shange who began it as a short story, turned it into a performance piece produced in 1979 at the Kennedy Center as *Boogie Woogie Landscapes*, and finally rewrote it as a novel. Shange and jazz trumpeter-composer Baikida Carroll approached Mann for help in reworking the piece for the stage. The result was a full-fledged collaboration, a musical whose 28 songs color and interweave the various strands of a distinctly contemporary story.

The eponymous Betsey Brown is a young African-American woman who comes of age in St. Louis of 1959. The first stirrings of the civil rights movement form the background for a number of issues the play explores. The most obvious is, of course, racism, both within the black community and from white society threatened by integration. At least as consequential is the question of a role model for teen-age Betsey. On one side is her mother, a "modern" woman who briefly abandons her family to pursue her own intellectual needs. Notwithstanding, she is genuinely concerned about educating her daughters to become cultivated members of a society which hardly encourages the self-actualization of black women. On the other side is the comforting figure of the Browns' housekeeper, a traditional woman who sings gospel songs with exquisite conviction. Her other accomplishments include commonsensical strategies for pleasing a man and consoling a crying child. Reviews of *Betsey Brown*'s premiere prove the success of the work in moving beyond its delineation of the tensions and beauties of black life to dramatize universal problems of parental responsibilities to children in a radically changing world.

In addition to her work for the stage, Mann has written three screenplays (none yet produced). *Naked* (1985), based on the book by Jo Giese Brown, is subtitled *One Couple's Intimate Journey Through Infertility*. *Fanny Kelly* (1985) dramatizes the true story of an intrepid pioneer woman captured by the Sioux. *You Strike a Woman, You Strike a Rock* (1990) is a script on the Greensboro Massacre, commissioned by NBC Theatre. These scripts are distinguished by tight, suspenseful plots as well as the credible characterizations that Mann has made her signature.

—Ellen Schiff

MAY, Elaine.

American. Born Elaine Berlin in Philadelphia, Pennsylvania, 21 April 1932; moved to Los Angeles, California, 1942. Daughter of theatre director Jack Berlin and actress Jeannie Berlin. Attended University of Chicago and Playwrights Theatre in Chicago, 1950. Married 1) Marvin May, 1949; daughter: Jeannie Berlin; 2) the lyricist Sheldon Harnick (divorced 1963). Studied acting under Maria Ouspenskaya, 1947; member of the improvisational theatre group, The Compass Players, 1953–57; performed in New York clubs with Mike Nichols, 1957; made several TV appearances, 1960; wrote, directed and acted in the theatre, also wrote and performed for radio, and recorded comedy albums, 1960s. Address: c/o Julian Schlossberg, Castle Hill Productions, 1414 Avenue of the Americas, New York 10019, USA.

Publications

PLAYS

An Evening with Mike Nichols and Elaine May (sketches; produced 1960).
A Matter of Position (produced 1962).
Not Enough Rope (produced 1962).
Adaptation (also director; produced 1969). 1971.
Mr Gogol and Mr Preen (produced 1991).

SCREENPLAYS: *A New Leaf*, 1970; *Such Good Friends* (uncredited), 1971; *Mickey and Nicky*, 1976; *Heaven Can Wait*, with Warren Beatty and Buck Henry, 1978; *Tootsie*, with Larry Gelbart (uncredited), 1982; *Ishtar*, 1987.

THEATRICAL ACTIVITIES
DIRECTOR: **Plays**—*The Third Ear* (revue), 1964; *Adaptation, and Next* by Terrence McNally, 1969. **Films**—*A New Leaf*, 1970; *The Heartbreak Kid*, 1972; *Mickey and Nicky*, 1976; *Ishtar*, 1987.
ACTOR: **Plays**—debut as child actor; also *An Evening with Mike Nichols and Elaine May*, 1960; Shirley in *The Office* by María Irene Fornés, 1966. **Films**—*Enter Laughing*, 1966; *Luv*, 1967; *A New Leaf*, 1970; *California Suite*, 1978; *In the Spirit*, 1990. **Television**—since 1959. **Cabaret**—at The Second City, Chicago, and The Compass, Chicago and New York, 1954–57; Village Vanguard and Blue Angel, New York, 1957; Town Hall, New York, 1959.

Although in the 1980s and 1990s there has been a proliferation of women directors in Hollywood, Elaine May, along with Dorothy Arzner and Ida Lupino, paved the way for these contemporary careers. May entered show business at the age of six as an actor spending her childhood on the road with her father's travelling theatre company. From 1954 to 1961, she had a stage partnership with Mike Nichols. May then became more interested in playwriting and went on to film acting roles and screenwriting. She was valued in Hollywood as a 'script-doctor' and used her considerable ability in this area when other more prestigious film-work was not available. Her films fall into the conventional Hollywood genres, mainly comedy, although her work usually has a subtext of darker psychological depth and resonance.

Some critics have seen her work as derogatory to women but her male characters are also weak and dependent. They exhibit mutual needs (see, for example, May and Matthau in *A New Leaf*). Her main protagonists are openly neurotic victims who, like the protagonists in Woody Allen's films, triumph by achieving what they want, namely, a love relationship earned through pain. The secondary characters in May's films are generally pragmatists who get on in life by using other people. She sees this social pragmatism as a neurotic weakness, and once again like Woody Allen, has more admiration for sensitive people who make no secret of their vulnerability.

The plots of her films explore the way in which men see women as objects who can be used to fulfil a fantasy or 'save' them. Both Matthau in *A New Leaf* and Grodin in *The Heartbreak Kid* see their 'love-objects' as a means of gaining money, sex, and security but have their defensive pragmatism stripped away from them until they are exposed as equally dependent and vulnerable as the women. In both of the films, the women appear to be the victims but end up triumphant.

However, Elaine May's work is not restricted to exploring male/female conflicts. In *Mickey and Nicky*, she enters the world of mobsters, *film noir* terrain, and provides a bitter and complex exploration of male friendship. *Ishtar* (made at Columbia in 1987 with the largest budget ever entrusted to a woman director) is a film about male-buddies-on-the-road rather in the Bob Hope and Bing Crosby vein—a genre which took her back to her show-business origins.

Elaine May believes above all in comedy—she says, 'You can drink this wine straight or you can drink it funny. You can kill somebody straight or you can kill them funny. Funny is closer to life . . . Humour is just a way of looking at things. I mean you can look at it this way and it's a disaster. And you can look at it this way, and it's funny'. But in all her films, the humour is subversive, revealing a remarkably dark and injured world where everyone betrays everyone else.

—Sylvia Paskin

McINTYRE, Clare.

British. Member, Nottingham Playhouse TIE Company, 1977–78, The Women's Theatre Group, London, 1979–81, and Common Stock, London, 1981. Recipient: Beckett award, 1989; *Evening Standard* award, 1990; London Drama Critics award, 1990. Agent: Leah Schmidt, Curtis Brown Group, 162–168 Regent Street, London W1R 5TB, England.

Publications

PLAYS

Better a Live Pompey than a Dead Cyril, with Stephanie Nunn, adaptation of the poems and writings of Stevie Smith (produced 1980).
I've Been Running (produced 1986).
Low Level Panic (produced 1988). In *First Run*, edited by Kate Harwood, 1989.
My Heart's a Suitcase (produced 1990). 1990.

RADIO PLAY: *I've Been Running*, 1990.

THEATRICAL ACTIVITIES

ACTOR: **Plays**—role in *Better a Live Pompey than a Dead Cyril*, by McIntyre with Stephanie Nunn, 1980; Mrs. Kendal in *The Elephant Man* by Bernard Pomerance, 1982; Dawn in *Steaming* by Nell Dunn, 1985; Gwendolen in *The Importance of Being Earnest* by Oscar Wilde, 1985; Jane in *Crystal Clear*, 1986; Jan in *Bedroom Farce* by Alan Ayckbourn, 1987; Linda in *Kafka's Dick* by Alan Bennett, 1988. **Films**—*The Pirates of Penzance*, 1981; *Krull*, 1982; *Plenty*, 1984; *Empire State*, 1986; *Security*, 1987; *A Fish Called Wanda*, 1988. **Television**—*Hotel du Lac*, 1985; *Splitting Up*, 1990.

Clare McIntyre was an actress working in theatre and film for several years before she turned full-time to writing. As a member of the Women's Theatre Group she produced a delightful compilation of the work of Stevie Smith. Her first original play was *I've Been Running*, directed by Terry Johnson and performed at the Old Red Lion in London. It focuses on a female health freak whose fears are kept at bay by feverish activity. McIntyre is one of a long line of female playwrights whose work has been encouraged and nurtured by a combination of the Women's Playhouse Trust and Max Stafford-Clark at the Royal Court. Both *Low Level Panic* and *My Heart's a Suitcase* reveal an uncanny ability to reflect the obsessions and anxieties of contemporary women. Like Caryl Churchill, her plays attract a huge female following, but there is no reason why men shouldn't also enjoy her wit and shrewd observation.

The panic in *Low Level Panic* is engendered in a couple of female flat-sharers when confronted with the images of women peddled by advertising and pornography. The territory is similar to Sarah Daniels's but without her aggression. Mary, Jo, and Celia are preparing for a party. McIntyre cleverly sets all but two of the play's scenes in the bathroom, the very place where women minutely examine their bodies and almost invariably find them wanting. Lying in the bath, Jo imagines herself as the heroine of a sexual fantasy, a leggy model gliding through the cocktail bars of London's hotels, clinking glasses of Martini and meeting the admiring eyes of a rich handsome stranger across a crowded room. Such glacial perfection and anonymity is in complete contrast with Jo's vision of herself as overweight and over-talkative, especially when confronted with a roomful of people at a party. Far from being an expression of her own sensuality, her fantasy makes her feel both humiliated and undesirable. It is also in sharp contrast with the reality experienced by Mary when, in one of just two scenes set outside the bathroom, she is stopped on her way home and raped. As a result she can no longer dress up for a party without feeling she is asking to be attacked again. The pornographic magazine she discovers in their dustbin appears to her to be a legal incitement to men to attack women. In contrast, Celia, the third member of the flat and the least developed as a character, dishes out advice on the right colour of eyeshadow as though life simply consists of trapping the right man. The intimate dialogue about spots, herpes, and even unattractive clitorises is sharply observed and very amusing. But above all it is the confusion and naïvety of her characters that McIntyre captures so accurately.

Anxiety is also a theme in *My Heart's a Suitcase*. Chris is 30 years old, a waitress and distinctly unhappy about it: "What's wrong with being a waitress is that it's a shit job with shit money, no shitting pension and zero fucking prospects." She has a capacity to complain that rivals Jimmy Porter's in Osborne's *Look Back in Anger*. *My Heart's a Suitcase* is a play of the 1980's, a time when everybody was supposed to be getting richer but Chris, who is middle-class, articulate, has a degree, and could presumably earn money if she set her mind to it, is paralysed. Her life is drifting by while she is obsessed with the horrors of the world, an obsession intensified after being attacked by a man with a gun on the tube. Her more placid friend Hannah faces the possibility of real paralysis in the form of multiple sclerosis. The two of them travel down to the seaside together, invited to spend the weekend in an empty flat belonging to a rich ex-boyfriend of Chris's. Thus Chris is given plenty of opportunity to rail against the injustice of some people having money while she has a pittance. She is confronted with real riches when Colin's wife, Tunis, arrives at the flat trailing her consumer goods behind her and throws a tantrum when she discovers her specially made curtains don't fit. Tunis doesn't even have to work for her money but fritters her time away in endless shopping sprees. McIntyre, however, avoids drawing too neat a moral; Tunis is indolent but not a villain and is discontented without being wildly unhappy. It is not that Chris is particularly greedy; it is more that she imagines that wealth would make her happy, although a strange religious phantom called Luggage suggests that it is a woman's role in life to make do with her lot. This phantom, together with that of the man who attacked her, are the least engaging aspects of the play. Most enjoyable is Chris's ability to articulate her discontent with such ferocious gusto. She may be maddening but it is hard to dislike her, and McIntyre makes a rare attempt to present the rich complexities of female friendship onstage. She is a humorous, observant playwright with a deep understanding of the female psyche, and, if she is not diverted into television, could well produce a major play in the future.

—Jane Edwardes

MILLER, Susan.

American. Born in Philadelphia, Pennsylvania, 6 April 1944. Educated at Pennsylvania State University, University Park, B.A. 1965; Bucknell University, Lewisburg, Pennsylvania, M.A. 1970. Instructor in English, Pennsylvania State University, 1969–73; lecturer in playwriting, University of California, Los Angeles, 1975–76; playwright-in-residence, Mark Taper Forum Theatre, Los Angeles, 1975. Recipient: Rockefeller grant, 1975; National Endowment for the Arts grant, 1976; Obie award, 1979. Agent: Joyce Ketay Agency, 334 West 89th Street, New York, New York 10024, U.S.A.

Publications

PLAYS

No One Is Exactly 23. In Pyramid 1, 1968.
Daddy, and A Commotion of Zebras (produced 1970).
Silverstein & Co. (produced 1972).
Confessions of a Female Disorder (produced 1973). In Gay Plays, edited by
    William M. Hoffman, 1979.
Denim Lecture (produced 1974).
Flux (produced 1975; revised version produced 1977).
Cross Country (produced 1976). In West Coast Plays , 1978.
Nasty Rumors and Final Remarks (produced 1979).
Arts and Leisure (produced 1985).
For Dear Life (produced 1989).
It's Our Town, Too (produced 1992).

TELEVISION PLAYS: Home Movie (Family series); One for the Money, Two for the Show, with Nedra Deen; A Whale for the Killing; Visions series.

In Susan Miller's Arts and Leisure, the character J.D. Salinger inquires of the Professor—about a student's films—"Does her work astonish you?" Miller's startling explorations of women's minds and hearts do just that, especially creating the shock of recognition in spectators who, like her characters, write, teach, or experience turbulent relationships. Miller's plays most frequently explore issues of intimacy and of evolving sexual identity. In contrast to her self-protective Dina in Flux, who pleads "I'm not eager to expose private agonies," Miller persists in such probing, in plays characterized by their whimsy yet potential violence, passion yet playfulness.

Most of Miller's full-length plays include a tap dance, and nearly all her funny dramas or poignant comedies end on an upbeat note—with Jake's optimism, with Ronnie's self-discovery, with Jess regaining her confidence, with Salinger gladly relinquishing his manuscripts, with Perry beginning a new life; in fact, the last line of *Cross Country* finds Perry greeting new companions. Although the title of *Nasty Rumors and Final Remarks* suggests that Raleigh's demise concerns Miller, actually the dramatist focuses on the life of this quicksilver woman, who can't be confined by her hospital bed or defined by her friends, lovers, or offspring; hence, even Raleigh after her stroke seems affirmative. So does Miller's reply to the Republican's 1992 convention; although *It's Our Town, Too*, because it follows the structure of her model by Thornton Wilder, ends at the graveyard, it affirms respect for those who are different, for values other than those of fundamentalist Christians, and for families other than the old-fashioned model of homemaker mother, wage-earning father, two children, and a dog.

Miller's language provides part of her plays' fascination. She builds her rhythms into her lines so their catchy cadences prove actor-proof. In natural dialogue, fragmented but also filled with expressive turns of phrase, her characters fumble to express their panic or pleasure, occasionally achieving eloquent accuracy. *Cross Country*, for instance, says of Perry's wrenching herself out of her marriage to take off in search of professional and personal fulfilment: "There is a moment, like the black holes in space, of complete and irrevocable loss. To allow that moment is to let go of the sides of time, to fall into another place where it is not likely any of your old friends will recognize you again." Often Miller's lines provide witty insights into women's lives, as when a character remarks that, because we are so often interrupted while looking after others, "Women live longer just to finish their conversations."

Miller chooses as her characters writers and others in the arts, usually women in crisis or transition, experiencing problems living with others or in their own skin. One of several protagonists bearing names unusual for women, Ronnie in *Confessions of a Female Disorder* makes the transition from puberty to marriage and career while struggling to avoid confronting her attraction to women. The title expresses both Ronnie's love of women and a female penchant for abnegation. Perry leaves her marriage to find herself. *Flux*'s iconoclast Jess, on the edge and unable to contain her emotions or control those she inspires in others, turns on her students to her considerable charms instead of to English, making a mess in the classroom and in her personal life as well. *Nasty Rumors and Final Remarks* takes dying Raleigh on an adventure of self-discovery; nobody else could tame her enough to know her. Catherine and Jake in *For Dear Life* differ too profoundly to sustain their relationship: she always expects the worst, while her husband flees her pessimism, which begins to infect him. Yet, ironically, she proves correct in her fears that their marriage will crumble.

Such early Miller works as the Jewish-American rites-of-passage black comedy *Silverstein & Co.* and her one-act *No One is Exactly 23* employ absurdist styles. As her craft developed, however, Miller suited her form to her objective, often combining presentational and representational conventions in the same play and varying her structure to fit her purpose. Although frequently employing surface verisimilitude, Miller sticks to that style throughout only in *Arts and Leisure*, in which the Professor and Ginny break into the New Hampshire farmhouse of J.D. Salinger—"the Greta Garbo of American letters"—threatening to blow up his home unless the reclusive but compulsive writer turns over all his unpublished manuscripts. Establishing immediate suspense and then sustaining it throughout, Miller confines the action to less than 24 hours on a single set.

At the other extreme, Miller's most surprising play structurally, *Cross Country*, employs huge chunks of narration (distributed among the cast, rather than assigned to a single narrator) as well as stage directions which the actors speak aloud, as in chamber theatre. This highly episodic play dramatizes some scenes in a single sentence, or gives one line to two characters who interact on stage simultaneously, but in fact separately, with protagonist Perry. Miller begins by describing what happens after the play's middle, and the narrative occurs mostly in the past tense. After repeatedly jumping around in its chronology, however, *Cross Country* eventually moves forward to Perry's new life on the West Coast.

Miller experiments with chronology in another fashion with *For Dear Life*, which disrupts linear progression through time by moving from a "present" in Act I, to 18 years later in Act II, to 16 years before that in Act III. In other words, Act III occurs about two years after Act I, but the intervening act flashes far forward. The style, meanwhile, moves from mostly representational to often presentational. Miller unifies the unusual construction with a speech which we watch Jake prepare during the first act and which his son quotes at the end of the play, when he's supposed to be one year old—but we see him then as the teenager he was in the previous act. The disrupted chronology of the play's construction permits Miller to show us in Act III the problems which cause the divorce which Act II has already shown us does occur. The couple in the third act wait for their happiness to end—as we know it must. Not only Act II but the title also tells us that they are hanging on for dear life, clinging to a relationship as though to a lifeline, even though logic dictates letting go.

Confessions of a Female Disorder, perhaps the most fluid of all Miller's unconventionally constructed plays, takes Ronnie from her first menstrual period and the start of her search for a man through her gathering with other women in her kitchen to begin exploring facets of themselves. So presentational and episodic is this play that Miller hops Ronnie out of a shower straight into her shrink's office in mid-lather and pops husband David in "out of sequence," a line which acknowledges to spectators that we all know this is a play, not a slice of life. "Cheerleaders" and "Lettermen" jump in and out of the action both to comment and to take minor roles (such as the guys who offer her a sexual experience superior to her first time); when coercing her into marriage, Ronnie's shrink turns into a minister.

Although Miller has revised *Flux* several times, each version employs presentational, episodic scenes conveying the quality of dreams and nightmares which do for the collapse of female self-esteem what Arthur Miller (no relation) did for male disintegration in *Death of a Salesman*. Moving freely from the classroom, Saul's bedroom, Jess's house, Jess's office, and her mentor's office or classroom, Miller dramatizes Jess's disorienting mismatch of expectations with those of her students and partner. Such construction and style convey what Jess and her students experience emotionally rather than factually; thus, the mentor performs a con artist's shell game, the students don pyjamas and brush their teeth in the classroom, and a voice-over about student evaluations accompanies an orgy. Clearly Jess and her students populate each other's dreams.

Miller's most unusual temporal distortions occur in *Nasty Rumors and Final Remarks*; while Raleigh experiences a cerebral haemorrhage on one side of the stage, others elsewhere deal with its aftermath. Only one preliminary scene has established Raleigh's personality before the stroke. As time passes, Raleigh begins narrating and describing herself in the third person, past tense (somewhat like *Cross Country*); while she's supposed to be in a coma and dying, we see her talking to us and eavesdropping on her male lover, her female lover, her friend. Raleigh's ramblings round the hospital are intersected by flashbacks which dramatize her relationships to these people who have gathered to wait for her death. These presentational episodes connect so seamlessly in a montage of past events and present passions that we scarcely notice the technique, till everyone gathers to bid goodbye to the dead woman.

Raleigh has proven unreliable, unpredictable, unfaithful, and unnerving to all who care about her. Yet when the play ends, we miss her, as we do all Miller's protagonists—usually brilliant, beautiful, bisexual women who fascinate and bewilder their admirers, who cannot tame their whirlwind natures. In dramatizing them Miller explores such themes as how to couple successfully, how to balance professional and personal fulfillment, how to know and be oneself, and how to behave responsibly towards others without betraying oneself. Miller balances her evocation of anxiety and loneliness with a sense of elation at rising to the challenges of intimacy and career. Repeatedly she achieves the trademark Miller effect of locating our hidden lacerations, then tickling those wounds till we're convulsed.

—Tish Dace

MUNRO, Rona.

Scottish. Born in Aberdeen, 7 September 1959. Educated at Mackie Academy, Stonehaven; Edinburgh University, 1976–80, M.A. in history (honours). Married Edward Draper in 1981; one son. Writer-in-residence, Paines Plough Theatre Company, London, 1985–86. Recipient: McClaren award for radio, 1986; Susan Smith Blackburn prize, 1991; *Evening Standard* award, 1991; London Theatre Critics Circle prize, 1992; *Plays and Players* award, 1992. Agent: Casarotto Ramsay Ltd., National House, 60–66 Wardour Street, London W1V 3HP, England.

Publications

PLAYS

The Salesman (produced 1982).
The Bang and the Whimper (produced 1982).
Fugue (produced 1983). 1983.
Touchwood (for children; produced 1984).
The Bus (for children; produced 1984).
Ghost Story (for children; produced 1985).
Piper's Cave. In *Plays by Women: Five*, edited by Michelene Wandor and Mary Remnant, 1985.
The Biggest Party in the World (produced 1986).
Dust and Dreams (produced 1986).

The Way to Go Home (produced 1987).
Winners (produced 1987).
Off the Road (produced 1988).
Saturday at the Commodore (produced 1989). In*Scot Free*, edited by Alasdair
    Cameron, 1990.
Bold Girls (produced 1990). In *First Run 3*, edited by Matthew Lloyd, 1991.
Your Turn to Clean the Stair (produced 1992).

RADIO PLAYS: *Kilbreck* series, 1983–84; *Watching Waiters*, 1986; *Dirt under the Carpet*, 1987; *Citizens* series, 1988; *Elsie*, 1990; *Elvis*, 1990; *Eleven*, 1990; *Three Way Split*, 1992.

TELEVISION PLAYS: *Hardware*, 1984; *Biting the Hands*, 1989; 3 episodes in *Dr. Who* series, 1989; *Say It with Flowers* in *Casualty* series, 1990.

Rona Munro comments:

I am a Scottish playwright, a woman playwright, and an Aberdonian playwright, not necessarily in that order. All of these facts inform my writing but don't define it. Up till now a lot of my writing has concerned itself with issues around gender and sexual politics and as yet there's no sign of that preoccupation wearing off. I'm concerned to address these issues from a broad, human perspective, and as far as possible to write entertainingly and honestly, reflecting women's and men's lives as I perceive them rather than as I would choose them to be. I'm concerned to assert my place as part of a living tradition, a distinctive Scottish culture, and to explore the possibilities of writing in Scots as well as in English. I am also apparently incapable of writing anything without slipping a few gags in and will probably always choose to write drama that is liberally laced with comedy.

Rona Munro is one of Scotland's most innovative young playwrights. Her use of language and particularly of Aberdonian dialect in some of her work, and her creative weaving of Celtic myth into her contemporary scenarios, both serve to enrich her theatre writing immensely. Her own experiences as a student, cleaner, and experienced traveller have also influenced her work, lending it a voice which is at once true to her working-class origins and informed by world affairs and global issues.

An early play, *Fugue*, was commissioned in 1982 and staged at the Traverse Theatre, Edinburgh in 1983. Another early work, *Ghost Story*, was staged at the Tron Theatre, Glasgow, in 1985. She has also written for television and radio, but her theatre work is her true forte, and has been influenced by her work with (and has been influential upon the work of) both Paines Plough Theatre Company and her own women's comedy duo, the Msfits, founded with colleague Fiona Knowles. But her best-known plays—and deservedly so—are *Piper's Cave* and *Saturday at the Commodore*.

Piper's Cave is a curiously surreal play, a two-hander between a young woman (Jo) and a mysterious man who appears to be older than his 30-odd years (Alisdair). A third "character" of sorts is the unseen spirit of the landscape. Munro gives this spirit a "local habitation and a name," as well as a good number of lines in the script: the landscape is called "Helen." Helen is present from the opening of the play, but she comes into her own about half-way through, when she speaks as frequently as do the two "real" characters. Whether or not she is speaking, however, Helen's presence is crucial through-out, for this is a play about the power of the environment, and one which challenges ingrained essentialist notions about "Mother Nature." At the same time, it addresses the issues of gender and power, sex and violence.

Piper's Cave, as Rona Munro reveals in the published afterword to the play, "actually exists," though she exercised some creative licence in terms of its location. Similarly, the issues which Munro deals with in the play are quite real. Yet the play experiments with reality and myth by combining them, drawing on one to enrich the other. The play introduces young Jo as a modern woman, and Alisdair as a version of the legendary "piper who walked into the hill and never came out." Helen is the natural world, and she has a mighty wit. But Jo and Alisdair also have their "other-worldly" sides: Alisdair is, or thinks he is, the legendary piper; Jo becomes, or thinks she becomes, the Selky, the seal woman of Celtic myth. At the play's end, we hear splashing: the sound of waves which could be made by Jo, or by Helen, or which might be the sound of curtains closing on a thought-provoking play.

While in *Piper's Cave* only Alisdair spoke regularly in dialect, all of *Saturday at the Commodore* is written to be performed in a strong Aberdonian. The play is quite short (only five pages in the published version); a one-woman monologue of sorts, commissioned by 7:84 Scotland as part of a series of short pieces by "Voices of Today's Scotland." The use of dialect is crucial, due to the setting of both the play and its performances (it was first performed at the Isle of Skye in 1989).

Lena is the 30-year-old central character, or narrator, who relates the story of *Saturday at the Commodore*, a story of one woman's memories of child-hood and adolescence in Scotland. The play is a story, a narrative which somehow conjures up vivid images of other places and people, most notably Nora, Lena's "best mate" and the girl she fancied as well. The development into womanhood, from being a student to being a teacher, through one heterosexual relationship to a life of independence—all this is told in a narrative which is relaxed, wry, witty, and immensely engaging. The dialect makes it Lena's story, and a uniquely Scottish story. Yet Munro's ability to create likeable characters and familiar, evocative situations makes it a larger story as well, one worth staging and re-staging to see what different communi-ties and different audiences may make of it.

—Lizbeth Goodman

MURDOCH, (Jean) Iris.

British. Born in Dublin, Ireland, 15 July 1919. Educated at the Froebel Education Institute, London; Badminton School, Bristol; Somerville College, Oxford, 1938–42, B.A. (first class honours) 1942; Newnham College, Cambridge (Sarah Smithson student in philosophy), 1947–48. Married the writer John Bayley in 1956. Assistant principal in the Treasury, London, 1942–44; administrative officer with the United Nations Relief and

Rehabilitation Administration (UNRRA) in London, Belgium, and Austria, 1944–46; fellow, St. Anne's College, Oxford, and university decturer in philosophy, Oxford university, 1948–63; honorary fellow of St. Anne's College from 1963; lecturer, Royal College of Art, London, 1963–67. Recipient: James Tait Black Memorial prize, 1974; Whitbread award, 1974; Booker prize, 1978; Shakespeare prize (Hamburg), 1988; National Arts Club (U.S.A.) medal of honor, 1990. D. Litt.: Oxford University, 1987. Member, Irish Academy, 1970; honorary member, American Academy, 1975, and American Academy of Arts and Sciences, 1982; honorary fellow, Somerville College, 1977, and Newnham College, 1986. Companion of literature, Royal Society of Literature, 1987. C.B.E. (Commander, Order of the British Empire), 1976; D.B.E. (Dame Commander, Order of the British Empire), 1987. Lives in Oxford. Agent: Ed Victor Ltd., 162 Wardour Street, London W1V 4AT, England.

Publications

PLAYS

A Severed Head, with J.B. Priestley, adaptation of the novel by Murdoch (produced 1963). 1964.
The Italian Girl, with James Saunders, adaptation of the novel by Murdoch (produced 1967). 1969.
The Servants and the Snow (produced 1970). With *The Three Arrows*, 1973.
The Three Arrows (produced 1972). With *The Servants and the Snow*, 1973.
Art and Eros (produced 1980). In *Acastos*, 1986.
The Servants (opera libretto), adaptation of her play *The Servants and the Snow*, music by William Mathias (produced 1980).
Acastos: Two Platonic Dialogues (includes *Art and Eros* and *Above the Gods*). 1986.
The Black Prince, adaptation of her own novel (produced 1989). In *Three Plays*, 1989.
Three Plays (includes *The Servants and the Snow*, *The Three Arrows*, *The Black Prince*). 1989.

RADIO PLAY: *The One Alone* (in verse), music by Gary Carpenter, 1987.

NOVELS

Under the Net. 1954.
The Flight from the Enchanter. 1956.
The Sandcastle. 1957.
The Bell. 1958.
A Severed Head. 1961.
An Unofficial Rose. 1962.
The Unicorn. 1963.
The Italian Girl. 1964.
The Red and the Green. 1965.
The Time of the Angels. 1966.
The Nice and the Good. 1968.
Bruno's Dream. 1969.
A Fairly Honourable Defeat. 1970.

An Accidental Man. 1972.
The Black Prince. 1973.
The Sacred and Profane Love Machine. 1974.
A Word Child. 1975.
Henry and Cato. 1976.
The Sea, The Sea. 1978.
Nuns and Soldiers. 1980.
The Philosopher's Pupil. 1983.
The Good Apprentice. 1985.
The Book and the Brotherhood. 1987.
The Message to the Planet. 1989.
The Green Knight. 1993.

VERSE

A Year of Birds. 1978.

OTHER

Sartre, Romantic Rationalist. 1953; as *Sartre, Romantic Realist,* 1980.
The Sovereignty of Good over Other Concepts (lecture). 1967.
The Sovereignty of Good (essays). 1970.
The Fire and the Sun: Why Plato Banished the Artists. 1977.
Reynolds Stone (address). 1981.
The Existential Political Myth. 1989.
Metaphysics as a Guide to Morals. 1992.

BIBLIOGRAPHY: *Iris Murdoch and Muriel Spark: A Bibliography* by Thomas T. Tominaga and Wilma Schneidermeyer, 1976; *Iris Murdoch: A Reference Guide* by Kate Begnal, 1987.

MANUSCRIPT COLLECTION: University of Iowa, Iowa City.

CRITICAL STUDIES: *Iris Murdoch* by Rubin Rabinovitz, 1968, *Iris Murdoch* by Frank Baldanza, 1974; *Iris Murdoch* by Donna Gerstenberger, 1974; *Iris Murdoch: The Shakespearian Interest,* 1979, and *Iris Murdoch,* 1984, both by Richard Todd, and *Encounters with Iris Murdoch* edited by Todd, 1988; *Iris Murdoch: Work for the Spirit* by Elizabeth Dipple, 1981; *Iris Murdoch's Comic Vision* by Angela Hague, 1984; *Iris Murdoch: The Saint and the Artist* by Peter J. Conradi, 1986; *Iris Murdoch* edited by Harold Bloom, 1986; *A Character Index and Guide to the Fiction of Iris Murdoch* by Cheryl K. Bove, 1986; *Iris Murdoch* by Deborah Johnson, 1987; *Iris Murdoch: Figures of Good* by Suguna Ramanathan, 1990.

Iris Murdoch has published one volume of plays, *Three Plays,* which includes *The Servants and the Snow, The Three Arrows,* and her adaptation of her novel *The Black Prince.* In addition, she has published *Acastos,* a volume containing two philosophical plays in the form of Platonic dialogues, *Art and Eros* and *Above the Gods.* The drama critic Harold Hobson praised Andrew Cruickshank's performance of *Art and Eros,* saying that he conducted "a Socratic enquiry with philosophic zeal and illuminating theatrical skill."

Above the Gods inquires into the differences between morality and religion. Murdoch wrote both her Platonic plays so that they could be performed either in modern dress or in period costume. In a period version of *Above the Gods*, she suggests casting the servant as a black man born of a Nubian mother. This choice on her part shows her willingness to unsettle a modern British audience, questioning religion, values, British ideas of empire, and slavery. Before Murdoch tried her own playwriting, she collaborated with J.B. Priestley in the stage adaptation of her novel *A Severed Head*, and with James Saunders on the adaptation of *The Italian Girl*. The experienced hands of her collaborators made these plays more actable than her own later ones—indeed, *A Severed Head* was a theatrical success. Her play *The Black Prince* is her first attempt to adapt one of her own novels into a play without the benefits of an experienced theatrical collaborator. It is a witty, fast-paced drama, about love, death and art that testifies to her sure hand as a master of the dramatic as well as the narrative mode.

The play version of *A Severed Head* diminishes the complexity and obscurity of Murdoch's novel while it preserves its zany, quick-paced, very British high comedy. Physical farce, unexpected entrances, surprise discoveries, and unanticipated twists of plot all contribute to the effect. In "Against Dryness," Murdoch described her own novel as one in which Sartre's "facile idea of sincerity" is tested against the "hard idea of truth." When Martin is confronted by his wife's affair with her analyst, he tries broadmindedly to take it in his stride. Unwilling to confess his own affair, and himself attracted to the American analyst, he suffers passively as his wife flaunts her infatuation and asks his approval of her plan to move into her lover's home. It takes Honor Klein, the half-sister of the analyst and a Cambridge anthropologist, to function as the "dark god" of this play. Manipulating all the other characters, she forces Martin to submit to irrational and primitive forces, to understand the "hard idea of truth," and to give himself over to his love for her, however temporary and however imperfectly understood. The play rivals Restoration comedy in the variety of its sexual pairings. Martin passes through the stages of the outraged husband, latently homosexual lover to his wife's lover, complacent cuckold, violent lover, and lover surrendering to a higher, more mysterious, primitive love. Variations of incest are explored in the relationship between Honor and her half-brother and Antonia and her brother-in-law. In many ways *A Severed Head* is a modern *The Cocktail Party*. T. S. Eliot's one-eyed Reilly becomes Murdoch's Honor Klein. Both plays examine religious feeling and neurotic obsessions.

Murdoch's other plays, with the exception of *The Black Prince*, confirm that her gifts are as a novelist; nevertheless, they are also interesting in their own right. In her novels, Murdoch the storyteller and Murdoch the moral philosopher, struggling with ideas of freedom and contingency and accident and pattern, live fairly comfortably together. In her plays, the two fight each other and conspire to flatten her characters in ways that the novel can accommodate or avoid. She is often unable to find the dialogue that believably captures her hybrid characters—half-mythic, half-natural. She strikes the best balance in *The Black Prince* but she does so at the expense of her intellectual inquiry into the nature of art, love, and ethics.

The Servants and the Snow is a compact play which, like Strindberg's *Miss*

Julie, depends for its effect on the pressure that the environment and past exert on the characters. The snow madness imprisons the characters; it covers and holds the blood guilt of the past. Basil, a landowner who returns to the isolated country house of his father who has died six months earlier, finds himself accountable for his father's crimes. He feels unequal to the task of being master to his 200 or more servants. Too anxious to play benevolent master, and too scrupulously "sincere" in his efforts to examine his own situation and motives, he finds himself forced to atone for his father's affair with a servant girl, Marina, which led to the death of the girl's husband at the hand of her jealous master. To prevent the erosion of his own authority, Basil is persuaded to re-enact his father's crime—to deflower the servant girl on her nuptial night. Neither Marina nor Oriane can tolerate weak men. Like the girl in Sylvia Plath's poem "Daddy," they prefer the "boot in the face" administered by the brute Daddy/husband. Marina consents to the marriage because it will figuratively give her back her dead master and dead husband. Oriane loathes Basil's sentimentality and misguided sense of guilt and cannot abide the injury to her pride posed by Marina. In a jealous rage, Oriane kills her husband during Marina's wedding vows and welcomes the arrival of her brother, the General, who knows how to treat servants as swine and give commands. The play examines the nature of power and the relationship of past to present. It also examines moral character. The final action fulfills Murdoch's ideas about accident and free will, but it cannot wholly contain the ideas. The characters in the play are too reductive.

The Three Arrows depends heavily for its effect upon ritual action and theatricality. Some of its moments are brilliant. Set in medieval Japan, the play explores the choices available to Prince Yorimitsu, a political prisoner held captive by the Emperor and a pawn of the Shogun, the real ruler. Yorimitsu's avowed ambition is to be a leader of the forces of the North and seize the power of the Shogun. The play abounds with deceits and stratagems. Necessity conspires to defeat moral purpose and free will. Yorimitsu is forced to choose between the contemplative life, an honorable death, love, or his ambition for power. The choices he ultimately exercises are constrained: he acts without properly knowing the motives of those who act against him, or understanding the meaning of the choices put to him. At the end of the play he is free, the Shogun dead, the princess he loved dead, and the young Emperor the willing accomplice in his escape. Intellectually the play is fascinating, but its plot unfolds too slowly and the motives behind certain actions are incompletely conceptualized.

Murdoch's most recent play, presented at the Aldwych Theatre in 1989 to considerable critical acclaim, is adapted from one of her finest and most difficult novels, a novel more novelistic than any she has written. Offering her most protracted and penetrating examination of aesthetics and the relation of art to human behavior, *The Black Prince* is a highly self-reflexive and elaborately mediated novel. It tells the story of Bradley Pearson, a fussy, aging, recently retired taxman and blocked writer, and his ordeal with love and art. It is introduced by two forewords and concluded by five postscripts, four written by the principal dramatic characters: Christian, Pearson's ex-wife; Francis, his "unfrocked" physician brother-in-law; Rachel, the battered and vengeful wife of Pearson's literary rival, Arnold Baffin, and mother of Julian; and Julian, the

Baffin's 20-year-old daughter with whom the 58-year-old Pearson (53 in the play version) falls absolutely in love. The fifth postscript is written by Pearson's mysterious editor and cell-mate, Loxias, his alter ego and muse, the god Apollo in disguise, who finally compels Pearson to answer to Apollonian truth and goodness, replacing the dark creative god Eros with the higher god Apollo. Murdoch's play could hardly do justice to the intricacy of the novel's struggle with form and formlessness. She does, in her play version, combine the dramatic and narrative modes, allowing Pearson to step forward and address the audience directly, with veiled references to his final transformation. She also concludes the play with an epilogue where four characters offer their highly eschewed and self-serving interpretations of the play's central action, the murder of Baffin. Notably missing from the play is any reference to Loxias, the editor and Apollo figure. No doubt Murdoch's instincts were right in this regard. The novelistic techniques and the ambiguous, often tortuous structure, could not but damage the play. She does treat the theme of *The Black Prince* in her play version, developing the relationship between Julian, decked out in her Hamlet costume, and Hamlet, and also enabling the audience to understand the relationship of Bradley Pearson's struggle to write with Shakespeare's. However, without a familiarity with the novel these references in the play may not adequately convey the theme. What does succeed, and very well, is her highly comic and ironic treatment of the three interwoven crises: Pearson's struggles with his sister's failed marriage and suicide; his rivalry with Baffin, over both women and art; and his immersion in his love for Julian which leads to the play's denouement, Rachel's murder of Baffin for which Pearson is tried and convicted.

Murdoch's wit and irony and gift for character, her fondness for patterning and artifice, serve her well when she adapts her novels for the stage.

—Carol Simpson Stern

N

NORMAN, Marsha (née Williams).

American. Born in Louisville, Kentucky, 21 September 1947. Educated at Durrett High School, Louisville; Agnes Scott College, Decatur, Georgia, B.A. in philosophy 1969; University of Louisville, 1969–71, M.A. 1971. Married 1) Michael Norman in 1969 (divorced 1974); 2) Dann C. Byck, Jr., in 1978 (divorced 1986); 3) Tim Dykma in 1987. Worked with disturbed children at Kentucky Central State Hospital, 1969–71; teacher, Brown School, Louisville, from 1973; book reviewer and editor of children's supplement (*Jelly Bean Journal*), Louisville *Times*, mid-1970's; playwright-in-residence, Actors Theatre, Louisville, 1977–78, and Mark Taper Forum, Los Angeles, 1979; since 1988 treasurer, the Dramatists Guild. Recipient: American Theater Critics Association prize, 1978; National Endowment for the Arts grant, 1978; Rockefeller grant, 1979; John Gassner award, 1979; Oppenheimer award, 1979; Susan Smith Blackburn prize, 1983; Pulitzer prize, 1983; American Academy award, 1986; Tony award, 1991. Lives in Long Island, New York. Agent: Jack Tantleff, The Tantleff Agency, 375 Greenwich Street, New York, New York 10013, U.S.A.

Publications

PLAYS

Getting Out (produced 1977). 1980.
Third and Oak: The Laundromat (produced 1978). 1980.
Third and Oak: The Pool Hall (produced 1978). 1985.
Circus Valentine (produced 1979).
Merry Christmas, in *Holidays* (produced 1979).
'Night, Mother (produced 1982). 1984.
The Holdup (produced 1983). 1987.
Traveler in the Dark (produced 1984; revised version produced 1985).
Four Plays (includes *Getting Out, Third and Oak, The Holdup, Traveler in the Dark*). 1988.
Sarah and Abraham (produced 1988).
The Secret Garden, music by Lucy Simon, adaptation of the novel by Frances Hodgson Burnett (produced 1990).
D. Boone (produced 1992).
The Red Shoes, from the 1948 movie, music by Jule Styne, lyrics by Marsha Norman and Paul Stryker (produced 1993).

TELEVISION PLAYS: *It's the Willingness* (*Visions* series), 1978; *In Trouble at Fifteen* (*Skag* series), 1980.

NOVEL
The Fortune Teller. 1987.

BIBLIOGRAPHY: *American Playwrights since 1945: A Guide to Scholarship, Criticism, and Performance* by Philip C. Kolin, 1989.

CRITICAL STUDIES: *American Voices: Five Contemporary Playwrights in Essays and Interviews* by Esther Harriott, 1988; "'I thought You Were Mine': Marsha Norman's *'Night, Mother*" by Sally Browder in *Mother Puzzles: Daughters and Mothers in Contemporary American Literature*, edited by Mickey Pearlman, 1989; 'Marsha Norman's She-Tragedies' by Jenny S. Spencer in *Making a Spectacle: Feminist Essays on Contemporary Women's Theatre*, edited by Lynda Hart, 1989; *Taking Center Stage: Feminism in Contemporary US Drama*, 1991.

THEATRICAL ACTIVITIES
DIRECTOR: **Play** — *Semi-Precious Things* by Terri Wagener, 1980.

When *Performing Arts Journal* printed a symposium on "The 'Woman' Playwright Issue" in 1983, the opening contributor began with a broadside on Marsha Norman, then a recent recipient of a Pulitzer prize: "For all intents and purposes, *'Night, Mother* was written in 1949 by Arthur Miller. . . . By canonizing these works, effectively suppressing alternative visions, we are . . . crippling an art form . . .". The critic, Colette Brooks, went on to invoke the spirit of Hrotsvitha, who would be "appalled at our current state of confusion".

If Norman has not exactly been ostracised by feminist scholarship, she has certainly been neglected in many analyses of women playwrights, left to fend for herself in the male theatre world where she has, accidentally, found success. Ironically, it is only in *Traveler in the Dark*, her major work since *'Night, Mother*, that she begins to converge on the tradition of patriarchal saga that has been staked out as the territory of Miller and O'Neill. Even this play, though, is anything but masculinist in its study of the transmission of values, such as gentleness and spirituality, through three generations between polarities of individuality.

The social consciousness that permeates most of Norman's work from *Getting Out* to *The Holdup* is a reflection of her early career, but is not contained by gender boundaries. Certainly, the victim-protagonist of the first play can only be female, and the suffering she endures in her first 24 hours of parole (essentially the play's whole action) places her as the target of male power and exploitation. Arlene's landlord, pimp, father, and prison guard all appear as real or memory figures to construct a pattern of entrapment that is just as strong outside the prison as within, leaving her the product of conditioning forces that almost defy resistance. That Arlene has some capacity to survive such pressures, in a way that Willy Loman in Miller's *Death of a Salesman* cannot, shows Norman's assertion of the power of female individuality. The play's weakness lies not in any traditional value-structure but in its dramaturgy, which pivots on the theatrical cliché of representing the protagonist by two actors, showing two facets of identity. Though this appears as a clumsy device, not uncommon in a first play, it does establish Norman's interest in psychological dissection on stage, which she would perfect in 'Night, Mother.

Not all of Arlene's oppressors, however, are males, and the most keenly-felt rejection is by her mother, who some would see as perpetrating patriarchal domesticity. Similarly, Thelma, the mother of Jessie in 'Night, Mother, is sustaining a structure of dependence, but this play is remarkable in that the concluding behaviour (Jessie's suicide) is in no way predicated on the information flow between mother and daughter that has occupied most of the play: the play is structured in defiance of Aristotle as much as of Arthur Miller, and its crisis is totally devoid of any hint of *anagnorisis* in Jessie. Also, whereas for Sophocles, Ibsen, Pinero, or Miller, suicide is a simplifying gesture, freeing society of someone who has violated fundamental taboos, the central action of 'Night, Mother is placid, organising, and structured, but the suicide is an action raising problems, suddenly making the mother's world very complex indeed; this is much more than a mere dilemma, and is more intense in production than the end of *Ghosts* because there is no simple choice left.

For Jessie, self-knowledge is a state rather than an event. In the last year she has "gained control of her mind and body", and this includes her physical debility (epilepsy), the fragmented relationships that surround her, and her attitude to her parents. Though Norman does not causally relate it to the suicide, Jessie has an acute curiosity about what she looks like during her fits, to see herself as "other", just as she sees her own baby photographs as representing "somebody else, not me"; here, the playwright addresses the problem of treating alterity in drama which she dealt with clumsily in *Getting Out*.

As with Hedda Gabler, it is important to Jessie that she kills herself with her father's gun, and especially in this respect the play invites a neo-Freudian reading: both women use their fathers' guns to annihilate themselves as women and as daughters at the point that they are stepping outside of the passivity that is their place in the symbolic. They have asked questions, they have disturbed the nature of things under patriarchy, and because patriarchy only offers women absence, it seems appropriate that it is a phallic symbol that blows Jessie away.

Not all would subscribe to such a reading, and perhaps least of all Hrotsvitha, the 10th-century religious writer invoked by Colette Brooks. But there is a fascinating similarity between Jessie's undeviating course towards death and the constancy of Hrotsvitha's female martyrs in the face of the highly inventive oppression of the pagan male emperors of her plays. Neither they nor Jessie seem to have any awareness of a theatre of "confusion".

—Howard McNaughton

See the essay on *'Night, Mother.*

O

O'MALLEY, Mary (Josephine).

British. Born in Bushey, Hertfordshire, 19 March 1941. Resident writer, Royal Court Theatre, London, 1977. Recipient: *Evening Standard* award, 1978; Susan Smith Blackburn prize, 1978; Plays and Players award; Pye award, for television play. Address: c/o Salmon Publishing, The Bridge Mills, Galway, Republic of Ireland.

Publications

PLAYS

Superscum (produced 1972).
A 'nevolent Society (produced 1974).
Oh If Ever a Man Suffered (produced 1975).
Once a Catholic (produced 1977). 1978.
Look Out . . . Here Comes Trouble (produced 1978). 1979.
Talk of the Devil (produced 1986; revised version produced 1986).

TELEVISION PLAYS: *Percy and Kenneth*, 1976; *Oy Vay Maria*, 1977; *Shall I See You Now?*, 1978; *On the Shelf*, 1984.

OTHER

A Consideration of Silk. 1990.

Mary O'Malley came into the public eye with her mischievous play *Once a Catholic*, which premiered at the Royal Court Theatre in 1977, and then transferred to the West End. The play won awards from the London *Evening Standard* and *Plays and Players*. The play is a warm but sharply retrospective look at a Catholic girls' convent in the 1950's, with the youth rebellion of that decade given added edge by the repressiveness of the nuns. All the girls are called "Mary," and the play is a witty and perceptive extended sit-com, which is such good fun that it would undoubtedly offend no-one. In its way it even was able to test the taboos of the commercial theatre, in a scene where one of the shocked nuns discovers a packet of Tampax hidden in the lavatory, and a final act of sacrilege when one of the girls affixes a plasticine penis to a statue of Christ in the school chapel—for which Mary the scape-goat (the only one who genuinely wants to become a nun) is blamed.

There is a satirical edge to O'Malley's writing which derives from a sensitivity to the very ordinary pains and ironies of daily life—and also to the iconography of domestic experience, which is so important to people. This latter was the main feature of her play *Look Out . . . Here Comes Trouble*, staged by the Royal Shakespeare Company at the Warehouse in London in 1978. The play was set in a psychiatric ward, but floundered in the material detail, and although the comic pain was a feature in the lives of the characters, it never became part of the structural fabric of the play. Somehow O'Malley appears to be caught between the potentialities of a more ruthless satirical approach and a familiar, lightly comic sit-com approach.

—Michelene Wandor

OWENS, Rochelle.

Pseudonym for Rochelle Bass. American. Born in Brooklyn, New York, 2 April 1936. Educated at Lafayette High School, Brooklyn, graduated 1953. Married George Economou in 1962. Worked as a clerk, typist, telephone operator. Founding member, New York Theatre Strategy. Visiting lecturer, University of California, San Diego, 1982; adjunct professor, and host of radio program *The Writer's Mind*, University of Oklahoma, Norman, 1984; distinguished writer-in-residence, Brown University, Providence, Rhode Island. Recipient: Rockefeller grant, 1965, 1975; Ford grant, 1965; Creative Artists Public Service grant, 1966, 1973; Yale University School of Drama fellowship, 1968; Obie award, 1968, 1971, 1982; Guggenheim fellowship, 1971; National Endowment for the Arts grant, 1974; Villager award, 1982; New York Drama Critics Circle award, 1983. Agent: Dramatists Guild, 234 West 44th Street, New York, New York 10036. Address: 1401 Magnolia, Norman, Oklahoma 73072, U.S.A.

Publications

PLAYS

Futz (produced 1965). 1961; revised version in *Futz and What Came After*, 1968, in *New Short Plays 2*, 1969.

The String Game (produced 1965). In *Futz and What Came After*, 1968.

Istanboul (produced 1965). In *Futz and What Came After*, 1968.

Homo (produced 1966). In *Futz and What Came After*, 1968.

Beclch (produced 1968). In *Futz and What Came After*, 1968.

Futz and What Came After. 1968.

The Karl Marx Play, music by Galt MacDermot, lyrics by Owens (produced 1973). In *The Karl Marx Play and Others*, 1974.

The Karl Marx Play and Others (includes *Kontraption, He Wants Shih!, Farmer's Almanac, Coconut Folksinger, O.K. Certaldo*). 1974.

He Wants Shih! (produced 1975). In *The Karl Marx Play and Others*, 1974.

Coconut Folksinger (broadcast 1976). In *The Karl Marx Play and Others*, 1974.

Kontraption (produced 1978). In *The Karl Marx Play and Others*, 1974.

Emma Instigated Me, in *Performing Arts Journal 1*, Spring 1976.

The Widow, and The Colonel, in *The Best Short Plays 1977,* edited by Stanley
   Richards. 1977.
Mountain Rites, in *The Best Short Plays 1978,* edited by Stanley Richards.
   1978.
Chucky's Hunch (produced 1981). In *Wordplays 2,* Performing Arts Journal
   Publications, 1982.
Who Do You Want, Peire Vidal? (produced 1982). With *Futz,* 1986.

SCREENPLAY: *Futz* (additional dialogue), 1969.

RADIO PLAYS: *Coconut Folksinger,* 1976 (Germany); *Sweet Potatoes,* 1977.

TELEVISION PLAY (VIDEO): *Oklahoma Too: Rabbits and Nuggets,* 1987.

SHORT STORIES
The Girl on the Garage Wall. 1962.
The Obscenities of Reva Cigarnik. 1963.

VERSE
Not Be Essence That Cannot Be. 1961.
Four Young Lady Poets, with others, edited by LeRoi Jones. 1962.
Salt and Core. 1968.
I Am the Babe of Joseph Stalin's Daughter. 1972.
Poems from Joe's Garage. 1973.
The Joe 82 Creation Poems. 1974.
The Joe Chronicles 2. 1979.
Shemuel. 1979.
French Light. 1984.
Constructs. 1985.
Anthropologists at a Dinner Party. 1985.
W. C. Fields in French Light. 1986.
How Much Paint Does the Painting Need? 1988.
Paysanne: New and Selected Poems 1961–1988. 1990.

RECORDINGS: *A Reading of Primitive and Archaic Poetry,* with others,
Broadside; *From a Shaman's Notebook,* with others, Broadside; *The Karl
Marx Play,* Kilmarnock, 1975; *Totally Corrupt,* Giorno, 1976; *Black Box 17,*
Watershed Foundation, 1979.

OTHER
Editor, *Spontaneous Combustion: Eight New American Plays.* 1972.

MANUSCRIPT COLLECTIONS: Mugar Memorial Library, Boston University;
University of California, Davis; University of Oklahoma, Norman; Lincoln
Center Library of the Performing Arts, New York; Smith College,
Northampton, Massachusetts.

CRITICAL STUDIES: *American Playwrights: A Critical Survey* by Bonnie
Marranca and Gautam Dasgupta, 1981; *Women in American Theatre* edited
by Helen Krich Chinoy and Linda Walsh Jenkins, 1981; *American Women*

Writers by Linda Mainiero, 1981; article by Owens in *Contemporary Authors Autobiography Series* 2 edited by Adele Sarkissian, 1985; Len Berkman, in *Parnassus*, 1985.

THEATRICAL ACTIVITIES

DIRECTOR AND ACTOR: **Television**—*Oklahoma Too: Rabbits and Nuggets*, 1987.

Rochelle Owens comments:

I am interested in the flow of imagination between the actors and the director, the boundless possibilities of interpretation of a script. Different theatrical realities are created and/or destroyed depending upon the multitudinous perceptions and points of view of the actors and director who share in the creation of the design of the unique journey of playing the play. There are as many ways to approach my plays as there as combinations of people who might involve themselves.

The inter-media video *Oklahoma Too* uses poetry and images juxtaposed. The structures both linguistic and visual offer exciting projections of my continuous investigation of making art.

Rochelle Owens came to the attention of the theatre public with her first play, *Futz*, whose shocking subject and inventive language launched her theatrical career. Owens's plays are distinguished by intense poetic imagery that springs from primordial human impulses of the subconscious and by the passionate and often violent struggle of her characters to survive within their repressive societies. Although a moralist who satirizes human frailty with parody, dialect, and the comic grotesque, Owens is also a compassionate observer who imbues her characters with tragic dimensions.

Futz is preceded by a quotation from Corinthians: "Now concerning the things whereof ye wrote to me: It is good for a man not to touch a woman." Cyrus Futz loves his pig, Amanda, and is persecuted by the community. Majorie Satz lusts for all men and wheedles an invitation to share Futz's sexual pleasure with his pig. Oscar Loop is driven to madness and murders Ann Fox when they inadvertently witness the Futz-Amanda-Majorie orgy. Majorie kills Amanda for revenge. Oscar is condemned to hang and Futz is sent to prison where he is stabbed by Majorie's brother. Puritanical society punishes innocent sensuality.

The String Game also explores the conflict between puritanism and natural impulse. Greenland Eskimos play the string game to ward off winter boredom. They are admonished for creating erotic images by their Italian priest, Father Bontempo; yet he longs for his own string game: warm spaghetti. Half-breed Cecil tempts Bontempo with a promise of pasta in exchange for the support of Cecil's commercial schemes. While gluttonously feasting, the priest chokes to death. The saddened Eskimos refuse to comply with Cecil's business venture and stoically return to their string games.

Istanboul dramatizes a cultural clash and *Homo* a class struggle. In *Istanboul* Norman men are fascinated by hirsute Byzantine women, and their wives by the smooth-skinned Byzantine men. In a religious frenzy St. Mary of Egypt murders the barbaric Norman, Godfrigh, and sensual Leo makes love to Godfrigh's wife as they wait for the Saracens to attack. *Homo* presents the mutual greed and contempt of Nordic and Asiatic. A surrealistic exploration of racial and class conflict the dramatic energy of the play in which revolution comes and goes, and workers continue their brutality.

Human perversion and bloody primitive rites prevail in Owens's most savage play, *Beclch*. In a fantasy Africa, four white adventurers intrude upon the natural innocence of a village. Queen Beclch, a monster of excess, professes her love for young Jose, then introduces him to the cruelty of cock-fighting. She promises Yago Kingship, if he will contract elephantiasis. When Yago cannot transcend the pain of his deformity, he is forced mercilessly by the villagers to strangle himself. Beclch moves further into excess, and Jose flees in disgust. Since a queen cannot rule without a male consort, Beclch prepares herself for death as voluptuously as she lived.

A promise of social progress resides in Owens's first play with music, *The Karl Marx Play*. As in *Homo*, linear time is ignored and through a montage of scenes, past and present, a human portrait of Marx emerges in this, Owens's most joyful play. Her Marx is drained by illness, poverty, and lust for his aristocratic wife. All those who surround him demand that he complete *Das Kapital*, particularly his friend Engels and a 20th-century American black, Leadbelly. Though Marx denies his Jewish heritage, he invokes Yahweh for consolation, but it is finally Leadbelly who actively ignites the man of destiny to fulfill his mission.

He Wants Shih! is an elegant poetic tragedy. Lan, son of the last Empress of the Manchu dynasty, abdicates the warlike legacy of his mother, ignores the adoring Princess Ling, loves his stepbrother Bok, and is enthralled with his stern mentor Feng. Steeped in Eastern philosophy and the supernatural, this surrealistic archetypal myth of individuation is dramatized with ritual, masks, and pseudo-Chinese dialect. The dismembered head of the Empress continues to speak on stage while Western imperialists decimate the Chinese. Acknowledging his homosexuality in the final scene, Lan-he transforms into Lanshe. Total renunciation of sex and empire ends this fantastic play.

As *He Wants Shih!* explores the quest for selfhood, *Kontraption* examines dehumanization in a technological world. On an empty terrain Abdul and Hortten share their lives and sexual fantasies. Abdul's intolerance of their repulsive laundryman, Strauss, drives him to murder, and he is in turn transformed by a magician into a mechanical contraption. When Abdul attempts to transcend his own grotesque condition he falls to his death, leaving behind a disconsolate Hortten.

Owens returns to historical biography in *Emma Instigated Me*. The life of Emma Goldman, the 19th-century anarchist, is juxtaposed against a contemporary Author, Director, and female revolutionaries. Once again linear time is dissolved. The characters change from one to another, from character into actor into bystander. The theatricality of the play becomes its most important objective.

Owens continues to experiment. *Chucky's Hunch* was acclaimed by New York critics as hilarious and impelling. In contrast to her multi-character dramas, the solitary Chucky, a middle-aged failure, narrates a series of recriminating letters to one of his three ex-wives. Similarly in *Who Do You Want, Peire Vidal?*, two characters assume multiple roles. In this play-within-a-play a Japanese-American professor is among the transformational characters in a series of episodic confrontations. Owens's fantastic imagery, charged language, and daring confrontation with subconscious impulse remains unique in American theatre.

—Elaine Shragge

P

PAGE, Louise.

British. Born in London, 7 March 1955. Educated at High Storrs Comprehensive School, Sheffield; University of Birmingham, 1973–76, B.A. in drama and theatre arts 1976; University of Wales, Cardiff, 1976–77, postgraduate diploma in theatre studies 1977. Yorkshire Television fellow in creative writing, University of Sheffield, 1979–81; resident playwright, Royal Court Theatre, London, 1982–83; associate director, Theatre Calgary, Alberta, 1987. Recipient: George Devine award, 1982; J.T. Grein award, 1985. Agent: Phil Kelvin, Goodwin Associates, 12 Rabbit Row, London W8 4DX. Address: 6–J Oxford and Cambridge Mansions, Old Marylebone Road, London NW1 5EC, England.

Publications

PLAYS

Want-Ad (produced 1977; revised version produced 1979).
Glasshouse (produced 1977).
Tissue (produced 1978). In *Plays by Women 1*, edited by Michelene Wandor, 1982.
Lucy (produced 1979).
Hearing (produced 1979).
Flaws (produced 1980).
House Wives (produced 1981).
Salonika (produced 1982). 1983.
Falkland Sound/Voces de Malvinas (produced 1983).
Real Estate (produced 1984). 1985.
Golden Girls (produced 1984). 1985.
Beauty and the Beast (produced 1985). 1986.
Goat (produced 1986).
Diplomatic Wives (produced 1989). 1989.
Plays: One (includes *Tissue, Salonika, Real Estate, Golden Girls*). 1990.
Adam Was a Gardener (produced 1991).
Like to Live (produced 1992).
Hawks and Doves (produced 1992).

RADIO PLAYS: *Saturday, Late September*, 1978; *Agnus Dei*, 1980; *Armistice*, 1983.

TELEVISION PLAY: *Peanuts* (*Crown Court* series), 1982.

Although Louise Page's work may lack the strident militancy expected of modern women writers, her contribution lies in her singling out the experiences of women as keystones to an examination of social conditioning. These women are unexceptional, lacking in unique personality traits. Their right to be the centre of the drama stems from the situations they are in, unremarkable situations in themselves, but personal crises to the characters through whom we see the contradictions between our socially conditioned expectations and our private experience of life. By isolating these ordinary women and their mundane crises, Page explores and exposes the social preconceptions by which people define and judge, analysing the ways in which these assumptions limit our lives, complicate our decisions, and contradict our experiences.

Page adopts different theatrical styles to highlight this tension between socially conditioned expectations and private experience. In plays as different in form as *Tissue*, *Salonika*, and *Real Estate*, the most frequent single word is "expect," and the action of the plays is played out against a background of expectations, making the audience aware of the contradictions and distortions these ingrained preconceptions place upon individual behaviour. *Tissue*, for example, is not so much a play about breast cancer as a play in which the crisis of breast cancer serves as a focus for the examination of assumptions about female sexuality and value.

A straight narrative about a woman fighting breast cancer would, by definition, imply themes of personal heroism. The structure of *Tissue* changes the emphasis from personality and the fact of cancer to the associated ideas that make facing breast cancer more difficult for both victim and associates. Scenes from Sally's life, unconnected by time or space, irrelevant in themselves, are magnetized by Sally's cancer; their juxtaposition highlights the complex socially conditioned assumptions which create the feminine mystique. Their sequence has the logic of memory, setting each other off through association of word, image, or emotional logic and building an analysis of the obsessive connections between breasts and sexuality, sex and love, and the evaluation of women by physical appearance we absorb from childhood. Sally herself is barely a character at all. She displays no individual personality traits; her thoughts and reactions are not so much personal as situational, the responses of a woman who has breast cancer.

Breasts define womanhood. They are assumed to be the measure of attractiveness, synonymous with sexuality and prerequisites for love, happy partnership, and future. The mystique created round the female body is shown through the play to prevent realistic and healthy attitudes towards oneself and others. Sally's mother, who treated Sally's growing breasts as objects of magical impurity, is afraid to touch her own to test for cancer. Sally's boss tells of his wife who "wrecked her life trying to keep her body whole. I did not ask her to be beautiful but to be there." Although we would consciously reject the evaluation of a woman solely on the size of her breasts, the progress of the play illuminates the way these assumptions infiltrate our lives and inform our behaviour.

Through stylistic choices, Page depersonalizes the characters in order to accentuate their situations and responses. All the men and women, except

Sally, are meant to be played by the same actor and actress. Direct speeches to the audience and other theatrical devices like the content-related sequence of scenes and the quick-fire lists (the "possible causes" of cancer in Scene 28) serve to demystify by removing the personal elements and emphasizing the situational behaviour and its constriction through preconceptions. The construction of the play encourages audiences to go beyond their fear of cancer and recognize the social conditioning which exacerbates their fears but which, through unravelling and understanding, can be overcome. Cancer, terrifying as it is, becomes not the end of the road, but a pathway through distorted preconceptions of femininity and the examination of the taboos of both cancer and sexuality.

Sally's greatest fear when she finds she has cancer is not that she will die, but that she will cease to be attractive to men and thus be unable to love and be loved. Only at the end, when she has a new lover, and after she has confronted, with us, the moments of her life which make up the fearful, complex confusion between her appearance and her value as a woman does she take joy in the very fact of living.

Salonika, too, celebrates the indefatigable life force which defies physical limitation, while making us aware of our assumptions and their limiting effect on our lives. The play's dream-like quality not only stems from the World War I soldier's ghost rising from the sands; the situation itself flies in the face of expectation. The mother and daughter on holiday to visit the father's grave are 84 and 64 years old. The mother has a 74-year-old lover who has hitch-hiked to Greece to be with her. In a world where love is assumed to be the reserve of the young and beautiful, these very facts cause a sense of unreality and demand that we take note of our preconceptions.

Within the play, too, the characters are constantly evaluating the expectations they held in the light of experience:

Ben   — (the ghost) I didn't think you'd be a daughter.
Enid   — Didn't you?
Ben   — No. That's why I said to call a girl Enid. Because I thought you'd be a boy.
Leonard — You expect everything in you to shrivel. All the hate and the longing. The lust. You don't expect to have them any more. But there isn't much else so you have them all the more. I could kill now. If I had the strength. . . . That's not what you expect.

Life as we live it defies expectation. The young man on the beach suddenly dies, leaving the old to bury him.

This dichotomy between social preconceptions and personal experience is elaborated in a more realistic form in *Real Estate*. Here Gwen, a middle-aged woman, lives with Dick, her second husband, outside Didcot where she runs a small estate agency. Her daughter Jenny, a successful London buyer, returns for the first time since she ran away 20 years before. Jenny is pregnant and has come to claim the care and attention mothers are expected, automatically, to provide. Gwen, conventional as she appears, does not revert to type. Although she dreads losing contact with Jenny again, she resists her intrusion into her life.

We assume, without thinking, that the younger, modern woman would introduce a life-style free from preconceptions and conventions. But Jenny, the very image of the modern independent woman, demands conventional responses from others. The "modernness" she brings with her is calloused, self-centred, and totally material. She carelessly lets the dog out; she refuses to marry Eric, the child's father, while demanding his attention. When she insinuates herself into the business Gwen has founded on honesty, loyalty, and personal concern, Jenny's first act is to encourage a client to gazump.

Almost by definition, we expect a middle-aged, middle-class woman's life to be circumscribed by convention and socially approved roles, but, without proselytizing, Gwen and Dick have evolved a life-style that suits them both: "I can't ask you to stay for supper because I don't know if there's enough. Are you expecting to be asked to stay? Dick's province, not mine. He's the one who knows how long the mince has been in the freezer. How many sheets there are which haven't been turned edge to edge." Dick even embroiders tapestries! Indeed, the men in the play could not be more amenable. Eric, though divorced, appears sympathetic to his wife and is actively committed to the care of his daughter. Jenny considers this a liability; when her needs conflict with the child's, she demands priority although she refuses Eric her commitment. While Gwen has no desire to be a mother, again, nor a grandmother, Dick longs for a baby on whom to lavish loving care.

Gwen cannot share her life with Jenny. Their expectations and values are mutually exclusive. Without fuss, leaving to Dick the traditional role she once imagined for herself, Gwen takes the little acorn she planted at the play's start and plants it in the forest; like Jenny, it is well able to continue its growth on its own, though probably more willing. The placing of Gwen at the centre of the play challenges our assumptions. We are led to consider the limitations these preconceptions force upon individual lives and their lack of validity as bases for judgement and the evaluation of human behaviour. While retaining our sympathy, Gwen foils our expectations, setting them in relief so we might evaluate them.

Page structures her plays to call into question our assumptions about character, behaviour, and role and to stress that the roots of these automatic expectations and responses are in social conditioning rather than personality and psychology. Her choice of unexceptional women in unexceptional circumstances places emphasis on the way these preconceptions infiltrate the very fabric of our lives, laying bases for misunderstanding and regret and corrupting moments of crisis and decision.

—Elaine Turner

PARKS, Suzan-Lori.

American. Educated at Mount Holyoke College, South Hadley, Massachusetts, B.A. in English and German literature (Phi Beta Kappa) 1985; the Drama studio, London, 1986. Guest lecturer, Pratt Institute, New York, 1988, University of Michigan, Ann Arbor, 1990, and Yale University, New Haven, Connecticut, and New York University, both 1990 and 1991; playwriting professor, Eugene Lang College, New York, 1990; writer-in-residence,

New School for Social Research, New York, 1991–92. Recipient: Mary E. Woolley fellowship, 1989; Naomi Kitay fellowship, 1989; National Endowment for the Arts grant, 1990, and playwriting fellowship, 1990, 1991; New York Foundation for the Arts grant, 1990; Rockefeller Foundation grant, 1990; Obie award, 1990. Agent: Wiley Hausam, International Creative Management, 40 West 57th Street, New York, New York 10019, U.S.A.

Publications

PLAYS

The Sinner's Place (produced 1984).
Betting on the Dust Commander (produced 1987). 1990.
Imperceptible Mutabilities in the Third Kingdom (produced 1989).
Greeks (produced 1990).
The Death of the Last Black Man in the Whole World (produced 1990). In*Theatre*, Summer/Fall 1990.
The America Play (produced 1991).
Devotees in the Garden of Love (produced 1991).

SCREENPLAY: *Anemone Me*, 1990.

RADIO PLAYS: *Pickling*, 1990; *The Third Kingdom*, 1990; *Locomotive*, 1991.

VIDEO: *Poetry Spots*, 1989; *Alive from Off Center*, 1991.

A playwright with the linguistic sensibilities of a Gertrude Stein or James Joyce, who recognizes that "the world is in the word" and attempts to stage that world following the example of Samuel Beckett; who eschews stage directions, citing the model of Shakespeare: "If you're writing the play—why not put the directions in the writing"; and who draws on her own experiences as an African-American woman living in a white, male culture but who denies that her works are only about being black: "I don't want to be categorized in any way." This is Suzan-Lori Parks.

Parks sees her main task as writer to "Make words from world but set them on the page—setting them loose on the world." Others may employ neologisms, lexical transformations, phonetic shifts, spelling variations, and repetitions to further the plot and point to the theme. In Parks's plays language is the theme, and the omission of even a letter can change the direction of a play or the life of a people. "Before Columbus thuh worl usta be *roun* they put uh /d/ on thuh end of roun makin roun. Thusly they set in motion thuh end. Without that /d/ we coulda gone on spinnin for ever. Thuh /d/ think ended things ended" says Queen-then-Pharaoh Hatshepsut in *The Death of the Last Black Man in the Whole Entire World*. Fixed in place by an imposed language that defines them but is not their own, Parks's people—just as Joyce's and Beckett's—seek to get out from under the weight of words. "Talk right or you're outa here," Molly is told by her boss in *Imperceptible Mutabilities in the Third Kingdom*. A phoneme, the /sk/ in ask, defeats her as she struggles against a language—and a world—in which "Everything in its place."

Parks's first produced play is a tetraptych, whose title she carefully defines:

Imperceptible: "That which by its nature cannot be perceived or discerned by the mind or the senses"; *Mutabilities*: "things disposed to change"; *in the Third Kingdom*: ". . . that of fungi. Small, overlooked, out of sight, of lesser consequence. All of that. And also: the space between." The four playlets— *Snails, Third Kingdom, Open House, Third Kingdom (reprise)*, and *Greeks*— offer a composite picture of African-American experience, starting with contemporary time, moving backward to a mythic retelling of the black forced journey from Africa and concluding with two "family plays" depicting the terrible results of such displacement and estrangement from both language and self.

The absence of traditional narrative is counteracted by formal structures: all have five characters whose names either rhyme or are the same; *Snails* is divided into six sections; *Open House* and *Greeks* into seven. Each makes use of slides and photographs offering an intertextual archival history. In each the angle of vision is, to invoke Beckett, "trine: centripetal, centrifugal and . . . not": the characters seen by white society, see themselves thus reflected but still struggle to see beyond the stereotype, the "not."

Snails describes three roommates, each wounded by words and each carrying two names: the one she chooses and the one by which she is known in the white community, names that "whuduhnt ours." They are visited by a robber who "didn't have no answer cause he didn't have no speech" and his opposite, a loquacious Naturalist named Lutsky, spouting the latest anthropological terminology, who comes to study the habits of the women, disguised as cockroach, the contemporary version of the fly on the wall, and who also doubles as the "exterminator" called to rid the women of the pest. Of the two it is Lutsky, Parks suggests, who is the true thief: he steals their voice by fixing them with his words the better to classify and study them.

Third Kingdom offers a melodic, mythic retelling of the black voyage from Africa to America, chanted by characters whose names range from Kin-Seer, Us-Seer, Shark-Seer, Soul-seer, to Over-seer. A refrain opens the section and punctuates the piece and the reprise: "Last night I dreamed of where I comed from. But where I comed from diduhnt look like nowhere like I been." The speakers evoke images of a lost home, of a voyage, and of the boat that carried them. While Shark-Seer denies their collective experience, "But we are not in uh boat!" Us-Seer insists, "But we iz."

Open House is a composite black/white family portrait in which Aretha Saxon, a black servant/surrogate mother to a white girl and boy is being "let go because she's gone slack." But before she leaves/expires she is subjected to "an extraction" in which her teeth are tortuously yanked from her mouth by the efficient Miss Faith, who records in the process the parallel extraction/ eradication of African-American history from white memory.

Parks's last play, *Greeks*, is her most powerful. The modern retelling of the Odysseus legend, focuses on the Smith family—Sergeant, Mrs. Sergeant, Buffy, Muffy, and Duffy—the mother and children awaiting the return of the father who will bring with him "his Distinction" won by faithfully serving his country in the white man's army. While they make periodic visits to "see their maker" each furlough followed by the birth of a child, and Mrs. Smith takes pride in her own mark of distinction—looking as if "You ain't traveled a mile nor sweated a drop"—Sergeant Smith waits in vain, returning finally in old age, like Odysseus, to a family that barely recognizes him. Legless, broken, he helplessly explains his dream: "Always wanted to do me somethin noble. . . . Like what they did in thuh olden days." The only glory open to him, however, is to break the fall of "that boy fallin out thuh sky. . . . I saved his life. I aint seen him since." This section ends where the first play began: the character recognizing the position of blacks in America: "we'se slugs."

The Death of the Last Black Man in the Whole Entire World is even more experimental and language-centered: a series of poetic phrases or melodious riffs depicting the life and times of Parks's composite African-American couple —Black Man with Watermelon and Black Woman with Fried Drumstick— surrounded by characters with names evoking black soul food—Lots of Grease and Lots of Pork—literary figures—And Bigger and Bigger and Bigger (after Richard Wright), and ancient times—Queen-then-Pharaoh Hatshepsut.

Beginning with the line, "The Black man moves his hands," Parks takes her people on a linguistic voyage back through African-American experience, historic and literary, animating her characters as she plays with a set of phrases and transformations, concluding with "Thuh black man he move. He move. He hans," words carved on a rock to be remembered: "because if you dont write it down we will come along and tell the future that we did not exist." Unlike the earlier play, the characters laugh at the end, having thrown off and stomped on the controlling "/d/."

Again strict form undergirds the work. The title is repeated nine times through the seven sections of the play, the first six times ending in "world," the last three "worl," allowing the Black Man to go from a fixed figure in a borrowed language to a self-animated speaker. The commensurate female experience moves from provider of chicken to supporter and encourager. Her words end the play.

Parks's work is audacious, upending traditional dramaturgy and replacing action with language shifts. Building on the earlier experiments of Ntozake Shange and Adrienne Kennedy, Parks moves even further, creating a theatre of poetry, in which the very power of language is reaffirmed by showing its potential to stand as subject and theme.

—Linda Ben-Zvi

PINNOCK, Winsome.

British. Born in London in 1961. Educated at Goldsmiths' College, London, B.A. (honours) in English and drama 1982. Playwright-in-residence, Tricycle Theatre, London, 1989–90, and since 1991 Royal Court Theatre, London. Recipient: Unity Theatre Trust award, 1989; George Devine award, 1991; Thames Television award, 1991. Agent: Lemon, Unna, and Durbridge, 24 Pottery Lane, Holland Park, London W11 4LZ, England.

Publications

PLAYS

The Wind of Change (produced 1987).
Leave Taking (produced 1988). In *First Run*, edited by Kate Harwood, 1989.
Picture Palace (produced 1988).

A Rock in Water (produced 1989). In *Black Plays: Two*, edited by Yvonne
   Brewster, 1989.
A Hero's Welcome (produced 1989).
Talking in Tongues (produced 1991).

TELEVISION PLAYS: episode in *South of the Border* series, 1988; episode in
Chalkface series, 1991.

Winsome Pinnock is widely acknowledged as one of the leading young talents
currently writing for the British theatre. She is also known as one of a very
small circle of black women playwrights whose work is regularly produced at
mainstream theatres in Britain, most notably at the Royal Court.
   Though Pinnock was born and educated in London, her work is influenced
by an awareness of the role of a Caribbean heritage in the lives of black
communities in England. Some of her most recent work has also dealt with the
theme of civil rights. These two interests combine and enrich the language, as
well as the themes, of her plays.
   One of Pinnock's best-known plays is *A Hero's Welcome*, first presented as a
rehearsed reading at the Royal Court in 1986, and given a full production—in
a revised version—at the Theatre Upstairs in 1989 (produced by the Women's
Playhouse Trust). The play is set in Jamaica and tells a story of family tension
and young love, framed in the traditions and expectations of West Indian
culture but informed by the British context of its writing and production. It
centres on three young women, Minda, Sis, and Ishbel. All three grow up in a
small Caribbean community in 1947. All are looking for a way out of poverty,
for better lives, and Len, the returning "hero" (charged with a strong sexual
drive which is exciting and enticing to the young women) seems to symbolize
that kind of possibility and hope. Only the two older women characters, Nana
and Mrs. Walker, are able to offer the wisdom of age and experience which
keeps the girls in line, in their community. That such a play found a wide and
diverse audience is itself an achievement, but more important was the national
recognition which this production brought to Pinnock.
   Also in 1989—in fact, one month before *A Hero's Welcome* was given its
full production—the Theatre Upstairs premiered Pinnock's *A Rock in Water*.
This play broke new ground for Pinnock and for London audiences, in its
powerful evocation of a recent historical figure: Claudia Jones, the founder of
the Notting Hill Carnivals in the mid-1950's and a dedicated worker at one of
the first black presses, the *West Indian Gazette*. In bringing Jones to public
attention, Pinnock engaged in a process of "writing [black] women into
history." And as Jones was not just any woman, the play also engaged
audiences in a recognition of the importance of location and cultural identity
in the lives of black women and men. The play chronicles the life of Claudia
Jones in Trinidad and Harlem as well as in London, where she lived only after
she was exiled to England after being accused of "un-American activities."
   A Rock in Water was commissioned by the Royal Court's Young People's
theatre and was developed through workshops with actors. But Pinnock also
did her own research by interviewing people who had known Claudia Jones:
she brought the woman to life through the memories of contemporaries and
co-workers, including the actress Corinne Skinner-Carter (who was featured in

A Hero's Welcome). The play was performed by 14 members of the Young People's Theatre, all of whom had been closely involved in the development of the ideas which Pinnock wove into the play.

Leave Taking was first produced at the Liverpool Playhouse Studio in 1988, the same year which saw the national tour of *Picture Palace*, produced by the Women's Theatre Group. While *Picture Palace* focused on the roles which women play and the images which are used in advertising and the media in Britain, *Leave Taking* followed on from *A Hero's Welcome* in its cross-cultural focus. *Leave Taking* was given a revival in 1990, when it was directed by Jules Wright and produced by the Women's Playhouse Trust at the Royal Court. The play's popularity is related to its scope and its intelligent yet humorous view of relationships between individuals and their cultural identities. *Leave Taking* also introduced the theme of cultural difference in the coming of awareness of individuals and groups of black women and men, a topic which is rarely dealt with in British theatre. *Leave Taking* was revived for a run at the Belgrade Theatre, Coventry in May 1992.

Pinnock's most recent play, *Talking in Tongues*, was performed at the Royal Court Theatre (directed by Hetty MacDonald), when Pinnock was writer-in-residence there in 1991. In this play, Pinnock's concern with the intermingling of cultures, identities, and voices is further developed within the story of a number of black and white friends and colleagues who come together at a New Year's Eve party. Sexuality and inter-racial relationships are represented, as are the themes of competition and identification between blacks and whites, women and men. As in her other work, the use of dialect frames the play with the sound and rhythm of another language. The film adaptation of *Talking in Tongues* is already underway.

In these plays, as in most of Pinnock's work to date, the realist drama focuses on the central dilemma of the black woman coming to terms with (predominantly) white British society. Pinnock's talent as a playwright is enriched in all of her work by her keen awareness of the nuances of language, and by her ability to reach out to and communicate with the many different "communities" and individuals who make up the audiences of her plays.

—Lizbeth Goodman

POLLOCK, Sharon (née Chalmers).

Canadian. Born in Fredericton, New Brunswick, 19 April 1936. Educated at the University of New Brunswick, Fredericton, 2 years. Married Ross Pollock in 1954; six children. Actor in New Brunswick, and with touring group, Prairie Players, Calgary; head of the playwriting division, Department of Drama, University of Alberta, Edmonton, 1976–77; director of the Playwrights' Colony, Banff School of Fine Arts, Alberta, 1977–81; playwright-in-residence, Alberta Theatre Projects, Calgary, 1977–79, National Arts Centre, Ottawa, 1981, 1982, and Regina Public Library, Saskatchewan, 1986–87; dramaturge, 1982–83, associate artistic director, 1983–84, and artistic director, 1984, Theatre Calgary. Member, 1979–80, and chair 1980–81, Canada Council Advisory Arts Panel; vice-chair Playwrights Canada National Executive, 1981–83. Recipient: Dominion Drama Festival award, for acting, 1966; Nellie award, for radio play, 1981; Governor-General's award, 1981, 1986; Alberta award of excellence, 1983; Chalmers award, 1984; Canada Council Senior Arts grant, 1984; Alberta Writers Guild award, 1986; Alberta Literary Foundation award, 1987. Honorary Doctorate: University of New Brunswick, 1986. Address: 319 Manora Drive N.E., Calgary, Alberta T2A 4R2, Canada.

Publications

PLAYS

A Compulsory Option. 1970; revised version (produced 1972; as *No! No! No!* produced 1977), 1972.

Walsh (produced 1973). 1972; revised version (produced 1974), 1974.

New Canadians (for children; produced 1973).

Superstition Throu' the Ages (for children; produced 1973).

Wudjesay? (for children; produced 1974).

A Lesson in Swizzlery (for children; produced 1974).

The Rose and the Nightingale (for children), adaptation of the story by Oscar Wilde (produced 1974).

The Star-child (for children), adaptation of the story by Oscar Wilde (produced 1974).

The Happy Prince (for children), adaptation of the story by Oscar Wilde (produced 1974).

And Out Goes You? (produced 1975).

The Komagata Maru Incident (produced 1976). 1978.

Blood Relations (as *My Name Is Lisbeth*, produced 1976; revised version, as *Blood Relations*, produced 1980). In *Blood Relations and Other Plays*, 1981; in *Plays by Women 3*, edited by Michelene Wandor, 1984.

Tracings: The Fraser Story (collective work), with others (produced 1977).

The Wreck of the National Line Car (for children; produced 1978).

Mail vs. Female (produced 1979).

Chautauqua Spelt E-N-E-R-G-Y (for children; produced 1979).

One Tiger to a Hill (produced 1980; revised version produced 1981). In *Blood Relations and Other Plays*, 1981.

Generations, from her radio play (produced 1980). In *Blood Relations and Other Plays*, 1981.

Blood Relations and Other Plays. 1981.

Whiskey Six (produced 1983).

Doc (produced 1984; revised version, as *Family Trappings*, produced 1986). 1986.

OTHER PLAY: *The Great Drag Race; or, Smoked, Choked, and Croaked* (for children).

RADIO PLAYS: *Split Seconds in the Death Of*, 1971; *31 for 2; We to the Gods; Waiting; The B Triple P Plan; In Memory Of; Generation*, 1980; *Sweet Land of Liberty*, 1980; *Intensive Care; Mary Beth Goes to Calgary; Mrs. Yale and Jennifer* (8 episodes); *In the Beginning Was; One Tiger to a Hill*.

TELEVISION PLAYS: *Portrait of a Pig*; *The Larsens*; *Ransom*; *Free Our Sisters, Free Ourselves*; *The Person's Case*; *Country Joy* (6 episodes), with others, 1979–80.

MANUSCRIPT COLLECTION: University of Calgary, Alberta.

THEATRICAL ACTIVITIES

DIRECTOR: **Plays**—some of her own plays, and *Betrayal* and *A Slight Ache* by Harold Pinter; *The Mousetrap* by Agatha Christie; *Scapin* by Molière; *The Gingerbread Lady* by Neil Simon; *The Bear* and *A Marriage Proposal* by Chekhov; *Period of Adjustment* by Tennessee Williams; *The Indian Wants the Bronx* by Israel Horovitz; *The Effect of Gamma Rays on Man-in-the-Moon Marigolds* by Paul Zindel; *Buried Child* by Sam Shepard; and others.

ACTOR: **Plays**—roles in some of her own plays, and title role in *Lysistrata* by Aristophanes; Nancy in *The Knack* by Ann Jellicoe; Amanda in *Private Lives* by Noël Coward; Miss Cooper in *Separate Tables* by Terence Rattigan; Bunny in *The House of Blue Leaves* by John Guare; Nell in *Endgame* by Samuel Beckett; Maddy in *All That Fall* by Arthur Miller; Polina in *The Seagull* by Chekhov; title role in *Miss Julie* by Strindberg; Alison in *Look Back in Anger* by John Osborne; The Psychiatrist in *Agnes of God* by John Pielmeier; and others.

Sharon Pollock's early plays are typical of the large branch of Canadian theatre which directly explores the country's history, employing documents but moving from them in a subjective response to events and an investigation of character and political process. In a note to the text of *The Komagata Maru Incident*, Pollock posits that drama "is a theatrical impression of an historical event seen through the optique of the stage and the mind of the playwright."

Her first play, *A Compulsory Option*, is a rather simple exercise in farce which does not fit this documentary model and which has been overshadowed by the later plays which do. It is, however, an amusing play with witty insights, especially into predictable academic character traits.

In her second play, *Walsh*, Pollock began to experiment with what has been considered her typical form. In the first version of the play, for example, broadcasted speeches taken from historical sources preceded each scene to provide necessary background; this rather awkward attempt at documentation was replaced in the published version by a Prologue which occurs out of time and which shows us the eventual moral decline of the protagonist while simultaneously providing fewer but more easily assimilated historical details. The play recreates the dilemma of Major John Walsh of the Northwest Mounted Police who, in 1876, is caught in the middle between the Canadian government of Sir John A. MacDonald (symbolized by Queen Victoria as Great White Mother) and the American Indian nations as symbolized by Chief Sitting Bull. Sitting Bull is cast as a shamanistic figure, and when critics have sometimes found the character overly pious to the point of unreality, they have ignored the fact that he is intended not as rounded character in a drama but as mystical *exemplum* of his dying race, caught in a modern European world it cannot resist and true to the primitive but doomed values of the "Sacred Hoop" of life. Major Walsh, a strict militarist, attempts to extend white logic to the Indian view of the world and discovers that he does not himself wish to accept the detached political logic of his white superiors. He also discovers that considerations other than reason and fair play motivate the Canadian government. In one short and highly dramatic speech, however, he capitulates in the face of these discoveries, reverting to his background and his sense of duty, and by doing so seals his own moral doom. The young recruit, Clarence, functions in the play as a mirror to Walsh's spiritual decline, learning to see the Indians as human beings even as Walsh forces himself to manage them as political pawns. The interesting discussion which these two figures embody becomes a central theme of the play: the man without responsibility can remain idealistic and humane; the bureaucrat trapped between forces he cannot control but must administer suffers and often falls victim to the events of history. The staging echoes this stark reality—a few representative figures on an almost bare stage play out a tiny portion of the larger event and do so in an unadorned and internalized landscape.

The same trapped figure reappears in *The Komagata Maru Incident* in the person of the spy, William Hopkinson. In this play, Pollock returns to a form similar to that of *Walsh* after an experiment in history seen as burlesque in *And Out Goes You? Komagata Maru* concerns the historic refusal of the turn-of-the-century provincial government to allow a boatload of East Indian refugees to enter the country. The ship remains in harbour for two months, and the play explores the racial and legal aspects of the event. Sent as a spy, Hopkinson is forced to come to terms with his own racial self-image (he is half-East Indian) and with his attempts to survive in a white world by denying his cultural background. The rendering of Hopkinson is rounder than that of Walsh; the issues are not as clear cut and the protagonist fights not only the social values which surround him but the weaker side of his own personality. The stagecraft is similarly more sophisticated than it was in *Walsh*: the action moves back and forth from the ship to other locales; the secondary characters and motives are interesting in themselves; and the thematic action is less directly stated. The theme, though it centres on a serious local problem of a particular time, is universal enough to affect other audiences and its considerations of the roles of fear, envy, and ambition speak to us all.

Although these first plays concern the reactions of men to historical events, the later plays show a growing interest by Pollock in the reactions of women in general and herself in particular. Her most successful play, *Blood Relations*, a reworking of an idea she first wrote as *My Name Is Lisbeth*, is a study of the American murderer Lizzie Borden in the context both of her feminine struggle to resist a role carved out for her by 19th-century society and her attempt to discover her own identity as a agent with Will. The play makes its point not only in the text, but by a powerful staging in which Lizzie switches roles with her Actress friend and watches "herself" repeat the action which led to the murder. The question of her guilt is played out in this mirror world and extended through an elaborate pattern of blood imagery to include the audience. As part of the folklore which condemns her, the play suggests, Americans and even Canadians are as guilty of the murder as is Lizzie. This contention is supported not only in the double action, but in Pollock's most successful writing, a well-designed and intricate web of language which demonstrates a significant leap from the earlier dialogue.

The most recent major play, the semi-autobiographical *Doc*, continues Pollock's search into the feminine memories of family. Although the play has not attracted the critical attention of *Blood Relations*, it has reinforced the notion that Pollock has, in the later plays, found a more literary voice. The writing here is highly compelling, the speeches often beautiful in themselves, and the general tone softer and more intimate. By moving steadily away from the directly documentary and away, as well, from the heroes themselves (be they male or female) into the philosophical implications of her events and characters, Pollock is creating plays which exist beyond the confines of the history they employ; her new plays have become more important than the subjects which have inspired them.

—Reid Gilbert

See the essay on *Blood Relations*.

R

RAYSON, Hannie.

Australian. Born in Brighton Beach, Melbourne, 31 March 1957. Educated at Brighton High School, Melbourne, 1969–72; Melbourne Church of England Girls Grammar, 1973–74; University of Melbourne, Parkville, Victoria, B.A. 1977; Victorian College of the Arts, Melbourne, Victoria, diploma of art in dramatic art 1980. Lives with James Grant; one son. Co-founder, writer and actor, Theatre Works, Melbourne, 1981–83; writer-in-residence, The Mill Theatre, Geelong, 1984, Playbox Theatre, Melbourne, 1985, LaTrobe University, Bundoora, Victoria, 1987, Monash University, Clayton, Victoria, and Victorian College of the Arts, Melbourne, 1990. Recipient: Queen Elizabeth II Silver Jubilee award, 1981; Australian Writers Guild award, 1986, 1990; Victorian Green Room award, 1990; New South Wales Premier's Literary award, 1990. Agent: Hilary Linstead and Associates, Suite 302, Easts Tower, 9–13 Bronte Road, Bondi Junction, New South Wales 2022, Australia.

Publications

PLAYS

Please Return to Sender (produced 1980).
Mary (produced 1981). 1985.
Leave It Till Monday (produced 1984).
Room to Move (produced 1985). 1985.
Hotel Sorrento (produced 1990). 1990.

TELEVISION PLAYS: *Sloth*, 1992; episode in *Sins* series, 1993.

Hannie Rayson comments:

My plays to date have been a response to particular contemporary social phenomena which at the outset I want to understand more fully. I seek subject matter which is full of contradiction and spend large tracts of time doing research. I begin with a big question, for example, in *Room to Move*, how has feminism affected Australian men or in *Hotel Sorrento*, how does the experience of expatriation alter one's perception of home?

Articulating the intellectual context occurs in tandem with the process of immersing myself in the world of the play: the characters, their lives, relationships, and so on. I am neither polemical nor didactic but I do want my work to be dense with ideas which have a critical relationship with the narrative. My ambition is to write plays which send audiences into the night with much to talk about.

Hannie Rayson's early work was in collaborative and community theatre, and the influence of that experience is evident in the problem-based plots and episodic structures which are characteristic of her writing. The first of her plays to achieve publication and some prominence, *Mary*, was directly a product of that involvement, and was developed in close consultation with relevant interest groups. Rayson acknowledges in her foreword to the published text both their contribution to the project, and the challenge which she herself faced as a fifth-generation Australian in dramatizing authentically the experience of a teenage Greek girl caught between her parents' culture and the very different expectations and rituals of Australian adolescents. *Mary* works very effectively, though, to catch sympathetically and with some humour the painfulness of the conflict.

Room to Move marked Rayson's transition into the mainstream subsidized theatre, and it has proved a very popular piece. It was hailed at the time as representing a belated recognition of feminist concerns in the Australian theatre, though that seems a partial distortion of the real achievement of the play. Rayson's subject is less the reappraisal of the role of women in relationships and the wider society than the impact which such reappraisals have had in those areas, particularly on the men who have been challenged with adjusting to them. The practical consequence of this approach is, in a sense, the reinforcement of the privileged status which men have enjoyed (or suffered from) in recent Australian plays as the principal agents of wit and momentum in the dialogue; reviewers frequently likened Rayson's presentation of the comedy of marital strife to that of David Williamson. But *Room to Move* has a further dimension, through the mediating presence of the elderly Peggy, who demonstrates that age and a warm cardigan offer no exemption from the need for challenge and intimacy in relationships. Like the more routine business of gender politics, her situation is treated with a nicely balanced sense of its pain and poignancy and its potential for farce.

Hotel Sorrento is Rayson's most ambitious play, and established her as a playwright of real substance. At its centre is the interaction, past and present, between three sisters; it has suitably Chekhovian elements of wryness and compassion, and establishes credibly a number of lines of conflict, most of them unresolvable. There are other aspects reminiscent of Chekhov: a strong sense of nostalgia for a lovelier and more innocent past, which in Rayson's depiction of the little seaside town of Sorrento is allowed to pass largely without analysis; a lively and articulate range of surrounding characters with a tendency to pontificate on the state of the nation; and, most tellingly, a subtle and powerful sense of the dignity and beauty which can co-exist with the silliness of people. The central images of the beach and the pier are handled very evocatively here, and catch for the first time in Australian theatre something of the mythological importance which looking out from the fringes of the continent to the water has in constructions of the Australian identity; it is a way of seeing which is just as fundamental as the more characteristic literary stance which looks inward to the arid centre.

Hotel Sorrento has more than its share of good conversation, and now and then the debate structure, and the much-canvassed matter of Australian identity, becomes a little stodgy; another limitation is the skeleton in the cupboard which underlies the sisters' wariness, which seems at once too prosaic and too melodramatic to account for the intricacies of their relationship. But it is a very moving and intelligent piece, impressive in its reach, and almost certainly built to last; it testifies to Rayson's growing stature in the contemporary Australian theatre.

—Peter Fitzpatrick

REID, Christina.

Irish. Born in Belfast, 12 March 1942. Educated at Everton Primary School, 1947–49, Girls Model School, 1949–57, and Queens University, 1982–83, all Belfast. Married in 1964 (divorced 1987); three children. Worked in various office jobs in Belfast, 1957–70; writer-in-residence, Lyric Theatre, Belfast, 1983–84, and Young Vic Theatre, London, 1988–89. Recipient: Ulster Television Drama award, 1980; Thames Television Playwriting award, 1983; George Devine award, 1986. Agent: Alan Brodie Representation, 91 Regent Street, London W1R 7TB, England.

Publications

PLAYS

Did You Hear the One About the Irishman . . .? (produced 1982). With *The Belle of Belfast City*, 1989.
Tea in a China Cup (produced 1983). With *Joyriders*, 1987.
Joyriders (produced 1986). With *Tea in a China Cup*, 1987.
The Last of a Dyin' Race (broadcast 1986). In *Best Radio Plays of 1986*, 1986.
My Name, Shall I Tell You My Name (broadcast 1987; produced 1990).
The Belle of Belfast City (produced 1989). With *Did You Hear the One About the Irishman . . .?*, 1989.
Les Miserables, adaptation of the novel by Victor Hugo (produced 1992).

RADIO PLAYS: *The Last of a Dyin' Race*, 1986; *My Name, Shall I Tell You My Name*, 1987; *The Unfortunate Fursey*, adaptation of the novel by Mervyn Wall, 1989; *Today and Yesterday in Northern Ireland*, for children, 1989.

TELEVISION PLAY: *The Last of a Dyin' Race*, 1987.

Christina Reid comments:

I come from a long line of Irish storytellers. The women of my mother's family didn't just sit still and tell tales, they dressed up and enacted a mixture of fact and fiction through song, dance, and dialogue, as much for their own enjoyment as to entertain us children. It is my earliest memory of theatre. In my plays, characters often tell their story as naturally in song and dance as they do in words, and much of my writing to date has been about the women and children of Northern Ireland. There are strong parts for men in the plays, but there are usually more women in the cast, and the main storyline tends to be mostly theirs. I don't set out to do this in any causal way; it is simply how I write, but I do think that too often Northern Ireland is portrayed on stage and screen as if "the troubles" and male violence is the whole rather than a part of life there, and that this leaves too many songs unsung.

Much as the weaver of homespun interlaces strands of yarn, Christina Reid alternates the tragedies of Belfast life with her ironic humor. Her plays are at once soft and abrasive, delicate and resilient, and they blanket us in warmth. Her portraits of working-class people are well crafted, their characters revealed quickly and neatly by series of humble incidents. Woven into the comfort of the ordinary is the horror of the extraordinary; entwined in the pain is the ache of laughter. The effect is outrageous: prejudice, deprivation, and death are reduced to commonplace events that we can understand, no matter where we live.

Outrage is a natural reaction to Reid's first play, the one-act *Did You Hear the One About the Irishman . . .?*. It is a 1980's romance à la Victor Hugo in that "the sublime and the grotesque" co-exist. Allison, a Protestant, and Brian, a Catholic, are idealists in an imperfect world. Neither can understand why it could be dangerous for them to marry, even though Brian's father was murdered and both have relatives in the Long Kesh prison where political prisoners are held. Their dialogue is witty and gentle, in contrast to the pleading of their families and the warnings of the prisoners. Periodic appearances are made by an Irishman who reads from a list of "Permitted Christmas Parcels" for the prison, thereby injecting reality, and by a comedian whose anti-Irish jokes are increasingly ominous. In counterpoint to Allison's and Brian's joke about forming their own peaceful "Apathy Party," the comedian talks of the inevitable violent deaths the Irish must suffer. The tragic conclusion is expected, yet the theatrical impact is not diminished. Reid makes effective use of black humor.

Tea in a China Cup is a lovely, quiet play. Though it takes place during the Troubles, it is concerned more with pride—making the proper impression and not airing dirty linen in public. It is the maintenance of dignity that obsesses Beth's working-class Protestant family, and fear of becoming caught in the same domestic trap that motivates Beth. In the first scene Beth must buy a grave plot for her mother, Sarah, who is dying of cancer. Reid's ironic faculty is evident immediately as Beth must decide between the Catholic and Protestant sections of the new cemetery, lest her mother stand out "like a sore thumb." Always aware of tradition, Sarah hopes only to live until 12th of July, when the Orangemen will again march past her window. She cautions Beth to remember all the family stories after she is gone, and Beth tells us about the men who went to war, the women who laid out the dead, her own friendship with a Catholic girl, and the importance of having what her grandmother called "a wee bit of fine bone china." But the china which to Sarah symbolizes the last vestige of civilization in a city of soldiers and Catholics is a bane to Beth. As Reid leads us through 30 years in the life of this family, Beth matures. In the end, still loving them all, she is able to break free of the restrictions which bound the women to home and custom. Superstition, prejudice, and tradition are cast aside in one last ironic act; hope is possible.

Less optimistic is *Joyriders*, a spirited evocation of what it means to be a poor Catholic teenager in Belfast. Sandra, Maureen, Arthur, and Tommy are four residents of the deplorable Divis Flats housing development who are given a chance to prove themselves in a youth training program. Two are young offenders, one was scarred when the army accidentally shot him, and one lives alone with her glue-sniffing brother. Reid first places these characters in a theatre, watching the end of Sean O'Casey's *Shadow of a Gunman* with their social worker Kate. By their reactions to the dialogue, their characters are instantly defined. Tommy, possibly a half-caste, is defensive; the disfigured Arthur is a joker; Sandra is practical; Maureen is a romantic. Together, they form a kind of family which Kate leads through various vicissitudes to a conclusion even she cannot control. The startling reversal is reminiscent of the well-made play. *Joyriders* is a particularly ironic title, since the activity brings this group only momentary joy and lasting misery. More ironic still is Kate's realization that the entire training course is the ultimate joyride because, when it ends, the participants have little chance of finding jobs. The course itself is constantly threatened with extinction. Sandra, Maureen, Arthur, and Tommy will all rejoin the cycle of hopelessness. In several ways, the play ends by coming full circle. Reid creates a sensitive portrait of teenagers trying to find their identities in a society that has no place for them. The issue is the fate of children from what Reid quotes as "the worst housing development in Western Europe."

The Belle of Belfast City takes its title from a music-hall song sung by Dolly, the ageing child star and matriarch of this play's family. As three generations gather, their reunion is marred by Jack, a loyalist who protests against the Anglo-Irish Agreement with the Reverend Ian Paisley. All of Dolly's women— Belle, the half-caste granddaughter; niece Janet, the victim of her brother Jack's incestuous attentions; the brave Vi and the idealistic Rose, Dolly's daughters—are subject to the males in power. Jack, the conservative Protestant zealot, and Tom, a strong-arm English "businessman," both harass the women. Each copes in her own valiant way, but is swept along on the political undercurrent which ripples through this play. Eventually Vi is persuaded to sell her shop. Rose fears the right-wing Catholic stand, so like Jack's, which limits women's rights. Reid is more straightforward about her politics than usual.

Reid's themes are women and their submissive role in Northern Ireland, their families, and the damage caused to both by the Troubles. She speaks sympathetically yet unsentimentally, and with the authority of one who knows the people and the customs about which she writes. It is a tribute to her skill that we can receive her message while being entertained. In no sense do we feel we have been subjected to a lecture, and yet we are filled with rage. In the midst of a lovely story is the inescapable presence of oppression, of a cycle of hopelessness despite courage. It is Reid's humor which gives resilience to her characters and provides a fascinating contrast to degradation and horror. Her frequent use of music also adds texture to her plays.

—Carol Banks

RENÉE.

New Zealander. Born Renée Gertrude Jones in Napier, 19 July 1929. Educated at primary schools to age 12; extra-mural study at Massey University, Palmerston North, from 1967: B.A. (University of Auckland) 1979. Married in 1949 (divorced); three sons. English and drama teacher in secondary schools, Wairoa, and at Long Bay College, Auckland, 1975–81; member, Womenspirit Collective, 1979–85, and Broadsheet Collective, Auckland, 1982–84; organised and led several writing workshops, 1983–85; playwright-in-residence, Theatre Corporate, Auckland, 1986; Robert Burns fellow, Otago University, Dunedin, 1989. Actress and director with Napier Repertory Players, Wairoa Community Theatre, and in Auckland. National vice-president, P.E.N., 1992. Recipient: Queen Elizabeth II Arts Council grant, 1982, and award, 1986. Lives in Dunedin. Agent: Play-market, P.O. Box 9767, Wellington, New Zealand.

Publications

PLAYS

Secrets: Two One-Woman Plays (produced 1982; revised version produced 1987). With Setting the Table, 1984.
Breaking Out (produced 1982).
Setting the Table (produced 1982). With Secrets, 1984.
What Did You Do in the War, Mummy? (also director: produced 1982).
Asking for It (also director: produced 1983).
Dancing (produced 1984).
Wednesday to Come (produced 1984). 1985.
Groundwork (produced 1985).
Pass It On (produced 1986). 1986.
Born to Clean, songs by Jess Hawk Oakenstar and Hilary King (produced 1987).
Form (for children). 1990.
Jeannie Once (produced 1990). 1991.
Touch of the Sun (produced 1991).
Missionary Position (produced 1991).
Te Pouaka Karaehe (The Glass Box) (also director: produced 1992).
Tiggy Tiggy Touchwood (produced 1992).

TELEVISION PLAYS: Husbands and Wives (Country G.P. series), 1985; Beginnings and Endings, Strings, and Sheppard Street (Open House series), 1986.

NOVEL
Willy Nilly. 1990.

SHORT STORIES
Finding Ruth. 1987.

MANUSCRIPT COLLECTION: University of Canterbury, Christchurch; Play-market, Wellington.

THEATRICAL ACTIVITIES

DIRECTOR: **Plays**— *What Did You Do in the War, Mummy?*, 1982; *Asking for It*, 1983; *Te Pouaka Karaehe (The Glass Box)*, 1992.

In the decade since Renée began writing plays, she has remained true to the principles which first inspired her. These are to celebrate the lives of ordinary working women and to give prominence to their undervalued struggles in times of social change, whilst writing with humour and a light touch. She is widely respected as New Zealand's most prolific and versatile woman dramatist, exploring themes of gender, class, and race. Perhaps because her work coincided with the upsurge in feminist thinking, and because it certainly filled a need for more and better parts for women in plays, all the major professional theatres performed her plays during the 1980's.

Setting the Table, written in January 1981, shows women as intelligent, humorous, and strong, in a naturalistic play that also handles radical feminist questions. Set in the kitchen and revolving around four women who run a refuge for battered women, the action arises out of an angry husband who follows one of the workers home while looking for his wife. Sheila, who works at a public hospital, has become so angered by living in a culture which accepts rape that she takes the opportunity to intimidate a violent man. She injures him with a knife, ties a yellow ribbon around his penis, and hangs a sign on him saying "This man is a rapist." The central issue which follows from this action is whether it is ever necessary—or acceptable—to retaliate with violence in a violent situation.

Her best-known work is a historical trilogy which began in 1984 with *Wednesday to Come* (set in the 1930's), followed with *Pass It On* (set in 1951), and completed in 1990 by *Jeannie Once* (set in 1879). The stories of four generations of working-class women during times of upheaval are told. *Wednesday to Come* is also set in a kitchen but this time during the Depression, while a march of the unemployed to Parliament passes the house. Inside a young woman is waiting for the body of her husband (who has committed suicide in a work camp) to be returned to her. Four generations of women live together, represented by five well-drawn characters who retain their individuality while signifying class oppression and working women's invincibility.

Pass It On takes the action forward, while keeping the teenagers Jeannie and her brother from the previous play, to the 1951 waterfront confrontation when men fought each other in the streets and it was against the law to help strikers or to publish any news about them. A hand-written broadsheet is being printed and distributed (hence the title) and the technique this time is Brechtian rather than naturalistic. Several actors are used to fill many smaller roles and the effect is more didactic than in the earlier play.

Jeannie Once goes back to the first Jeannie, the old grandmother of *Wednesday to Come*, and explores her first years in New Zealand in 1879. Again Renée tries new ways of telling her story, using music-hall songs and many characters in shorter scenes. Women are the strong centre of this group of people from Britain trying to make a new life in a distant colony. Issues of racial prejudice appear in the victimisation of 19-year-old Martha, a Maori accused of stealing.

A racial theme is also obvious in *Groundwork*, set during the 1981 South African Springbok rugby tour of New Zealand, which takes the play inside prison and in flashback to a suburban home. Lesbian relationships are also thematic in this play, as they were covertly in *Setting the Table* and *Breaking Out*, and more overtly in *Belle's Place*.

Missionary Position is a full length play in which three bag-ladies seek refuge from life's realities at the bottom of the social heap by living in a film-star fantasy, casting themselves as Garbo, Monroe, and Dietrich. As she has often done, Renée uses music to counterpoint the action. *Touch of the Sun* is a comedy with strong roles for two women playing sisters sorting through the extensive wardrobe of their dead mother and discovering that things were not quite as they imagined in her life. The dominant presence of the dead mother looms over their lives, and always will.

Maori values set alongside success in the European world is the theme of *Te Pouaka Karaehe* (*The Glass Box*). "I think people get caught up in the glass box [of the city] and that becomes a barrier. Just living in the city and learning city ways and playing city games, you forget some of the things about home," Renee said of this play. Handicapped by three off-stage characters who do not appear but are constantly talked about, *The Glass Box* gives good opportunities for Maori women actors but the focus is diffused over several cultural and political issues, weakening the impact. *Tiggy Tiggy Touch Wood* is a tragi-comedy about a woman who, as the result of a vicious attack years before, has been brain-damaged. Cared for by a friend who loves her, the time has come when a decision has to be made about putting her in a home.

Renée has added television scripts, a collection of short stories (*Finding Ruth*), a film treatment, and a novel (*Willy Nilly*) to her output, while plays continue to be her first line of creative communication with a society not by any means fully adjusted to the feminist point of view.

—Patricia Cooke

RIDLER, Anne (Barbara, née Bradby).

British. Born in Rugby, Warwickshire, 30 July 1912. Educated at Downe House School; King's College, London, diploma in journalism 1932. Married Vivian Ridler in 1938; two sons and two daughters. Member of editorial department, Faber and Faber publishers, London, 1935–40. Recipient: Oscar Blumenthal prize, 1954, and Union League Civic and Arts Foundation prize, 1955 (*Poetry*, Chicago). Address: 14 Stanley Road, Oxford OX4 1QZ, England.

Publications

PLAYS

Cain (produced 1943). 1943.
The Shadow Factory: A Nativity Play (produced 1945). 1946.
Henry Bly (produced 1947). In *Henry Bly and Other Plays*, 1950.
Henry Bly and Other Plays. 1950.
The Mask, and The Missing Bridegroom (produced 1951). In *Henry Bly and Other Plays*, 1950.

The Trial of Thomas Cranmer, music by Bryan Kelly (produced 1956). 1956.
The Departure, music by Elizabeth Maconchy (produced 1961). In *Some Time After and Other Poems*, 1972.
Who Is My Neighbour? (produced 1961). With *How Bitter the Bread*, 1963.
The Jesse Tree: A Masque in Verse, music by Elizabeth Maconchy (produced 1970). 1972.
Rosinda, translation of the libretto by Faustini, music by Cavalli (produced 1973).
Orfeo, translation of the libretto by Striggio, music by Monteverdi (produced 1975). 1975; revised edition, 1981.
Eritrea, translation of the libretto by Faustini, music by Cavalli (produced 1975). 1975.
The King of the Golden River, music by Elizabeth Maconchy (produced 1975).
The Return of Ulysses, translation of the libretto by Badoaro, music by Monteverdi (produced 1978). In *The Operas of Monteverdi*, edited by Nicholas John, 1992.
The Lambton Worm, music by Robert Sherlaw Johnson (produced 1978). 1979.
Orontea, translation of the libretto by Cicognini, music by Cesti (produced 1979).
Agrippina, translation of the libretto by Grimani, music by Handel (produced 1982).
La Calisto, translation of the libretto by Faustini, music by Cavalli (produced 1984).
Così fan Tutte, translation of the libretto by da Ponte, music by Mozart (produced 1986; broadcast, 1988). 1987.
Don Giovanni, translation of the libretto by da Ponte, music by Mozart (produced 1990).
The Marriage of Figaro, translation of the libretto by da Ponte, music by Mozart (produced 1991).
The Coronation of Poppea, translation of the libretto by Busenello, music by Monteverdi (produced 1992). In *The Operas of Monteverdi*, edited by Nicholas John, 1992.

Television play: *Così fan Tutte*, 1988.

Verse
Poems. 1939.
A Dream Observed and Other Poems. 1941.
The Nine Bright Shiners. 1943.
The Golden Bird and Other Poems. 1951.
A Matter of Life and Death. 1959.
Selected Poems. 1961.
Some Time After and Other Poems. 1972.
Italian Prospect: Six Poems. 1976.
Dies Natalist: Poems of Birth and Infancy. 1980.
Ten Poems, with E.J. Scovell. 1984.
New and Selected Poems. 1988.

OTHER

Olive Willis and Downe House: An Adventure in Education. 1967.
A Victorian Family Postbag. 1988.
Profitable Wonders: Aspects of Thomas Traherne, with A.M. Allchin and Julia
   Smith. 1989.

Editor, *Shakespeare Criticism 1919–1935.* 1936.
Editor, *A Little Book of Modern Verse.* 1941.
Editor, *Time Passes and Other Poems*, by Walter de la Mare. 1942.
Editor, *Best Ghost Stories.* 1945.
Editor, *The Faber Book of Modern Verse*, revised edition. 1951.
Editor, *The Image of the City and Other Essays*, by Charles Williams. 1958.
Editor, *Selected Writings*, by Charles Williams. 1961.
Editor, *Shakespeare Criticism 1935–1960.* 1963.
Editor, *Poems and Some Letters*, by James Thomson. 1963.
Editor, *Thomas Traherne: Poems, Centuries, and Three Thanksgivings.* 1966.
Editor, with Christopher Bradby, *Best Stories of Church and Clergy.* 1966.
Editor, *Selected Poems of George Darley.* 1979.
Editor, *The Poems of William Austin.* 1983.
Editor, *A Victorian Family Postbag.* 1988.
Editor, *A Measure of English Poetry: Critical Essays.* 1991.

MANUSCRIPT COLLECTION: Eton College Library, Buckinghamshire.

CRITICAL STUDY: *The Christian Tradition in Modern British Verse Drama* by
William V. Spanos, 1967.

Anne Ridler comments:

(1977) It is a great advantage for a dramatist to know the cast and place he is
writing for, the audience he is addressing. Only rarely have I had this opportunity, and this is perhaps why *Thomas Cranmer*, commissioned for performance in the church where Cranmer was tried, has been judged my best play.

   Writing words for music, however, gives a rare opportunity for a contemporary poet to use his particular talents in the theatre, and it is in this field
(whether by original words, or fitting a translation to a musical line) that I
prefer to work at present. Libretto-writing, as W.H. Auden said, gives the poet
his one chance nowadays of using the high style.

Although Anne Ridler has to her credit a number of plays which have their
place in the postwar revival of blank verse drama, it is more likely that she will
be remembered for her volumes of poetry than for her work in the theatre. She
began by tackling the forbidding theme of Cain, presenting the characters from
Genesis with the archangels Michael and Gabriel serving as chorus to the
tragedy. *The Shadow Factory*, a most unusual nativity play, is altogether more
interesting as it juxtaposes reflections on the birth of Christ and some sharp
criticisms of contemporary issues. In the factory the workers are reduced
almost to robots, endlessly repeating the same pointless actions in the pro-

duction line. The jingle "The Piece-Work Way/Means Better Pay" sums up the futility of it all, and the director is no doubt intentionally something of an Orwellian Big Brother. He has, however, had the idea of commissioning a large mural painting as an example of corporate sponsorship which will enhance the company's image. The artist who undertakes the work soon sizes up the situation and, having taken the precaution of obtaining a promise that nobody shall see what he is doing until it is finished, paints a picture which portrays the director as a masked figure playing chess heartlessly with the lives of his work people. Meantime, a parson, who is also admitted to the factory as part of a policy of good treatment for the staff, rehearses a nativity play with the workers. The two strands come together as the director swallows his pride and accepts the mural and its message, or rather the message of the nativity. With its concern for social injustice the play strikes a chord, and if the director is a little too wooden in his attitudes and expression, there is certainly life in the portrayal of the workers, especially William, whose reactions to the birth of his first child are observed with affectionate accuracy. All the same, the mixture of realism and allegory is not altogether persuasive, and the optimism, as with many nativity plays, is a little difficult to swallow except on Christmas Eve.

Henry Bly is more successful because its engaging plot, based on the Grimm Brothers' fairy tale "Brother Lustig," is realistic only in its depiction of characters, not of milieu. Henry is a picaresque rogue, always keen to enjoy a drink or to cadge a coin. On his feckless way through life he falls in with a Tramp who never explains himself very fully but whom we soon come to recognise as some sort of Christ-figure when he works miracles without hope of any material reward. For Henry he is at first merely a simpleton to be exploited, but by the end the ne'er-do-well comes to realise that what he is being offered is his chance for salvation. Folklore is also used as the basis for *The Mask* which takes the form of a reworking of the moving Somerset folksong "The Shooting of His Dear" and manages to modernise the tale without destroying its charm.

Ridler turned to history with *The Trial of Thomas Cranmer*, written to mark the 400th aniversary of his death. When played in the University Church, Oxford, near so many of the sites mentioned by the characters, the tragedy must have been particularly moving, but even without local knowledge this simple and yet very sympathetic chronicle of inhumanity strikes home. Ridler's method is first to show Cranmer as a complete human being, naturally anxious to avoid the challenge of martyrdom, so that she can enlist all our sympathies as he goes to his death. His persecutors seem all the more ignoble since he is not cast in the heroic mould, and his courage and faith impress us all the more since we know he would sooner not be tested. There is, of course, also Cranmer's magnificent control of language, and this, perhaps as much as an obvious Oxford connection and reverence for one of the martyrs of the English church, must have attracted Ridler.

For her, verse drama is not a matter of grand phrases and extravagant imagery. Instead she prefers a sober style, rarely enlivened by metaphor and spiced with just occasional dry wit. She knows the power of monosyllables and has enough confidence in the power of her verse to avoid gross effects. It is the rhythm, close to that of prose yet subtly more strict, that repeatedly lifts the speeches she puts into the mouths of her characters above the mundane matters they may be discussing and gives her dialogue the extra strengths of poetry. In her plays her constant concern is to present images of redemption within contexts which portray the pains, problems, and little joys of mankind. Her verse serves as one more element in the bridge that she seeks to build between two worlds.

After her verse plays, Anne Ridler did not only continue to write poetry herself and edit a variety of other works; she also turned towards the world of opera. For the composer Elizabeth Maconchy, for instance, she provided the libretto for *The Departure* and for *The King of the Golden River* (after Ruskin), and for Robert Sherlaw Johnson she refashioned a popular County Durham folktale for his opera *The Lambton Worm*. In recent years she has also produced translations—or, as she significantly prefers to call them, "singing versions"—of the texts of Monteverdi's *The Return of Ulysses*, Cavalli's *La Calisto*, Handel's *Agrippina*, and Mozart's *Così fan Tutte*. These meticulously worked versions, which reveal a rare combination of verbal and musical sensitivity, have set high standards in this very testing art form. They have made an important contribution to the growing trend, exemplified at its best by Kent Opera, of performing, both in the theatre and on television, the masterpieces of the operatic repertory in English.

—Christopher Smith

RITTER, Erika.

Canadian. Born in Regina, Saskatchewan in 1948. Educated at McGill University, Montreal, B.A. 1968; University of Toronto, M.A. in arts and drama 1970. Teacher, Loyola College, Montreal, 1971–74; playwright-in-residence, Stratford Festival, 1985; host of *Dayshift*, CBC radio program, 1985–87. Recipient: Chalmers award, 1980; ACTRA award, 1982. Agent: Shain Jaffe, Great North Artists, 350 DuPont Street, Toronto, Ontario M5R 1V9, Canada.

Publications

PLAYS

A Visitor from Charleston (produced 1975). 1975.
The Splits (produced 1978). 1978.
Winter 1671 (produced 1979). 1979.
The Automatic Pilot (produced 1980). 1980.
The Passing Scene (produced 1982).
Murder at McQueen (produced 1986).

RADIO PLAYS: *The Road to Hell*; *Dayshift*; *Miranda*, 1985; *Smith and Wesson*; *The Girl I Left Behind Me*.

OTHER

Urban Scrawl (essays and sketches). 1984.
Ritter in Residence (essays and sketches). 1987.

CRITICAL STUDY: *The Work: Conversations with English-Canadian Playwrights*, edited by Robert Wallace and Cynthia Zimmerman, 1982.

Erika Ritter's first published play, *A Visitor from Charleston*, produced in 1975, concerns Eva, a youngish divorcée and frustrated would-be actress, who drowns the tedium of a routine library job and a dull ex-husband in a world of romantic fantasy created by repeated viewings of *Gone with the Wind*, viewings which continue after her separation from her husband and which number 47 as the play opens. Eva is deterred from seeing the film for the 48th time by a door-to-door cosmetic salesman pushing a line called "Instant Fantasie," promising rejuvenation and glamour, all the things Eva experiences vicariously in Rhett and Scarlett, who are eternally young, frozen in time on film. For the period of the play, Eva heckles and badgers the salesman, distracting him from his patter to reveal her life's disappointments and expose his frauds and weaknesses, all in the hope that "Instant Fantasie" products will somehow prove to be her own personal *Gone with the Wind*. Peering into the mirror as she tries out the new blushers and mascaras, recalling the face of her youth, triggers a series of three memory scenes, each one increasing her disillusionment, and confirming her sense that love and artistic fulfilment are impossible except in the movies.

The two major themes of male/female relationships and the creating of art, along with a number of motifs and technical devices introduced in *A Visitor from Charleston*, continue with variations throughout the five following plays, all (with the exception of the anachronistic historical play, *Winter 1671*) contemporary, urban, and full of corrosively witty one-liners and self-deprecating anecdotes.

The Splits, Ritter's next play, produced in 1978, is about Megan, a television script writer, trying to organize her career as well as come to terms with the three men in her life—Hal, the Tuesday-Thursday lover she met in group therapy; David, her story editor and well-meaning, though weak friend; and Joe, her boorish, abusive, cadging ex-husband. In the end they all split, Hal willingly, Joe by force, trashing Megan's apartment while declaring she's the only woman he ever loved, and David by default. Most important is Megan's departure. The play closes with her picking up her purse and typewriter from the wreckage and walking out, the upbeat ending of a courageous woman who has rejected palliatives and mediocre solutions for a creative life on her own terms.

The Automatic Pilot is Ritter's most accomplished work to date. It concerns Charlie, a writer of soap operas by day and a stand-up comedienne by night, who uses the disasters of her personal life as material for her comic routines. Again Ritter deals with male/female relationships, but this time from both perspectives: Charlie's (the female lead) in the first act and Gene's (her lover) in the second. Because Ritter refuses to oversimplify the difficulties of the current situation for unattached, self-supporting, successful professional women who also want a fulfilling and secure love relationship with a decent man who can accept equality of the sexes, her plays never take a straight feminist direction. She refuses just to blame "patriarchal" society, and insists that many women (like Charlie) are their own worst enemies. This leads to a very shrewd analysis of elements of character which are self-defeating in women. Yet while Ritter sees their unhappiness as "largely a product of their own mentality and their attitude about themselves", she does recognize that there is a link between this and society as a whole: "My characters tend to do a lot of wistful wandering;

they tend to be indecisive people because they live in an indecisive age." Both men and women are affected by this modern indecisiveness, as even macho Nick, one of Charlie's pick-ups in *The Automatic Pilot*, slumps wearily and says he feels old. And the root of Charlie's difficulty (as both Gene, her lover, and Alan, her ex-husband, point out) is that, despite her independence and apparent cynical toughness, ultimately she depends on other people for respect and a sense of self. In reaction against this dependency, Charlie tries constantly to see herself as the victim of the people whose respect she feels she has lost. As Ritter explains, "[Charlie] wants to contrive circumstance so that she, in her own mind, is free from guilt or blame . . . . She manipulates situations so that the other person is responsible, because she's more comfortable with the role of the person who is acted upon."

The form that this self-contempt takes is her routine as a stand-up comedienne at the Canada Goose, a night club employing amateurs. On one level, joking is Charlie's method of coming to terms with the harshness of experience by laughing at herself, but on another level it is an appeal for the audience's approval and sympathy. The technique of comic self-deprecation that started as a defense mechanism becomes an emotional necessity for her. Gradually she starts to see her actual experience in terms of the show, instead of vice versa. As the audience watches Charlie's routine in the "show within the play," it sees creation in process at the same time as the destruction of Charlie's life. The saddest result is that when she does win the love of a totally decent man, Gene, she can't accept it; she has to spoil it because she only feels comfortable and safe in her habitual mixture of self-contemptuous misery, projected as comedy to win admiration of an audience.

In the meantime, Gene, the only male character in all the plays who represents Ritter's point of view, also turns his personal experience into a novel, comically entitled *Deathless Prose*. However, he is not hooked into the process as Charlie is, but uses his art to try to understand. Beneath the often farcical situations and constant wisecracks are extremely perceptive comments on human behaviour and art, typical of the bitter-sweet, comic-sad mixture of most of Ritter's work.

Six years later *Murder at McQueen* was produced, a play again focusing on women and their relations with men and with their own particular forms of self-expression. Three of the four women, each a decade apart in age, has an affair with a macho, amoral talk-show host, appropriately named Rex. The eldest, Mitzi, founds a successful women's club, The McQueen, as therapy following the break-up, but after five years she still yearns for him. Secretly her best friend, Norah, a beautiful young lawyer in her 20's, annoyed by the chauvinist tack Rex takes in his talk show, telephones her protest and, both intrigued, they meet and end up in bed, Rex enthralled for the first time despite numerous affairs, and Norah attracted, but feeling she has betrayed Mitzi. Ultimately she rejects Rex, to his astonishment and dismay, but also leaves the club and Mitzi.

This plot is framed by a chorus figure, Blythe, a writer and teacher of detective fiction, and non-member of the club who observes and receives confidences from members. She suffers from the same unsatisfactory love experiences as the others—separation, rejection, fulfilment through fantasy. When her fictional detective, Butler, appears in the flesh investigating a fire at the club and crank calls to Rex, she finds illusion merging wonderfully with reality at first until fantasy is overwhelmed by sordid facts. The "Murder" in the play's title refers to the betrayal of friendships, the death of hope and trust, and concomitantly, the growth of cynicism, despair, and loneliness.

Ritter's plays are all written in the style and tradition of the Comedy of Manners, where her shrewd eye for modern "yuppie" attitudes and ear for ways of talking are captured in often brilliant verbal wit. In fact, the wit is so ubiquitous and sharp that the audience sometimes forgets Ritter's technical skill. The juxtaposing of two modes of fantasy, the movie and the cosmetics, in her first play, *A Visitor from Charleston*, creating a kind of literary *trompe d'oeil*, and the mode of sliding into memory through the mirror, are effects which she varies imaginatively in later plays, creating clever transitions from one level to another so that we see the relationship between real life and performance, fantasy and human need that is central to Ritter's vision.

—Dorothy Parker

S

SÁNCHEZ-SCOTT, Milcha.

American. Born in Bali in 1955. Lived in Colombia and Mexico until 1969.
Educated in London and in California. Has lived in California since 1969.
Member of New Dramatists, New York. Recipient: Drama-logue award
(seven times); Vesta award, 1984; Rockefeller award, 1987. Agent: George
Lane, William Morris Agency, 1350 Avenue of the Americas, New York, New
York 10019. Address: 2080 Mount Street, Los Angeles, California 90068,
U.S.A.

Publications

PLAYS

Latina (produced 1980). In *Necessary Theater: Six Plays About the Chicano
Experience*, edited by Jorge A. Huerta, 1989.
Dog Lady and The Cuban Swimmer (produced 1984). In *Plays in Process*,
vol.5, no.12, 1984.
Roosters (produced 1987). In *On New Ground: Contemporary Hispanic-
American Plays*, edited by M. Elizabeth Osborn, 1987.
Evening Star (produced 1988). 1989.
Stone Wedding (produced 1989).
El Dorado (produced 1990).

Of pan-American and pan-Pacific ancestry, Milcha Sánchez-Scott has felt the
shock of sexist prejudice as a Latina in California. Since 1980 she has drama-
tised the humor and resolution of the disempowered. These qualities, along
with the devotion of displaced communities, hold back for a moment the
relentless oppression of economics and negative assumptions. Sánchez-Scott
finds holes within harsh realities through which stream magical visions, spells,
miraculous cures, transformations, and an old religious faith in past and
future. Dual language allows her characters an alternative to the dominant
one, whether Spanish or English. Words let them escape from mundanity into
unique eloquence. Such language supplies a textual correlative for the immediately visualized and physicalized images.

In *Latina*, her first play, a remarkable playwriting voice made
Sánchez-Scott's bilingual and bi-level dramatic visions clear, rich, and effective
—even for materialistic, English-speaking audiences. In the prologue to *Latina*,
New Girl journeys from a Peruvian mountain village to cross the barbed-wire
American border. The originally plaintive Peruvian flute resounds "trium-

212

phantly" with American pop music and traffic, as we see a bus stop in front of FELIX SANCHEZ DOMESTIC AGENCY on Wilshire Boulevard in Los Angeles. Two tanned mannequins stand in the window of the comically sleazy entrepreneur's agency; the maternal dummy in white holds a pink doll, and the naughty maid in black holds a feather duster. Dressed carefully in the American style, Sarita enters briskly to say how embarrassing it is to be thought car-less, a maid-for-hire, Latina, or available at 23 in Los Angeles. Overhearing this but speaking no English, old Eugenia the yu-yu vendor and cleaning lady offers "niña Sarita" a cure for her malady. Sarita, still denying, answers in effortless Spanish, rebukes in English, and translates for the audience. Eugenia ritually sprinkles water to sweep, and Sarita, hearing a rooster, admits she sees her grandmother sweeping a dirt road in 1915 Juarez. Then, joking bawdily about using Lava soap, they reveal Sarita's frustrated television-acting career and the old woman's affectionate pride in it. New Girl, dressed in the Peruvian style, furtively seeking domestic work, panics at the word "immigration" in Sarita's reassurance, and bites the hand that places Latinas in WASP households. As Don Felix approaches to open his shop, Eugenia still prays before they make their daily bet: is he wearing his Mickey Mouse or sailboat pajama top today? What's the point of praying? Sarita blurts in Spanish, and before going in, pauses to assure her audience, "I let her win."

These first few moments of *Latina* typify Sánchez-Scott's career. Seven comically disparate Latin women (eight, including Sarita), awaiting jobs in the agency, gossip about their desperate realities and party. The mannequins appear in Sarita's mind, mock her abject servility to WASP's and failure to defend Alma, and don rebozos to go to the park as sisters. What one lets oneself be called is important. New Girl lets them reduce her five names to "Elsa Moreno," accepts Sarita's exchanging her carefully chosen disguise for her Peruvian clothes, and with the help of Eugenia's charm and prayer and everyone's generosity, gets a placement. Sarita—in learning to accept Eugenia's prayer and bet (that her own audition overcame television's prejudice against "exotics") and divest herself of her disguise in order to help others—gets beyond her "mal educada" status to find her own dignity. "Sarita Gomez" will play her television role, and she attacks the intolerable Mrs. Camden. *Latina* ends with an immigration raid arresting all the "illegal" women as another New Girl creeps toward the barbed wire.

The Cuban Swimmer shows the Suarez family from Long Beach in the Pacific Ocean halfway to Catalina Island. Daughter Margarita is swimming in the invitational race, and her father (coach), mother (a former Miss Cuba), the praying Abuela (grandmother), and the younger brother with binoculars and punk sunglasses follow on their boat. Margarita, losing concentration, is apparently drowned by exhaustion, the oil slick ("rainbows"), and the family's hopes and demands, but mostly by the condescension of being called a simple Cuban amateur and brave little loser by the sexist American television reporter in a helicopter. Sinking to the bottom, she swims to the rhythm of "Hail Mary" into blackout. Abuela, who shouted "Assholes!" after the vanishing helicopter, invokes ancestors and saints as the grieving family reports the swimmer lost: "My little fish is not lost!" The same television reporter, in a nicely ambiguous phrase, describes to the family and the world "a miracle!" —

the lost, little Cuban swimmer "is now walking on the waters, through the breakers," first "onto the beach." Abuela recognizes "sangre de mi sangre"— blood of my blood.

In *Dog Lady*, pretty, 18–year-old Rosalinda Luna will successfully and literally "run like a dog" to win the big race, and run on beyond the barrio's Castro-street—with the prayerful support of her decorous mother and the yu-yu spell and incantation of old Luisa Ruiz, the mentally and physically unkempt dog-keeper and "healer" next door. But Jesse, the 15–year-old tomboy, receives the audience's attention, her mother's scolding, her sister's trust, and half the bouquet an infatuated 18–year-old intended for the star. Suddenly transformed into a beautiful señorita, Jesse asks, "You really turn into a dog?" Rosalinda puts the yu-yu around Jesse's neck, explaining, "You have to work very hard." The two actions—winning and reluctantly coming-of-age—frame soaring fantasies, functional but very funny misunderstandings, and sparkling dialogue.

Evening Star offers another two houses on Castro Street and another reluctant coming-of-age; Olivia Peña, aged 14, in parochial school uniform, and Junior Rodriguez, aged 16, search for stars from his roof. A 30–year-old male vendor is the keeper of lore and cures (like Eugenia, Abuela, the dog lady, and *Our Town*'s Stage Manager). Grandmother Tina Peña puzzles with the vendor over the significance of a white rose miraculously appearing in her garden that morning. It should signify birth, they agree—before the old man Peña, throwing rocks, drives the vendor off. Both hardworking households are impoverished and have problems with daughters. Peña drove off their lost Sarita who left behind her child Olivia, and the abandoned Mrs. Rodriguez at first does the same when her lanky 15-year-old admits her own pregnancy. However, as Lilly Rodriguez gives birth upstairs in the Peñas' house, little epiphanies, tendernesses, and strengths bloom like roses. Mama Rodriguez rushes in to help her baby, and old Peña, who can't go in and can't pray, throws a humanistic rock at heaven. The vendor is heard: "The sun is rising. Another day of life. Try not to abuse it." Despite gritty details, poetic mono-logues, Old Peña's comic grouchiness and his daily ritual with Olivia (pains-takingly, penuriously crossing off from his mailing list Hispanic names found in the obituaries), real theatrical magic seems slight, and too much of the affirmation gratuitous.

In *Roosters*, a multi-levelled conflict is set among farm workers who are laboring to achieve some dignity and respite. Sánchez-Scott divides allegorically-named males and females into contrasting types and lets the drama bring them to fertile reconciliation. In a prologue the handsome Gallo, in his forties, explains how, at the cost of a prison term for manslaughter, he "borrowed" a high-flying ("like dark avenging angels") Filipino bolina named MacArthur to breed with his old red Cuban hen ("a queen" to whom you would never give "a second look" yet who killed every "stag") to create the prize-fighting cock Zapata. As he stalks and pricks his crossbred Hispanic-Pacific rooster (a male dancer) with a stiletto, Gallo croons "Show Daddy watcha got" and delights when "son" Zapata attacks and draws blood. Now, all anxiously await the homecoming of husband-lover, brother and father. Willed the bird by his grandfather during his father's absence, Gallo's 20-year-old son Hector plans to first-fight Zapata tonight and sell him to finance a better life for his mother (Juana), tortilla-rolling aunt (Chata), and mystical younger sister (Angelita). The women preparing food anticipate more hardship and loneliness. Angelita with her cardboard wings and tombstones, prayers to saints, disappearances, and imaginary tea-parties can see the shadows stalking her father and brother and must choose sides. The predicted cockfight between Hector and Gallo allows rightful shares of nobility to each generation, character, and way of living. Sánchez-Scott achieves this persuasively.

—John G. Kuhn

SCHENKAR, Joan M.

American. Born in Seattle, Washington, 15 August 1946. Educated at St. Nicholas School, Bennington College, Bennington, Vermont, and a collection of graduate schools. Advertising copywriter, social worker, and researcher, all New York, 1960's; coffee and doughnut vendor, 1973, and church organist, Congregational Church, 1974, both Vermont; playwright-in-residence, Joseph Chaikin's Winter Project, New York, 1977 and 1978, Polish Laboratory, New York, 1977, Florida Studio Theatre, Sarasota, Florida, 1980, Changing Scene, Denver, Colorado, 1982, Centre d'essai des auteurs dramatiques, Montreal, and Composer-Librettist's Workshop, New York, both 1985, Minnesota Opera New Music Theatre Ensemble, Minneapolis, 1986–88, and Kentucky Foundation for Women, Louisville, Kentucky, 1988. Visiting fellow, Cummington Community Arts, Cummington, Massachusetts, 1978, Ragdale Foundation, Lake Forest, Illinois, 1979, and MacDowell Art Colony, Peterborough, New Hampshire, 1980; teacher, School of Visual Arts, New York, 1978–91; founder and artistic director, Force Majeure Productions, New York, from 1987. Since 1992 director, The Performance Series, North Bennington, Vermont. Recipient: National Endowment for the Arts grant, 1977, 1978, 1980, 1982, fellowship, 1981; Creative Artists Public Service fellowship, 1979–80; Lowe Foundation grant, 1983; Playwrights Forum award, 1984; Arthur Foundation grant, 1984, 1989; New York State Council on the Arts grant, 1986, 1989, 1992; Schubert Travel grant, 1988; Vermont Community grant, 1991. Agent: Casarotto Ramsay Ltd., National House, 60–66 Wardour Street, London W1V 3HP, England. Address: P.O. Box 814, North Bennington, Vermont 05257, U.S.A.

Publications

PLAYS

The Next Thing (produced 1976).
Cabin Fever (produced 1976). 1984.
Last Words (produced 1977).
Signs of Life (produced 1979). In *The Women's Project Anthology* edited by Julia Miles, 1980.
The Lodger (produced 1979).
Mr. Monster (produced 1980).
The Last of Hitler (also director: produced 1981).
Between the Acts (also director: produced 1984).

Fulfilling Koch's Postulate (also director: produced 1985).
Joan of Arc (produced 1986).
Family Pride in the 50's (produced 1986). In *The Kenyon Review*, Spring 1993.
Fire in the Future (produced 1987; also director: produced 1988).
Hunting Down the Sexes (includes *Bucks and Does, The Lodger*) (produced 1987).
Nothing Is Funnier than Death (produced 1988).
The Universal Wolf (produced 1991). 1992.

CRITICAL STUDIES (SELECTION): "Foodtalk in the Plays of Caryl Churchill and Joan Schenkar" by Vivian M. Patraka, in *The Theatre Annual*, 1985; "Mass Culture and Metaphors of Menace in Joan Schenkar's Plays" by Vivian M. Patraka, in *Making a Spectacle, Feminist Essays on Contemporary Women's Theatre* edited by Lynda Hart, 1989; "History and Hysteria, Writing the Body in *Portrait of Dora* and *Signs of Life*" by Ann Wilson, in *Modern Drama*, March 1989; "Crossing the Corpus Callosum" by Elin Diamond, in *The Drama Review*, Summer 1991.

THEATRICAL ACTIVITIES

DIRECTOR: **Plays**—*The Last of Hitler*, 1981; *Between the Acts*, 1984, 1989; *Fulfilling Koch's Postulate*, 1985; *Fire in the Future*, 1988.

Joan Schenkar comments:

My most serious intention as a writer for the stage is to enter a clear condition of nightmare thru the comedy of precise vernacular . . . Some truths are so terrible they can only be approached by laughter—which is why I write comedies of menace. In the best of all possible productions, I will have made you laugh at something horrible.

Dreams, history, and fantasy serve as raw material for the elliptical, determinedly non-naturalistic plays of Joan Schenkar. Her style is heavily influenced by cartoons, comic strips, feminist theory and literature, radio, television, circus, and sideshow. Schenkar's stated purpose "is to make comedies of tragic subjects," and she wields her macabre, demonic sense of humor like a scalpel, dissecting varied topics—the Victorians' destructive attitude toward women, the insidious spread of anti-Semitism, the power and precariousness of a scientific outlook, and the surreal normality of American suburbia.

Schenkar gives a number of her plays the subtitle "a comedy of menace." Her three primary works in this vein—*Cabin Fever, Fulfilling Koch's Postulate*, and *Family Pride in the 50's*—all share this subversive manic humor. *Cabin Fever*, the funniest and most menacing, reads like a Stephen King story as dramatized by Samuel Beckett. Three characters, called One, Two, and Three, never move from their dilapidated New England front porch as they try to stave off the dreaded disease of the title. Underneath their reserved, almost formal manner, terror lurks: they know "it comes in threes." "What does?" one character asks. "Death," assures another. With each repetition of this litany their anxiety spirals. When talk turns to the cannibalism that's been running rampant in this backwoods community, One twitches in her seat as Two and Three recall the last time they sampled human flesh. Although they jocularly threaten to eat One, she gets the last laugh, and the play ends with her brandishing knife and fork.

Influenced by the Katzenjammer Kids comic strip, Schenkar purposefully confines herself to a 300-word vocabulary for *Fulfilling Koch's Postulate*. Like *Cabin Fever*, Schenkar provides her characters with a one-line litany: "Nothing is funnier than death." Her sets are always exaggerated metaphors that serve as an extra character and this one is no exception, featuring a lip-shaped proscenium and a playing space made into an esophagus. Within this frame the stage is split between the kitchen, from which a household chef, based on the infamous historical figure known as Typhoid Mary, spreads her deadly contagion, and the laboratory in which Dr. Koch tries to track down the disease's root. As the cook cooks and the scientist probes, the culinary activities take on shades of sinister experimentation while Koch's dissections become utterly domestic. *Family Pride in the 50's* is a heavy-handed satire on an easy target: the idyllic post-war decade dominated by frosted flakes, family holiday dinners, and fights over the television set. Everyone resembles everyone else—two brothers married two sisters, each with two children. As the eldest child Joan retches violently, everyone blithely continues their family squabbles. When the children play "doctor," they use real knives and instruments, much like the dramatist did: "When I was a kid I used to collect knives. . . . I had a surgeon's puncture tool. . . . And I'd take people's blood samples." The play ends with the children sitting around the table:

> Maureen: You gonna deal those cards? Or do I have to cut 'em with my knife.
> Joan: Tch tch. Such language sis. Tch tch tch. Such *language* at the *dinner* table.

Schenkar's preoccupation with science—or what she calls "false science"—underlies two other historically based plays, *The Last of Hitler* and *Signs of Life*. The former is a dream play picturing the Führer in what Schenkar envisions as his version of Hell—a "Kozy Kabin" in Florida, a state with a large population of Jews. Once again, Schenkar works with a split stage, but this one is divided by an enormous 1940's radio that spews anti-Semitism, less visible than Typhoid Mary's infection but just as deadly. As Dr. Reich and his office skeleton perform ventriloquist routines reminiscent of Charlie McCarthy's, Hitler and Eva Braun fight off cancer and their own Jewishness. *Signs of Life*, the most successful of Schenkar's imaginative treatments of history, features Henry James and Dr. Sloper, the inventor of the "uterine guillotine," taking tea and toasting "the ladies" who Schenkar believes helped make the men famous—Henry's invalid sister Alice, and Jane Merritt, P.T. Barnum's sideshow star dubbed the "Elephant Woman," on whom Sloper performed experimental surgery. The play clearly demonstrates how both women were transformed into freaks, victims of Victorian patriarchy's male-volence toward women.

Between the Acts, an absurdist surreal fairytale set in the garden of the wealthiest man in the world, gives allegorical voice to Schenkar's feminist and political concerns. At a climactic moment, the rich capitalist Martin Barney and his daughter's lesbian lover the artist Romaine Brooks, circle each other like boxers. Instead of trading physical blows, they shout out famous names. When Barney yells "J.P. Morgan" Romaine is momentarily staggered, but she strikes back with "Emily Brontë, Emily Dickinson, Virginia Woolf!" and crumples the industrialist, who wails, "Genius! Good God! I have nothing to fight genius with." Featuring a gigantic Venus Fly Trap that serves as a trysting spot, a riding crop that spews magic dust, and a dog in a tutu performing bourrées in silhouette, this is one of Schenkar's wildest efforts.

Hunting Down the Sexes, composed of two compact and vicious one-acts, literalizes these gender wars. Part One, *Bucks and Does*, focuses on three men, Rap, Ape, and Ab, at their hunting cabin. The play opens with Rap masturbating in synchronized motion with Ab's ritualistic cleaning of the guns. Schenkar then takes Freud's theories to their harrowing extreme: Rap, who insists on calling does "pretty brown girls," tells his mates, "There's nothing like pulling a trigger and watching 'em drop. I always come when they drop." Of course, the does, portrayed by actresses, get their final revenge when Rap staggers into the cabin with his crotch bloodied by a stray bullet. In Part Two, *The Lodger*, a pair of spinsterish women debate the tortures they'll inflict on their male prisoner, captured in the guerilla war between genders raging around their Victorian New England home.

Schenkar's works all limn the body/brain duality. Images of blood, ritualistic "bloodings," and blood samples appear in virtually every play, while the fragile intellectual systems holding reality together go haywire. Schenkar's stagecraft, using varied performance traditions—from cartoons to shadow-puppets—and structural devices—from entr'actes to epilogues—matches her imagination to provide, in the best of her work, insightful entrées to the dualities duelling for body and soul in Western society.

—John Istel

SHANGE, Ntozake.

American. Born Paulette Williams in Trenton, New Jersey, 18 October 1948; took name Ntozake Shange in 1971. Educated at schools in St. Louis and New Jersey; Barnard College, New York, 1966–70, B.A. (cum laude) in American studies 1970; University of Southern California, Los Angeles, 1971–73, M.A. in American studies 1973. Married David Murray in 1977 (2nd marriage; divorced); one daughter. Faculty member, Sonoma State College, Rohnert Park, California, 1973–75, Mills College, Oakland, California, 1975, City College, New York, 1975, and Douglass College, New Brunswick, New Jersey, 1978. Since 1983 associate professor of drama, University of Houston. Artist-in-residence, Equinox Theatre, Houston, from 1981. Recipient: New York Drama Critics Circle award, 1977; Obie award, 1977, 1980; Columbia University medal of excellence, 1981; Los Angeles *Times* award, 1981; Guggenheim fellowship, 1981; New York State Council of the Arts award, 1981. Address: Department of Drama, University of Houston–University Park, 4800 Calhoun Road, Houston, Texas 77004, U.S.A.

Publications

PLAYS

For Colored Girls Who Have Considered Suicide When the Rainbow Is Enuf (produced 1975). 1976; revised version, 1977.

A Photograph: Lovers-in-Motion (as *A Photograph: A Still Life with Shadows, A Photograph: A Study of Cruelty*, produced 1977; revised version, as *A Photograph: Lovers-in-Motion*, also director: produced 1979). 1981.

Where the Mississippi Meets the Amazon, with Thulani Nkabinda and Jessica Hagedorn (produced 1977).

Spell #7 (produced 1979). In*Three Pieces*, 1981; published separately, 1985.

Black and White Two-Dimensional Planes (produced 1979).

Boogie Woogie Landscapes (produced 1980). In*Three Pieces*, 1981.

Mother Courage and Her Children, adaptation of a play by Brecht (produced 1980).

From Okra to Greens: A Different Kinda Love Story (as *Mouths* produced 1981; as *From Okra to Greens*, in *Three for a Full Moon*, produced 1982). 1983.

Three Pieces: Spell #7, A Photograph: Lovers-in-Motion, Boogie Woogie Landscapes. 1981.

Three for a Full Moon, and Bocas (produced 1982).

Educating Rita, adaptation of the play by Willy Russell (produced 1983).

Betsey Brown, adaptation of her own novel, with Emily Mann, music by Baikida Carroll, lyrics by Shange, Mann, and Carroll (also director: produced 1986).

Three Views of Mt. Fuji (produced 1987).

The Love Space Demands: A Continuing Saga (produced 1992). 1991; included in *Plays: One*, 1992.

Plays: One (includes *For Colored Girls Who Have Considered Suicide When the Rainbow Is Enuf, Spell #7, I Heard Eric Dolphy in His Eyes, The Love Space Demands: A Continuing Saga*). 1992.

NOVELS

Sassafrass: A Novella. 1977.

Sassafrass, Cypress and Indigo. 1982.

Betsey Brown. 1985.

VERSE

Melissa and Smith. 1976.

Natural Disasters and Other Festive Occasions. 1977.

Nappy Edges. 1978.

A Daughter's Geography. 1983.

From Okra to Greens: Poems. 1984.

Ridin' the Moon West in Texas: Word Paintings. 1988.

OTHER

See No Evil: Prefaces, Essays, and Accounts 1976–1983. 1984.

THEATRICAL ACTIVITIES

DIRECTOR: Plays—*The Mighty Gents* by Richard Wesley, 1979; *The Spirit of Sojourner Truth* by Bernice Reagon and June Jordan, 1979; *A Photograph: Lovers-in-Motion*, 1979; *Betsey Brown*, 1989; *Fire's Daughter* by Ina Césaire, 1993.

ACTOR: Plays—The Lady in Orange in *For Colored Girls Who Have Considered Suicide When the Rainbow Is Enuf*, 1976; in *Where the Mississippi Meets the Amazon*, 1977; in *Mouths*, 1981.

Ntozake Shange is best known as the creator of the choreopoem form for the stage. The choreopoem, a uniquely African-American form of performance, is a collection of related poems combined with song and dance. Shange's famous choreopoem, *For Colored Girls Who Have Considered Suicide When the Rainbow is Enuf*, allowed the seven women performers, each dressed in a color of the rainbow, to express their emotional experiences in dance, song, and poetry written in African-American dialect. When Shange played the part of the Lady in Orange in the Broadway production, she created a uniquely African-American grammar of gestures and strides to accompany the dialect. Shange has created an innovative, distinctive style of oral and visual presence for the African-American performer.

Shange has also pioneered a sucessful rebellion against the hegemony of the well-made play through creating innovative narrative strategies and through parodying racist representations. In *Spell #7*, a giant minstrel mask, suggesting both the horrific minstrel shows performed by whites in black-face and a black African mask, hangs over the stage. The plot of the play consists of struggling actors and actresses taking up the position of narrator as the remaining cast enact the story, so that the actors do not retain fixed identities, but are portrayed as fluid constructions, subjects-in-process. The performers dress up and play racist stereotypes such as "picaninnies", the stereotype of African-Americans as happy farmers. Lou, dressed as the traditional inter-locuter of the minstrel show, intervenes between the audience's complicity in accepting the black performers as minstrels by citing black history, confronting them with the implications of racism. In this play, all are under the spell of the black minstrel mask, the sceptre of white culture's appropriation and degra-dation of African-American art forms, and yet African-American men and women can dis-spell the spell through black magic. This black magic consists of coding "whiteness" as an ethnic category in a reversed minstrel show, as the black cast put on white face and perform "white experience".

In *A Photograph: Lovers-in-Motion*, Sean's camera functions as the techno-logical equivalent of the minstrel mask in *Spell #7*. Sean, a photographer, tries to take control of the means of representation. Shange reveals the camera as a tool that can record the unrepresented, freeing them from domination, at the the same time as the camera itself is a tool of objectification and oppression. In the play, Sean objectifies the female Michael, and his desire to photograph her becomes a means of possessing and dominating her. The play suggests that the camera, which can produce images in black-and-white or color, still can photograph only in black and white; African-Americans cannot merely appro-priate the means of representation without subjecting the structure of represen-tation, whether it be the well-made play or photography, to reconsideration.

Boogie Woogie Landscapes dramatizes a woman's dreams, memories, and experiences in a stream-of-consciousness style. As in *Spell #7*, Layla and the other six characters are night-life performers who sing, dance, and narrate their emotional experiences in a powerful, lyrical form. As Layla sleeps, the other characters present scenes of her life and dramatize her thoughts. With this formal innovation, Shange again provides an alternative to the notion of character as a stable identity performed by only one performer.

In the American theatre, any one image of an African-American character can become representative of the entire race of African-Americans. To subvert the white liberal assumption that one fictional story of an African-American facilitates an understanding of the African-American experience, Shange's characters tell many different stories within each choreopoem, all imaginative constructions of the devastating effects of racism and sexism. None of these stories can be subsumed beneath one hegemonic notion of what it means to be an African-American. Similarly, in *For Colored Girls Who Have Considered Suicide When The Rainbow is Enuf*, seven women tell their own stories. The play does not amount to one narrative but is composed of conflicting stories which do not give rise to a mythic notion of the African-American woman. The spectator leaves the theatre with a plurality of women's voices ringing in her ear. Shange herself stresses: "I feel that as an artist my job is to appreciate the differences among my women characters . . . what is fascinating is the multiplicity of individual responses to this kind of oppression [racism]". Instead of producing myths, stereotypes, or positive images of African-Americans, Shange's plays examine how the representations of African-Americans both determine and obfuscate their real existence.

In her foreword to *Three Pieces*, Shange reveals that she has been influenced by Frantz Fanon's theory of "combat breath", the lived struggle of the colonized subject contending with foreign occupation and surveillance. She admits that Fanon's descriptions of a colonized existence made her conscious of her own status as a victim of American colonization: "although Fanon was referring to francophone colonies, the schema he draws is sadly familiar". All of Shange's work reflects her astute consciousness that the means of representation, including the English language and the theatrical stage, are mechanisms of colonialism bearing traces of a violent history.

In her plays, Shange writes a different history, a history of resistance, which requires linguistic and formal innovations. Her use of lower-case letters, contractions, transcriptions of oral speech, and slashes reflect her desire to "attack deform and maim the language that i waz taught to hate myself in". She speaks of deconstructing language: "i haveta fix my tool to my needs/ i have to take it apart to the bone/so that the malignancies/fall away/leaving us space to literally create our own image". Shange writes with the consciousness that she is at war with the symbolic order, with the pre-constituted, colonizing representations which inform African-American experience.

Sandra L. Richards notes that Shange's style is rooted in the spiritual African perspective, in which the world is conceived "as animated by the interplay of energy fields or forces . . .". The language, music, dance, props, and costumes function as *mojos*, spiritual fields of energy which allow the subject to experience cosmic wholeness. For Richards, Shange's plays are extraordinary because they portray a dialectic between social oppression and spiritual resistance and transcendence. "In Shange's drawing upon this black aesthetic lies the will to divinity, an impulse which her characters experience as an opposition to combat breath".

—Karen Cronacher

See the essay on *For Colored Girls Who Have Considered Suicide When the Rainbow is Enuf.*

SHEARER, Jill.

Australian. Born in Melbourne, 14 April 1936. Secretary, Japanese Consulate-General, Brisbane, 1966–79. Recipient: Big River Festival prize, for poetry, 1973; Monash Alexander Special award, 1976; New South Wales Society of Women Writers award, 1976; Utah Cairns Centenary award, 1976; McGregor Literary award, 1987; Australia Council grant, 1989. Address: c/o Playlab Press, P.O. Box 185, Ashgrove, Brisbane 4060, Queensland, Australia.

Publications

PLAYS

The Trouble with Gillian (produced 1974).
The Foreman (produced 1976). 1979.
The Boat (produced 1977). In *Can't You Hear Me Talking to You*, 1978.
The Kite (produced 1977). In *Echoes and Other Plays*, 1980.
Nocturne (produced 1977). In *Echoes and Other Plays*, 1980.
Catherine (produced 1978). 1977.
Stephen (produced 1980). In *Echoes and Other Plays*, 1980.
Echoes and Other Plays (includes *The Kite, Nocturne, Stephen*). 1980.
Release Lavinia Stannard (produced 1980).
A Woman Like That (produced 1986).
Shimada (produced 1987). 1989.
Comrade (produced 1987). 1987.

RADIO PLAY: *A Woman Like That*, 1989.

MANUSCRIPT COLLECTION: Fryer Library, University of Queensland, St. Lucia, Brisbane.

CRITICAL STUDY: "Telling It in Multiple Layers: an interview with Jill Shearer" by Helen Gilbert, in *Australasian Drama Studies*, 21, October 1992.

Jill Shearer comments:

Whilst I'm interested in all aspects of contemporary society, I'm drawn to writing about individuals and families often caught up in larger events. Living and working in Australia I'm increasingly interested in exploring Asian cultures (as I did in my play *Shimada*) increasingly linked as they are with my own.

Beginning with numerous one-act plays written in the 1970's and produced mostly by amateur companies, Jill Shearer's work exhibits a passionate concern with social issues and tackles such wide-ranging and often controversial topics as abortion, industrial work practices, conservation, race relations, and foreign economic influence in Australia. Most often, these broader issues are played out in localized settings through the representation of ordinary people and family situations. *The Foreman*, for example, condemns racism not through a primary focus on interactions between Aboriginal and non-Aboriginal Australians but by revealing the effects of prejudice on an Aboriginal family whose relationships become strained when the breadwinner is rejected by his white "mates" after he receives a well-deserved promotion.

Other plays such as *Echoes*, *The Trouble with Gillian*, *Stephen*, and *The Boat* also foreground family tensions, although these are often more powerfully suggested by the characters' desperate attempts to sustain some semblance of harmony or normality than by any overt confrontations. *The Boat* depicts a man's regression into a child-like fantasy world after he loses his job and sense of purpose. His wife and son choose not to disabuse him of his belief that the daily fishing trips played out in the living room of their conventional suburban home are mere fictions. In *Echoes*, the representation of a family on holiday at the beach is similarly energized by a forced but unsustainable congeniality which side-steps problems and masks hostilities. In both texts, subterranean conflict is kindled by an outsider who threatens to fracture the fragile integrity of the family unit, but despite its fissures, this structure proves resistant to the "truths" the outsider might offer. Short, sharp, and narrowly focused, both plays construct vivid impressions of the roles people play in order to cope with difficult situations. Characterized by deft touches of the bizarre combined with a vague sense of threat, they are strongly evocative of Pinter's work, as is *Nocturne*, a very short scenario which positions a cellist at the top of a mountain road playing with wild abandon, oblivious to all else but the music, while a walker becomes increasingly frustrated and aggressive as she tries to make conversation. Here, Shearer's use of silence and the unfinished line or trail-away phrase also owes much to Pinter's influence.

To the extent that she evokes clearly recognizable images of tropical Australia, Shearer could be called a regionalist writer. *Nocturne* owes something of its uncomfortable ambience to the disjunction between a highly minimalist set, an abstract tree beside a white strip of road, and the dialogue's insistent references to the panoramic view from the tangled rainforest where the antagonists sit to the nearby coastline and beyond. *Echoes* features the Great Barrier Reef as a deceptively calm retreat wherein nature's bounty is balanced only by its potential destructiveness. This dual aspect of nature which represents both threat and promise acts here as a metaphorical parallel for the characters themselves while in *The Kite*, the healing powers of the beach and the sand are harnessed to dissuade a young woman from committing suicide.

Though not pursuing an obvious feminist agenda, Shearer consistently creates strong women characters and her one historical play, *Catherine*, clearly argues for a reconsideration of women's roles in Australia's past and present. Constructed as a play within a play, *Catherine* explores the relationship between a female convict on the second fleet and a rakish upper-class gentleman who has taken her by intimidation, if not force, for his mistress. While the viewer's interest is directed toward this tale, the framing narrative questions the passivity attributed to Catherine when the actor who plays her insists on presenting a character with more verve than the director sees fit. Primarily, the play sets out to rescue Catherine and other convict women from the margins of imperial history, but it also voices a powerful indictment of the convict system even while celebrating the tenacity of the oppressed and dispossessed who were transported to Australia to found a nation.

Stylistically, Shearer's recent work strives towards heightened expression through spare dialogue and dramatic uses of the mise en scène. *Shimada*, her most acclaimed play, shows the theatrical influences of Japanese forms such as Nō and Kabuki. Also set on Queensland's tropical coast, *Shimada* tackles the difficult issue of Asian-Australian relations. Eliding past and present, the play interweaves two narratives of cultural conflict. The contemporary scenes focus on a group of Australians struggling to avoid Japanese control of a small bicycle factory, but their efforts are clearly motivated less by a commitment to national economic growth than by xenophobic fears, inflamed by wartime memories, for the ending looks to American capital investment to keep the factory viable. One of the older workers, Eric, believes that the Japanese businessman Toshio, who comes to discuss the merger, is the dreaded guard of the camp in Burma where he was interned during World War II. Through flashbacks and effective uses of role doubling the text does indeed suggest that Toshio might be Shimada, but it is equally probable that the two are only related in Eric's mind. While the Australian's suspicion of the cultural "other" is matched by Toshio's inscrutability, suggesting that relationships between the two nations are destined to remain problematic, *Shimada*'s primary appeal lies in precisely those differences which make interactions between characters and the cross-fertilization of forms so theatrically charged.

Thematically and stylistically, Shearer's work is not easily categorized as it ranges freely through diverse topics, and experiments with a number of dramatic modes of expression. One recurrent element in her work, however, is a cautious celebration of Australians' abilities to cope with the vicissitudes of modern life.

—Helen Gilbert

SIMONS, Beverley (née Rosen).

Canadian. Born in Flin Flon, Manitoba, 31 March 1938. Educated at Banff School of Fine Arts, Alberta, 1956; McGill University, Montreal, 1956–57; University of British Columbia, Vancouver, 1958–59, B.A. (honours) in English and theatre 1959. Married to Sidney B. Simons; three sons. Lived in Europe, 1959–61. Recipient: Canada Council grant, 1967, and award, 1972. Lives in Vancouver. Address: c/o Playwrights Union of Canada, 8 York Street, 6th Floor, Toronto, Ontario M5J 1R2, Canada.

Publications

PLAYS

Twisted Roots (as Beverley Rosen), in *First Flowering*, edited by Anthony Frisch. 1956.
The Birth (produced 1957).

A Play (produced 1957).
The Elephant and the Jewish Question (produced 1968). n.d.
Green Lawn Rest Home (produced 1969). 1973.
Crabdance (produced 1969). 1969; revised version (produced 1972), 1972.
Preparing (produced 1973). In *Preparing* (collection), 1975.
Preparing (includes *Prologue, Triangle, The Crusader, Green Lawn Rest Home*). 1975.
Prologue, Triangle, The Crusader (produced 1976). In *Preparing*, 1975.
If I Turn Around Quick, in *Capilano Review*, Summer 1976.
Leela Means to Play (produced 1978). In *Canadian Theatre Review* 9, Winter 1976.

TELEVISION PLAY: *The Canary*, 1968.

CRITICAL STUDY: "Beverley Simons Issue" of *Canadian Theatre Review* 9, Winter 1976.

Crabdance is Beverley Simons's best-known work and remains her outstanding achievement. In it the commonplace world is transformed by Sadie Golden's hyper-sensitive perceptions, salesmen becoming sons, lovers, and husband as Sadie projects onto them her feelings about sex, motherhood, and her femaleness. At the critical hour of 3 p.m. she dies out of the lacerating existence in which "Mama's gone a-hunting/She's taken off her own white skin. . . ." The salesmen are recognizably objective figures as well as emanations from Sadie, and the play's relation to experience is powerfully present through distorted images. The great success of *Crabdance* lies in the perilous balance between observation and feeling, the known world and Sadie's vision of it.

In an earlier one-act play, *Green Lawn Rest Home*, less ambitious than *Crabdance* but the most finished and unified of her plays, Simons also makes the internal perceptions of the characters modify the presentation of outward reality and brilliantly fuses lyrical and satirical perspectives. Society's prettification of senility and dying is critically observed while, at the same time, the mortifications before death, the leaking away of life in anguish, the tiny passions of the geriatrics, are seen and felt from within. A "date" which consists of a walk to the gate of the rest home becomes, for the old couple subjectively presented, the equivalent of the most violent adolescent sexuality. Simons conveys feelingly the real hardness of the green pebbles which, from a little distance away, give the illusion of lawns.

Leela Means to Play presents, sporadically, clear moral views of the operations of legal justice through a kind of trial-by-encounters of a judge. The play is a full-length aggregation of very short scenes, related in theme but not through plot or sequence—gobbets of allegory in which the representation of modern life is distorted by an intensely feeling consciousness. There is no equivalent of Sadie Golden, however, to give focus and coherence in this play. In this work Simons relies too naïvely on her audience's recognition of the personality *behind* it. The play seems to have been untimely snatched from the authorial womb, still trailing unsynthesized bits of Beckett, Genet, Albee, and Nō-via-Yeats, unfinished though very much alive.

The title piece of *Preparing* gives us (like *Crabdance*) a dramatization of the passionately sensitive perceptions of Simons. This monologue requires an actress skilled in mime and with a set of voices adequate to portray the several ages of woman. From adolescence to womanhood the speaker undertakes preparations for imposed sexual roles ending with ultimate resistance ("fuck 'em all") to all the impositions. Two other short pieces in this collection are too clamantly "experimental"; one, *The Crusader*, employs masks in a novel but clumsy way; in the other, *Triangle*, light and movement give us the geometry of bonding and victimage in the relationships of three characters. In both the moral view is rather heavily imposed and not offset by studious "theatricality."

In an earlier play, *The Elephant and the Jewish Question* (published only in mimeographed form), Simons showed herself capable of handling a conventional structure and natural speech, though the piece is rather stickily embedded in "Jewish atmosphere." The great development from this to *Crabdance* is an indication of Simons's strengths. Her work is marked by her exploration of various ways of presenting lyrical, internalized characters within an objective framework. But her genuine distinctiveness seems to be still overlayed and obscured by studious imitation and anxiety about form.

—Michael Sidnell

SMITH, Dodie (Dorothy Gladys Smith).

British. Born in Whitefield, Lancashire, 3 May, 1896. Attended Whalley Range High School, Manchester; St Paul's Girls' School, London; studied acting at Royal Academy of Dramatic Art, London, 1914–15. Married Alec Macbeth Beesley in 1939 (died 1987). Actor, 1915–22; buyer, Heal and Son, London, 1923–32; then full-time writer. *Died 24 November 1990.*

Publications

PLAYS

British Talent (as C.L. Anthony) (produced 1923).
Autumn Crocus (as C.L. Anthony) (produced 1931). 1931.
Service (as C.L. Anthony) (produced 1932). 1932.
Touch Wood (as C.L. Anthony) (produced 1934). 1934.
Call It a Day (produced 1935). 1936.
Bonnet over the Windmill (also co-director: produced 1937). 1937.
Dear Octopus (also co-director: produced 1938). 1938.
Lovers and Friends (produced 1943). 1947.
Letter from Paris, adaptation of the novel *The Reverberator* by Henry James (produced 1952). 1954.
I Capture the Castle, adaptation of her own novel (produced 1954). 1955.
These People, Those Books (produced 1958).
Amateur Means Lover (produced 1961). 1962.

SCREENPLAYS: *Schoolgirl Rebels* (as Charles Henry Percy), 1915; *The Uninvited*, with Frank Partos, 1944; *Darling, How Could You!*, with Lesser Samuels, 1951.

NOVELS

I Capture the Castle. 1948.
The New Moon with the Old. 1963.
The Town in Bloom. 1965.
It Ends with Revelations. 1967.
A Tale of Two Families. 1970.
The Girl from the Candle-Lit Bath. 1978.

FICTION (FOR CHILDREN)

The Hundred and One Dalmations. 1956.
The Starlight Barking: More about the Hundred and One Dalmations. 1967.
The Midnight Kittens. 1978.

OTHER

Autobiography:
  1. *Look Back with Love: A Manchester Childhood.* 1974.
  2. *Look Back with Mixed Feelings.* 1978.
  3. *Look Back with Astonishment.* 1979.
  4. *Look Back with Gratitude.* 1985.

THEATRICAL ACTIVITIES

DIRECTOR: **Plays**—*Bonnet over the Windmill* (co-director, with Murray Macdonald), 1937; *Dear Octopus* (co-director, with Glen Byam Shaw), 1938. ACTOR: **Plays**—in the sketch *Playgoers* by Pinero, 1915; *Kitty Grey* by J.S. Piggott and *Mr Wu* by H.M. Vernon and Harold Owen, 1915; *Ye Gods* by Stephen Robert and Eric Hudson, and *Jane and Niobe*, 1916–17; *When Knights Were Bold* by Charles Marlowe, 1917; in music-hall sketches and in a concert party, 1918; Claudine in *Telling the Tale*, 1919–20; *French Leave* by Reginald Berkeley, 1921; *The Shewing Up of Blanco Posnet* and *You Never Can Tell* by Shaw, 1921; *Ann in The Pigeon* by Galsworthy, 1922.

Cynthia – Is that a teddy-bear there (Taking it.) Why, it's Symp.
Scrap   – (Following Her). Symp?
Cynthia – We called him that because he was extra sympathetic. We
         used to hug him whenever we were miserable—when we were
         in disgrace or the rabbits died or when nobody understood us.

The quotation is from Dodie Smith's best-known play, *Dear Octopus*, a play about a family, its feuds and friendships, first performed in 1938 with one of those casts publicists call 'glittering' (with good reason—included in the Queen's Theatre company were Marie Tempest, John Gielgud, Madge Compton, Angela Baddeley, among others). The theme of sympathy in fact might be Smith's principal key—in all her plays she seems to comprehend the very well-springs of her characters. She builds them surely and with understanding; they emerge as palpable beings, ordinary people who are more-than-ordinarily believable. And that's quite a talent.

Starting with an early screenplay written while studying at RADA (*Schoolgirl Rebels*—written under a male pseudonym) the playwright first went on stage in 1915 at the age of 19, but it did not bring her the golden fruits her pen was later to harvest for her—after a series of depressing tours she left the stage and became a buyer for Heal's. Fortunately while shopping for toys and pictures for middle-class kids she did not stop writing, and in 1923 *British Talent* was given an amateur airing. In 1931 came *Autumn Crocus*—a huge success—and she was launched. She wrote a number of plays in the 1930s, a gilded era when style and construction were of supreme value and audiences expected a well-made play. Smith constructed her plays like boxes, solid, secure, each line leading to another line, each situation growing and blossoming within the classic three-act mould. In fact as one reads them now it is the strong sense of craftsmanship that still comes across—a professional and enviable ability to forge a story so that the shape of the play, from opening curtain to closing line, is all of a piece. You can read her plays like novels—and with a little imagination see the situations developing before you. It isn't surprising that she turned to novel writing, and her first, *I Capture the Castle*, was later turned into a play. She also adapted a Henry James story, *The Reverberator*, to become *Letter from Paris*. It is a play that, unlike some of the others, has a musty air of datedness, and the characters, although still firmly handled and well presented, have a slight edge of melodrama—which may of course be a Jamesian legacy.

It's not just a lucky chance that makes Smith's work so often the choice of enthusiastic amateur groups, for perhaps more than professional actors they seize quickly onto these ready-formed characters which are so near completion on the printed page. Smith liked to write about good, middle-class homes and people with values—taking that sensible but often ignored advice, to write about what one knows. She undoubtedly knew her people and put them into human situations which cleverly avoid being sentimental. Her ear for the comfortably-off family in *Dear Octopus* is very sound; indeed her dialogue has an authentic natural running ring that rarely bogs down.

—Michael T. Leech

SOFOLA, Zulu.

Nigerian. Born in Issele-Uku, 22 June 1935. Educated at Virginia Union University, Richmond, B.A. in English (cum laude) 1959; Catholic University of America, Washington, D.C., M.A. in drama 1966; University of Ibadan, Ph.D. in tragic theory 1977. Married J.A. Sofola in 1960; four sons and one daughter. Coordinator of extra-mural programme, University of Ibadan, 1968–70; acting head of the performing arts department, 1985–87, and since 1989 head of department, University of Ilorin, Kwara State; senior visiting professor, State University of New York, Buffalo, New York, 1988–89. Recipient: African-American scholarship, 1961–62; Ford Foundation fellowship, 1969–72; University of Missouri award, 1971; African Writers Project award, 1980; Ife International Book Fair award, 1987; Fulbright fellowship, 1988. Address: c/o Department of the Performing Arts, Faculty of Arts, University of Ilorin, Ilorin, Kwara State, Nigeria.

Publications

PLAYS

The Disturbed Peace of Christmas (produced 1969). 1971.
Wedlock of the Gods (also director: produced 1971). 1973.

The Operators (produced 1973). In *Lost Dreams and Other Plays*, 1992.
King Emene (produced 1975). 1974.
Old Wines Are Tasty (produced 1975). 1981.
The Sweet Trap (produced 1975; also director: produced 1988). 1977.
The Wizard of Law. 1976.
The Deer and the Hunters Pearl (produced 1976).
Memories in the Moonlight (produced 1977). 1986.
Song of a Maiden (produced 1977). 1991.
Queen Omu-Ako of Oligbo (also director: produced 1989).
Eclipso and the Fantasia (produced 1990).
Lost Dreams (produced 1991). In *Lost Dreams and Other Plays*, 1992.
The Showers (produced 1991). In *Lost Dreams and Other Plays*, 1992.
The Love of the Life. In *Lost Dreams and Other Plays*, 1992.
Lost Dreams and Other Plays (includes *Lost Dreams*, *The Operators*, *The
    Love of the Life*, *The Showers*). 1992.

OTHER PLAYS
The Ivory Tower; *A Celebration of Life*.

THEATRICAL ACTIVITIES
DIRECTOR: **Plays**— *Wedlock of the Gods*, 1971; *King Emene*, 1978; *The Sweet
Trap*, 1988; *Queen Omu-Ako Oligbo*, 1989.

Zulu Sofola comments:

My main areas of research are into the African concept of tragedy, the creative
process, the artist in traditional societys and African aesthetics. In my plays I
explore the tragic factor in African cosmology in a search for an Afro-centric
theory that may help the African scholar to better define African humanity.
Consequently in my plays I have treated the aspects in traditional society where
customs and moral precepts set themselves at war against individual citizens, as
is the case in: *Wedlock of the Gods*; *Song of a Maiden*, where a university
intelligentsia reject the philosophy of "town and gown" and become irrelevant;
Queen Omu-Ako of Oligbo, where the traditional female arm of government
confronts the warring camps of the Federal Government of Biafra in defence of
the citizens in the Ani'ocha area of Delta State; and in *The Sweet Trap* where a
misguided elite engage in a meaningless gender debate, a battle of the sexes.

Zulu Sofola is the first published and established female Nigerian dramatist
and theatre practitioner of English expression. The main thematic concerns
and preoccupations of her textual/dramatic output are the utilization of tradition to address various other contemporary issues and concepts such as the
state and status of women in modern society, the individual in contending
western and indigenous African cultures, and individual and group moralities
as influenced and determined by religious persuasions, social and communal
ethics, and history.
   Zulu Sofola's plays employ elements of magic, legend, myth, ritual, and
folklore to explore the enduring conflicts between indigenous African traditionalism and Western-induced modernism with an often undisguised

preference for the former. In her exploration and examination of this conflict, the patriarchal male supremacy survives or is at best gently admonished to accommodate and recognize the importance of women in a male-dominated society. Some of her major plays also manifest her vision of individual and group tragedy, mainly derived from her indigenous African perception and cosmology. Again, this conception of tragedy arises from individual protagonists and female representatives of the women's liberation movement who attempt to break the existing harmonious culture of patriarchy. Her most produced play, *Wedlock of the Gods*, explores the repercussions of an attempt to violate traditional lores and order. Her other important plays which examine traditional issues include *King Emene, Old Wines Are Tasty*, and *Memories in the Moonlight*. Her more contemporary plays which deal with women's struggle for liberation and the conflict between academia (gown) and the macro-society (town) are *The Sweet Trap* and *Song of a Maiden* respectively.

Myth, legend, and magic enrich and structure her dramaturgy in traditional themes where characters who defy age-old conventions are revealed as treading tragic paths. Uloko and Ugwoma in *Wedlock of the Gods* are passionate and genuine lovers who cannot consummate their love in marriage because an older and more acceptable (to the parents) suitor exists. As it turns out, the older suitor dies shortly after marrying Ugwoma and the two lovers return to their original purpose of getting married without waiting for the prescribed traditional mourning period and rites for the late husband to pass. As expected, the enraged mother-in-law makes it her responsibility to set tradition back on course by evoking her magical powers to destroy the new couple. Here is an oversimplified mythopoesis in which tragedy equates defiance of traditional codes and mores.

This tradition of imposing an elderly man on an unwilling young girl who has already chosen her partner recurs in the play *Memories in the Moonlight*. In the end, Abiona marries her dream man and the plot is resolved via metaphysics and traditional contrivance where an arranged parent/suitor reconciliation takes place.

The Sweet Trap employs a traditional cleansing ceremony (Okebadan Festival, an exclusive male cult accomplished by licence and permitted abuse of the female sex) to celebrate a traditionally Nigerian supremacy of the man over his wife or wives. In this play, using the three-act dramatic structure, Sofola counsels—against the growing wave of feminism in the country, particularly in university circles where she teaches—that harmonious matrimony requires that a wife recognize and accept her husband's supremacy, with, of course, a gentle appeal to husbands to accord their wives due emotional regard. The plot takes off in Femi Sotubo's university residence. Femi applies brute force and chauvinism to deny his wife the right to celebrate her birthday. Encouraged by her friends and with the promise of a venue to celebrate the birthday, Clara Sotubo changes from an initial position of docility and submission to one of violent defiance and self-assertion. The party goes on. As it turns out, the birthday party ends in a fiasco and humiliation as the Okebadan celebrants intrude on the arena and generously dole out abuse to the women, who in confusion blame each other for being responsible for initiating the party. After the disruption, the resolution of the play comes from Dr. Jinadu, who advises Clara to apologise to her husband, advice she gleefully takes and complies with. She cringes on her knees for stubbornly going against "tradition." The thesis of the play is an advocation of female submission in order to avert matrimonial disharmony.

Sofola's conceptual vision of tragedy grows out of her traditionalist vision of a particular African world view which emphasizes that iconoclasm and unorthodoxy disrupt cosmic harmony and wreak historical discontinuity on the communal psyche. An individual in this perception is independent within a communal equilibrium. Tragedy occurs when that independence is extended beyond the communal ethos and cosmos. Tragedy can be averted through conformity or atonement and expiation. In the play *King Emene*, a usurpation of the throne has taken place through intrigue and a murder contrived by Emene's mother in order to deprive the deceased of his due right of ascendancy and place his own son on the throne. Inevitably, disharmony occurs and the kingdom is troubled. King Emene aggravates the situation when he rejects the admonition of elders that he should not perform the rites which usher in the Peace Week because a heinous crime needing cleansing and propitiation has been committed. Oblivious of the facts of the situation, Emene interprets this as a plot against him and proceeds with the rites during which he is suddenly and mysteriously attacked by a boa. He is shamed and inevitably commits suicide. Thus, unexpiated crime and defiance of traditional wisdom occasion the tragedy of King Emene.

Sofola's thematic concerns with tragedy, metaphysics, gender problems, and individual and societal conflict with a growing Western modernism are all anchored structurally and perceptually in certain traditionalist aesthetics. Technically, her plays are simple and accessible, at times bordering on over-simplification. Her dialogue and characterization oscillate between the sketchy and the profound. Her language is clear and unobtrusive, ranging between standard English usage and direct translation from her vernacular African linguistic sources and background, and partly responsible for audience interest in her theatre.

—Olu Obafemi

SUNDE, Karen.

American. Actor, Colorado Shakespeare Festival, Boulder, Colorado, 1967, The New Shakespeare Company, San Francisco, 1967–68, Arrow Rock Lyceum, Arrow Rock, Missouri, 1969–70, and CSC Repertory, New York, 1971–85; associate director, CSC Repertory, New York, 1975–85. Recipient: Bob Hope award, 1963; American Scandinavian Foundation travel grant, 1981; Finnish Literature Center Production grant, 1982; Villager award (three times), 1983; McKnight fellowship, 1986; Aide de la Création grant, 1987. Address: 23 Leroy Street, Number 8, New York, New York 10014, U.S.A.

Publications

PLAYS

The Running of the Deer (produced 1978).

Balloon (produced 1983). 1983.

Philoctetes, adaptation of the play by Sophocles (also director: produced 1983).

Dark Lady (produced 1986). 1985.
Kabuki Othello (produced 1986).
To Moscow (produced 1986).
Quasimodo (musical), adaptation of Victor Hugo's *The Hunchback of Notre Dame*, with Christopher Martin (produced 1987).
Anton, Himself (produced 1988). In *Moscow Art Theatre*, edited by Michael Bigelow Dixon, 1989.
Kabuki Macbeth (produced 1989).
Haiti: A Dream (produced 1990).
Masha, Too (produced 1991).
Achilles (produced 1991).
In a Kingdom by the Sea (produced 1992).

RADIO PLAYS: *The Sound of Sand*, 1963; *Balloon*, 1987; *Haiti: A Dream*, 1991.

MANUSCRIPT COLLECTION: Lincoln Center Library for the Performing Arts, New York.

THEATRICAL ACTIVITIES

DIRECTOR: **Plays**—*Exit the King* by Ionesco, 1978; *Philoctetes* by Sophocles, 1983.
ACTOR: **Plays**—some 60 roles performed Off Broadway including: Ruth in *The Homecoming* by Pinter, 1972–76; Celimene in *The Misanthrope* by Molière, and Viola in *Twelfth Night*, 1973–74; Hedda in *Hedda Gabler* by Ibsen, 1974–77; Antigone in *Antigone* by Anouilh, 1975–77; Isabella in *Measure for Measure*, 1975; Hesione in *Heartbreak House* by Shaw, 1976–77; Rebekka West in *Rosmersholm* by Ibsen, 1977–78; Countess Aurelie in *The Madwoman of Chaillot* by Giraudoux, 1978; Portia in *The Merchant of Venice*, 1980; Jocasta and Antigone in *Oedipus Rex*, *Antigone*, and *Oedipus at Colonus* by Sophocles, 1980–81; Aase in *Peer Gynt* by Ibsen, 1981–82; Lotte in *Big and Little* by Botho Strauss, 1983–84; Alice in *Dance of Death* by Strindberg, 1984; Clytemnestra in *The Orestia* by Aeschylus, 1984–85. **Television**—Mary Brewster in *The Mayflower*, 1980.

Karen Sunde comments:

I follow my nose—and here's all I know: that rhythm is important to me. And economy. And passion. That the live current between audience and stage is everything.

With a voice both poetic and theatrical, Karen Sunde's plays dramatize historical epochs in epic scope, making hers a distinctive, even unique, contemporary American drama, more akin to European than to other American plays. She tackles topics of war and politics to produce usually presentational, often explosive theatre which many would swear could not have been created by a woman. Yet she imbues her mythic vision of the bellicose and patriarchal nature and direction of the United States and the world with a sense of what women can or do contribute to modifying these.

Sunde's twenty works for stage and screen fall into three related groups: the historical plays, the treatments of classics, and the glimpses of a painful present shaping a deplorable, but possibly salvageable future.

The first of her three consecutive plays set during or immediately after the American Revolution, *The Running of the Deer*, with its huge canvas and varied vistas, dramatizes the ravages of cold, starvation, and battle on George Washington's troops in order to probe the character of American male heroes, while the second, *Balloon*, achieves the same goal by setting in a theatrical framework worthy of Jean Genet another American founding father, Ben Franklin, so he can spar with his Tory son and woo his French mistress, Helvetius, who fears losing her autonomy in marriage to a man as passionately committed to his vocations as to his lovers. An appropriate protagonist for a play about hope and progress, Franklin strives and achieves, yet his painful interpersonal relations have diluted his triumphs.

Deborah: The Adventures of a Soldier (an unproduced television play), like several of Sunde's subsequent plays, investigates female heroism, or, in this case, the male model of heroism achieved by an astonishing woman warrior, Deborah Sampson, who enlists in the Continental Army as "Robert Shurtliffe," and rises to leadership among men while battling with the British. As Sunde remarks of her version of this actual historical woman's triumphs, "When war is real, issues confused, deaths bitter, a woman has to finally decide who she is." This one can outshoot, outthink, and outrun the men, but should she continue to do so? Sunde humorously recounts Deborah's adventures both as a soldier and as a woman trying to pass for a man (with women coming on to "him") and falling in love with a sergeant who thinks she's male. Sunde's background as an actor in Shakespeare's plays certainly sensitized her to the comedic possibilities of employing a woman playing a man. But the dramatist also conveys the war's pathos, its pain, and its cost in lives lost.

Sunde continues to explore female heroism in *The Flower's Lost Child* (an unproduced play), which portrays what the playwright describes as "America's romance with violence." Instead of colonists resisting taxation without representation and throwing off an oppressor's rule, Sunde chooses hippie revolutionaries in 1970 New York. The shift in period changes our perspective, forcing us to distance ourselves from terrorists, to question the appropriateness of bombs in the pursuit of peace. Yet she dramatizes these idealists sympathetically. A resourceful and brave leader, Anne had worked with Martin Luther King and embraced non-violence. Now, disillusioned by his assassination, she has abandoned marches and rallies in favor of dynamite. This tragedy creates a powerful sense of fate because Sunde frames the entire play as flashback by beginning with firemen sifting through rubble and dismembered bodies, and then enhances the suspense by surrounding her characters with explosives.

In her as yet unproduced and untitled gothic thriller about British serial killer John George Haigh, set in 1948, Sunde builds tension by hinting at a murder and the threat to the lives of two courageous women, a spirited teenager and another more mature woman, who struggle to foil their amoral terrorizer.

Sunde again depicts a female hero in *Dark Lady*, which, set against the plague's slaughter, dramatizes the relationship between Shakespeare and Renaissance England's best-known woman poet, Emilia Bassano. Sunde creates in her a passionate woman whose humanity, courage, spirit, and generosity equal—and ultimately exceed—the Bard's.

In three further plays, Sunde dramatizes actual characters in events which plausibly might have occurred. *To Moscow* concerns Chekhov, his actress wife Olga Knipper, Konstantin Stanislavsky, and the beginnings of the Moscow Art Theatre. The title evokes Chekhov's three sisters' unrealized intention to return from their provincial backwater to Moscow. Sunde chooses as four of the six central characters women whom Chekhov exploits. But in one, Olga, he finds (like Shakespeare in Emilia) his equal. Sunde completes her Russian trilogy with two matching one-act portraits, one of the narcissist Chekhov titled *Anton, Himself*, the other, *Masha, Too*, of his sister, as she struggles to summon the courage to tell him she plans to marry. We conclude from *Anton* that her brother will not let her leave him. While viewers need know nothing about Chekhov to enjoy these three, Sunde interlards the action with jokes about the plays and stories, especially intriguing to knowledgeable viewers.

While penning her history plays Sunde undertook a related approach to indicting human folly, by means of our literary myths, one from Victor Hugo, three from Shakespeare's plays, and one from Homer's *Iliad*. Sunde's musical version of *The Hunchback of Notre Dame*, which she wrote with director Christopher Martin, fashions the novel into a fluid work which contrasts with the long, carefully demarcated scenes in that other Hugo musical, *Les Misérables*. More opera than musical and boasting a score ranging from ecclesiastic to gypsy, the galvanic *Quasimodo* dramatizes the theme that people should experience, not repress, their passions: "Man is man, not stone."

Providing further evidence of her versatility, Sunde created four Kabuki plays for Japanese director Shozo Sato, who has staged them in Kabuki style but with American performers. Although *Kabuki Othello* preserves the Shakespearean outlines, Sunde makes Iago's motivation clearer and eliminates the Bard's racism and sexism. Asian ritual reinforces the tragedy's inevitability. Far from inviting any unfavorable comparisons to the original, Sunde creates her own distinctive imagery—delicate, tender, and eventually heroic for Desdemona, demonic for the Ainu Othello—and, in Emilia's lines, a healthy sarcasm about machismo and female subservience. In her *Kabuki Macbeth* and, the as yet unproduced, *Kabuki Richard* the dramatist also evokes a theatrical mixture of the original plots and their archetypes with Eastern culture—samurai, shoguns, karma, and Shiva intertwined with ghosts, witches, and severed heads.

In *Achilles* Sunde converts material from *The Iliad* into a mythic anti-war tragedy. She emphasizes the macho lust for glory which leads to the razing of Troy and massive, senseless slaughter, reminding us of the continuing cost of personal and international bravado. Sunde's searing script dramatizes pride, arrogance, and savagery—and their aftermath of grief, when Achilles joins Priam in mourning Hector's death after the bereaved father kisses the "victor's" hand. Focusing her work for us through the eyes of the enslaved Briseis, "only a woman," a prize of battle, who has learned "the purpose of life is war," Sunde employs an archetypal example to promote peace and recognition of our common humanity.

Sunde likewise dramatizes conflicts from a humanist perspective in a series of prescient plays looking towards the global future. *House of Eeyore* (an unproduced play), which takes its title from A. A. Milne's *Winnie the Pooh* stories, employs dream research, a gubernatorial campaign, and an ageless native American psychic (named after the female spirit Gaia) to awaken a prominent American family to its spiritual and social responsibilities.

Whereas the visionary middle-class women in *House of Eeyore* works as a research physician, Gaye in *Countdown: Earth* (an unproduced screenplay), saves the western half of the planet because of her skill as a geophysicist—not to mention her bravery in carrying out a daredevil rescue while dangling above a volcano starting to erupt. Still a third woman scientist, this one discovering a cure for cancer, plays a prominent role in *Over the Rainbow* (another unproduced screenplay), but here Sunde chooses as her protagonist another healer, the scientist's little girl. Both *Countdown: Earth* and *Over the Rainbow* employ science fiction to arouse concern about our planet's survival.

In three further plays Sunde hopes for a better tomorrow even as she explores the roots of misery today. The prophetic *Haiti: A Dream* dramatizes the flight to Florida of Haitian boat people by focusing on a man and his wife and the Old Woman empowered by voodoo who tries unsuccessfully to inspire them both to recognize their own strength to lead their people. In a similar spirit of fantasizing about a better way, *How His Bride Came to Abraham* (an unproduced play), creates an extraordinary modern pacifist myth in which a wounded male Israeli soldier and a female Palestinian terrorist experience each other's passionate hunger for their homes and rights. Sunde describes this tragedy as "today's violent news stories in fairy-tale form," but it indelibly etches itself upon viewers' souls because of the human encounter, as wary people drop their guard with an enemy.

The multi-media *In a Kingdom by the Sea*, based upon the abduction of Marine Lt. Col. William Higgins, presents simultaneously the efforts of the UN peacekeepers to free one of their own—here named Hogan—and Hogan himself, who appears in both past and present, in both monologue and dialogue, to share with us the "key to America," and to his character: football and women—in Hogan's case the woman whom, since high school, he has tried to impress with a uniform. In contrast to *How His Bride Came to Abraham*'s wartime dream of peace and love, *In a Kingdom by the Sea* dramatizes the subversion of the UN peacekeeping forces' efforts in Lebanon by those on both sides for whom macho bravado means more than would an end to hostility.

A balloon will rise, but what, Sunde inquires in *Balloon*, of humanity? Her plays consider whether we have reason to hope.

—Tish Dace

SUTHERLAND, Efua (Theodora, née Morgue).

Ghanaian. Born in Cape Coast, 27 June 1924. Educated at St. Monica's School and Training College, Cape Coast; Homerton College, Cambridge, B.A.; School of Oriental and African Studies, London. Married William Sutherland in 1954; three children. Schoolteacher in Ghana, 1951–54. Since 1958 founding director, Experimental Theatre Players (now Ghana Drama Studio), Accra. Founder, Ghana Society of Writers (now the University of Ghana Writers Workshop) and Kusum Agoromba children's theatre group, Legon. Co-founder, *Okyeame* magazine, Accra. Address: Institute of African Studies, University of Ghana, P.O. Box 25, Legon, Ghana.

Publications

PLAYS

Foriwa (produced 1962). 1967.
Edufa, based on *Alcestis* by Euripides (produced 1962). 1967; in *Plays from Black Africa*, edited by Fredric M. Litto, 1968.
Anansegoro: You Swore an Oath, in *Présence Africaine 22*, Summer 1964.
Vulture! Vulture! Two Rhythm Plays (for children; includes *Tahinta*), photographs by Willis E. Bell. 1968.
Ananse and the Dwarf Brigade (for children; produced 1971).
The Marriage of Anansewa: A Storytelling Drama (produced 1971). 1975.

OTHER PLAYS: *Odasani*, version of *Everyman*; adaptation of Chekhov's *The Proposal*; *The Pineapple Child*; *Nyamekye*; *Tweedledum and Tweedledee*, adaptation of *Alice in Wonderland* by Lewis Carroll.

RADIO PLAYS: devised plays for Ghana Radio's *The Singing Net* series.

VERSE (FOR CHILDREN)

Playtime in Africa, photographs by Willis E. Bell. 1960.

OTHER

The Roadmakers, with Willis E. Bell, photographs by Bell. 1961.
The Original Bob: The Story of Bob Johnson, Ghana's Ace Comedian, illustrated by Willis E. Bell. 1970.
The Voice in the Forest: A Tale from Ghana. 1983.

Efua Sutherland brought playwriting and theatrical production together in Ghana. The few plays that predate Ghanaian independence in 1957 and the founding of her Experimental Theatre Group in 1958 were essentially closet dramas. Moreover, from the start she was concerned to bring drama to the people. She was, thus, also concerned with bringing drama to children and encouraging their participation in drama, by drawing upon local folk stories, lyrics and dances, and by performing in Twi as well as English. Her work attracted American support from the Rockefeller Foundation and the Fund for Tomorrow. With their funding, and government support, the first professional theatre, the Ghana Drama Studio, was built and opened in 1961. In 1962 the Drama Studio became a part of the newly established School of Music and Drama at the University of Ghana. Continuing her concern with reaching the ordinary person, Sutherland designed a courtyard theatre derived from traditional performance areas. From the Studio she sent out a company to tour schools and colleges performing, in Twi and English, original works and her own adaptations of *Everyman* and *Alice in Wonderland*.

The example and influence of Sutherland's production work is likely to prove to be of greater significance than her plays. Indeed, one wonders how concerned she is for publication; of all her work for children, for example, she has published only the extremely brief *Vulture! Vulture! Two Rhythm Plays*. The skilful dramatization of a traditional tale of a deer-woman, *Anansegoro: You Swore an Oath*, appeared without her advance knowledge. Of her three full-length plays the first, *Edufa*, is an adaptation of Euripides' *Alcestis*—or, rather, since the values given to many of the characters are reversed, a counter-argument to *Alcestis*. While there are various critical interpretations of Euripides' play, to see it as a celebration of hospitality makes sense of the play as a whole. It is because of his reputation for hospitality that Admetus is allowed to let someone else die for him—his wife, Alcestis—and that even in the midst of his grief for Alcestis he plays host to the visiting Heracles, who then pursues Death and wrestles Alcestis away from him and returns her to Admetus. The play was presented not as a tragedy but in place of a satyr play. *Edufa*, however, is a tragedy, with the Alcestis-figure's death ending the play. Moreover, with heavy irony, the action is set against an annual ceremony in which funeral songs are sung as evil is expelled from the town. The evil is in Edufa, Sutherland's Admetus-figure, a selfish member of the new class of privileged *nouveaux riches*, who, behind his facade of a man emancipated from traditional beliefs by his education, secretly resorts to diviners in terror at the coming of death. Similarly, the Heracles character is a seedy intellectual. In contrast the father, a self-centered hypocrite in Euripides' play, becomes a representative of the dignity and wisdom of the older generation. The focus, as the title suggests, is on the educated modern man and the loss of moral orientation in his alienation from traditional values.

Foriwa is more didactic. Labaran, a university graduate, has come to transform a provincial town. He tells the audience:

> I am keeping vigil here, placing my faith in some daybreak after this long
> night when the townsmen shall wake and shake my soul with vibrant talk
> . . . I was impatient at the beginning: in haste. Seeing the raggedness of
> my people's homes, I was ashamed, even angry. I heard it screamed:
> Progress! Development! I wanted it far and everywhere.

From this straightforward statement of the theme, we expect—quite correctly—that the play will end with his triumph. Yet the play is distinctively original. First, Sutherland eschews the conflicts between generations, tradition and modernization, on which many African plays about social change are based. Labaran's ally is the retired postmaster, the Queen-Mother is herself a reformer, and the climax is her use of a traditional ceremony to win endorsement for change. Second, the tone of the play is set not by the struggle for social change, but by the joyous youthfulness and self-discovery of the title character, the Queen-Mother's daughter. She and Labaran take the length of the play to fall in love. Since he is a Hausa from the distant north, this is yet another symbol of unity for progress.

The Marriage of Anansewa is a divertissement on the theme of the rascally father who encourages various wealthy suitors to woo his daughter. When the juggling of visitors becomes too complicated, the only way to end the solicitations is for Anansewa to "die" and, after a final round of generous gifts to the "dead" girl from the other suitors, to be miraculously revived by the messenger of the Chief-Who-is-Chief. Since the wooing is all by messenger, and since Anansewa is silent while she is "dead", Sutherland can keep her untainted by her father's mercenary schemes. By keeping her uninvolved, however, Sutherland also leaves her character undeveloped. The effect is rather as if Jonson, in his *Volpone*, had given Celia to Mosca to hustle for instead of to Volpone.

Sutherland's interest is, one suspects, in the traditional story-telling manner of presentation of this play rather than the subject. Each of her plays experiments with the involvement of the spectators. *Edufa* keeps the chorus from *Alcestis* and was intended for presentation in the Ghana Drama Studio's courtyard theatre, with spectators and actors entering through the same gate. *Foriwa* was written for performance "in a street in any of many small Ghanaian towns" and the hero explains his intentions directly to the audience. Most ambitiously, *The Marriage of Anansewa* attempts to recapture the atmosphere of traditional story-telling sessions by keeping the performers onstage throughout as an onstage audience with whom Sutherland hopes the real audience will "feel as one."

—Anthony Graham-White

T

TERRY, Megan.

American. Born Marguerite Duffy in Seattle, Washington, 22 July 1932. Educated at Banff School of Fine Arts, Alberta, summers 1950–53, 1956; University of Washington, Seattle, 1950, 1953–56, B.Ed. 1956; University of Alberta, Edmonton, 1951–53. Drama teacher and director of the Cornish Players, Cornish School of Allied Arts, Seattle, 1954–56; founding member, 1963, and director of the playwrights workshop, 1963–68, Open Theatre, New York; writer-in-residence, Yale University School of Drama, New Haven, Connecticut, 1966–67; founding member, Women's Theatre Council, 1971; founding member and treasurer, New York Theatre Strategy, 1971; Bingham professor of humanities, University of Louisville, 1981; Hill professor of fine arts, University of Minnesota, Duluth, 1983; visiting artist University of Iowa, Iowa City, 1992. Since 1971 resident playwright and literary manager, Omaha Magic Theatre. Recipient: Stanley award, 1965; Office of Advanced Drama Research award, 1965; ABC-Yale University fellowship, 1966; Rockefeller grant, 1968, 1987; Obie award, 1970; National Endowment for the Arts grant, 1972, fellowship, 1989; Earplay award, 1972; Creative Artists Public Service grant, 1973; Guggenheim fellowship, 1978; Dramatists Guild award, 1983; Nebraska Artist of the Year Governors award, 1992. Agent: Elisabeth Marton, 96 Fifth Avenue, New York, New York 10011. Address: 2309 Hanscom Boulevard, Omaha, Nebraska 61805; or, c/o Omaha Magic Theatre, 1417 Farnam Street, Omaha, Nebraska 68102, U.S.A.

Publications

PLAYS

Beach Grass (also director: produced 1955).
Seascape (also director: produced 1955).
Go Out and Move the Car (also director: produced 1955).
New York Comedy: Two (produced 1961).
Ex-Miss Copper Queen on a Set of Pills (produced 1963). With *The People vs. Ranchman*, 1968.
When My Girlhood Was Still All Flowers (produced 1963).
Eat at Joe's (produced 1964).
Calm Down Mother (produced 1965). 1966.
Keep Tightly Closed in a Cool Dry Place (produced 1965). In*Four Plays*, 1967.
The Magic Realists (produced 1966). In *Three One-Act Plays*, 1972.
Comings and Goings (produced 1966). In *Four Plays*, 1967.

The Gloaming, Oh My Darling (produced 1966). In *Four Plays*, 1967.

Viet Rock: A Folk War Movie (also director: produced 1966). In *Four Plays*, 1967.

Four Plays. 1967.

The Key Is on the Bottom (produced 1967).

The People vs. Ranchman (produced 1967). With *Ex-Miss Copper Queen on a Set of Pills*, 1968.

Home; or, Future Soap (televised 1968; revised version, as *Future Soap*, produced 1987). 1972.

Jack-Jack (produced 1968).

Massachusetts Trust (produced 1968). In *The Off-Off-Broadway Book*, edited by Albert Poland and Bruce Mailman, 1972.

Changes, with Tom O'Horgan (produced 1968).

Sanibel and Captiva (broadcast 1968). In *Three One-Act Plays*, 1972.

One More Little Drinkie (televised 1969). In *Three One-Act Plays*, 1972.

Approaching Simone (produced 1970). 1973.

The Tommy Allen Show (also director: produced 1970). In *Scripts 2*, December 1971.

Grooving (produced 1972).

Choose a Spot on the Floor, with Jo Ann Schmidman (produced 1972).

Three One-Act Plays. 1972.

Couplings and Groupings (monologues and sketches). 1973.

Susan Peretz at the Manhattan Theatre Club (produced 1973).

Thoughts (lyrics only), book by Lamar Alford (produced 1973).

Nightwalk, with Sam Shepard and Jean-Claude van Itallie (produced 1973). In *Open Theater*, 1975.

St. Hydro Clemency; or, A Funhouse of the Lord: An Energizing Event (produced 1973).

The Pioneer, and Pro-Game (produced 1973). 1975.

Hothouse (produced 1974). 1975.

Babes in the Bighouse (produced 1974). 1979.

All Them Women, with others (produced 1974).

We Can Feed Everybody Here (produced 1974).

Hospital Play. 1974.

Henna for Endurance. 1974.

The Narco Linguini Bust (produced 1974).

100,001 Horror Stories of the Plains, with others (produced 1976). 1979.

Sleazing Towards Athens. 1977; revised version (produced 1986), 1986.

Willie-Willa-Bill's Dope Garden. 1977.

Brazil Fado (produced 1977). 1977; revised version (produced 1978), 1979.

Lady Rose's Brazil Hide Out (produced 1977).

American King's English for Queens (produced 1978). 1978.

Goona Goona (produced 1979). 1985.

Attempted Rescue on Avenue B: A Beat Fifties Comic Opera (produced 1979). 1979.

Fireworks, in Holidays (produced 1979). 1992.

Running Gag (lyrics only), book by Jo Ann Schmidman (produced 1979). 1981.

Objective Love I (produced 1980). 1985.

Scenes from Maps (produced 1980). 1980.
Advances (produced 1980). 1980.
Flat in Afghanistan (produced 1981). 1981.
Objective Love II (produced 1981). 1985.
The Trees Blew Down (produced 1981). 1981.
Winners (produced 1981).
Kegger (produced 1982).
Fifteen Million Fifteen-Year-Olds (produced 1983). 1983.
Mollie Bailey's Traveling Family Circus, Featuring Scenes from the Life of Mother Jones, music by Jo Anne Metcalf. 1983.
X-rayed-iate (produced 1984).
Katmandu, in *Open Spaces*, 1985.
Family Talk (produced 1986).
Sea of Forms (collaborative work), text and lyrics with Jo Ann Schmidman (produced 1986). 1987.
Walking Through Walls (collaborative work), text and lyrics with Jo Ann Schmidman (produced 1987). 1987.
Dinner's in the Blender (produced 1987). 1987.
Retro (produced 1988).
Amtrak (produced 1988). 1990.
Headlights (produced 1988).
Do You See What I'm Saying? (produced 1990). 1991.
Body Leaks, with Sora Kimberlain and Jo Ann Schmidman (produced 1990).
Breakfast Serial (produced 1991).
Sound Fields: Are We Hear (produced 1992).

RADIO PLAYS: *Sanibel and Captiva*, 1968; *American Wedding Ritual Monitored/Transmitted by the Planet Jupiter*, 1972.

TELEVISION PLAYS: *The Dirt Boat*, 1955; *Home; or, Future Soap*, 1968; *One More Little Drinkie*, 1969.

OTHER

Editor, with Jo Ann Schmidman and Sora Kimberlain, *Right Brain Vacation Photos: New Plays and Production Photographs 1972–1992*, 1992.

MANUSCRIPT COLLECTIONS: Kent State University, Kent, Ohio; Hope College, Holland, Michigan; Lincoln Center Library of the Performing Arts, New York; Omaha Public Library.

CRITICAL STUDIES: "Who Says Only Words Make Great Drama?" by Terry, in *New York Times*, 10 November 1968; "Megan Terry: Mother of American Feminist Theatre," in *Feminist Theatre* by Helene Keyssar, 1984; "(Theoretically) Approaching Megan Terry" by Elin Diamond, in *Art and Cinema 3*, 1987; "Making Magic Public: Megan Terry's Traveling Family Circus" in *Making a Spectacle*, edited by Lynda Hart, 1989.

THEATRICAL ACTIVITIES

DIRECTOR: Plays—with the Cornish Players, Seattle: *Beach Grass*, *Seascape*, and *Go Out and Move the Car*, 1955; with the Open Theatre's Playwrights Workshop, New York, 1962–68; *Viet Rock*, 1966; *The Tommy Allen Show*, 1970; and other plays. Television—*The Dirt Book*, 1955.

ACTOR: (as Maggie Duffy) Plays—Hermia in *A Midsummer's Night Dream*, title role in *Peter Pan* by J.M. Barrie, Kate in *Taming of the Shrew*, and other roles, Banff School of Fine Arts, Alberta, 1950–53; (as Megan Terry): roles in *Body Leaks*, 1991, and *Sound Fields*, 1992.

Megan Terry comments:

I design my plays to provoke laughter—thought may follow.

"Roughly political, generally unintelligible, devoutly gymnastic." Walter Kerr's assessment seems strikingly at odds with the playwright who has more recently been acknowledged as the "Mother of American Feminist Drama." Yet the energy, vitality, and diversity of Megan Terry's work in the 1960's was often mistaken for lack of control or purpose, especially as many of those plays seemed to merge with the cultures of pop, protest, and the hippies. She became best known for *Viet Rock: A Folk War Movie*, a pivotal theatrical rallying-point against the Vietnam War, but one which could also too easily be dismissed as politically superficial, without acknowledging the dramaturgically innovative features it shared with most of her early work.

Calm Down Mother, Terry's first major contribution to a feminist theatre, is subtitled "A Transformation for Three Women," referring to an improvisatory technique developed by Terry and Joseph Chaikin in the early period of the Open Theatre. To the audience, a transformation simply appeared as a dissolving of character, location, or any other apparently concrete reality, so that the given circumstances that might be thought to define role would be constantly protean. Many different fragments of identity crystallize briefly in *Calm Down Mother* to provide a tapestry of female experience similar to Ntozake Shange's notion of the choreopoem. Though some found the play shocking for its upfront physicality, it was also generally received as celebratory of women reclaiming their bodies in the theatre.

The transformation was, more intellectually, conceptualized within psychoanalysis to reveal fragments of personality or role that are not easily integrated into one's preferred identity, so that the "tapestry" of *Calm Down Mother* is also a condensation. This becomes clearer in two plays dealing with male criminals, *The People vs. Ranchman* and *Keep Tightly Closed in a Cool Dry Place*. The latter has three actors in a prison cell working through a murder and a trial in which they were complicit; the clustering of responses to the event, the exposure of repressed self-images, and the merging of figures from history and the screen, constitute the central action, with the notion of transformation being facilitated by the actors occasionally connecting to form a machine.

Other plays of the 1960's experiment with other styles. *Ex-Miss Copper Queen on a Set of Pills* can be read as Gothic realism in its picturing of two female scavengers encountering the title character in a New York street at night, but it also has an hallucinatory fabric as the Queen "fights through drugs and drink" to make contact with them. *The Magic Realists* is transformational in its whimsical presentation of a businessman paranoiacally in retreat from his family and other responsibilities, but it also has elements of dream, jazz, male fantasy, and the consoling retreat into an ersatz pioneering ethos, derived from stage and screen more than from history books. *Home; or, Future Soap*, written for television and rescripted for stage, is a science-fiction vision of population explosion carried to an extreme in which its nine characters are born and die in the same room; yet it too has a social concern as it scrutinizes principles such as home, family, and children.

Terry's most lasting play, as a reading script, has been *Approaching Simone*, ostensibly a stage biography of Simone Weil. The play's seriousness and appeal to authenticity certainly acted as a corrective to those who had found her earlier work trite; it was widely praised for its audacity in presenting an affirmative portrait of a genius, and also for finding theatricality in an apparently untheatrical life. Yet Terry also saw the play as the culmination of 15 years of developing her dramatic technique. In its combination of stark statements to the world, couched in a context of sometimes severe or shocking stylization, there is a boldness of dramatic strategy that matches the choice of subject.

At the height of her New York success, and having won an extensive international reputation, Terry joined the Omaha Magic Theatre in the early 1970's; with that group, she has remained highly productive, but much of her work has been local or regional in its application. Her "social action theatre" or "community problem plays" are extensively researched and workshopped within the community that they in a sense document, and on tour their performance is accompanied by a "scholar" such as a psychiatrist or historian who will facilitate discussion with the audience after the show. Subjects like juvenile alcohol abuse (in *Kegger*), domestic violence (in *Goona Goona*), and incarceration of women (in *Babes in the Bighouse*) are of obvious community concern, but her plays also deal with issues such as illiteracy (in *Headlights*), how behaviour is shaped by language imbalance (in *American King's English for Queens*), and communication within families (in *Family Talk* and *Dinner's in the Blender*). But seriousness of social commitment could be found in Terry from the start: there is a case study in *Copper Queen* that might almost offer a gloss to *Kegger*. And neither has sheer playfulness deserted her in the face of earnestness: she is still writing plays such as *Amtrak*, about a pick-up on a train, which combines satire, iconoclasm, and a self-reflexive structure, with a hint of the artistic anarchy of the 1960's.

—Howard McNaughton

THOMPSON, Judith.

Canadian. Born in Montreal, 20 September 1954. Educated at Queen's University, Kingston, Ontario, 1973–76, B.A. in English drama 1976; National Theatre School, Montreal, 1976–79. Married Gregor Campbell in 1983; two daughters and one son. Nurse aide, Ongwanada Hospital, 1974, and social worker, Ministry of Social Services, 1977, both Kingston, Ontario; private tutor, Toronto, 1979. Recipient: Governor-General's award, 1984,

1990; Chalmers award, 1988, 1991; Nellie award, for radio, 1989; Toronto Arts award, 1990. Lives in Toronto. Agent: Great North Artists, 350 Dupont Street, Toronto, Ontario M5R 1V9, Canada.

Publications

PLAYS

The Crackwalker (produced 1980; also director: 1987). 1988.
White Biting Dog (produced 1984). 1984.
Pink (produced 1986). In *The Other Side of the Dark*, 1989.
Tornado (broadcast 1987). In *The Other Side of the Dark*, 1989.
I Am Yours (produced 1987). In *The Other Side of the Dark*, 1989.
The Other Side of the Dark. 1989.
Lion in the Streets (also director: produced 1990). 1991.
Hedda Gabler, adaptation of the play by Ibsen (also director: produced 1991).

RADIO PLAYS: *Quickening*, 1984; *A Kissing Way*, 1986; *Tornado*, 1987.

TELEVISION PLAYS: *Turning to Stone*, 1986; *Don't Talk*, 1992.

CRITICAL STUDY: "'Cause You're the Only One I Want: The Anatomy of Love in the Plays of Judith Thompson" by George Totes in *Canadian Literature*, 118, 1988.

THEATRICAL ACTIVITIES

DIRECTOR: **Plays**—*The Crackwalker*, 1987; *The Crucible* by Arthur Miller, 1989; *Lion in the Streets*, 1990; *Hedda Gabler*, 1991.

Judith Thompson comments

I believe that the voice is the door to not only the soul of an individual, but the soul of a nation, and within that, the soul of a culture, a class, a community, a gender. When I write a play it is as if I am walking into dark woods—do not know what I will find, but the most interesting stories happen when I stumble on raw mythology. I have worked in radio, television, and film, but I believe that the stage has by far the most power. There is a rock, an actor and words—when the technology all collapses—the play will survive.

Judith Thompson's haunting and challenging plays evaluate love relationships and betrayals, the destructive force of cities and contemporary lifestyles, and physical and spiritual pain. Dreams and the effects of dreams expressionistic- ally shape the plays which have had a considerable impact in Canada in the last decade. The evil beast that exists in every subconscious—sometimes resulting in murder—confronts good, though not in a didactic manner. Thompson's plays refer to worms, snakes, and lions, and are sometimes punctuated by screams of agony which are frequently difficult to decipher. The characters try to deal with their evil, peeling back the layers of the selves they have con- structed to hide the nightmares. Because of the self protection that many characters engage in, they do not listen to the seers and psychics.

Class and generational tensions exist in every play, with birth being a recurrent image of the search for love, acceptance, and belonging in this world. The characters of Thompson's plays are people for whom life means psychic hardship and pain, but they are not extraordinary people: they are merely undisguised versions of Everyman, and thus deserving of empathy. Reflecting both this tension and the ordinariness of the characters, bodily functions and fluids, epilepsy, and cancer are not modestly overlooked.

The plays are not naturalistic in style. But much of the dialogue is naturalistic and the accents and pronunciations clearly indicate the ages, education, and frames of mind peculiar to each character. Thompson talks of standing in her characters' blood to really feel who they are.

The Crackwalker centres on two couples who are friends. Sandy and Joe are working-class, while Theresa and Alan are unable to hold jobs and to react independently. They unsuccessfully imitate Joe and Sandy: a desperate Alan helplessly kills his baby in fear and in an ironic gesture of protection. As Alan slips down between the cracks to the world "below" the sidewalk, he finds the company of the Crackwalker, a "drunken Indian" who symbolizes, among other things, social and economic failure. Joe and Sandy—sickened by Alan and by the naïve Theresa's acceptance of the horrifying world around her— escape to Alberta, but they will never escape from their fear of the Crackwalker.

Pink is a brief monologue about Lucy, a white South African girl, whose black nurse, Nellie, is killed in an uprising. It explores the insidiousness of apartheid through Lucy's insistence that the pink colour of her favourite cake is real, and through her demands that nothing, insidious or not, is her fault. Pink is not real: black is.

The radio drama *Tornado* pursues the struggle of having babies and stealing babies that is developed in *I Am Yours*. Dee in *I Am Yours* must accept her mother's death, represented by the evil blob she paints that lives behind the wall. Encephalitis is the metaphor Dee uses to describe the nightmarish control that her subconscious has over her, and Toilane also talks of his head filling with water. Dee's one-night stand with Toilane produces a baby that Toilane abducts, with the help of his mother, because he needs to care for someone. The title, from a locket Dee's father gave to her, refers to all the characters, each of whom seeks love, understanding, and belonging.

White Biting Dog is also about possession and fear of losing one's self and others. Pony, a psychic, arrives at the Race household, feeling that she is on a mission. Her dog, recently dead, appeared to Cape Race, who was about to jump to his death. The dog convinced him that if he saved his father from death, Cape too would experience a salvation. Dogs reappear throughout the play, and Pony especially misses her white biting dog. Desperately searching for his release, Cape tries to bring his estranged parents back together. The only two surviving characters are Cape and his mother, Lomia, who hope that the deaths (one metaphoric, two literal) will at least provide the hope that they need to keep living. Pony's suicide is the blood sacrifice that will, she hopes, effect the change in Cape. The play uses music, particularly drum beats and song, to provide a rhythm. Once again the nightmares terrorize many of the characters who frequently try to create other selves to survive, covering up the "bad" implicit in everyone.

Lion in the Streets presents another devilish creature who is haunting a murdered, intellectually disadvantaged Portuguese girl who must both warn others of the lion and decipher what happened to her, before she can be released from its clutches and the hold that life still has on her. She becomes a Cassandra figure to the many other characters who attempt to cope with cancer, poverty, childcare, and weight problems. The play ends with the girl's crucifixion-cum-wedding which expiates her lion only. The other characters must fight their own lions.

Thompson's plays are also visually exciting. Favouring a staging that allows for different levels, the plays graphically demonstrate the evils that everyday life uncovers in the world and in the characters considering ways to exorcize the beasts.

—Joanne Tompkins

TOWNSEND, Sue (Susan Lilian Townsend).

British. Born in Leicester, 2 April 1946. Educated at South Wigston Girls High School, Leicestershire. Married 1) in 1964 (divorced 1971), two sons and one daughter; 2) Colin Broadway in 1985, one daughter. Member of the Writer's Group, Phoenix Arts Centre, Leicester, 1978. Recipient: Thames Television bursary, 1979. Lives in Leicester. Agent: Anthony Sheil Associates, 43 Doughty Street, London WC1N 2LF, England.

Publications

PLAYS

In the Club and Up the Spout (produced 1979).
Womberang (produced 1980; as *The Waiting Room*, produced 1982). In *Bazaar and Rummage, Groping for Words, and Womberang*, 1984.
The Ghost of Daniel Lambert, music by Rick Lloyd (produced 1981).
Dayroom (produced 1981).
Bazaar and Rummage (produced 1982). In *Bazaar and Rummage, Groping for Words, and Womberang*, 1984.
Captain Christmas and the Evil Adults (produced 1982).
Groping for Words (produced 1983; revised version, as *Are You Sitting Comfortably?*, produced 1986; as *Groping for Words*, produced London, 1988). In *Bazaar and Rummage, Groping for Words, and Womberang*, 1984.
Clients (produced 1983).
Bazaar and Rummage, Groping for Words, and Womberang. 1984.
The Great Celestial Cow (produced 1984). 1984.
The Secret Diary of Adrian Mole Aged 13³/₄, songs by Ken Howard and Alan Blaikley (produced 1984). 1985.
Ear, Nose and Throat (produced 1988). 1989.
Ten Tiny Fingers, Nine Tiny Toes (produced 1989). 1990.
Disneyland It Ain't (produced 1990).

RADIO PLAYS: *The Diary of Nigel Mole Aged 13³/₄*, 1982; *The Growing Pains of Adrian Mole*, 1984; *The Great Celestial Cow*, 1985; *The Ashes*, 1991.

TELEVISION PLAYS: *Revolting Women* series, 1981; *Bazaar and Rummage*, 1984; *The Secret Diary of Adrian Mole* series, 1985; *The Growing Pains of Adrian Mole*, 1987; *The Refuge* series, with Carole Hayman, 1987; *Think of England* series, 1991.

NOVELS

The Adrian Mole Diaries. 1985.
   The Secret Diary of Adrian Mole Aged 13³/₄. 1982.
   The Growing Pains of Adrian Mole. 1984.
Rebuilding Coventry: A Tale of Two Cities. 1988.
Adrian Mole from Minor to Major. 1991.
The Queen and I. 1992.

OTHER

The True Confessions of Adrian Albert Mole, Margaret Hilda Roberts, and Susan Lilian Townsend. 1989.
Mr. Bevan's Dream. 1989.

Sue Townsend comments:

I suppose I write about people who do not live in the mainstream of society. My characters are not educated; they do not earn high salaries (if they work at all). I look beneath the surface of their lives. My plays are about loneliness, struggle, survival, and the possibility of change.

Strangely, they are also comedies. Comedy is the most tragic form of drama.

Sue Townsend writes compassionate comedy whose power comes from its intermittently hard edge. A comedy with serious intentions is nothing new. But what is distinctive about the sometimes gentle, sometimes tough comedy Townsend writes is her ability to balance buoyant laughter with biting social commentary. In what she has called "problem plays," Townsend presents groups whose troubles are conventionally ignored: agoraphobics, adult illiterates, Asian women immigrants. In her most recent work, she has written increasingly on politically volatile issues like national health and institutional attitudes to childbearing and children. She is optimistic that by comically encouraging awareness of such groups and issues in a diverse audience (she hopes to attract working-class people back to the theatre) her theatre can contribute to social change.

In *Bazaar and Rummage* genial comedy cushions the revealing and disturbing study of three agoraphobics and their two social workers. Here Townsend refines the tendencies already apparent in her early theatre script *Womberang*, tendencies which characterize most of her plays: a group and not an individual is at the center of the action, the play refuses conventional descriptions of its plot, and the comedy is generated by community and concern. Townsend describes plays like *Bazaar*, which offer a "group against the world," as "closet plays," "enclosed plays," to emphasize her focus on neglected social problems. In *Bazaar* she engages her predilection for dealing with "the change in [such] a group" by presenting a trio of agoraphobics venturing from home for the first time in years, flanked by the two amateur social workers attempting to aid them. Instead of focusing on one of the characters and her progress toward health, Townsend balances the advances and setbacks in the lives of all five women; progress toward self-understanding is not a function of individual awareness but of group members supporting one another through crises. The plot which such communal character development creates is more circular than linear. There is a passing of awareness from one character to another until the group's collected courage allows for a collective exit onto an Acton street. Townsend's approach to comedy in this play occasioned a notable critical debate. The marriage of very funny lines to a feminist message moved some reviewers to dismiss the effort as "glib," "quirky," or "not too seriously meant," and motivated Michael Billington to warn the playwright that laughter "can't be used simply to decorate." But Townsend herself describes the combination of comedy and women as natural. Laughter, she explains, is "how women cope and have coped for centuries." She sees comedy as the most powerful tool available to her as an aid in reaching people; and in *Bazaar*, by allowing her audience to laugh with the agoraphobics, she encourages compassion and enables reflection. While theatre critics have found comedy variously revolutionary or reactionary, Townsend uses it to approach tough social issues and sees it—perhaps for that reason—as "a basic need of the human body."

Townsend's concern turns from women's special problems to the class issue of illiteracy in *Are You Sitting Comfortably?* (an earlier version was called *Groping for Words*). The play shares its class-conscious focus with *The Secret Diary of Adrian Mole Aged 13³/₄*, the play version of Townsend's successful novel. Both plays portray working-class characters seeking personal and social validation, but to the very light touch of *Adrian Mole* Townsend adds, in *Are You Sitting Comfortably?*, a pointed political message—a condemnation of the British class structure which seems to require illiterates. The play's class conflict is manifest in the encounter of the well-positioned, middle-class Joyce —the novice literacy instructor—and her three working-class students, George, Thelma, and Kevin. As in *Bazaar*, Townsend again keys the play's action to the symbiotic developments within this group. By the end of the play Joyce must acknowledge that her liberalism effects little social change, but Kevin vocalizes what all the others are scared to. In the play's chilling ending, he realizes that the world doesn't "want us to read! There ain't room for all of us is there?" This painful truth gels not just in Kevin, however, but also in the group. The audience, too, must join in this difficult collective realization, for as it laughs, it is being asked, 'are *you* sitting comfortably?" This play may be the clearest example of Townsend's comic gifts, but also evidence of her commitment to using comedy to urge re-thinking and re-considering.

In two recent works, Townsend moves further in her engagement with political issues. *Ten Tiny Fingers, Nine Tiny Toes* is set in a future where two couples are curiously joined in their attempt to maintain some control over their offspring. In a right-wing society strictly compartmentalized by class, Lucinda and Ralph, the equivalent of an upper-working-class couple, conceive a baby in a government-sanctioned laboratory procedure. In distinct contrast, Dot and Pete, unskilled labourers relegated to perish on the fringes of organized society, conceive naturally—and illegally. When the two mothers meet, awaiting childbirth in a shared hospital room, they bond through recognition of how much the institutions around them devalue both women and the life they produce. Their connection empowers them to challenge the government hegemony. When Lucinda's daughter is destroyed by the authorities because of a deformity (a missing toe), the two conspire to share the breastfeeding and rearing of Dot's baby boy. With both husbands rejected (for their failure to behave admirably to the stress of births gone wrong), the two women face an uncertain future together; yet, as in previous plays, Townsend provides an upbeat ending in which these women brave the future on their own terms. In the one-act *Disneyland It Ain't*, children again provide the focus as Maureen pleads with "Mr. Mouse" to visit her dying 10–year-old daughter. As the British mother and the American carnival worker puzzle through his reluctance to help, her rage and his fear frame a discussion which ranges from national health insurance to consumerism to religious apostasy. All the while, the grim specter of the dying child shadows the caustic and clever dialogue. In theatrical shorthand, Townsend displays her ability to combine the trials of day-to-day survival with a hope she and her most burdened characters manage to eke out.

In fiction as well as in drama, Townsend continues to fuse comedy and serious matter. In her novel *Rebuilding Coventry*, Townsend creates a slightly bizarre, often comic, but deadly serious narrative centered on a woman who discovers she has options in her life only as a result of unintentionally murder-ing a man strangling his wife. Townsend's feminism and class consciousness— active in both genres—are leading her on a constant quest for new forms and formats. But it is in her plays especially where she has worked, through her comedy, to bring people together both inside and outside of the play's frame.

—Susan Carlson

V

VOGEL, Paula (Anne).

American. Born in Washington, D.C., 16 November 1951. Educated at Bryn Mawr College, Pennsylvania, 1969–70, 1971–72; Catholic University, Washington, D.C., 1972–74, B.A.; Cornell University, Ithaca, New York, 1974–77, A.B.D. Various jobs including secretary, moving van company packer, factory packer, computor processor, electronics factory worker, 1969–71; lecturer in women's studies and theatre, Cornell University, Ithaca, New York, 1977–82; artistic director, Theater with Teeth, New York, 1982–85; production supervisor, theatre on film and tape, Lincoln Center, New York, 1983–85; associate professor and director of graduate playwriting program, Brown University, Providence, Rhode Island, from 1985. Since 1990 artistic director, Theatre Eleanor Roosevelt, Providence, Rhode Island; since 1992 board member, Circle Repertory Company, New York. Recipient: Heerbes-McCalmon award, 1975, 1976; American College Theatre Festival award, 1976; Samuel French award, 1976; American National Theatre and Academy-West award, 1977; National Endowment for the Arts fellowship, 1980, 1991; MacDowell Colony fellowship, 1981, 1989; Bunting fellowship, 1990; Yaddo fellowship, 1992; McKnight fellowship, 1992; Bellagio fellowship, 1992; AT&T award, 1992. Agent: Peter Franklin, William Morris Agency, 1350 Avenue of the Americas, New York, New York 10019. Address: c/o Box 1852, Brown University, Department of Creative Writing, Providence, Rhode Island 02912, U.S.A.

Publications

PLAYS

Swan Song of Sir Henry (produced 1974).
Meg (produced 1977). 1977.
Apple-Brown Betty (produced 1979).
The Last Pat Epstein Show Before the Reruns (produced 1979).
Desdemona: A Play About a Handkerchief (produced 1979).
Bertha in Blue (produced 1981).
The Oldest Profession (produced 1981).
And Baby Makes Seven (produced 1986).
The Baltimore Waltz (produced 1992). 1992.
Hot 'n' Throbbing (produced 1992).

THEATRICAL ACTIVITIES
DIRECTOR: Plays—*The Lower Rooms* by Eliza Anderson.
ACTOR: Plays—Sister George in *The Killing of Sister George* by Frank Marcus, 1972.

Paula Vogel's plays, while imaginatively dramatizing the conflict between the life force and death, prompt us to re-examine such topics as the feminization of poverty, the non-traditional family, the AIDS epidemic, and domestic violence (both in late 20th-century America and in the context of a revisit to Shakespeare's *Othello*). Despite the topicality of her comedies sporting a sting, these plays tend to salute the salutary nature of fantasy. Although clearly writing from a feminist perspective, Vogel does not portray her women uncritically or her men unsympathetically.

Nevertheless Vogel laments the unnecessarily Darwinian nature of people's odds of survival—a sort of law of the jungle by which the more muscular, wealthy, or powerful white, Protestant men enjoy the advantage. Prodigy Cecil, one of three fantasy children in *And Baby Makes Seven*, quotes Darwin to this effect: "Never forget that every single organic being around us strives to increase in numbers; that each lives by a struggle at some period in its life; that heavy destruction inevitably falls either on the young or the old. . . . Thus, from war or nature, from famine and death, all organic beings advance by one general law—namely, Multiply, Vary, Let the Strongest Live, and the Weakest Die. . . ."

The Oldest Profession depicts the effects wrought by the feminization of poverty among the elderly during the Reagan years. In a tiny New York City park at 72nd and Broadway, four still-working prostitutes in their 70's and their madame, aged 83, quietly chat about their fees, their clients and their simple meals—which provide a precarious pleasure and sustenance, given their low incomes. These hookers preserve their self-respect and their dignity except for the occasional necessity of beating off the incursions of a rival's encroachment on their territory. Although Vogel's premise that ladies of the night keep plying their trade till they drop might seem far-fetched, *The Oldest Profession* reflects the reality that senior citizens do service their own generation in this manner—what else are they trained to do and how else, deprived of health insurance and Social Security payments, can they eke out an existence? Vogel's shrewd social criticism even locates them in the building occupied by Zabar's Delicatessen, which really did evict the elderly tenants living upstairs when it expanded into selling housewares.

Vogel evinces a keen ear for her characters' colloquial speech, an intuitive understanding of their honor, pride, and enjoyment in their work, and subtlety in dramatizing their deprivations, ambitions, conflicts, and mutual nurturing. She gives us 10 minutes or so to warm to these women before we learn that they are anything more than just widows enjoying the sun. By this time we're perfectly prepared to recognize their importance to their clients and their value as people—for this represents the most respectful play ever written on this topic. As we laugh at such quips as "Vera's not just a woman with a Past; she's a woman with an Epic," we respond to Vogel's views of their struggle to survive on income insufficient to meet expenses, their efforts to exercise some control over their destinies, their compassion, their sisterhood, their respect for others and themselves, and their loneliness as, one by one, they die.

Although a comedy (especially in its, as yet unreleased, cinematic version, which takes the women away from their park bench and includes their satisfied customers), *The Oldest Profession*, like Vogel's other plays, stresses the women's mortality. *And Baby Makes Seven* initially seems a more carefree comedy about a contented though non-traditional family composed of Ruth, her pregnant partner Anna, Peter (the gay man who has fathered Anna's child), and three imaginary children made quite real to the adults (and to us) by Ruth and Anna. The situation quickly grows sinister, however, after Peter insists the kids must go before baby arrives. Once more Vogel hooks us with her characters' charm before telling us the truth about them. When we hear the boys talking in the dark about how babies are made, we can't resist lovable Henri from Albert Lamorisse's 1955 film *The Red Balloon*, prodigy Cecil, and Orphan—a wild boy brought up by a pack of dogs, who wants to name the baby Lassie. Soon infanticide occupies the grown ups. Combining whimsy and menace, the fantasy threatens to career off into violence while still encompassing the playful interaction of the lesbian lovers and their friend. After eight-year-old Henri tries to blackmail Anna into buying him a pony by claiming to be the father of her child, all three kids are killed off. (Orphan, most amusingly, dies of rabies, while quoting dog references from Shakespeare, such as "Out, damned spot.") Yet the parents come to appreciate their need for both illusions and playfulness and, in Vogel's happiest ending, quickly recapture both.

Vogel repeats this mingling of fantasy and death in *The Baltimore Waltz*, this time replacing the earlier plays' realism with a fluid presentational approach which combines narrative, lectures, language lessons, a slide show, and quick two- and three-person scenes set in the United States and Europe. Vogel creates simultaneously a compassionate comedy about death, a bedroom farce, and a satire on American AIDS policy, which fails urgently to pursue a cure because so many of the victims have been those "different" (from our rulers) and powerless. "If just one grandchild of George Bush caught this thing during toilet training, that would be the last we'd hear about the space program," laments a character.

But Vogel conjures a disease which targets single elementary school teachers, because they haven't a mother's immunity to their pupils' viruses. Although set in a ward at Baltimore's Johns Hopkins Hospital, this fantasy waltzes protagonist Anna around Europe in a two-fold quest: to find a cure for Acquired Toilet Disease and to enjoy sex, so that she can, before her untimely demise, make up for all those years of celibacy while forcing herself to remain a good little girl. Vogel forces spectators not in a high-risk group to consider for the first time the possibility of their own impending deaths, struck down by a mysterious illness the government doesn't care to fight fiercely. An AIDS play for those unaware souls who ignore the epidemic's ravages, *The Baltimore Waltz* proves another Vogel comedy which wins our sympathies before showing its hand: only after we can't help caring about Anna does the play, by substituting slides of Baltimore for views of Europe, let us know she's merely a surrogate for her dying sibling, AIDS-victim Carl (Vogel's brother, to whose memory she dedicates the play "because I cannot sew"). This ferocious comedy, playful and poignant, written in lieu of a panel for the AIDS memorial quilt, veers quickly then from nightmarish satire of medical quackery, to bereavement, to a magical waltz.

The plays which tackle violence, however, cannot offer such an upbeat conclusion. *Hot 'n' Throbbing* tells the truth: domestic violence escalates to murder. And *Desdemona* creates no happy ending to avoid its protagonist's death. We're stuck with how Shakespeare ends his play—though Vogel stops her comedy's action prior to that tragedy's crisis. Yet the intersection of their plots at *Desdemona*'s conclusion in the hair-brushing scene renders chilling the loss of life awaiting the high-spirited woman we've been delighting in earlier.

Vogel's imaginative recreation of Desdemona provides us with everything which Shakespeare denies us: full portraits of the three women (the only characters here), high spirits which do not willingly suffer their men's foolishness, no easy acquiescence to being victimized, even a lusty, frank sexuality. This provocative, startling comedy takes from Shakespeare its setting in Cyprus, Amelia's theft of the handkerchief, and the women's names. But where Shakespeare's Desdemona today must appear foolish to endure Othello's violent and unwarranted jealousy, Vogel's gives him cause to be jealous by exulting in an earthy, exuberant sexuality as she beds every man on the island save Cassio. Weaving such irony through her short, pithy episodes Vogel depicts women as often coarse, mainly honest, and so sensual they seem on the verge of seducing each other. The women's relations are marred, however, by petty jealousies, betrayals, and rivalries.

Vogel shows us we must blame the social system, implicitly responsible for denying the women sisterhood in a common cause, forcing them instead to depend on destructive men who exercise over them the power of life and death. Denied meaningful, remunerative employment, a woman can slave in a kitchen while promoting the advancement of a husband she despises (Amelia's choice), run a bawdy house (Bianca's choice), or prostitute herself (Desdemona's choice). Separated by class, financial status, and education (like the women in Wendy Kesselman's *My Sister in This House*), the women trust each other too little, too late—and therefore Desdemona will die, ironically having just made plans to leave her husband the next morning.

Ostensibly more in control, *Hot 'n' Throbbing*'s Charlene, an empowered, professional woman and feminist, has obtained a restraining order against the husband who has beaten her for years. At her computer, she supports herself and her kids by writing women's erotica for a feminist film company; like Desdemona's hooking, this has earned her independence. Yet gender power imbalances leave her vulnerable to violence. The husband breaks down the door, manipulates both her compassion for him and their teenagers' responses, and finally kills her.

Charlene has created powerful images of a dominant woman and submissive partner, but later, just before she is murdered, a male crew reverse the roles and turn the script into a snuff film. Even the daughter has fantasized about bondage and pain. If Vogel permits us any hope for women at this funny but dark and frightening play's conclusion, it emerges when the daughter dons knee-socks, flannel shirt, overalls, and heavy boots, thereby ensuring she's no sex object, before taking her own place at the computer. There she begins to write the play we've just seen, the sort of play Paula Vogel dramatizes, with the power to transform people and thus alter the world.

—Tish Dace

See the essay on *The Baltimore Waltz*.

WANDOR, Michelene (Dinah).

British. Born in London, 20 April 1940. Educated at Chingford Secondary Modern School, 1954–56, and Chingford County High School, 1956–59, both Essex; Newnham College, Cambridge, 1959–62, B.A. (honours) in English 1962; University of Essex, Colchester, 1974–75, M.A. in sociology 1975. Married the literary agent Ed Victor in 1963 (divorced 1975); two sons. Poetry editor, *Time Out* magazine, London, 1971–82; regular contributor, *Spare Rib* magazine, London, 1972–77; reviewer, *Plays and Players, Listener,* and *New Statesman,* all London, and *Kaleidoscope* programme, BBC Radio. Playwright-in-residence, University of Kent, Canterbury, 1982–83. Currently student, performers' course in Renaissance and Baroque music, Trinity College of Music, London. Recipient: Arts Council bursary, 1974, 1983; Emmy award, 1987. Address: 71 Belsize Lane, London NW3 5AU, England.

Publications

PLAYS

You Too Can Be Ticklish (produced 1971).

Brag-a-Fruit (produced 1971).

The Day after Yesterday (produced 1972).

Spilt Milk, and Mal de Mère in *Point 101* (produced 1972). In *Play Nine,* edited by Robin Rook, 1981.

To Die among Friends (includes *Mal de Mère, Joey, Christmas, Pearls, Swallows*) (produced 1974). In *Sink Songs,* 1975.

Friends and Strangers (produced 1974).

Sink Songs, with Dinah Brooke. 1975.

Penthesilia, adaptation of the play by Heinrich von Kleist (produced 1977).

The Old Wives' Tale (produced 1977). In *Five Plays,* 1984.

Care and Control (produced 1977). In *Strike While the Iron Is Hot,* edited by Wandor, 1980.

Floorshow, with others (produced 1978).

Whores d'Oeuvres (produced 1978). In *Five Plays,* 1984.

Scissors (produced 1978). In *Five Plays,* 1984.

Aid Thy Neighbour (produced 1978). In *Five Plays,* 1984.

Correspondence (broadcast 1978; produced 1979).

Aurora Leigh, adaptation of the poem by Elizabeth Barrett Browning (produced 1979). In *Plays by Women 1,* edited by Wandor, 1982.

Future Perfect, with Steve Gooch and Paul Thompson (produced 1980).

The Blind Goddess, adaptation of a play by Ernst Toller (produced 1981).
Five Plays (includes *To Die among Friends*, *The Old Wives' Tale*, *Whores
   d'Oeuvres*, *Scissors*, *Aid Thy Neighbour*). 1984.
The Wandering Jew, with Mike Alfreds, adaptation of a novel by Eugène Sue
   (produced 1987). 1987.
Wanted (produced 1988). 1988.

RADIO PLAYS AND SERIALS: *Correspondence*, 1978; *The Unlit Lamp*, from the
novel by Radclyffe Hall, 1980; *Precious Bane*, from the novel by Mary Webb,
1981; *Lolly Willowes*, from the novel by Sylvia Townsend Warner, 1983; *An
Uncommon Love*, 1984; *Kipps*, from the novel by H.G. Wells, 1984; *Venus
Smiles*, from the story by J.G. Ballard, 1985; *The Brothers Karamazov*, from a
novel by Dostoevsky, 1986; *The Nine Tailors*, from the novel by Dorothy L.
Sayers, 1986; *Persuasion*, from the novel by Jane Austen, 1986–87; *Helbeck
of Bannisdale*, from the novel by Mrs. Humphry Ward, 1987; *Gardens of
Eden*, 1987; *Whose Body?*, from the novel by Dorothy L. Sayers, 1987; *The
Dwelling Place*, from the novel by Catherine Cookson, 1988; *Frenchman's
Creek*, from the novel by Daphne du Maurier, 1989; *Ben Venga Maggio*,
1990; *The Courtier, the Prince and the Lady*, 1990; *The Mill on the Floss*,
from the novel by George Eliot, 1991; *A Summer Wedding*, 1991; *Killing
Orders*, from the novel by Sara Paretsky, 1991; *A Question of Courage*, from
the novel by Marjorie Darke, 1992; *The King's General*, from the novel by
Daphne du Maurier, 1992; *Deadlock*, from the novel by Sara Paretsky, 1993.

TELEVISION PLAYS: *The Belle of Amherst*, from the play by William Luce, 1987;
The Story of an Hour, adaptation of a story by Kate Chopin, 1988.

NOVEL
Arky Types, with Sara Maitland. 1987.

SHORT STORIES
Tales I Tell My Mother, with others. 1978.
Guests in the Body. 1986.
More Tales I Tell My Mother, with others. 1987.

VERSE
Upbeat: Poems and Stories. 1982.
Touch Papers, with Judith Kazantzis and Michèle Roberts. 1982.
Gardens of Eden: Poems for Eve and Lilith. 1984.
Gardens of Eden: Selected Poems. 1990.

OTHER
The Great Divide: The Sexual Division of Labour; or, Is It Art?, with others.
   1976.
Understudies: Theatre and Sexual Politics. 1981; revised edition, as *Carry On,
   Understudies*, 1986.
Look Back in Gender: Sexuality and the Family in Post-1956 British Drama.
   1987.

Wandor on Women Writers: Antonia White, Elizabeth Barrett Browning, Hannah Culwick, Dorothy Richardson, Jean Rhys. 1988.
Once a Feminist: Stories of a Generation. 1990.

Editor, *The Body Politic: Writings from the Women's Liberation Movement in Britain 1969–1972.* 1972.
Editor, with Michèle Roberts, *Cutlasses and Earrings* (poetry anthology). 1977.
Editor, *Strike While the Iron Is Hot: Three Plays on Sexual Politics.* 1980.
Editor, *Plays by Women 1–4.* 4 vols., 1982–85.
Editor, *On Gender and Writing.* 1983.

CRITICAL STUDIES: "The Personal Is Political: Feminism and the Theatre" by Wandor, in *Dreams and Deconstructions* edited by Sandy Craig, 1980; *Feminist Theatre* by Helene Keyssar, 1984.

Michelene Wandor comments:

I began writing plays in 1969, when the "fringe" began. I also was writing poetry and theatre reviews. For me the activities of fiction/non-fiction have always been complementary. At that time I became aware of, and developed, socialist and feminist convictions. For about ten years I wrote plays just for the stage, in a variety of forms—social realism, collage, surreal, comedy, abstract: whatever. Since 1979 I have written extensively for radio, a stimulating medium. I have dramatised/transposed a number of texts for radio—a way of working with the voices and styles of other writers that is both exciting and rewarding. I have absolutely no pre-conceived ideas about the appropriateness or otherwise of dramatic form. For me the appropriate form arrives as a combination of content and my approach to it. Having said that, I can also be lured by any subject. I have written a lot of female-centred work and male-centred work, and am always as aware as I can be of the way an inevitable (though variable) gender-bias operates in every drama.

Michelene Wandor is a playwright who is also known for her poetry and fiction, and for her writing about the theatre. In her theatre writing, Wandor established her reputation with two key texts: *Understudies: Theatre and Sexual Politics* and *Look Back in Gender: Sexuality and the Family in Post-1956 British Drama.* These books, and others to which she has contributed, have earned her a reputation as one of England's most flexible writers, adept at producing critical essays and overviews of the state of the theatre and at writing plays for theatre, radio, and television.

As a playwright, Wandor has worked in a wide variety of different contexts, from her early work with feminist collectives and fringe theatre companies, to her work for the Royal National Theatre and the BBC. Some of her plays have been published in anthologies with playwrights such as Howard Brenton and Frank Marcus, marking her as one of the most notable "political playwrights" of her generation. She is also one of the few women—along with more "mainstream" playwrights such as Caryl Churchill, Pam Gems, and Louise Page—who was in on the watershed of women's alternative theatre in the 1970's. She has worked with and for Monstrous Regiment, Mrs. Worthington's Daughters, and Gay Sweatshop, as an independent playwright, and as a commissioned writer of radio and television drama.

Wandor is best known for a few early stage plays and for a number of highly successful radio dramas. She attributes the high profile of her radio plays to the fashion in contemporary theatre for "conservative" forms, styles, and themes, including the current popularity of dramatic adaptations. In her words:

> If theatre had not become so conservative so quickly, and if the theatre had retained its early 1970's openness, more of my work would be done in the theatre. Basically, to be successful in the theatre as a woman playwright, you need to have patrons who will bandwagon you. To work well in radio some similar things apply, but I genuinely believe that there are more radio producers whose commitment is to the work rather than to the fashion.

The comment reflects on the nature of Wandor's writing, which is always informed by politics; whether social, cultural, sexual, or personal. Thus, it has been Wandor's adaptations which, on the whole, have best suited the "conservative" trend of theatre production. Her best radio work includes *Ben Venga Maggio*, a dramatic poem in the voice of the popular character Columbina; it is a play which blends spoken language and Italian carnival music. Another notable radio play of the same period is *The Courtier, the Prince and the Lady*, which is set in Renaissance Italy and draws on Machiavelli and Castiglione as source material, while incorporating the music of Josquin and his contemporaries. In 1991, Wandor adapted George Eliot's *The Mill on the Floss* in a five-part serial dramatization. She has since adapted feminist detective stories by Sarah Paretsky and some of the writings of Marjorie Darke.

Wandor has also had considerable success in television drama. She won an Emmy award for her television adaptation of William Luce's play about the life of Emily Dickinson, *The Belle of Amherst*. In 1988, she wrote a short film adaptation of Kate Chopin's *The Story of an Hour*. *The Well Woman*, her television adaptation of Radclyffe Hall's *The Well of Loneliness*, has yet to be produced.

Yet Wandor's most characteristic work is found in her own original stage plays. One important contribution to British theatre was her scripting, from devised and group-researched material, of Gay Sweatshop's *Care and Control* in 1977. That play was among the first political theatre pieces to address the issue of the state and motherhood. It had a considerable social impact as well as theatrical and critical success, as did *Aid Thy Neighbour*, produced at London's New End Theatre in 1978. The latter play offered a frank treatment of the process of artificial insemination by donor, another crucial issue for contemporary women. In these and many of her other stage plays, Wandor combined her feminist politics and social activism in her writing for the stage. While some of her work could be described by labels such as "agitprop" or "social realism," Wandor herself would be the first to qualify and explain these terms. In fact, analysis of the influence of politics on the theatre of the 1970's and 1980's is one of the threads running through Wandor's critical writing about the theatre. For Wandor, playwriting and political involvement (real and representational) tend to go hand in hand.

Partly for reasons related to the politics (and "fashionability") of radio and theatre production, Wandor wrote more and more adaptations in the 1980's, including *Aurora Leigh*—an adaptation of Elizabeth Barrett Browning's poem —produced by Mrs. Worthington's Daughters in 1979 and revived at the Royal National Theatre in 1981. Her major mainstage theatre success was also an adaptation: *The Wandering Jew*, co-written with Mike Alfreds and adapted from Eugène Sue's novel about the Jesuits, given a mainstage production at the Royal National Theatre in 1987.

Yet in the late 1980's and early 1990's, Wandor's stage plays have begun to convey more of her own distinct voice. In *Wanted*, for instance, she took an experimental tack in her depiction of a mixed bag of characters (an angel, an unborn being, and the biblical Sarah), all engaged in a witty and topical theatrical representation of the issue of surrogacy. Here, as in her earlier plays *Care and Control* and *Aid Thy Neighbour*, the concern for gender relations and family structure are central themes. Yet the style of *Wanted* reveals a developmental shift in Wandor's work, a move away from social realism and the structure of adaptations, to the refinement of a distinctive personal voice. That voice, fractured in *Wanted* into three, is still shifting too quickly to predict the next phase in Wandor's career as a playwright. Yet it does seem clear that her current work is developing in conjunction with (and sometimes in a challenging opposition to) current debates about post-modernist and post-structuralist theatres.

—Lizbeth Goodman

WASSERSTEIN, Wendy.

American. Born in Brooklyn, New York, 18 October 1950. Educated at Calhoun School, Manhattan; Mount Holyoke College, South Hadley, Massachusetts, B.A. 1971; City College, City University of New York, M.A. 1973; Yale University School of Drama, New Haven, Connecticut, M.F.A. 1976. Recipient: Pulitzer prize, 1989; New York Drama Critics Circle award, 1989; Susan Smith Blackburn award, 1989; Tony award, 1989; National Endowment for the Arts grant; Guggenheim grant. Lives in New York. Agent: International Creative Management, 40 West 57th Street, New York, New York 10019, U.S.A.

Publications

PLAYS

Any Woman Can't (produced 1973).
Happy Birthday Montpelier Pizz-zazz (produced 1974).
When Dinah Shore Ruled the Earth, with Christopher Durang (produced 1975).
Uncommon Women and Others (produced 1975). 1979.
Isn't It Romantic (produced 1981; revised version produced 1983). 1985.
Tender Offer (produced 1983).

The Man in a Case, adaptation of a story by Chekhov, in *Orchards* (produced 1985). 1986.

Miami, music and lyrics by Bruce Sussman and Jack Feldman (produced 1986).

Smart Women/Brilliant Choices in *Urban Blight* (musical revue), based on an idea by John Tillinger, music by David Shire, lyrics by Richard Maltby, Jr. (produced 1988).

The Heidi Chronicles (produced 1988). 1990.

The Heidi Chronicles and Other Plays (includes *Uncommon Women and Others*, *Isn't It Romantic*). 1990.

The Sisters Rosensweig (produced 1992). 1993.

TELEVISION PLAY: *The Sorrows of Gin*, from the story by John Cheever, 1979.

OTHER

Bachelor Girls (essays). 1990.

THEATRICAL ACTIVITIES

ACTOR: **Play**—in *The Hotel Play* by Wallace Shawn, 1981.

Identity is the theme in all of Wendy Wasserstein's plays, but is most fully integrated in her major works—*Uncommon Women and Others*, *Isn't It Romantic*, and *The Heidi Chronicles*. Wasserstein's commercial success with *The Heidi Chronicles*, which received both the Pulitzer prize and the Tony award for best play in 1989, has placed her in the slippery position of championing women's causes and feminist concerns. However, the playwright is more concerned with genetics than gender; and more likely to employ humor than humanism in creating her female characters. Her early works, which are not published, are precursory exercises exploring themes of sexuality, marriage, and relationships using episodic structure, music, and comic caricatures. Male characters are primarily used as foils and are rarely fully developed. Most of Wasserstein's female characters are not traditionally developed either, and are often representative of types. What unifies and sustains her dramaturgy is Wasserstein's coy sense of humor supported by keen observations of everyday life.

Wasserstein uses traditional American rituals as a means to exploit traditional roles. In two early plays, *When Dinah Shore Ruled the Earth* and *Any Woman Can't*, she uses a beauty pageant in the former and a dance audition in the latter to both exhort and extol the eclectic roles of ambitious females in a male-dominated society. In *Happy Birthday, Montpelier Pizz-zazz*, the college party scene is the backdrop for the exploitation of both stereotypical roles and stereotypical expectations of college students. The primary issues center around women's options but the play depends too much on caricature to be taken seriously. *Uncommon Women and Others*, Wasserstein's first major work, makes better use of college rituals as a means to explore both character and issue.

Uncommon Women and Others is not unique but it is risky in terms of subject matter. The reunion format of five women who meet in 1978 and then travel back six years to their final year at Mount Holyoke College provides the structure of the all-female play. What makes the play compelling are the concerns that each of the five women have regarding their role in society, in relation to each other, and to themselves. There is no real plot that unifies the play, and no real ending. A disembodied male voice is heard between each scene reciting extracts from a traditional graduation address. The technique serves to unify the play not only structurally but also thematically, since each excerpt raises issues that the women are trying to work through and choices that they are facing in the future.

Isn't It Romantic is similar to *Uncommon Women and Others* in terms of episodic structure, the use of music to create mood and exploit ritual, and in terms of the disembodied voice, which takes the form of telephone messages from various characters in the play and characters who are not physically present. *Isn't It Romantic* offers a better developed plot, characters with more dimension, and thematically the strongest philosophical bent of any Wasserstein work. The play, benefiting from some major rewrites after its initial New York première, contains the best linguistic foreplay of wit and wisdom stemming from Wasserstein's keen sense of irony and honest portrayal of the two major characters.

The central character, Janie Blumberg, is "a little kooky, a little sweet, a little unconfident." By contrast, her best friend Harriet Cornwall could be "the cover girl on the best working women's magazine." With Janie, her friends, and her parents along with Harriet and her mother, Wasserstein creates a Chekhovian *Cherry Orchard* where the plot is simple and the characters, each of whom is a bit eccentric and lives in his or her own world, discover that each must fulfill his or her own desires; that each must have his or her own dream. Janie grows by recognizing the discrepancies in everyone else's desires. The final tableau shows Janie as she begins to dance to "Isn't It Romantic" while the audience hears the voice of a friend leaving a desperate message on the telephone machine. Janie's dancing becomes more confident until she is "dancing beautifully," symbolizing her growth and celebrating an optimistic future.

The final tableau in Wasserstein's most celebrated work, that of Heidi sitting in a rocker singing softly to her adopted child, is in stark contrast to that of Janie's ebullient face and dancing silhouette. Unfortunately, *The Heidi Chronicles* overshadows the merits of *Isn't It Romantic*. The plays are similar, both dealing with a single woman looking for her place in society and in life. However, Heidi more closely resembles Harriet or Kate from *Uncommon Women and Others*. All are successful in their careers, but all have paid a price for success.

Wasserstein's most prize-winning play is not without merit, but it does not live up to its potential as a well-documented play that promises a comparison of "lost women painters" from the 16th century to the "lost feminists" of the 20th century.

Heidi, an art historian, opens the play in mid-lecture in front of a slide screen of a Sofonisba Anguissola painting. The painting and the lecture serve as both a literal and symbolic framing device. Scenes move back in time from 1965 to 1977, and from 1980 to 1989. The play explores Heidi's disillusionment with the women's movement, dramatizing its history at the same time. It raises serious and important issues only to undercut them with a loosely constructed plot and a contrived ending. Homosexuality, single parenting, politics, and art are all subjects that remain unexplored. As the heroine of the play, Heidi has an unusual role in that much of the time she is a spectator. And most of the action is that of encountering and re-encountering the various people in her life who have influenced her. The humor is closer to that of television sit-com and lacks the risqué verbiage of *Uncommon Women and Others* or the strong philosophical wit of *Isn't It Romantic*. Wasserstein's strengths lie in her ability to create characters who laugh at themselves while questioning others. She serves as a role model for women who wish to be successful in the New York theatre venue. All her plays are quirky and interesting and offer strong roles for women.

—Judy Lee Oliva

See the essay on *The Heidi Chronicles*.

WERTENBAKER, (Lael Louisiana) Timberlake.

British and American. Educated at schools near St. Jean-de-Luz, France; attended university in the United States. Journalist in London and New York; teacher of French in Greece, one year. Resident writer, Shared Experience, 1983, and Royal Court Theatre, 1985, both London. Recipient: Arts Council of Great Britain bursary, 1981, grant, 1983; Thames Television bursary, 1984, 1985; *Plays and Players* award, 1985; *Evening Standard* award, 1988; Olivier award, 1988; Whiting award, 1989; London Theatre Critics Circle award, 1991, 1992; Writers Guild Macallan award, 1992. Lives in London. Agent: Michael Imison Playwrights, 28 Almeida Street, London N1 1TD, England.

Publications

PLAYS

This Is No Place for Tallulah Bankhead (produced 1978).
The Third (produced 1980).
Second Sentence (produced 1980).
Case to Answer (produced 1980).
Breaking Through (produced 1980).
New Anatomies (produced 1981). In *Plays Introduction*, 1984.
Inside Out (produced 1982).
Home Leave (produced 1982).
False Admissions, adaptation of a play by Marivaux (produced 1983).
Successful Strategies, adaptation of a play by Marivaux (produced 1983).
Abel's Sister, based on material by Yolande Bourcier (produced 1984).
The Grace of Mary Traverse (produced 1985). 1985.
Léocadia, adaptation of the play by Jean Anouilh (broadcast 1985). In *Five Plays*, by Anouilh, 1987.
Mephisto, adaptation of the play by Ariane Mnouchkine, based on a novel by Klaus Mann (produced 1986).
Our Country's Good, adaptation of *The Playmaker* by Thomas Keneally (produced 1988). 1988; revised edition, 1990.
The Love of the Nightingale (produced 1988). With *The Grace of Mary Traverse*, 1989.

Pelléas and Mélisande, adaptation of the play by Maeterlinck (broadcast 1988;
   produced 1989).
Three Birds Alighting on a Field (produced 1991). 1991.
The Thebans, adaptation of three plays by Sophocles (includes *Oedipus
   Tyrannos, Oedipus at Colonus, Antigone*) (produced 1992). 1992.

RADIO PLAYS: *Léocadia*, 1985; *La Dispute*, from the play by Marivaux, 1987;
Pelléas and Mélisande, from the play by Maeterlinck, 1988.

TELEVISION PLAYS: *Do Not Disturb*, 1991; *The Children*, adaptation of a novel
by Edith Wharton, 1992.

Timberlake Wertenbaker comments:

I like monologues. I think they are an unused and rather beautiful form of
communication. I do not like naturalism. I find it boring. My plays are an
attempt to get away from the smallness of naturalism, from enclosed rooms to
open spaces, and also to get ideas away from the restraints of closed spaces to
something wider. My plays often start with a very ordinary question: If women
had power, would they behave the same way as men? Why do we seem to want
to destroy ourselves? Is the personal more important than the political? If
someone has behaved badly all of their lives, can they redeem themselves?
Parallel to this will be some story I may have heard, some gossip about
somebody, a sentence heard or read. A friend of mine once told me his mother
had been taught how to be a good hostess by being made to talk to empty
chairs. I used that as the opening scene of *The Grace of Mary Traverse*. I once
heard about a young couple where the woman, for no apparant reason, had
come out of the bath and shot herself. That became *Case to Answer*.
Somebody showed me a print of the Japanese courtesan Ono No Komachi. I
wrote a play about her. Everything gets collected and used at some point. I'm
sure it's the same for all writers, but I haven't asked. Once I have the idea and
the people, I do a lot of research. I think plays should be accurate, whatever
their subject. Then the imagination can be let free, but only after a solid
knowledge of the world, the people, the age, whatever is the world of the play.
   I don't think you can leave the theatre and go out and make a revolution.
That's the naïvety of the 1970's. But I do think you can make people change,
just a little, by forcing them to question something, or by intriguing them, or
giving them an image that remains with them. And that little change can lead
to bigger changes. That's all you can hope for. Nor do I think playwrights
should have the answers. A play is like a trial: it goes before the jury, the
audience, and they decide—to like or not like the people, to agree or not to
agree. If you really have the answers, you shouldn't be a writer but a politician.
And if you're only interested in slice of life, then you should make documentaries. The theatre is a difficult place, it requires an audience to use its imagination. You must accept that and not try to make it easy for them. You must
give them language, because it is best heard in the theatre and language is a
potent manifestation of hope. In some theatres in ancient Greece, the number
of seats corresponded to the number of adult males with voting rights. I think
that is right: theatre is for people who take responsibility. There is no point in

trying to attract idiots. Theatre should never be used to flatter, but to reveal, which is to disturb.

There is a wonderful continuity in the work of Timberlake Wertenbaker, which is none the less full of surprise, invention, and a delight in inversion. It is never possible to predict how she may wish to say something, though familiarity with her work shows themes and preoccupations which are part of her powerful personal identity as a writer. In form and setting, however, her dramas roam freely over historical periods and cultures: from antique Greece to a Japanese story which spans centuries; from an Australian penal colony to Islamic cross-dressing and the art world in London in the 1990's.

With the worldwide success of her major play, *Our Country's Good*, originally performed at London's Royal Court Theatre, Wertenbaker moved from the ranks of the much courted and professionally admired (for she is that rarity, a "writers' writer" who repeatedly demonstrates the potential of dramatic writing) to the genuinely popular. The play came about when the theatre's director, Max Stafford-Clark, brought her Thomas Keneally's novel, *The Playmaker,* an historical retelling of a production of Farquhar's *The Recruiting Officer* by prisoners at a penal settlement in Australia.

Although it springs from Keneally's novel, *Our Country's Good* is richly original theatre in its own right. A densely populated play, it maintains a constant focus on the individuals in the story and finds in the convict population a creative and positive energy which is lacking in the British officers who oppress them. As much as any of her plays, it demonstrates her sure instinct for the theatrical situation, for instance, her development of the character of a woman rehearsing her role despite a sentence of death which will mean her execution before the first performance.

Such skills did not come about overnight, although they seem to flower spectacularly in the collaborative creative atmosphere of the Royal Court. Before her first four major plays, *The Grace of Mary Traverse*, *Our Country's Good*, *The Love of the Nightingale*, and *Three Birds Alighting on a Field*, she had established an intriguing and peculiar body of work. There was individuality and dramatic inversion in even the most straightforward of her plays, such as *Home Leave*, which she wrote about women working in a factory at the end of World War II. Her opening stage directions present her leading character with calculated ambiguity: "She's in overalls, her hair hidden in a cloth cap and it should be impossible to tell she's a woman." Often the tilt of her writing explores a fluidity between the sexes that is far more revolutionary than any declaration of equality, and she does not hesitate to subvert legend or history in her examinations of human nature.

Perhaps the most elaborate statements about the intentions of her early work appear in her play *Inside Out*, borrowed from the Japanese legend of Komachi, a famous beauty and poet who was doomed to suffer because of the task undertaken by one of her admirers which led to his death. Unable to match the poetic speech of Komachi in his declaration of love, he vowed to return from an arduous journey every night for 100 nights, but returned only 99 times. In Wertenbaker's version, Komachi first appears as an old woman who has survived into our present, and who has become interchangeable with

Shosho, the lover. When the story of the love affair is retold, the old woman becomes Shosho and another actress plays the young Komachi who first rebuffs him and then, through desire, regrets the delay. Shosho remains steadfast in his promise.

As if that were not enough sexual ambiguity, it is by draping Shosho in her clothes and exchanging roles with him that Komachi extracts the promise of the 100 visits. Because it is by imagining himself as Komachi that Shosho has invented the idea of the poetic action, it is forever unclear who really suggested the task, but what remains equally unclear is the function of gender in Wertenbaker's version of the story.

The chorus reports: "They say a woman is a man turned inside out. Most evident in the genitals, his turned out, hers turned in, hers waiting for his, waiting for completion, that's what they say." But while that may be what "they say," it is obvious that Wertenbaker is not convinced. The chorus also asks: "Question: what is the anatomy of a woman?" and is answered by Komachi's companion Li: "Not what you imagine through your genitals."

Another of Wertenbaker's plays, *New Anatomies*, tackles that physical question more directly. It tells the story of Isabelle Eberhardt, a young woman who dresses as a male Arab to find acceptance among the Muslims and, ironically, is persecuted by the French. In her Arab persona as Si Mahmoud she seeks spiritual enlightenment and though the Arabs have more than a fair idea that she is actually a woman, they befriend her and accept her own determination of her sex. In the stage version, written for a women's theatrical troupe, all the roles, male and female, are taken by women. That ambiguity was not helpful as the issue of Isabelle's self-determined sexuality is profound, and the dressing-up of other women undermines both the spiritual search and the intended clash of western and oriental cultures. However, as a text it carefully and provocatively defines its arguments.

As a woman of American heritage, educated in France and resident in Britain, Wertenbaker herself juggles cultures and influences and in addition to her original work she has already made significant contributions to translation from the French, particularly with her translations from Marivaux. His stylish comic knowingness about sexuality and faithlessness has been well reflected in her English versions of *False Admissions*, *Successful Strategies*, and *La Dispute*, where she has maintained a cool ironical posture which admirably suggests the French originals. Although she has also provided convincing versions of Jean Anouilh's *Léocadia* and Ariane Mnouchkine's *Mephisto*, it is in Marivaux's writing that her own preoccupations are best reflected.

Ancient Greek is another of her languages, and her notable plain-spoken version of the Oedipus plays of Sophocles, *Oedipus Tyrannos*, *Oedipus at Colonus* and *Antigone*, were presented successfully by the Royal Shakespeare Company as *The Thebans*.

Possibly the most straightforward of her original plays is *Abel's Sister*, written with material provided by Yolande Bourcier. It is none the less emotionally complex. Although set in the English countryside, it has some of the mythical aspirations of Sam Shepard's versions of the American family. Sandra, the spastic twin sister of Howard, has removed herself from the "centre" where she lives to move in on her brother and his girlfriend. When she announces that her favourite story is Cain and Abel, because it was right that

Cain should at least kill the brother who suffocated him, she prepares the way for an attack on her brother by an American neighbour who has been led to believe that Howard is dangerously violent.

It is typical of Wertenbaker that she should turn to a basic biblical source, again inverting the sexes, to explain the motivation of her characters. In addition to the Japanese Nō theatre and investigations of Muslim culture, she has also explored the radicalization of Electra in her short (and relatively minor) reshaping of the *Oresteia*, *Agamemnon's Daughter* (as yet unproduced).

Her own most radical historical revision is her dramatic fantasia *The Grace of Mary Traverse*, in which she portrays Lord Gordon, the disaffected peer accused of treason after the destructive "Gordon Riots" of 1780, as a man who discovers power through the impulsive rape of a woman in the streets. In her version of events, he is a peripheral character and the dramatic catalyst is Mary Traverse, a young woman trained only in polite conversation by her father. After witnessing the rape by Gordon, she determines not to be a victim and decides to enter Georgian London as an equal of the rapacious men. She gambles with them, hires a male whore to deflower her, prostitutes herself to her father, and buys the sexual services of a woman for her own pleasure. She, too, finds power a seduction, and helps reignite the hatred for Catholics, though the horrors of mass violence finally chill her.

The classicism and cosmopolitan dramaturgy of Wertenbaker's writing seemed to mark her out from most of her contemporaries as a writer who dealt with the present only through metaphor. Her play for the Royal Shakespeare Company, *The Love of the Nightingale*, enforced that perception but when she returned to the Royal Court for *Three Birds Alighting on a Field* she was to provide one of the most articulate "de-constructions" of the 1980's to appear on stage.

Her central characters are Biddy, an English society woman who is ordered by her wealthy Greek husband to become interesting, and Stephen, a painter of English landscapes who has been exiled for a decade in the countryside for being unfashionable. In the original production the play included scenes that retold the parallel story of Philoctetes, the Greek hero abandoned on an island by Odysseus because of the smell of a wound. In order to win the Trojan War, Odysseus needed to trick Philoctetes back into his service, and in order for the gallery owner in Wertenbaker's play to survive the recession of the 1990's, he needs to lure Stephen back into his fold.

When the play was revived by the Royal Court a year after its first production, Wertenbaker dispensed with the enacted scenes of the Philoctetes story and allowed the modern story to stand on its own, secure in its parallels and confident of its own message. Events conspire to remove Biddy from her wealth and the limitations of her class while she becomes the agent who restores Stephen to the society of art. In the years covered by his exile, the world has changed. The ideological certainties of the left and the right have been vanquished by the collapse of Eastern Europe and western economies, and Wertenbaker's play is witty, knowing and eloquent in its depiction of the results.

Even in her most explicitly classical plays, Wertenbaker manages to wear her erudition lightly. What she demonstrates in *Three Birds Alighting on a Field* is the enduring strength of those classical values in the most topical of dramas. With her grasp of classical storytelling, her great gift of language and individuality of perception, she is likely to provide some of the most enduring drama of the late 20th century.

—Ned Chaillet

See the essay on *Three Birds Alighting on a Field*.

WYMARK, Olwen (Margaret, née Buck).

American. Born in Oakland, California, 14 February 1932. Educated at Pomona College, Claremont, California, 1949–51; University College, London, 1951–52. Married the actor Patrick Wymark in 1950 (died 1970); two daughters and two sons. Writer-in-residence, Unicorn Theatre for Young People, London, 1974–75, and Kingston Polytechnic, Surrey, 1977; script consultant, Tricycle Theatre, London; lecturer in playwriting, New York University; part-time tutor in playwriting, University of Birmingham, 1989–91. Member, Arts Council of Great Britain Drama Panel, 1980–84. Recipient: Zagreb Drama Festival prize, 1967; Actors Theatre of Louisville Best New Play award, 1978. Lives in London. Agent: Lemons Unna, and Durbridge, 24 Pottery Lane, Holland Park, London W11 4LZ, England.

Publications

PLAYS

Lunchtime Concert (produced 1966). In *Three Plays*, 1967; in *The Best Short Plays 1975*, edited by Stanley Richards, 1975.

Three Plays (as *Triple Image: Coda, Lunchtime Concert, The Inhabitants*, produced 1967; *The Inhabitants*, produced 1974). 1967.

The Gymnasium (produced 1967). In *The Gymnasium and Other Plays*, 1971.

The Technicians (produced 1969). In *The Gymnasium and Other Plays*, 1971.

Stay Where You Are (produced 1969). In *The Gymnasium and Other Plays*, 1971; in *The Best Short Plays 1972*, edited by Stanley Richards, 1972.

No Talking (for children; produced 1970).

Neither Here nor There (produced 1971). In *The Gymnasium and Other Plays*, 1971.

Speak Now (produced 1971; revised version produced 1975).

The Committee (produced 1971). In *Best Friends, The Committee, The Twenty-Second Day*, 1984.

The Gymnasium and Other Plays. 1971.

Jack the Giant Killer (produced 1972). In *The Gymnasium and Other Plays*, 1971.

Tales from Whitechapel (produced 1972).

Daniel's Epic (for children), with Daniel Henry (produced 1972).

Chinigchinich (for children; produced 1973).

Watch the Woman, with Brian Phelan (produced 1973).

The Bolting Sisters (for children; produced 1974).

Southwark Originals (collaborative work for children; produced 1975).

The Twenty-Second Day (broadcast 1975; produced 1975). In *Best Friends, The Committee, The Twenty-Second Day*, 1984.

Starters (collaborative work for children; includes *The Giant and the Dancing Fairies*, *The Time Loop*, *The Spellbound Jellybaby*, *The Robbing of Elvis Parsley*, *I Spy*) (produced 1975).

Three For All (collaborative work for children; includes *Box Play*, *Family Business*, *Extended Play*) (produced 1976).

We Three, and After Nature, Art (produced 1977). In *Play Ten*, edited by Robin Rook, 1977.

Find Me (produced 1977). 1980.

The Winners, and Missing Persons (for children; produced 1978).

Loved (produced 1978). 1980.

The Child (broadcast 1979). 1979.

Please Shine Down on Me (produced 1980).

Female Parts: One Woman Plays (includes *Waking Up*, *A Woman Alone*, *The Same Old Story*, *Medea*), adaptations of plays by Dario Fo and Franca Rame, translated by Margaret Kunzle and Stuart Hood (produced 1981). 1981.

Best Friends (produced 1981). In *Best Friends, The Committee, The Twenty-Second Day*, 1984.

Buried Treasure (produced 1983).

Best Friends, The Committee, The Twenty-Second Day. 1984.

Lessons and Lovers (produced 1985). 1986.

Nana, adaptation of the novel by Zola (produced 1987). 1990.

Strike Up the Banns (produced 1988). 1988.

Brezhnev's Children (produced 1991). 1992.

Mirror Mirror (opera; produced 1992).

RADIO PLAYS: *The Ransom*, 1957; *The Unexpected Country*, 1957; *California Here We Come*, 1958; *The Twenty-Second Day*, 1975; *You Come Too*, 1977; *The Child*, 1979; *Vivien the Blockbuster*, 1980; *Mothering Sunday*, 1980; *Sea Changes*, 1984; *A Wreath of Roses*, from the novel by Elizabeth Taylor, 1985; *Mothers and Shadows*, from a novel by Marta Traba, 1987; *Christopher Columbus*, from the novel by Elizabeth von Arnim, with Barbara Clegg, 1989; *Oroonoko*, from the novel by Aphra Behn, 1990.

TELEVISION PLAYS: *Mrs. Moresby's Scrapbook*, 1973, *Vermin*, 1974, *Marathon*, 1975, *Mother Love*, 1975, *Dead Drunk*, 1975, and *Her Father's Daughter*, 1984 (all in *Crown Court* series); *Oceans Apart*, 1984; *Not That Kind of People*, 1984.

Olwen Wymark comments:

I didn't start writing plays until my mid-thirties and for the first few years wrote only one-act, rather experimental plays; Harold Hobson called them "atonal." I also wrote about eight plays for children. Since 1977 I've written full-length plays in a more naturalistic form as well as some adaptations. I've recently written an opera which was performed in 1992 and hope I will write more. I'm currently concentrating on writing for television.

Olwen Wymark has written some three dozen plays for radio, television, and stage. These range from one-act plays through full-length ones, and her children's plays typify the playful side of her personality. Indeed smallness figures again and again in her work—though, like so much else, one has to unmask it from her work even as she herself relies on a series of unmasking for dramatic effect. *Find Me*, for example, is a documentary play about a mentally disturbed girl who had, in real life, died in a special hospital. Those expecting the play to concentrate sympathy on the little girl must have been disappointed: it is far easier to sympathize with the restaurant owners, friends, and family who have their peace and property destroyed by the girl's predilection for starting fires. Indeed, though she died in the hospital, viewers find themselves sympathizing with the desperate hospital authorities rather than with Verity. She is so small as to disappear in the maelstroms she creates. It is difficult to find her, let alone love her. For the play was sparked off by letters which the girl had written, and which her family had allowed Wymark to read; one began, "Dear Whoeveryouare. Please find me and have me as your beloved." Here, in Wymark's view, is everyman's dilemma: you feel unsure of yourself, and yet it is precisely that self-doubt which fuels creativity. At least it is so in her own case.

Her early plays are exteriorizations of internal anguish, games devised by the characters to reflect and exercise their griefs and dissatisfactions. In *The Gymnasium*, two friends begin a friendly boxing match, with the elderly and gentlemanly one requesting his pretty cockney partner not to talk. They have hardly commenced sparring when the boy turns on a stream of vitriolic abuse. There is plenty of time to attempt puzzling this through, before one realizes that this is a regular marriage therapy session, in which the cockney plays the gentleman's wife and incites his partner to beat him up instead of the wife who is protected by the fine walls of custom and civility.

Most of Wymark's plays are about boringly familiar situations, rooted as they are in the emotional hothouse of upper-middle-class life. What makes the plays dramatic is a lively sense of timing; she offers to her audience the pleasure of solving marvellously constructed puzzles. It is not always possible to sort out the stories, however; and, as in *Neither Here nor There*, "a series of false certainties recede in infinite perspective. Her characters fall through one trapdoor to the solid ground beneath, only to find that collapsing beneath them as well" (Irving Wardle's review in the *Times*). Is the play a comment on the nightmarish quality of experience? Hardly, because the schoolgirls are inventing the whole game themselves.

Situation and theme; anxieties, tensions, and emotional states; guilt, futility, and desperation—these come across in her bizarre and intense plays much more strongly than characters and situations, though these are presented starkly enough. Whenever it is possible to piece her stories together, one begins to care for her characters. Otherwise her plays remain merely ingenious. Witty, arresting at their best, their lack of shape reflects a deeper problem. *Stay Where You Are* shows us a girl at the mercy of two people who appear to be lunatics. Their lunacy turns out, however, to be designed to wake her from her complacency. Quasi-existentialism no longer brings the excitement it did in the 1960's, and this is Wymark's biggest problem: she needs to find something new or fresh or more substantial that she can say through the pressure and sparkle of her work.

What saves her work is that she is aware of this, and that she laughs at herself: *The Technicians* is a marvellous attack on technical cunning which operates in a moral vacuum. Modern experimental theatre is here hoist with its own petard, and what makes the attack poignant is that Wymark loves modern theatre; in it she lives and moves and has her being.

—Prabhu S. Guptara

Y

YANKOWITZ, Susan.

American. Born in Newark, New Jersey, 20 February 1941. Educated at Sarah Lawrence College, Bronxville, New York, B.A. 1963; Yale University School of Drama, New Haven, Connecticut, M.F.A. 1968. Married Herbert Leibowitz in 1978; one son. Recipient: Vernon Rice award, 1970; MacDowell Colony fellowship, 1971, 1973; National Endowment for the Arts fellowship, 1972, 1979; Rockefeller grant, 1973; Guggenheim fellowship, 1974; Creative Artists Public Service grant, 1974; New York State Council on the Arts grant, 1984; Japan/US Friendship Commission grant, 1985. Agent: Flora Roberts, 157 West 57th Street, New York, New York 10019. Address: 205 West 89th Street, New York, New York 10024, U.S.A.

Publications

PLAYS

The Cage (produced 1965).

Nightmare (produced 1967).

Terminal (produced 1969). In *Three Works by the Open Theatre*, edited by Karen Malpede, 1974.

The Ha-Ha Play (produced 1970). In *Scripts 10*, October 1972.

The Lamb (produced 1970).

Slaughterhouse Play (produced 1971). In *New American Plays 4*, edited by William M. Hoffman, 1971.

Transplant (produced 1971).

Basics, in *Tabula Rasa* (produced 1972).

Positions, in *Up* (produced 1972).

Boxes (produced 1972). In *Playwrights for Tomorrow 11*, edited by Arthur H. Ballet, 1973.

Acts of Love (produced 1973).

Monologues for *Wicked Women Revue* (produced 1973).

Wooden Nickels (produced 1973).

America Piece, with the Provisional Theatre (produced 1974).

Still Life (produced 1977).

True Romances, music by Elmer Bernstein (produced 1977).

Qui Est Anna Marks? (Who Done It?) (produced 1978).

A Knife in the Heart (produced 1983).

Baby (original story), book by Sybille Pearson, music by David Shire, lyrics by Richard Maltby, Jr. (produced 1983).

Alarms (produced 1987).
Night Sky (produced 1991). 1992.

SCREENPLAYS: *Danny AWOL*, 1968; *The Land of Milk and Funny*, 1968; *Silent Witness*, 1979.

RADIO PLAYS: *Rats' Alley*, 1969; *Kali*, 1969.

TELEVISION WRITING: *The Prison Game (Visions* series), 1976; *The Forerunner: Charlotte Perkins Gilman*, 1979; *Arrow to the Sun: The Poetry of Sylvia Plath*, 1987.

NOVEL
Silent Witness. 1976.

MANUSCRIPT COLLECTION: Kent State University, Kent, Ohio.

CRITICAL STUDIES: *Interviews with Contemporary Women Playwrights* edited by Kathleen Betsko and Rachel Koenig, 1987.

Susan Yankowitz comments (1973):

Most of my work for the theatre has been an attempt to explore what is intrinsically unique in the theatrical situation. That is, I've been interested in sound, gesture, and movement as a corollary to language; in the interaction between the visual and verbal elements of stage life; in the fact of live performers engaged with live audience members in an exchange; and in the development of a theatrical vocabulary. My work has been generally informed by the social and political realities which impinge on all our lives; these, to a large extent, influence and shape my plays. In addition, I have been interested in a collective or collaborative approach to evolving works for the theatre and in working improvisationally with actors and directors to "find" a play which is a creative expression of our shared concerns.

At present, I am growing more concerned with the question of language—its limits and possibilities—and am moving into the realm of fiction which I feel is a more appropriate medium for that adventure.

Susan Yankowitz enlivens non-realistic, highly theatrical images of sociological problems with music, dance, pantomime, patterned speech, bold sets and costumes. These devices reinforce her verbal attacks on such contemporary social sins as conformity, alienation, racism, and sexism. These devices also enable her to avoid didacticism. Yankowitz's emphasis on *theatre* was undoubtedly encouraged by the Open Theatre, whose ensemble work contributed to the several versions of the published text of *Terminal*. *Terminal* cannot be understood apart from the Open Theatre production; the text merely suggests the performance and may be altered by other groups.

Terminal achieves unity through ritual rather than through coherent plot. It argues that people must face their deaths, and satirizes people who do not. The dying in *Terminal* turn to "Team Members" who offer them a mass-produced panacea for death. The living conduct this impersonal ritual; they also embalm and touch up the dead to hide the fact of death. The dead pierce the subterfuge practiced by and upon the dying; they "come through" the dying to judge the living and themselves. The enactment of necrophilia or the graphic description of embalming involves the audience in this common human fate.

As ritual is the binding thread in *Terminal*, so the structure of a parable unifies *The Ha-Ha Play*. Like *Terminal*, this play exposes a general human failing, but emphasizes rectification rather than exposure. Children, abducted to a woods (in which the audience sits) by hyenas wearing masks, learn to communicate through laughter. Communication is thus not only possible between groups, but it also dissolves enmity between them.

In contrast to *Terminal* and *The Ha-Ha Play*, *Slaughterhouse Play* traces the growth of consciousness of a unifying character, the black slaughterhouse worker, Junius. *Slaughterhouse Play* attacks racism: its central symbol is the slaughterhouse, which whites run and in which blacks work, slaughtering black troublemakers and selling their "meat" to whites. As in *Terminal*, action and dialogue involve the audience. The most prized black meat is that of the male genitals, which a white butcher displays in his shop, and which Junius and other rebellious blacks steal to wear around their necks as symbols of their rebellion. *Slaughterhouse Play* ends with a sequence in which blacks stab whites and whites shoot blacks repeatedly.

Not only is *Boxes* in a much lighter vein than *Slaughterhouse Play*, but literal boxes function theatrically as a fictional slaughterhouse cannot. Characters carve windows in boxes, and from within those boxes define themselves according to type and speak in clichés. Yankowitz underlines this conformity by having the characters wear hats with boxes that match their box dwellings. People in their separate boxes perform their daily chores at the same time that others experience great pain or joy. Such caricature unifies *Boxes*. Ultimately the boxes become coffins.

Yankowitz dramatizes individual or social problems and involves her audience either by shock or mimicry. Once engaged, the audience is forced to admit its responsibility for such failures as avoiding death, alienation, conformity, and racism. And this is Yankowitz's aim.

—Frances Rademacher Anderson

WORKS

THE BALTIMORE WALTZ
by Paula Vogel.

First Publication: 1992.
First Production: 1992.

After nearly twenty years of crafting plays unusual in both form and content, Paula Vogel finally achieved fame with *The Baltimore Waltz*. This lesbian playwright compels us all to empathize with a male AIDS victim by taking as her protagonist, not a junkie, gay man, or a racial minority, but a heterosexual woman, a virgin suffering from acquired toilet disease (ATD) which she caught by sharing lavatory facilities with her first grade students. Except for being female, Anna qualifies as mainstream—the perfect surrogate to teach middle America empathy. A sister's salutary fantasy of her own approaching demise as she watches her brother actually die, *The Baltimore Waltz* doesn't give the game away until near the end, when we observe slides, not of Europe, where we think the pair have been traveling, but of Baltimore's Johns Hopkins Hospital.

Vogel begins by introducing us to gay Carl—who, because of his sexual orientation, has been fired from his position as children's librarian at the San Francisco Public Library—and his sister Anna, a teacher who would love to travel abroad but won't do so unless her brother accompanies her because foreign languages terrify her. The major language she must learn turns out to involve the medical jargon which an indifferent doctor babbles.

In a fluid, presentational style featuring only three performers, Vogel constructs her episodic play by combining narrative, lectures, language lessons, a slide show, and quick two- and three-person scenes set in the U.S. and in Europe. She enlists our sympathy for the victims of a disease for which no cure exists. ("I'm sorry," intones the doctor. "There's nothing we can do.")

Having won our allegiance to an innocent virgin struck down in her youth through no fault of her own by a toilet seat ("My God. Mother was right," Anna exclaims), Vogel then catapults her through a series of delicious sexual adventures, as she sows her wild oats prior to her premature death. ATD, we must believe, spreads from elementary school students only to their unmarried teachers, since mothers develop an immunity to the virus. But it cannot be transmitted by sex. Anna therefore sheds her unwanted virginity and, in a series of one-night stands, dallies with a waiter, the 50-year-old Little Dutch Boy, the Munich Virgin, and a radical student activist, all with appropriately hilarious dialogue and action.

Vogel satirizes the medical establishment's rationalizing of their indifference ("we think education on this topic is the responsibility of the NEA"), quacks exploiting patients' panic (Dr. Todesrocheln feeds them their own urine if he doesn't imbibe it first), and government indifference (which makes them seek out rip-off peddlers of hope in the form of worthless drugs). "If William Bennett sat on just one infected potty, the media would be clamoring to do articles on ATD. If just one grandchild of George Bush caught this thing during toilet training, that would be the last we'd hear about the space program. ATD would become a national priority overnight," complains Carl. U.S. red tape which prevents access to treatments available abroad provides one of their motives for travel to Europe. Vogel's most uproarious satire describes Operation Squat, which, recognizing ATD "as our 82nd national health priority," features "posters of a toilet seat in a circle with a red diagonal slash."

All Vogel's plays imaginatively dramatize the conflict between the life force and death. Although *The Baltimore Waltz* culminates in a touching death— not Anna's, but Carl's—Vogel nevertheless has grounded the play firmly in comedy featuring playful romance, sex farce, subversive satire, and parody of such mystery flicks as *The Third Man* and even of Elizabeth Kubler-Ross's "six stages the terminal patient travels in the course of her illness." A compassionate comedy about death and people who die because their qualities of "otherness" permit the government to regard them as peripheral and dispensable, the play achieves in Carl's death tragic catharsis. Lest our grief then lead us to despair, however, instead of stiffening our resolve to live, love, and combat AIDS, Vogel brings down the curtain on a magical, healing waltz, an affirmation of the life force.

Vogel compels those of us not in a high risk group to ponder the possibility of our own deaths from a disease the government doesn't make much effort to combat. She penetrates our denial about AIDS, our tendency to shrug it off and blame the victim, to assume if we're nice people it can't happen to us. She reaches those who lack the imagination to extend compassion to the suffering. And she accomplishes all this while entertaining and shattering us. She dedicates the play, however, not to our universal potential mortality, but to her brother Carl, who died of AIDS at Johns Hopkins Hospital, a dedication in lieu of a panel for the AIDS memorial quilt "because I cannot sew." She can, and does, however, write ferocious and moving comedy, and has used this gift to create a fresh, funny, sad, and passionate work, the finest American AIDS play and one of the more memorable achievements of the late 20th-century American theatre.

—Tish Dace

BLOOD RELATIONS
by Sharon Pollock.

First Publication: 1981.
First Production: as *My Name Is Lisbeth*, 1976; as *Blood Relations*, 1980.

Since its premiere, Sharon Pollock's play has been produced extensively across Canada and the United States. Acclaimed by Canadian critics as Pollock's most theatrically intricate and lyrical play, *Blood Relations* won the first Governor-General's award for drama in 1981.

Like several of Pollock's plays, *Blood Relations* focuses on an actual historical event—the Borden murders that took place in Fall River, Massachusetts, in 1892. Unlike her earlier work, however, this play goes beyond documentary realism in creating a world of its own on stage. In *Blood Relations* Pollock uses the medium of theatre not only as a vehicle for examining issues, but as a social institution, which by its very nature is paradigmatic of the society in which we live. The play reveals that the world on stage, which both actor and spectator have brought into being, is granted authenticity only when it mirrors the ideology of the society within which it is confined.

The play opens and closes in Lizzie Borden's parlour, ten years after the grisly axe-murder of her parents. Act I begins with Lizzie entertaining her guest and probable lover, the Actress, who is based on the historical character of Nance O'Neill. The Actress urges Miss Lizzie to confess, either to being a murderer or a "pretentious small-town spinster". In answer to the Actress's prodding, Miss Lizzie draws the Actress into another world by challenging her to play the role of Lizzie.

The challenge is picked up by the Actress in a play-within-the-play, which takes the characters back to 1892, where they become participants in events within the Borden household. Miss Lizzie assumes the role of Bridget, the maid, while the Actress becomes Lizzie. As figures from the past enter the "dream thesis", the fabric of the Bordens' family history begins to unravel. Miss Lizzie/Bridget acts as Actress/Lizzie's guide through the pattern of dependence and servitude that has been Miss Lizzie's experience of life within the Borden family. Through Miss Lizzie/Bridget's manipulations, Actress/Lizzie becomes caught up in the hostility and fear that permeate the home and, in this vulnerable position, she is open to subtle suggestions from Miss Lizzie/Bridget that offer hope of freedom through death, either her own or her family's.

In Act II, as Actress/Lizzie becomes more involved in the family's pathology; the dividing line between Actress/Lizzie and Miss Lizzie becomes harder to discern. As Miss Lizzie watches Actress/Lizzie absorb her ideology through Miss Lizzie/Bridget's manipulations, she comes to the realization that she too has been acting out the aspirations of her older, and conventional, sister, Emma. Miss Lizzie now perceives herself as a "puppet", acting not autonomously, but with Emma's desires controlling her every move.

The ending of the play is shrouded in mystery; while it establishes that Actress/Lizzie is capable of murder, it does not conclusively confirm Miss Lizzie's guilt. It veils culpability behind a myraid of characters. If Miss Lizzie did wield the hatchet, it was a hatchet forged by the heat of passion that arose from the greed of Mrs. Borden and her brother, the dehumanizing effect of Mr. Borden's insensitivity, and the manipulations of Emma. Even the audience is refused the position of the innocent bystander when Miss Lizzie "*looks to the hatchet—then to the audience*" and accuses them.

Pollock denies the spectator the right to sit passively and judge the reality on stage. Instead she demands that the audience acknowledge that the act of judging makes them active participants in the theatrical event. It is the audience's standards, beliefs, and prejudices—their ideology—that allow them to perceive, understand, and grant authenticity to the reality portrayed on stage. Through Miss Lizzie, Pollock turns the spectators' ideology back on themselves by making them examine their beliefs in the context of their ability to understand and credit the reality that *Blood Relations* illuminates.

The feminine perspective in *Blood Relations* does not merely point to the evolution of the women's movement from the horrific conditions women were subject to in the 19th century. Pollock goes beyond the obvious social statement to examine how the personal becomes political. Within the confines of the play, questions of personal identity are illuminated. The audience watches Lizzie's identity being created on stage and they are compelled to recognize the forces that go into creating that identity. The play's ambiguous ending is sustained by the spectators, who have come to the realization that these forces must take some responsibility for the actions of the character they have created.

—Mary Pat Mombourquette

THE CHAPEL PERILOUS;
or, The Perilous Adventures of Sally Banner
by Dorothy Hewett.

First Publication: 1972; revised edition, 1977.
First Production: 1971.

The Chapel Perilous, a musical play in two acts, and Dorothy Hewett's best-known work, chronicles the life of its central figure, the gifted and rebellious poet, Sally Banner, from her schooldays in the 1930s to late middle age. The prologue is set in Sally's school, a conservative, religious institution where she is a brilliant but disturbing pupil, whose rebelliousness against adult hypocrisy and conservatism is expressed in her iconoclastic climbing of the chapel tower and her refusal to bow to the altar. In Act I Sally seeks the independence of spirit which she craves through sexual freedom, first with her teenage lover, Michael, and later with her husband David and the political activist Saul. But in Act II, her disillusion with all these relationships sees her turn to left-wing politics for fulfilment, a commitment which ultimately proves as sterile as romantic love. Both her quests, through personal relationships in Act I and impersonal social commitment in Act II, lead to desperate losses in human terms, including estrangement from her family and lovers, isolation from her contemporaries, and, cruellest of all, the death of her child. The play's climactic scene—a surreal trial in which they all return to accuse her—brings her to a point of existential self-understanding from which she is able to return to the school chapel as a middle-aged celebrity, and bow to the altar which was once the focus of her schoolgirl rebellion. The ending, however, is far from Sally's submission to a conventional society. The occasion of her return to the school is her presentation of a stained-glass window of herself to the chapel in which she always refused to bow; the illumination of the window at the end of the play signals Sally's reclaiming of the chapel tower she once climbed as a schoolgirl, as well as her acceptance of herself and her contemporaries.

The play is a large-scale, even sprawling, epic work, written for an open stage, with a chorus which refracts into individual characters, multiple roles for many of the performers (excluding Sally and her lover Michael), a succession of briefly sketched scenes moving rapidly through place and time, sudden, and often ironic, changes in style and mood, and moments of music, song, and spoken poetry. The set is dominated by three, huge, totem-like "authority figures" from which emerge the significant figures in Sally's life, with some characters further refracted through disembodied voices played over an amplifier. The language ranges from often comic colloquialism to more elevated, poetic language and verse (from other writers as well as Hewett herself), while the music includes both popular ditties, such as the bawdy "Good Ship Venus", sung by the chorus on Sally's disappointing wedding night, and more lyrical and reflective songs. The eclecticism of the play's style makes for an extremely dense and rich work, though it is arguable that at times, as in much of Hewett's work, it is too densely written to be readily accessible in performance. Similarly, the doubling and trebling of roles according to a schema signifying the authority that various characters exert over Sally's development, which the author states is essential to the play's meaning, may not always communicate its significance to a theatre audience.

Sally's personal quest for artistic, sexual, and political freedom is given a much wider, idealistic context in the dominating image of the chapel and in the schoolgirl's chanting of the legendary quest for the Holy Grail (hence the "Chapel Perilous" of the title), and at times the language and quotations from literature appear to elevate the action to a quasi-symbolic level. But Sally's particular story also takes place in a specifically Australian, historical context from the 1930s to the 1960s. Through the songs and dances of various decades, performed by the chorus, and the representative figures into which the chorus refracts, *The Chapel Perilous* evokes a vivid sense of Australian society over several decades, often with a good deal of humour and ironic undercutting. In particular, the thumbnail sketches of Sally's conservative, but opinionated, parents; her hypocritical teachers; and minor characters such as the gushing Miss Funt, who conducts a culture program on national radio; all display an almost malicious wit at the expense of provincialism and pretension. This recreation of Australia's emergence from pre-war provincialism to a more aware, if less picturesque, society is one of the play's real achievements, often overlooked in the other issues *The Chapel Perilous* has tended to raise.

Although now accepted as a contemporary Australian classic, and often studied by secondary-school students, the play retains something of its initial reputation as an "immoral" piece. It shares with all of Hewett's work the qualities which have often polarised critical and audience responses to her—an affirmation of female sexuality, an iconoclastic attitude towards received authority and morality, and a free-wheeling, even apparently wayward, dramatic form. The character of Sally has also aroused both passionate identification and intense dislike; both views, however, overlook the ironically amused, and at times even savage, scrutiny of the central character, whose mistakes and gaucheries are as vividly portrayed as her courage and idealism. A taxing role for a performer, ranging as it does from adolescent precocity to middle-aged disillusion and acceptance, Sally Banner is one of the most memorable characters in Australian drama.

—Margaret Williams

CLOUD NINE
by Caryl Churchill.

First Publication: 1979.
First Production: 1979.

The first of the two thematically and chronologically related (but sharply dissimilar) acts of Caryl Churchill's play is set in the heyday of British imperialism in Victorian Africa. It gives a wildly satiric picture of the sexual confusions and entanglements of a colonial household presided over by Clive and his wife Betty. Its scenes reveal a chasm between social norms all characters subscribe to and try to keep up, and disruptive forces in their own natures manifesting themselves in adultery, homosexuality, and pederasty. The rigid code of behaviour required for their repression or concealment also obtains in the treatment of the native African population. The second act transposes the main characters of the first act (Clive and his family) into a contemporary metropolitan setting in London. The enforced unity of Victorian morality is dissipating in the main characters' attempts at personal emancipation, however partial and contradictory.

The play connects the theme of sexual politics with a perspective on the social conditions they presuppose or reinforce. The play's tone shifts from a wildly satirical view of Victorian people not meant to be more than caricatures, to a much more empathetic portrait of people struggling to liberate themselves from past and present oppression. In the first act the patriarchal system of the British Empire is mirrored in the upper middle-class family of Clive, his wife, and their children, Victoria and Edward. All are shown as victims of a rigid regime forcing them, at least outwardly, to conform to conventional role-patterns of a middle-class family. Any stability in this pattern is pre-empted by both personal and political realities. Clive has a violent affair with a visiting neighbour, Mrs. Saunders; his wife Betty falls in love with his best friend, the colonial explorer Harry; Harry is a homosexual who has taken up relations with Edward and his head servant Joshua, and even makes a mistaken attempt at the scandalized Clive; Betty, in her turn, is passionately loved by her servant Ellen. The marriage between Harry and Ellen, arranged to save appearances, is as unlikely to hold as any other relationship between people estranged from their real natures. Similarly, and for related reasons, the native African rebellion that Clive's colonial duty it is to quash eventually threatens to subvert his very household. The final scene in the first act has the Uncle-Tom figure of the servant Joshua overcome his alienation from his tribe and family and take aim at Clive, with Edward looking on unconcernedly, to indicate loyalties being dissolved from within as from outside.

Between the first and second acts 100 years of historical time have been compressed into just 25 years of the main characters' life-time. In many important respects Betty and her children have achieved their emancipation from the classical middle-class role-models. Betty is finally leaving her husband and is tentatively but determinedly trying to lead an independent life. Edward has come out in a gay ménage in which he soon adopts some traits typically ascribed to women, and Victoria, who in Act I had a fittingly symbolic representation as a puppet, has to reconcile marriage, motherhood, and a lesbian attachment to the working-class mother Lin. While not all tension is removed from the characters' lives, the resulting changes in behaviour are such as to make a bemused Clive—whose only brief reappearance occurs at the very end of the second act—yearn nostalgically for the lost certainties of the colonial past.

The play's major innovative device of syncopating individual and historical time inscribes political themes into personal development. While Act I gives a deliberately stereotyped view of a patriarchal Victorian family that only allows some flexibility in a few of the portraits of the system's victims (the adult women, the son), Act II allows more pyschological depth to its panorama of contemporary confusions and present lifestyles. Churchill enters a lot more into her characters' minds here, without, however, getting stuck in psychological realism since it is people's public behaviour that serves as a connecting link between the two acts. This insistence on the social dimension of the action is emphasized neatly by the device that has become important for some contemporary, feminist playwrights: cross-casting. By this means the boundaries separating male and female roles, children and adults, black and white, are symbolically transgressed to allow the audience more than the usual detachment from conventional processes of identification.

In its critical picture of Victorian upper-class life with its rigidly enforced codes, its double standards of morality, and excruciating conformist pressures, the play often utilizes farce to bring home general cultural points. Both the obvious unhappiness caused by suppressing people's identities and the idea of human happiness that the play's title ironically refers to, underpin a mischievous social system. However, at the end of the first act, the farcical props are removed to reveal naked aggression and force as a corollary of imperialist hegemony that can be turned against the aggressors as well as the victims. The second act of *Cloud Nine* has a much less unified dynamic because it tries to spell out the process of personal liberation as one involving difficult and even painful choices, as in Betty's separation from her uncomprehending husband, Clive, and in Victoria's gradual coming to terms with her social and sexual conditioning, and the resultant choices in her everyday life in which an equally tentative emancipation is recorded. It has rightly been said that the straightforward and seemingly didactic energy of Act I is replaced by a much less certain and more experimental dramaturgy in Act II. While there is an unmistakeable narrowing in the play's analytic connection of personal and social levels—only a hint at British involvement in Northern Ireland reminds us of the continuing legacy of the colonialist past—this shift in Churchill's preoccupations makes the play a much more intimate document of contemporary life and the plurality of possible lifestyles in it. The feminist perspective accordingly moves from larger political formations—in which a trace of the origins of the play in the workshop methods of the Joint Stock Theatre Company that first produced it can still be detected—to the level of day-to-day concerns. This change of emphasis was certainly in line with the impact of feminism on plays by women (and some men) in the late 1970s.

—Bernd-Peter Lange

CRIMES OF THE HEART
by Beth Henley.

First Publication: 1982.
First Production: 1979.

Beth Henley's 1981 Pulitzer prize winning play, *Crimes of the Heart*, remains her best work over a decade later. Her Southern characters have been compared to those of Flannery O'Conner and Eudora Welty; while her dramaturgical techniques have been compared to the likes of Chekhov and Tennessee Williams. Much has been written about *Crimes of the Heart* as a typically Southern play, about Southern women and familial bonds. Scholars of the text and reviewers of the production applaud Henley's storytelling ability, where the most bizarre and often the saddest tales create the most humour. Henley's attention to detail, her use of rhythmic colloquial language, and her seemingly haphazard manipulation of plot have been cited as unique elements in the play. However, given the longevity of the play, it becomes apparent that Henley offers more than just a humorous and regional treatment of Southern women in distress. Henley has a unique flair for balancing humor and pathos by exposing the eccentric and sometimes grotesque behavior of human beings. In *Crimes of the Heart* this dramaturgical strategy is implemented via the juxtaposition of action and language, and reinforced with polar thematic issues.

The play is set in Hazlehurst, Mississippi, in the kitchen of the Magrath sisters: Lenny, Meg, and Babe. Babe has just shot her husband, Zackery in the stomach, and Lenny has sent a telegram to Meg who "came on home to see about Babe". The central plot has to do with keeping Babe from going to prison. Henley creates secondary plot complications, all of which are linked to two significant absentee characters—granddaddy, who is in the hospital, and the sisters' mother, who committed suicide when the sisters were children. This use of physically absent characters is rarely noted, but it is a Chekhovian device that Henley exploits to advantage. Like Chekhov's *Three Sisters*, *Crimes of the Heart* includes well over twenty absentee characters, whose function in both plays is to enlarge the scope of the play, to establish additional complications, and to comment on the nature of society.

Henley uses the absentee character device in other more complex ways. The mother's suicide is a topic of conversation throughout the play and though the death haunts all three sisters; it also motivates them to live. The absent mother unifies the play by creating for the Magrath siblings a bizarre curiosity about why the mother chose to hang herself and her favorite cat. Just before Babe shot her husband she was planning on shooting herself, but decided against it because she didn't want to be like her mother. Meg forced herself to look at pictures of horribly disfigured people so that "she could stand it" and would therefore not be weak like her mother.

The absent granddaddy also serves to unify the play. However, unlike the mother who functions as a positive influence Henley uses granddaddy's absent presence to reveal how his influence has been negative on the sisters. Granddaddy pushed Babe to marry Zackery so that she would be financially secure. She ended up in an abusive marriage. Granddaddy dreamed that Meg, his favorite, would go to Hollywood and become a famous singer. Meg did go to Hollywood but ended up working for a dogfood company and becoming temporarily insane because she could never live up to granddaddy's expectations. For Lenny, who is unable to have children because of a "shrunken ovary", granddaddy's legacy was for her to serve as his caretaker in his old age. Lenny accepts the legacy and begins to wear grandmama's clothes and to work in the garden "wearing the lime green gloves of a dead woman".

The use of the absent mother and granddaddy advances polar thematic issues such as life and death; male and female; youth and age. These thematic issues and other lesser ones are also realized by juxtaposing them with the action of the play. While the Magrath sisters come to terms with their individual needs in the midst of Babe's forthcoming trial; their actions bespeak hope. Meg and Babe order a surprise birthday cake for Lenny. Meg stays out all night with her former lover who she wrongly assumes will dump his "Yankee wife and two half-Yankee kids" for her. However, Meg's reaction is not one of humiliation but rather of realization. "I realized I could care about someone". Lenny, with the encouragement of her sisters, calls Charlie, a man she use to date, but the relationship was spoiled by granddaddy. Babe's unsuccessful attempts to commit suicide, first by hanging and then by sticking her head in the oven are the most humorous moments in the play. We can laugh because she fails. The rope isn't long enough. The phone interrupts. And finally Meg intervenes saving her sister. Babe's failure is hopeful. Like Meg, Babe comes to realize something about herself when she understands why her mother killed the cat. Babe realizes that her mother killed the cat so that she would not die alone. Babe's realization is symbolic for all three sisters who realize, if just for a moment, that they are not alone.

Henley's linguistic technique goes beyond capturing the Southern colloquial rhythm. Her juxtaposition of words in a phrase not only establishes a personal voice for each character, but also provides a subtle commentary about the nature of this particular society. Phrases such as "cheap Christmas trash" or "mighty mild" are examples of Henley's linguistic counterpoint. The language establishes the world of the play where Billy Boy is a horse and Chick the Stick is the sisters' superficial cousin. The simplicity of the vocabulary corresponds with the simplicity of the action and creates a kind of theatricality by recognition. Henley's portrayal of the silly and often mundane actions people do for no apparent reason is selective and precise. Chick's nearly grotesque "dance" in the kitchen as she puts on a pair of too small pantyhose; Meg and Babe's exchange about how large Lenny's birthday cake should be; and Lenny's private celebration with the birthday cookies are representative examples. In *Crimes of the Heart* Henley's ability to make us laugh comes from the simple portrayal of people looking for love and what that search often makes people do.

—Judy Lee Oliva

FEFU AND HER FRIENDS
by María Irene Fornés.

First Publication: 1980.
First Production: 1977.

A plot summary would tell very little about *Fefu and Her Friends*. Rather, Fefu and her friends invite us to attend a little get-together. The play unfolds by letting us learn something about one character, then about another. Seven of the eight women who comprise the cast of the play are given speeches in which they philosophize, tell a dream, or recount an experience. There is not a sense of one action leading to and causing the next. Rather, when you have some understanding of the eight characters, the play ends.

The learning process is enlivened by a staging device. The first and last scenes are in Fefu's living room, but in between four scenes take place simultaneously in different locations. That is, the performers enact the scenes four times while different groups of audience members move from place to place. This suggests a circular form, since we start in and return to the same room. Perhaps, too, as we watch one of the four simultaneous scenes and we are aware that other scenes are going on simultaneously, and that the scene we are watching will be repeated, there is a sense that life flows around us and thus that our lives are no different from those onstage. With its three parts—set tidily in morning, afternoon, and evening—the play mocks the traditional three-act structure, with the second act offering spatial rather than plot complications. The play ends with a death by shooting that, on the one hand, fulfils the dictum that one cannot put a gun on stage without its playing a part in the action but, on the other, is not a conventional climactic action in that it does not grow out of the increasing tensions of a difficult relationship.

Fefu, who earlier in the play has been shooting at her husband in game, reminds us of another woman unfulfilled by marriage, Hedda Gabler. At the end she shoots a rabbit outside in the garden—and in the living room blood appears on the forehead of one of her friends, who is already confined to a wheelchair by an exactly parallel hunting incident, and who now, mysteriously, dies. The monologue of this friend, Julia, has been a hallucination which begins "They clubbed me. They broke my head. They broke my will". As she continues *they* becomes "the judges" and she tells of how "I was good and quiet. I never dropped my smile. I smiled to everyone. If I stopped smiling I would get clubbed because they loved me. They say they love me". *They* becomes *he*, which confirms that the judges are men. "He said that I had to be punished because I was getting too smart . . . I repented. I told them exactly what they wanted to hear. They killed me. I was dead. But I repented and they said, 'live but crippled'." María Irene Fornés has called Julia "the mind of the play—the seer, the visionary". Men's judgments on women can be paralyzing.

Fornés has deliberately avoided "a plot play [where] the woman is either the mother or the sister or the girldfriend or the daughter, [where] the purpose of the character is to serve a plot . . .". The mixture of the inconsequential and consequential evident in the manner of Julia's death is typical of the play. The lack of conflict, and lack of linear development that the four simultaneous scenes emphasize, allows Fornés to treat serious issues lightly. The intimacy of spirited conversation is never abandoned. *Fefu and Her Friends* started as "a kind of fantasy game", and the sense of that is still present for an audience. Fornés said, "I am delighted when something is not deliberate. I do not trust deliberateness. When something happens by accident, I trust that the play is making its own point. I feel that something is happening that is very profound and very important. People go far in this thing of awareness and deliberateness . . . They go see a play and they do not like it. So someone explains it to them, and they like it better. How can they *possibly* understand it better, like it better or see more of it because someone has explained it?" Whatever the seriousness of the issues in the play, Fornés' playfulness gives a rare buoyancy to the audience's experience.

Fefu gives the first line of the play: "My husband married me to have a constant reminder of how loathsome women are", although later another character tells us that Fefu and her husband love each other. Fornés has called *Fefu* a feminist play. At the same time she set it in 1935 to avoid the arguments current in the feminist movement. The focus of the play is on the treatment of women by men and on women's own relationships. It is these that are the subject of the solo speeches. Fornés has called the play "a homage to women, it enjoys the intelligence of women", and added, "My work is unusual . . . it's affectionate . . . tender". Exactly so.

—Anthony Graham-White

FOR COLORED GIRLS WHO HAVE CONSIDERED SUICIDE WHEN THE RAINBOW IS ENUF
by Ntozake Shange.

First Publication: 1977.
First Production: 1975.

For Colored Girls Who Have Considered Suicide When The Rainbow Is Enuf consists of twenty "choreopoems" that express different, complex experiences of African-American women in vibrant, explosive poetry punctuated by music and dance. The play established the importance of the choreopoem, a collection of related poems combined with song and dance, as a uniquely African-American form of performance. Seven African-American actresses, identified by the colors of their dresses (brown, yellow, orange, red, blue, purple, green), sing, dance, and recite poems that fuse personal, political, and spiritual concerns. The poems explore the personal torment of women victimized by both racism and sexism through addressing issues such as: the silencing of the African-American women's voice, feminine sexuality, date rape, abortion, life in Harlem, loneliness, the glory of the African heritage, wife-battering, and solidarity among African-American women. The women in the play struggle to affirm their heritage, race, and gender, for "bein alive & bein a woman & bein colored is a metaphysical dilemma". The gravity of this dilemma is dramatically realized in the climactic poem, "A Night with Beau Willie Brown". This poem describes the relationship of a psychically-damaged, Vietnam veteran with his young lover, Crystal. Shell-shocked and unable to work, Beau Willie vents his frustration on the racist country he served by brutalizing his wife and children. When Crystal refuses to marry him, he drops their two children from a fifth story window. The women in the play survive and transcend the devastating realities resulting from class, race, and gender difference. In the final scene of the play, "a laying on of hands", the women participate in a healing process by expressing collective solidarity and self-affirmation: "I found god in myself/& i loved her/i loved her fiercely".

The play portrays conflicting stories that represent a spectrum of women's experiences, rather than subsuming the different voices of African-American women beneath one definitive image, or myth, of the African-American experience. Shange is attentive to the differences among women, and the variety of their emotional responses to social, economic, and political constraints. In the first poem, the Lady in Brown celebrates music which expresses discontinuity, rather than the unity symbolizing the suppression of differences: "Half-notes scattered/without rhythm/no tune . . . it's funny/it's hysterical/the melody-less-ness of her dance". As the individual notes are not harmonized into one melody, so the different women are not localized into one space, but are disparate, free to express regional differences: "I'm outside chicago/i'm outside detroit/i'm outside houston".

In the second poem, the women each express different views of their sexuality. One woman reveals in her graduation/sexual initiation night: "WOW/by daybreak/I just cant stop grinnin", while another woman admits, "i never did like to grind". In another poem, a woman's sexuality is revealed as a masquerade of "orange butterflies and aqua sequins" which wash away in the bath: "Laying in water/she became herself/ordinary". She has no desire of her own, but is only the object of desire: "she glittered honestly/delighted she was desired". Her sexuality is revealed as a social construction, subject to patriarchal structures, rather than as a "natural", expressive reality.

Shange's play is also distinguished by its formal, structural, and linguistic innovations. The choreopoem form was influenced by the works of Sonia Sanchez, Beah Richards, Alexis De Veaux, and Judy Grahn. The choreopoem allows the different women in the play to express their material, historical situation in an emotional, lyrical, dynamic performance. The choreopoem breaks down the distinctions between the material and the spiritual, objective reality and subjective reality, psychological realism and Brechtian alienation. The subjective state of the performer is politicized, as the effects of history are played out as personal emotional experience.

Emotional experience is expressed not only in poetry and song, but also in dance. As a component of the choreopoem, dance challenges the opposition between interiority and exteriority, as the subjective world is expressed through bodily experience. When Shange played the part of the Lady in Orange in the Broadway production, she created a uniquely African-American grammar of gestures and strides to accompany the African-American dialect of the poems.

Shange's text is written in lower-case letters, contractions, and abbreviations, expressions of her rebellion against the colonizer's English. Shange's writing reflects her conscious war against the symbolic order, the pre-constituted, colonizing representational system which already informs African-American experience. Her "mutilations" of the written word suggest the brandings and markings the American colonizers inflicted upon African flesh. Shange uses language as a visual register of historical effects.

The choreopoem resists the rationality and empiricism of the well-made play, the colonizer's aesthetic; instead, Shange's play reflects the spirituality of the African tradition. Within the African tradition, language, music, and dance are *mojos*, spiritual force-fields of energy which allow the individual to transcend material reality and experience wholeness. Shange's choreopoem form, with its emphasis on *mojos*, is her response to a Western, Eurocentric system of aesthetics which gives priority to the spoken word.

For Colored Girls Who Have Considered Suicide When The Rainbow Is Enuf appeared as a controversial challenge to the predominantly white feminist movement and the predominantly male black power movement of the 1970s. The play's success helped both movements to question their exclusion of African-American women, to question their own complicity in racism and sexism.

—Karen Cronacher

FUNNYHOUSE OF A NEGRO
by Adrienne Kennedy.

First Publication: 1969.
First Production: 1962.

Before the curtain opens, a faceless, mumbling, female figure sleep-walks across the forestage carrying a bald head, and establishes that this is a nightmare play. The central action has a fluid texture, with time and place stretching and dissolving, defying conventional notions of cause and effect in behaviour, and substituting elements of associative linking between the brief scenes that are suggested. A number of these involve bedrooms, constantly reinforcing the dream motif, but the bedroom is not always obviously that of Sarah, the title character. In the opening scene it is, in fact, Queen Victoria and the Duchess of Hapsburg who are standing beside the bed, though their dialogue and identical, masked appearance immediately unsettle notions of identity. Victoria even refers to her father as a "black Negro" who, though dead, keeps returning to her. In a long monologue, the title character explains that Victoria, the Duchess, Jesus, and Patrice Lumumba are parts of herself and that the rooms on stage are "the places myselves exist in." None of these secondary characters has more than a trace of historical, individualising detail;

blackness is important to Lumumba, though also to the others, and the bond with his father is important to Jesus—as well as to the others. The murder of the father, by all of the sub-characters, is followed by Sarah hanging herself, and the play ends with brief, relatively objective, dialogue between a Funnyman and a Funnylady indicating that Sarah was out of touch with reality.

As a psycho-expressionistic, one-act play, *Funnyhouse of a Negro* stands by itself as its own statement: its simply represents the hallucinatory texture of a dream in which the tormented self is fragmented and recomposed with agonising conjunctions, to the point of annihilation. Like any staged dream, it challenges the audience's instinct towards interpretation, and this may follow any dream theory from the Strindbergian to the biological and the early Freudian notion of masochistic wish-fulfilment. But Kennedy's dramatic strategy subverts logic and interpretation in numerous ways. Not only are sub-characters, like Jesus, divorced from their received identity, but they collide and merge with one another so that they cannot even be taken as Sarah's distorted perception of them. Moreover, their constant merging makes troublesome any attempt to identify them as discrete parts of Sarah's psyche, so that even the term "alter ego" is unsatisfactory.

Two parts of the play introduce a somewhat incongruous element of objectivity. Sarah's early monologue presents her as a self-conscious narrator apparently offering a rationale of the action. Firstly, a quantity of mundane detail links her to Kennedy's own life as a student, and the noose around her neck hints that the entire action may represent her last thoughts at the point of suicide. On the other hand, her historical and geographical indeterminacy is also emphasised, and her "ancient" appearance suggests that she may be an archetype. Secondly, the two characters who clumsily diagnose her as psychotic at the end appear to be looking at her from outside, but because they are given some qualities of figures from a carnival funnyhouse there is the possibility that theirs is a mirroring function, reflecting Sarah's dislocated sense of identity.

Feminist criticism has produced some provocative approaches to this play. Kennedy wrote it shortly after living for a period in Ghana, which is clearly the source of the image of Jesus as a white, male colonizer. Yet Jesus also shares the constraints of living under a patriarchy, a phobic bondage which does not dissolve with the murder of the father. Sarah's dominant self constructs images of otherness in the form of masculinity and blackness, a construction which seems to be related to the rape of her mother by her (black) father. The opening scene (which taxes hard the resources of stagecraft) involves "great black ravens" flying over Victoria's bed, while Jesus's colonising mission has recurrent imagery of white doves and white stallions. Sarah's preferred self-image is that of Victoria who, like the Duchess, underscores her whiteness by being dressed in white satin and wearing an alabaster mask, all of it picked out by "strong white light". Sarah claims that she killed her father by bludgeoning his head with an "ebony mask" such as Lumumba carries through most of the play. Sarah's only "glaring negroid feature" is her "kinky hair"; on her first appearance, she is partially bald, and all the sub-characters lose their hair in prodigious quantities. In these terms of Sarah's frenzied aspiration to whiteness, the play is almost a literal illustration of a leading argument in Fanon's *Black Skin, White Masks*.

Disfigurement, self-effacement, and head mutilation recur throughout the play, from the severed head carried emblematically by the sleep-walker to the masks which constitute detached heads, and to the details of the father's death. Lumumba's head "appears to be split in two with blood and tissue in eyes." That this is Artaudian "theatre of cruelty" few would dispute, but the sensory aggression is nowhere gratuitous: it all contributes to the expression of the agony of a self that cannot accept her self.

—Howard McNaughton

HE AND SHE
by Rachel Crothers.

First Publication: 1917; revised version, 1925.
First Production: 1911.

Ann and Tom are a married couple, both of whom are sculptors. Tom is supportive of Ann's career—which is clearly subordinate to his—until she wins a first prize of $100,000 in a competition they have both entered (Tom is placed second). Initially Tom seems pleased but then begins to complain that fulfilling the prize commission will interfere with Ann's family obligations. A bitter argument ensues in which Tom asks, then demands, that she renounce the commission. The fight is interrupted by the appearance of their teenage daughter, Millicent, who has come home unexpectedly from boarding school. Millicent announces that she became engaged to a chauffeur when she was forced to spend a vacation at school while Ann worked on her models. Horrified, Ann determines that she must devote all her time to dissuading Millicent from her planned marriage. She asks Tom to execute the frieze for her, and he agrees.

Woven through the main story is a sub-plot involving Tom's assistant Keith McKenzie, Ann's friend Ruth Creel, and Tom's sister Daisy. Keith and Ruth are engaged, but Ruth breaks the engagement when Keith, who believes all wives should stay at home, balks at her accepting a career advancement she covets. With the help of Ann's father, Dr. Remington, Keith begins a romance with the far more domestic Daisy.

He and She has had a rocky stage history. No fewer than three productions of the drama (which was renamed *The Herfords* during its 1912 run but then reverted to its original title) were mounted before a fourth production finally arrived in New York City in 1920, this time with Crothers herself in the starring role. Despite mixed reviews, *He and She* had a run of only 28 performances. The play was first published in Quinn's *Representative American Plays* in 1917, but the more familiar version is the revised one, which Crothers prepared for later editions of the anthology and which reflects changes made for the 1920 production.

He and She is one of Crothers' most complex and provocative works, and it continues to intrigue scholars and directors. A play in which action and even character development are subservient to the presentation of varying points of view, *He and She* shows the influence of both Ibsen and Shaw. Most reviewers of the 1920 production saw Ann's giving up of her sculpting commission as Crothers' assertion that women belong in the home, not in the career world. Some critics applauded this apparently very conservative stance, while others expressed dismay. One reviewer was pleased that "Miss Crothers . . . wisely puts the task of wife and mother in the first place", but Heywood Broun complained, "We have always found that the soup tastes just the same whether it is opened with loving care or by the hired help. Nor are we convinced that young daughters tend to become entangled in unfortunate love affairs the instant a mother begins to paint a picture or deliver a series of lectures". There is much merit to Broun's objection, of course; it never occurs to the characters in the play—as it rarely occurred to anyone in the early part of the century— that someone other than a mother could care for a 16-year-old girl. In an interview Crothers claimed that "a profession need not necessarily upset a woman's home life", but *He and She* suggests the likelihood of conflict if the home life includes children. The climax of the work was particularly disappointing to those who admired her immediately preceding play, *A Man's World*, whose heroine is an outspoken defender of equality between the sexes.

Still, *He and She* is a more subtle and complicated drama than this debate would suggest. As the playwright herself once pointed out, Ann renounces the commission not because of her husband's desire but because of her daughter's perceived need: Tom's wishes are given no more validity than Ann's. Crothers also makes very clear that Ann will often, in future, regret the choice she has made. The playwright obviously considered this an important point, for she added a speech to the conclusion of the revised version in which Ann tells Tom: "And I'll hate you because you're doing it [the frieze]—and I'll hate myself because I gave it up—and I'll almost—hate—her". Like many of her generation Crothers had difficulty envisioning women with both successful careers and marriages, but she was sensitive enough to portray the painful decisions involved.

Moreover, the play does suggest that the home is not the "natural" place for all women, and that women artists are at least equal in talent to their male counterparts. Even the thoroughly misogynist Dr. Remington acknowledges that Keith has no right to ask Ruth to give up her promising career in journalism, and Ann wins a highly competitive contest, defeating both her husband and a (presumably) large number of other, prominent, male sculptors. Early in the play Tom dismisses Ann's work as not in "this class", but her victory proves him wrong.

For the most part Crothers keeps the dialogue lively and engrossing—no mean feat in a play so heavily dependent on discussion. Even if she sometimes sacrifices dramatic probability and character consistency to the demands of the debates, *He and She* remains an absorbing contribution to the genre of the problem play in America. And those debates themselves—about women's talents, rights, and obligations—continue to occupy us 80 years after Crothers put them on stage.

—Judith E. Barlow

THE HEIDI CHRONICLES
by Wendy Wasserstein.

First Publication: 1990.
First Production: 1988.

The Heidi Chronicles offers a truthful and slightly wistful comic look at the life and times of the fictional heroine, Heidi Holland, and of the "baby boom" generation. Heidi, like the play's author Wendy Wasserstein, is a young Jewish woman living in America in the 1980s. While it focuses on Heidi as the central character, and while women's relationships are treated sympathetically and humourously, the play is designed to appeal to both women and men.

The play opens with a Prologue, set in 1989. The eponymous Heidi delivers a lecture at Columbia University, New York. Slides of women painters and their work are projected behind her as she speaks; the audience is positioned as part of her class. She begins by discussing the marginalization of women in art history books, pointing out that: ". . . Although Sofonisba was praised in the seventeenth century as being a portraitist equal to Titian, and at least thirty of her paintings remain known to us, there is no trace of her or any other woman artist prior to the twentieth century in your current Art History Survey textbook. Of course, in my day, this same standard text mentioned no women, 'from the Dawn of History to the Present.' Are you with me? Okay."

Here, the lecturer Heidi, and through her the dramatist Wendy Wasserstein, engages in the feminist project of "writing women into history". She does so with humour and verve; with a mixture of academic argument and colloquial, conversational language. This opening speech is winning, amusing, convincing. So is the play as a whole.

The play's central theme is communication: between friends, between lovers, between a woman and her memory and understanding of her past. All the main characters demonstrate sharp wits and tongues. Heidi's responses are usually understated, and Wasserstein has created some wonderfully authentic scenes in which Heidi is repeatedly interrupted by men—even those who most love and respect her—contrasted quite effectively with the scenes in which she holds her own, in the authority position of lecturer. The characters are clearly and sympathetically drawn: Heidi, the strong independent woman; Peter, Heidi's closest friend, whose life experiences parallel Heidi's and with whom she might have formed a relationship if he were not gay; Scoop, the wise-guy journalist with whom Heidi first falls in love, and who remains a friend throughout; and a number of close women friends whose lives develop quite differently to Heidi's, showing the range and diversity of women's experiences, and of men's. For instance, Peter explains himself in this way in Act 1, scene 4, set in 1974 at the Chicago Art Institute: ". . . According to my mental health friends, we are moving into a decade of self-obsession. I am simply at the forefront of the movement." But Peter turns out to be less self-obsessed than other characters, each of whom is faced with decisions and changes indicative of the "me-first" baby boom generation in America. Indeed, Scoop's magazine is called "Boomer": it is a chronicle of the times, which develops alongside the lives of the characters in the play.

The Heidi Chronicles is episodic in form. The rest of Act One flashes back to significant moments in Heidi's past, all staged in public spaces in academic contexts. These scenes take us through Heidi's formative years: her college days; the forging of a significant friendship with Peter; her first romance with Scoop; her girlhood insecurities and young woman's friend- ships and alliances with a range of women, all of whom get involved in feminist consciousness-raising groups as well as each other's personal lives. Act Two takes us back to New York, but the time frame is Heidi's present (the 1980s) and the scenes contrast public and private spaces, moving from public lecture halls to TV studios, a restaurant, and a hospital ward (where privacy is both most necessary and hardest to come by), and finally to Heidi's apartment.

The device of using contemporary music helps to set the scene and mood of each episode, weaving together events and moods as they reflect on the central characters. Major events are mentioned, setting Heidi's life in context and allowing her personal chronicle to become something more universal.

At play's end: Scoop sells his magazine and sets out to do something else, perhaps politics (he ends up more self-obsessed than ever); Peter works as a successful pediatrician—"the most eligible Dr. under forty"—finds a partner and lives in the country, though this seemingly idyllic life is counterpoised by his job on a medical wing for immune-deficient children, and the revelation that his former partner "is not well" (he probably has AIDS); while Heidi adopts a daughter. We last see her rocking the child to sleep, singing the same song she sang as a younger woman:

> Darling, You send me.
> You send me.
> Honest you do, honest you do, honest you do.
> *Lights fade as Heidi rocks.*

In ending the play with this image and song, Wasserstein takes up the major theme of earlier women's drama such as Caryl Churchill's *Top Girls*, wherein the central character gave up her daughter in order to invest her time and energy in her career. Heidi adopts a daughter and has a career, but lacks a relationship, and is described as content rather than happy. Each generation gains and loses something. *This* generation gains something important in *The Heidi Chronicles*, which makes a major contribution to the field of drama.

—Lizbeth Goodman

THE KNACK
by Ann Jellicoe.

First Publication: 1962; revised version, 1964.
First Production: 1961.

Nancy, a naive young girl from the provinces, is in search of the local YWCA. She finds herself at the ground-floor window of a London house and is invited in by its three young, male occupants. She becomes the object of their sexual advances and the catalyst to their own power games. Tolen tries to demonstrate his "knack" with women in order to impress the shy and awkward Colin. Tom chooses to stay on the sidelines, encouraging Colin, deflating Tolen, and averting several nasty moments by way of funny animal stories. But the situation gets out of hand; Nancy becomes hysterical, faints, and then accuses the men of raping her while she was unconscious. The accusation soon centres on Colin who, flattered by the whole notion, chases Nancy around the room, at last impervious to Tolen's jeers. The final image is of Nancy and Colin alone, grinning at each other across the length of the bed.

The Knack is a witty, absurdist, comedy of menace that, in a light-hearted and exuberant way, examines ideas of gender, sexuality, and people's need to wield power over one another. Jellicoe's focus is character. She creates four young people, riddled with insecurities, each out to prove something. They become effective foils for each other. Tolen is a vulgar, motor-cycle-riding "smoothie", clearly the kingpin of the male trio. Tom needs his approval and Colin is in awe of his sexual prowess. He spouts the vilest of sexist attitudes:

"You must realize that women are not individuals but types. No, not even types, just women. They want to surrender, but they don't want the responsibility of surrendering. This is one reason why the man must dominate . . . In this world, Colin, there are the masters and there are the servants. Very few men are real men, Colin, are real masters. Almost all women are servants. They don't want to think for themselves, they want to be dominated."

Tolen suggests to Colin, the landlord, that he evict Tom in order to accommodate Tolen's own friend Rory; these two can then share their women. They will even throw Colin the occasional bone. In action Tolen is even more repulsive, terrorizing Nancy with his belt, grabbing her, and forcing himself on her. Jellicoe makes him so dreadful so as to keep him comic. She also has Tom alleviate dangerous situations with a thoroughly entertaining story or a cup of tea, effectively emasculating Tolen into the bargain.

Tom is the voyeur, seemingly a non-participant in the sexual games (he wants to remove the bed from his room), but in fact he controls much of the action, sexual and otherwise. Colin is Tolen's polar opposite and comic foil. He is shy, submissive to his male peers, and a total failure with women. Tolen delights in taunting him or sharing his vast experiences in a pompous lecture or a lesson in sexy walking. Nancy is hopelessly ingenuous, silly enough to get caught up in the men's games and idiotic enough to fall for Tolen's humiliating approaches. Her arrival sets the overtly sexual games in motion, but before that Jellicoe has subtly suggested the homoerotic nature of the male rivalries, their plays for dominance and control, their need to crush, please or assuage each other, and Nancy becomes a victim to these impulses as much as to Tolen's overt advances. With its complex sexual undercurrents the whole play takes on the quality of a ritualized mating-dance.

Jellicoe sets the play in male territory. It is Tom's room, emptied of most of its furniture while he paints it. All that is left are two chairs and a stepladder (used in the play to establish height, status or dominance), a chest-expander (the prop for a male strength—or ego—contest), and an all-important bed. Other beds are significant in the play. Tom wants his bed out, but finds it replaced by Colin's because the latter needs to make room for a new six-footer —as big as Tolen's. It is Colin's bed that dominates the room, taking on several functions: a cage, a prison, a safety-barrier, a push-toy, a piano. Only at the end of the play is it likely to serve a bed-like purpose.

Into this male territory comes Nancy, the female outsider, and the mating-dance already under way takes on a new dimension and urgency. Nancy is unresponsive to Colin's clumsy and more sincere overtures but is alternately attracted and terrified by Tolen's arrogance and sadistic toying with her. The ritualistic quality is reinforced by repeated action: Tolen disappearing out of the window to follow another woman and Tolen's outbursts of near-violence undercut by Tom's stories, for example. Tolen's cliché-ridden pronouncements and advances have the quality of a worn-out ritual. The language is often bizarre, and, in Nancy's case, fractured and monosyllabic, creating a rhythmic pulse to the play, particularly in Nancy's third-act repetition of "rape" and "I've been raped".

Nancy's accusation of rape turns the tables. Perched high atop the step-ladder, drinking tea, at first quietly and then with screams of jubilation and threats of making revalations to the tabloid newspapers, she claims power over the suddenly befuddled men. For the first time she speaks in articulate sentences with a new air of confidence. Soon she decides on Colin as her assailant, which prods him into an assertion of new-found masculinity. He chases Nancy around the bed to Tolen's jeers. Tolen grabs Nancy. Colin slams the bed into the wall and tells him, "If you touch her, I'll kill you". Tolen leaves. The macho-chauvinist has been rejected.

Jellicoe exposes and ridicules male sexist attitudes. She investigates the idea of subliminal homoeroticism at work in the cult of machismo. At the same time she attacks women who submit to male dominance, women who enter the male domain on men's terms. Nancy asserts herself at the end and may claim some form of a victory, but it is at the cost of collusion. Ultimately, it is a light-hearted attack, firmly in the realm of comedy, demanding high-energy and exuberant performance. By the standards of its time, *The Knack* stands out as a provocative feminist statement.

—Elizabeth Swain

THE LITTLE FOXES
by Lillian Hellman.

First Publication: 1939.
First Production: 1939.

It is 1900 and the "small town in the South" where Lillian Hellman sets *The Little Foxes* is on the brink of an unsettling future. The agrarian community is poised for the coming of industrialization. Ben Hubbard is about to realize his dream, "to bring the machine to the cotton, and not the cotton to the machine". To make this possible, he is forging a partnership with a Chicago enterprise.

Once, what he needed was to woo cotton and land. In those days, Ben and his brother Oscar were conniving shopkeepers; their own sister, Regina, threatening them with a lawsuit in front of a jury, is certain that "you couldn't find twelve men in the State you haven't cheated". Like Faulkner's Snopeses, these brothers benefited from the war between the states. They were eager to fill in the power vacuum when the aristocratic cotton barons answered the honor call to battle. Oscar married one of the baron's daughter's, Birdie and she gives birth to Leo, the crassest member of their clan. When the mother in Tennessee Williams's *Glass Menagerie* warns her daughter not to turn into one of those "little birdlike women without any nest", she is sure that marriage would protect a woman from the degradation of dependency. But Hellman depicts marriage as more terrifying than any condition of mere homelessness. All that is left for Birdie is to retreat into alcohol, music, and memories of Lionnet (where she grew up). Her romanticized vision of her childhood Eden acknowledges none of the horrors of a slave plantation: "We were good to our people . . . Poppa used to say that *nobody* had ever lost their temper at Lionnet, and *nobody* ever would. Poppa would never let anybody be nasty spoken, or mean". Yet one cannot even accept the veracity of her version of Southern pastoral.

Regina married Horace, a righteous banker who is not cut out for the predatory capitalism that his wife's voracious appetite for power demands. Banished from his wife's bed for a decade, he has been overwhelmed by the onslaught of the new age, and his heart is giving out. He cannot survive in a Hubbard world. All they need him for is to supply the financial backing for their new venture. But he is unwilling to come across, unwilling to be a partner to their factories because he envisions their starvation wages setting mountain Whites and town Blacks at each other's throats. First the brothers scheme to steal his bonds; then his wife stares icily ahead as he suffers a fatal collapse behind her back. It is the play's most chilling *coup de théâtre*. The decent man thought he could block the feral instincts of his wife to acquire great wealth at any human cost. He clearly under-estimated her. Unaided, he struggles to save himself. All he can occupy is a tenuous moment in the present; and then he is not allowed to have even that moment.

Regina lives for the future. Thwarted as a girl—Hellman depicts her frustration at not getting what she wants in *Another Part of the Forest*—she is now fixed in her determination: "I'm going to Chicago. And when I'm settled there and know the right things to buy—because I certainly don't know now—I shall go to *Paris* and buy them". She plays her game with complete ruthlessness. The reputation of Tallulah Bankhead's portrayal of Regina since the play's first production cannot be measured, but Bette Davis's performance in the 1941 William Wyler film is indelible. Davis's great moments, such as the chilling immobility of Regina's ice-maiden death-watch, are stage images demanded by the original script.

Alexandra, Horace and Regina's daughter, finds that she cannot continue both to adore her father and respect her mother. The play is one long awakening of her independence from the grasping single-mindedness of Regina. Her father instinctively knows that Alexandra will need someone when he is gone, and he is sure that person should be Addie, the African-American servant. Addie is given great moral weight when Hellman has her deliver the words that delineate the ethical center of the play: "Well, there are people who eat the earth and eat all the people on it like in the Bible with the locusts. Then, there are people who stand around and watch them eat it. (*Softly.*) Sometimes I think it ain't right to stand and watch them do it". In the end, Alexandra pledges to stand against the Uncle Bens of American capitalism. (Uncle Ben is also the name Arthur Miller goes on to use in *Death of a Salesman*; perhaps both he and Hellman are paying sly homage to the American prophet of enterprise, Benjamin Franklin.) When Alexandra makes her vow, she acknowledges that it is from Addie that she heard about those who "ate the earth": "Well, tell him for me, Mama, I'm not going to stand around and watch you do it. Tell him I'll be fighting as hard as he'll be fighting (*Rises* . . .) some place where people don't just stand around and watch". Horace proved to be ineffective at stopping the Hubbard clan. But by the end of the play, an alliance of strength against their greed has been formed between the Shavian young woman whose eyes have been opened and the alert mammy. Uncle Oscar had already been made uneasy by Addie's penetrating gaze: "You do a lot of judging around here, Addie, eh? Judging of your white folks, I mean". Though the play abandons the genteel lady, Birdie, as a captive, the young white woman and the mature black woman get out.

Earlier, before the final breaking away, the fine-souled but passive characters of the play have the house to themselves one rainy afternoon; they have a brief respite, elderberry wine and cakes with not a Hubbard in earshot. For once Birdie, Addie, and Horace can speak freely; Alexandra is taught to beware the model of her soft-spoken abused aunt. Alexandra's restlessness finds voice: "We sit around and try to pretend nothing's happened . . . We make believe we are just by ourselves". In the winter of 1939, America had not yet entered World War II, and Hellman was alerting her isolationist audience to the dangers of their stance. *Little Foxes* opened on 15 February 1939; Germany did not invade Poland until 1 September of that year. In Hellman's final act, Uncle Ben vividly clarifies the threat of what he represents:

"The century's turning, the world is open. Open for people like you and me. Ready for us, waiting for us. After all, this is just the beginning. There are hundreds of Hubbards sitting in rooms like this throughout the country. All their names aren't Hubbard, but they are all Hubbards and they will own this country someday. We'll get along."

Surely, he is speaking at least as much about the situation of fascism in 1939 as he is about the situation of capitalism in 1900. Yet Hellman's use of economics (like Ibsen's use of genetics) can be problematic. Horace recoils from the motivations of his wife's family to bring cotton mills to the South; he demands to know, is it only "to pound the bones of this town to make dividends for you to spend? You wreck the town, you and your brothers, *you* wreck the town and live on it". Whereas the Northern partner, Marshall, is indifferent to their motivations: "You want the mill here, and I want it here. It isn't my business to find out *why* you want it". Presumably, Hellman expects her audience to retreat from Marshall's commercial amorality and, instead, embrace Horace's outrage. But the depressed South desperately needed those jobs, and the audience today cannot wholeheartedly reject the opportunity to put men and women back to work. Nonetheless, Hellman's *mythos* of greed survives with glinting menace, just as melodrama itself has survived a century of pejorative connotation. *Little Foxes* provided inspiration for two forms highly adaptive to the melodramatic impulse—not only one of the best Hollywood movies, but also one of the only viable American operas, Marc Blitzstein's all-too-rarely heard *Regina*. *Little Foxes* deserves to regain its place on the stage.

—Roger Sorkin

MASTERPIECES
by Sarah Daniels.

First Publication: 1984.
First Production: 1983.

Masterpieces is, deservedly, a classic of feminist theatre. This issue play deals honestly and bravely with one of the most controversial subjects of our time: pornography, and does so with considerable style. Like Sarah Daniels' later play *Neaptide*, *Masterpieces* presents strong female characters at odds with male-dominated society. The play focuses on the representation of women, asking audiences to take a good look at the way women are viewed in society, using pornography as an example of the much larger cultural problem of the objectification of women.

The play is set in London. The events take place over a period of twelve months, in 1982 and 1983, though the scenes can be updated by inclusion of contemporary examples of news stories; Daniels has indicated the places where such updating would be appropriate in the text. The scenes shift back and forth in time, some before and some after the central event: the death of of a man, following his approach to the central character of the play, Rowena.

During the play Rowena is exposed to pornographic magazines for the first time and gradually becomes aware of the violence and degradation to which many women are routinely subjected. While she had never seen herself as a feminist, she is shocked by what she learns of the pornography industry, particularly after she watches a snuff film (in which women are mutilated and killed on camera. When Rowena leaves the cinema, she waits at a tube platform and is accosted by a man, whom she first ignores. When he accosts her again, she pushes him away. He falls on the tracks and is killed by an oncoming train. Rowena stands accused of murder. There is no doubt that Rowena will be found guilty, despite the circumstances. The tension of the play does not therefore revolve around the question of Rowena's fate but rather around the consciousness-raising which develops for all the female characters in the course of the play, and around the heated debate which the play tends to inspire in its audience.

The play opens with all the central characters gathered around a table for dinner in a restaurant: a decidedly public space, where the most private subjects are discussed. The scene, like the play as a whole, is very well crafted: comedy is interwoven with the most serious of points, as each couple interrupts and comments on themselves and each other. Sexist jokes are told, and one of the women, Yvonne, is angered. Then the subject of pornography is raised, and Yvonne—the feminist of the group—lets the others know what she thinks, to everyone's dismay. At the end of this opening scene, Yvonne speaks directly to the audience in the first of a series of interior monologues which enable Daniels to communicate views directly to the audience. Yvonne talks about herself and her perception of having been stereotyped as a "serious feminist". This monologue invites sympathy from the audience, particularly when she reveals: ". . . I was twenty-six before I learnt that the words 'I think' and 'I feel' were neither synonymous nor interchangeable . . . and there's no way I read that in any book". Here, Yvonne shows herself to be the most clear-headed of the characters in that opening scene: her viewpoint is the one which the other female characters come around to in time.

In the next scene, Rowena stands accused of murder. Asked how she pleads, she replies "neither", she sees herself as neither guilty nor not guilty; the terms are not adequate to express the complexity of the situation, nor is she confident that the court will be interested in that complexity. She knows she is doomed. The action does not dwell on the court room, but rather flashes back and forth, focusing on the relationship between Rowena and three women: her mother Jennifer, her friend Yvonne, and one of her clients, Hilary. All these women are represented alongside men: Rowena's husband Trevor, Jennifer's husband Clive, and Yvonne's husband Ron (who is also significant in Hilary's life, when he employs her as a secretary and then takes advantage of his position to rape her).

The doubling of characters is very well judged. Yvonne and Hilary are played by the same actress, so that the rape of the latter by the husband of the former takes on a double significance, revealed in the language which Ron uses to refer to all women: he sees them as interchangeable. Another effective device is Daniels' strategy of non-representation of the pornographic images discussed. For instance, when Rowena first looks at the magazines, the stage direction indicates that she holds them so that the images they contain will not be visible to the audience. This is more than a shielding of offensive images from the audience, or an attempt to engage interest by significant omission. This non-representation parallels the major theme of viewing women, expressed by the character Yvonne, who simply states that "it's all to do with the way men are taught to view women". She goes on to explain that she confiscates porn magazines at school, only to be criticised for the waste of money, as they are expensive: a link between exploitation of women and market forces which is reinforced later, when Jennifer reveals that she has angered Clive by soaking a pile of pornographic videos in water; he is angry because they're so expensive to replace.

As Rowena looks at the images, voice-overs are played to the audience. What they can not see they must imagine, but they can hear the voices of the women pictured, who tell their stories of exploitation, degradation, and ill-treatment by the men who "market" them. Here, Daniels literally gives voice to the women who are only pictured as disempowered bodies in the visual images, reminding the theatre audience that such women have stories to tell; that they are people, not objects. Rowena's disgust with the magazines leads her to confront her husband, Trevor, about his familiarity with such images, and Part One ends with a confrontation between them, leaving the audience to ponder their positions on the subject during the interval. Daniels is deliberate and creative in her inclusion of the audience in the debate: this is a play which evokes sympathy and anger and impassioned lines of identification from most who read or watch it.

Part Two opens with the same two actors on stage, but this time the male actor plays a psychiatrist, analysing Rowena and making assumptions about her character based on her style of dress. Here again, the doubling of characters is effective, for those in the audience who might have identified with Trevor as an individual are encouraged to re-view their positions when he is paralleled to the voice of patriarchal authority of the psychiatrist in the next scene. Throughout Part Two, the three women (Rowena, Jennifer, and Yvonne) find that they have more in common than they first thought, while the men become more and more marginal to the action. The women plan a holiday together, in a show of solidarity and affection which contrasts powerfully with the following "scene of the murder" which leads Rowena away from any hope of such a happy ending.

The judge in the trial scene is played by the actress who plays Jennifer, as is the policewoman who waits with Rowena for the verdict. The play ends before the verdict is announced, though all know what it will be. The policewoman asks Rowena about the snuff film, which is described in gory detail. Rowena ends her account with a statement which brings the play to a natural conclusion, bringing the action and imagery full circle, back to the opening dinner party scene, when the connections were first made between sex, violence, pornography, and misogynist jokes.

Masterpieces has generated considerable debate from audience and critics since its first production. Daniels has replied to some of the criticism in retrospect, explaining that the characters are not as finely drawn as she would like, because she saw the piece as "uanashamedly an issue-based play".

Now hailed as a feminist classic, *Masterpieces* arouses anger and irritation from many men, who see themselves implicated in the unpleasant and menacing male characters on stage. But to criticize the play for its representation of men is to miss the point. This is a play about women, and about men's views of women, and women's understanding of men's views of them. While it is a play about women, however, its message is—or should be—equally powerful for men. It is a play which sparks healthy debate and which should be performed again and again, for each new generation of women and men.

—Lizbeth Goodman

MY SISTER IN THIS HOUSE
by Wendy Kesselman.

First Publication: 1982.
First Production: 1981; revised version, 1987.

In the French town of Le Mans in 1933, two sisters, both domestic servants, were found guilty of the brutal murder of the two women they had served for for years. The case provided the inspiration and essential ingredients not only for Jean Genet's modern classic *The Maids*, but also for Wendy Kesselman's *My Sister in This House*.

In the 15 short scenes of Kesselman's play, just four characters, all female, appear on stage—the sisters and their employers Mme. Danzard and her daughter Isabelle. At the opening of the play, Christine, an experienced domestic, is aged 20, and her sister Lea, new to the world of service, is 15. They have grown up in the same local convent, and now Lea longs to be reunited with her sister. By the second scene this hope has become reality, as the sisters settle into the small room at the top of the Danzard house they have elected to share. The subsequent scenes, almost all set within the house, explore impressionistically the development of these four characters' relations with each other over a span of several years.

Accumulated tensions erupt fatally in the penultimate scene, when a verbal battle—ostensibly over a broken glass and a burnt blouse, but more fundamentally about deeply rooted frustrations and aspirations—explodes into the murderous acts committed by the sisters. The final scene has the offstage voices of the judge and the medical examiner describe, in gory detail, the specifics of the crime, and deliver judgements of death on Christine and long imprisonment on Lea. The play closes with Lea, in a reversal of roles with her sister, singing "*brokenly*" the same lyric Christine attempted to comfort her with at the start of the play ("Sleep my little sister, sleep/ Sleep through darkness . . .") while Christine cries out not to be separated from Lea. Ironically, the desire to be together in the same house has led to diverging fates being imposed upon them.

Kesselman keeps more closely to the known facts of this case than Genet did, but she uses the situation as a springboard for a sharply focused psychological and social study, conveyed in a carefully plotted style of heightened realism which gives the smallest of gestures, the most casual of words, a telling significance. There is nothing that is gratuitous, so that her deft touch evokes a subtext rich in psychological and social detail.

The play emphasizes the defining social contexts of its characters, the most obvious and significant element being class. Lea's first speech enthuses over the wonders of the middle-class lifestyle she has encountered in service ("duck with cherries", "chicken with champagne", her former mistress with her "skin like milk" who can play the piano), a world away from her own subsistent existence. In the next scene we enter the world of the Danzard household as the lights come up on a two-level setting: the comfortable sitting room/dining room downstairs, and the "*shabby, small*", unheated servants-room above, an ever-present visual reminder of social divisions.

Mme. Danzard and Isabelle soon reveal themselves to be overly self-conscious claimants to the status of *haute bourgeoisie*. But their claim is beset with contradictions. They, and especially Mme. Danzard, are constantly (and often comically) concerned with outward appearance, leading them to strained and often absurd gestures of social one-upmanship, as when Mme. Danzard scorns the idea of giving more money to the local convent until she wonders "how much the Blanchards are giving". Yet the efforts put into affirming a sense of status merely betray its hollowness. At dinner, Isabelle *"stuffs potatoes into her mouth"* while Mme. Danzard cleans her teeth loudly with her tongue; they wear hats that are *"particularly provincial"* and *"drab mauve dress"*; Isabelle plays the piano loudly but badly, and *"hums off key to the music"*. The play reveals the Danzards as inherently vulgar, and incapable of any useful or truly fulfilling activity.

Mme. Danzard, it appears, is widowed, while there are constant references to Isabelle's eligibility for marriage (although concrete signs of any movement in that direction are lacking). The implication is that the social conventions of the day demand that they, as middle-class women without men, largely confine themselves to the house, except for church and shopping. They are presented as frustrated hostesses with nothing to host. The essential failure of their lives is vital to understanding the play, for, their attention turns inwards: if the world outside remains unconquerable, then self-definition must be achieved by rigidly defining superiority over servants.

Economic and familial circumstances define the sisters' situation. They hope to save enough to free themselves of service, but the sparseness of their material possessions, the uncomfortableness of their small room, and their faded dresses are all testaments to the difficulty of achieving their dreams. Yet, ironically Kesselman portrays them, and especially Christine, as possessing manners, tastes, and abilities superior to their employers: Christine can crochet beautifully, and has a trunk full of delicate lace, and their work in the house is evidence of their practical ability and application. These qualities, together with their increasing appropriation of a more comfortable, freer lifestyle (they begin to dress more elegantly, and have their picture taken just as the Danzards did—but they do everything with greater taste than the Danzards can muster) challenge the subservient invisibility demanded of the servant class, and therefore challenge the Danzards' sense of their own identity.

Although the social dimension alone contains the potential for eventual conflict, the play does not present an inexorable movement towards an act of class war, for there are potent psychological and sexual forces which create alternative, if temporary, sympathies, alliances, and divisions, before they too contribute to the eventual calamity. In the early stages of the sisters employment, Kesselman juxtaposes the Danzards talking about their new servants with the sisters talking about their new employers, to reveal that Mme. Danzard and Christine share an almost identical conception of the mistress-servant relationship, and each expresses her happiness with the other. Mme. Danzard's praise of Christine's abilities contrasts, however, with Isabelle's evident inabilities (and an Isabelle/Christine parallel is emphasised by the fact they are the same age) to create an embryonic empathy between the ineffectual Isabelle and the somewhat clumsy Lea.

The twists and turns in the four characters relationships are then charted largely in indirect terms. This is partly because the Danzard's requirements for the sisters to be "invisible" means that the audience witnesses no actual verbal exchange among all four characters until the scene of the actual murders. It can also be seen in the Kesselman's careful use of simultaneous conversation and action to create striking counterpoints, and in her precise directions for stage choreography—several scenes are entirely non-verbal, and map out the obsessions and fears of the characters in physical manouevres.

Mme. Danzard's feelings towards her daughter are apparently more motivated by possessiveness and competition than love. When Mme. Danzard speaks of Isabelle's marriage prospects, which would leave Mme. Danzard alone in the house, she is keen to stress that Isabelle has "all the time in the world". Christine's attitude to Lea, although considerably more loving, smacks of the surrogate-mother, with indications of a similar possessiveness. When seen alone, Isabelle enacts little fantasies of a Parisian social life she can only dream of, while Lea is haunted by her own mightmare of claustrophobia: both sense a need for escape. Once Kesselman has suggested the Mme.Danzard/Christine and Isabelle/Lea parallels, and has engineered the competitiveness between mother-figures and daughter-figures, silent battles of will and dominance are enacted tangentially.

The threat to the sister's relationship represented by Isabelle rises to the surface in Scene 12. During a dress fitting for Isabelle, Mme. Danzard's barbed comments about the pleasures of marriage which "some people will never know" strikes at the core of Christine's fears. Later, alone with Lea, she emotionally voices her terror at being abandoned by Lea should Isabelle actually get married and leave. The suggestion of a growing sexual quality to the sisters relationship has been hinted at previously, and its consummation is finally confirmed in the next scene, in which they let down their hair in an act of sensual liberation, and Christine *pulls Lea down to her*. The uncertainty, fear, and strategic manouevering of previous scenes has given way, for the sisters, to a full realization of their love for one another, a love which the play articulates as a positive cathartic release and a genuine fulfilment.

If this point in the play is the pinnacle of the sisters' mutual fulfilment, then it also represents the more-or-less complete undermining of the Danzards. With Mme. Danzard's and Isabelle's battle with each other no longer able to be fought through manipulation of the servants, they position themselves against the servants, especially since apparent acts of rebellion become more noticeable—Lea's wearing of a pink sweater instead of her uniform, the failure of the sisters to hide their own pleasure in each other's company, their increased freedom about town. The sisters' increased security and confident self-sufficiency denies the invisibility and asceticism required of them. But clarification of the relations in the household, tragically, means that all the obstacles in the way of war between the two sides are removed.

This play has been cited as a prominent example of modern feminist playwriting. Yet, this point *is* debatable. Certainly, there are strong suggestions that the situation we see is determined by the norms of a male-dominated society. The use of the offstage male voices for the photographer, the judge, and the medical examiner suggests that the recorders and arbiters of history tend to be male. Yet the very shadowiness of these offstage figures, and the

absence of references to the male world outside the intense hothouse atmosphere the women inhabit, allows insufficient evidence from *within the play
itself* to draw conclusions about the wider social environment. Similarly, the
sisters' relationship has been viewed as almost entirely positive. Yet this would
be to miss the dark ironies that emerge. Ultimately, through the murders, they
destroy all hope of remaining together. And their sexual relationship must be
viewed in its context. While it does represent a genuinely loving relationship,
all they have known are all-female environments of confinement (the convent
and servants' quarters), and in this sense the play suggests that their form of
sexual expression has little alternative, that they have accepted the narrowness
of their world.

Kesselman's dramatic patterning is almost musical in its use of theatrical
motifs. Not only does she carefully create overlapping conversations and
reiterate certain visual images, but objects assume the status of symbols, their
connotations changing as the play progresses. Lea's crocheted blanket is
initially a metaphor for her dependence on the maternal bond; later she
unravels it and dances around the room weaving it around herself and
Christine, it becomes a metaphor for the sisterly union. The white glove, which
Mme. Danzard puts on to inspect the surfaces for dust, becomes a symbol of
her artificial bourgeois lifestyle; the sisters emergence, wearing similar white
gloves, yet using them in a natural, elegant manner, indicates their encroachment on the Danzards' social status and their subversion of it. The pewter
pitcher, in which Mme. Danzard keeps her dried flowers, and which is a
metaphor for the sisters' subservience and fear (Lea cries out in fear of the
consequences when she drops it one day) becomes the weapon of rebellion,
which Lea eventually brings crashing down on Isabelle's head. In these and
many other subtle details, Wendy Kesselman shows a mastery of the theatre's
resources—visual, aural, and verbal—to articulate meaning in her finely
crafted chamber piece.

—Mark Hawkins-Dady

'NIGHT, MOTHER
by Marsha Norman.

First Publication: 1983.
First Production: 1982.

Her daughter informs Thelma Cates five minutes into *'Night, Mother* that
Jessie plans to kill herself. Although Mama tries to josh her out of it, tries to
phone Jessie's brother Dawson, tries to argue her to reason, and begs her to
change her mind, nothing works. Right to the end, Jessie maintains her
determination to kill herself, and Mama keeps attempting passionately, but
ineffectually, to stop her. Along the way, Jessie prepares Mama for life alone,
shows her where kitchen supplies and detergent are stored, explains how to
have her favorite candies delivered, and advises her how, after Jessie's death, to

manage the police, the wake, and the food the neighbors will bring. She has thought of everything, has dry-cleaned the dress her mother should wear to the funeral, and now even rehearses Thelma in washing a pan until somebody arrives. Jessie also elicits from Mama the answers to her unanswered questions: Did Mama love Jessie's father? What does Jessie look like during her epileptic seizures—which Mama still refers to as "fits"? Mama, in turn, supplies unexpected news: Jessie's ex-husband cheated on her, and Jessie's epilepsy began years earlier than she has always thought.

After begging "Don't leave me, Jessie", Thelma's goal moves from saving Jessie to protecting herself—from guilt, from abandonment, from others' curiosity, from a lonely old age, from the disruption of a life she's ordered just the way she likes it. Thelma's survival after Jessie's death concerns them both in the daughter's final minutes. Jessie instructs Mama in how to deal with questions about motives; Thelma must ascribe the suicide to "something personal". By this time, Mama has run out of roadblocks to erect in front of a daughter rapidly approaching the moment when she will whisper "'night, Mother" and lock herself in her room. We know, of course, that a gunshot will quickly follow, and we dread that moment, even as we anticipate it. For, make no mistake, the play's tragic conclusion must arrive.

'Night, Mother could not be labeled melodrama. Norman provides no ranting and raving, no soap-opera accidents, no possibility of reprieve from the inexorable sweep towards Jessie's inevitable death. The 90-minutes run without intermission, which prevents anything from interfering with the cumulative tensions, from diluting the potent pity and fear which Jessie's final minutes alive generate in those of us who remain behind after she has pulled the trigger. We experience mounting suspense and dread and then, with Mama, heartbreak.

Norman's exceptionally linear plot construction contains two simultaneous actions: Jessie tries to prepare her mother for the daughter's suicide, and Mama tries to dissuade her or prevent it. This amounts to the irresistible force meeting the immovable object. Yet Mama's efforts also lead to both achieving some measure of understanding how Jessie arrived at the point where she would rather get off the bus than continue on the aimless ride which in the end would only drop her at the same destination—death.

Marsha Norman wrote 'Night, Mother to try to understand how someone could decide to take her own life. She selected as her protagonist a woman who chooses suicide as the logical step. "You're not even upset!" exclaims Mama, for Jessie does not feign ending her life as a disguised cry for help. Nor does she suddenly despair and impulsively grab a gun, aim it at her head, and pull the trigger. In her past, she has not even manifested self-destructive tendencies. Far from indicating she's out of touch with reality or has had a bad day, Jessie makes an existential choice—the exercise of her free will—from which she never waivers. She has examined her options, made a considered choice of what appeals to her most, and engaged in careful preparations, which conclude with her attempt to explain her decision to her horrified mother—and to us, the spectators.

By dramatizing an hour and a half of intense crisis and conflict, leavened by bursts of wry humor, Norman thrusts us inside the souls of both Jessie and

Thelma. We care for them, and we also come to align ourselves with both women, simultaneously. We accept that ending her life will please Jessie most and eventually we regard her position as not unreasonable. Yet even as we comprehend her motives we join traumatized Mama in aching to stop her daughter. Mama experiences the greater ordeal because nothing has prepared her for this, for the struggle to prevent her daughter's death, and also for its aftermath. By comparison, Jessie benefits from her conviction, her certainty that she has selected the proper course and soon will achieve peace. But *'Night, Mother* dramatizes, not only Jessie's will to die, but the efforts she makes to tutor her mother in survival.

Norman has not created eccentric oddballs such as Beth Henley might have imagined. Norman's Jessie and Thelma represent the ordinary "simple people" whose lives generally go unchronicled. Norman speaks for them. As she does so, she demonstrates an extraordinary ear for language, not highfalutin dialogue, but precisely the right words to convey what the characters would say—their mood, class, circumstances, gender, relationship—everything, in short, which makes them themselves. The spare, uncluttered and natural conversations move us readily to tears and laughter.

We respond to the women's experience so intensely in part because Norman has chosen a dramatic style so representational as to be termed naturalistic. The two women inhabit a fully realized living room and kitchen, with the menacing door to the room where Jessie plans to die clearly visible. We observe a slice of life—on a day which concludes that life—and it appears unusually real, as though we really were voyeurs at the actual event, peering through the fourth wall removed.

As we watch, we come to appreciate how the past has led these women to this moment. We can appreciate that Jessie doesn't enjoy life and has relinquished hope it will improve. Why should she stick around? Her mother can only try to tantalize her with suggestions they rearrange the furniture or go buy groceries at the A&P. When Jessie argues that the "self" she has hoped to become will never "show up, so there's no reason to stay," we can't refute her any more persuasively than Mama can.

Of course Mama must try, not just because any mother would, but because she has spent all Jessie's life controlling her daughter and expects she can do so now. One of the reasons Jessie has never before taken control of her life surely involves the fact Mama has never let her, but instead has always determined who Jessie has been, was, and would be—non-epileptic, even though Mama knew better, a wife to the man Mama chose for her, and eventually a comfort to Mama in her old age. Norman's astute psychological perceptions of this mother/daughter relationship lead the playwright to ascribe to Thelma the thought that Jessie belongs to her, "I thought you were mine", shorthand for the belief she has the right to meddle, manipulate, possess, and control her. When Mama insists she "won't let" Jessie take her life, however, Jessie reminds her "It's not up to you." She firmly insists her life belongs to her, not to Thelma. For *'Night, Mother* dramatizes Jessie taking control of her life by ending it. She has decided to escape prosaic circumstances she can't abide. Having "waited until I felt good enough," she now has marshalled the strength to declare about her life, "it's all I really have that's mine, and I'm going to say what happens to it." With exceptional emotional honesty and power, this modern masterpiece permits Jessie to do just that, and thus to achieve "everybody and everything I ever knew, gone."

—Tish Dace

QUEEN CHRISTINA
by Pam Gems.

First Publication: 1982.
First Production: 1977.

Like several of Pam Gems' other plays, *Queen Christina* opens with a visual trick, designed to destabilize standard ways of seeing things by playing off the audience's expectations. Accurate historical costumes and deliberate parallels with the build-up to the entry of Greta Garbo in the classic 1933 black-and-white film, foster anticipations of an ethereal and sentimentalized Queen. Her arrival from hunting is announced; and an elegantly dressed blond beauty sweeps onto the stage, followed by a mud-spattered, slouching, masculine figure in groom's clothing. Just like the impatient royal suitor, waiting for a first sight of his future wife, spectators automatically take the wrong one for the Queen. But the comic situation of mistaken identity has a serious, indeed tragic point: the incongruity of conventional gender stereotypes, which becomes the main focus of the first part of the play.

Reared as a man to fit the (male) role of ruler, Christina has taken the masculine ethos to the point of not only despising women, but even bedding young girls—her current love being Ebba, the beautiful lady-in-waiting. Yet now she is on the throne political stability requires her, as Queen, to produce an heir; and she is unable to adopt the female attitudes necessary to attract a husband. Scenes show her ordering military strategy and deciding state policy, as well as debating on equal terms with Descartes, the leading philosopher of the age. However, the eligible men who have been conditioned to see women as submissive sex-objects are repelled by her intellectual superiority as much as by her muscular strength and her plainness (which is accentuated by a minor physical deformity). The arranged marriage with the Prince of the opening scene falls through; and when she picks a handsome courtier, Christina discovers his sole motive for tolerating her is ambition. He prefers the conventionally feminine Ebba, whom he seduces. So, devastated through the rejection by her lovers of both sexes, Christina abdicates rather than demean herself by marrying, realizing that any man would be interested only in the crown.

The second half of the play shows Christina searching Europe for a different form of society in which she will be free from the stereotypes that had trapped her. In France a group of 18th-century "blue-stockings", proto-feminist intellectuals campaigning for sexual liberation and the right to abortion, hail her as their "inspiration". In Rome she is welcomed by the Pope when she seeks spiritual fulfilment as an alternative to sexuality. Offered the kingdom of Naples, she attempts—as a women—to take up a purely masculine role as a general leading an army to seize the crown. But each of these contrasting possibilities is revealed as a life-denying distortion. The feminists have simply reversed the standard pattern of male domination, while the celibacy praised by the Catholic Church is an unnatural denial of the body, and the logic of taking a man's place forces her to act against her personal interests in ordering the execution of her lover when he betrays her army. In the last scene, having retreated from the world to a hospital, she gains a radically different view of what it means to be female, based on maternal instinct.

This wide-ranging epic play, first produced by the Royal Shakespeare Company, marked Gems' emergence as a major playwright outside the bounds of the alternative women's theatre groups where her earlier work had been staged. Its large cast and historical setting provide a context for the discussion of significant philosophical issues. The action is framed by "the new scepticism" of the 18th-century, fuelled by Galileo's astronomy and Descartes' rationalism, which has overturned all traditional assumptions. This is seen as paralleling the conditions of modern life: and the analogy is clear between Queen Christina's identity crisis and the predicament of contemporary women puzzled by the mixed signals of today's culture. The stereotypes embodied in the Swedish scenes reflect the romantic novels, women's magazines and advertising, that all promote artificially constructed images of conventional femininity. The alternative avenues Gems' protagonist explores encapsulate different aspects of the new radical feminism and sexual revolution. Both extremes are rejected, in line with Gems' rejection of polemicism. Indeed, her view that drama can only influence society indirectly, and should therefore be "subversive", becomes a way of defining a specifically female approach, being echoed by the conclusion Christina draws from her experience. "Must it always be the sword? By God, half the world are women . . . they've learned subversion . . . why not try that?"

Queen Christina is didactic in structure, with the scenes organized to demonstrate a series of points that revolve around a central theme: gender roles and sexual identity. But the message is nowhere overt. Filtered through the experience of a relatively well-known historical protagonist, the play's statement is communicated by the way her personality and beliefs develop with each encounter. At the same time, it openly challenges the audience's socially-conditioned perceptions. Though reaching out to a broad general public, the play stands as a major contribution to the dominant trend of feminist drama in the 1970s: the reappropriation of history, previously presented solely from a male viewpoint. It is literally "her story". As Gems has asserted in the afterword to one of her other plays, "We have our own history to create, to write". And this play tackles the problem head-on in dramatizing the well-documented career of a woman whose anomalous position not only highlighted the issue, but had been given a highly sentimentalized—and stereotyped—interpretation in the Garbo film.

—Christopher Innes

A RAISIN IN THE SUN
by Lorraine Hansberry.

First Publication: 1959.
First Production: 1959.

Lorraine Hansberry was 28 when *A Raisin in the Sun* opened at the Ethel Barrymore Theatre in 1959. She was the first black woman to have her work produced on Broadway, and Lloyd Richards, the director, was the first black man to direct a play for the Broadway stage. The play won the New York Critics' Circle award, and Hansberry also became the first black writer and the first woman to receive that prize.

The title of the play, a line from Langston Hughes's poem "Dream Deferred", refers to both the subject and plot of the drama: the Younger family, trapped in poverty and overcrowded housing conditions, await the arrival of an insurance policy cheque for $10,000, following the death of the father. Act I deals with the family's situation and attitudes towards their condition and in a series of confrontations, members of the family reveal their different dreams in relation to the insurance cheque. The central tensions between Mama's dream and that of her son Walter, provide the axis and ultimately the action of the play. Walter proposes investing the money in a liquor-store business, which he believes to be the only way to break the cycle of servitude and poverty in which the family is trapped. His dream offers the potential to regain his pride and dignity, which has been eroded by his work as a chauffeur for a white man: "I open and close car doors all day long. I drive a man around in his limousine and I say, 'Yes, sir; no, sir; very good, sir; shall I take the Drive, sir?' Mama, that ain't no kind of job . . . that ain't nothing at all".

Mama begins to fulfil her dream in Act II when she announces that she has put a payment down on a house for the family, a place where she hopes the three generations of Youngers can thrive. The house is located in a white suburb, and this adds fuel to Walter's bitterness as his hope of opening a store fades. He articulates his anger in terms of his dream: "So you butchered up a dream of mine—you—who always talking 'bout your children's dreams". Fearful that his bitterness will destroy him, Mama entrusts the remainder of the $10,000 to Walter. Walter is duped by a friend who, instead of using the money to open the liquor store, steals it and disappears.

In Act III Walter, diminished and beaten as much by his failure of judgement as by the loss of the money, proposes to accept a lucrative bribe offered by a white man in an effort to keep the Youngers out of the white suburb where Mama has chosen their house. Walter plays out for the horrified family the full portrait of his humiliation, which is couched in terms of the social degradation to which black Americans are subjected and the roles which Whites expect them to play. Finally, Walter finds the strength and pride to reject the bribe, and the play ends with the Youngers moving out of their cramped apartment, on their way to their new home in the suburbs. An earlier draft of the play ended with the Youngers in their new home, preparing to face racial attack and, for some, the absence of a clear recognition of this future confrontation within the final draft of the play undermines the note of hope on which *A Raisin in the Sun* ends.

Interest in the play, at the time of its first performance, was undoubtedly fuelled by the unusual experience, for a Broadway audience, of watching a play in which all but one character was black. Furthermore, the tone of the play was not didactic. Its values were familiar, even if its characters and setting were not, and to some extent audiences and critics, both predominantly white, must have felt some relief that the protest implicit in the play was not belligerent. One of the dilemmas confronting black playwrights attempting to gain access to Broadway in 1959, was that their audiences were both the consumers and the object of the black writer's protest, and there is certainly, within the play, an acceptance of some of the myths inherent in the American dream and a lack of critical scrutiny of the values embedded in those aspirations. This led later critics to regard the play as middle-class and assimilationist. Opinions continue to differ as to whether it is a play of social protest or a soap opera. But, in 1959, the central tenet of the Civil Rights policy was to demand access to such aspirations, rather than to challenge them and, in this sense, *A Raisin in the Sun* is true to its cultural and political environment.

In form, the play is conventionally naturalistic, a three-act play within a single set. Dialogue and action are gently, even humorously, home-spun. The characters, whilst being affectionately drawn, are familiar types, only occasionally rising above the stock. There are, however, some fine moments of realisation and self-confrontation in the play, particularly when the aspirations of individuals encounter the constraints of social reality. The focus of the play centres on the characters' struggle to make choices of value, despite social constraints, and out of those choices to retain integrity. This may place *A Raisin in the Sun* within the tradition of Miller's *Death of a Salesman*, to which Hansberry acknowledged her debt, but the Younger family's search for dignity has a specific and inevitable resonance in relation to the political struggle current in black America in 1959.

—Glendyr Sacks

THE RIVERS OF CHINA
by Alma De Groen.

First Publication: 1988.
First Production: 1987.

The Rivers of China interweaves two complementary narratives. One story is of the last three months of the writer Katherine Mansfield's life. The other, set in Sydney, Australia, in the present time (although presented here as a dystopia dominated by women) concerns a young man who is brought back from the brink of death (probably a suicide attempt), given plastic surgery and, through hypnosis, a new, female mind—that of Katherine Mansfield.

Probably Alma De Groen's most successful play to date, *The Rivers of China* comes close to achieving her often-stated ambition to fuse form and content—

in other words, to have the audience experience directly, through the play's form, the thematic concerns of the play. De Groen proposes a feminist notion that women have no history—or, more accurately, that their history has been suppressed with the result that their concept of themselves is only a reflection of men's concept of women.

In the first narrative, Katherine Mansfield checks into Gurdjieff's Institute for the Harmonious Development of Man at Fontainebleau in the hope that she will be cured of her tuberculosis through his strict regimen of diet and physical and spiritual exercises. At the same time she is looking for enlightenment, or "the Truth", as she puts it. Gurdjieff's philosophy, however, pictures women as existing on a lower plane than men. Men and women have different roles and it is men who have the vocation to create and to undertake physical and spiritual journeys. Lidia, one of Gurdjieff's ostensible disciples (in fact, she confesses to Katherine that she stayed with him only because he could get her out of Russia) explains that, according to him, "for women there must be two people; that for a woman to progress in the work, she must have a man beside her". Katherine is not cured and is ultimately negated by Gurdjieff, her own uniquely feminine aesthetic ignored. This narrative is discontinuous, using flashbacks and extracts from journals and letters. In the end, Katherine records her own death and the two narratives come together.

The second narrative works in an ironic relationship to the first. In the dystopia of this narrative, it is the men who have no history. When the injured Man is brought into the hospital, a young wardsman, Wayne, takes an interest in him. Wayne writes poetry. This is illegal for a man and, in fact, the work of past male authors has been suppressed. Wayne goes around singing Keats' line "Much have I travelled in the realms of gold", thinking it only a piece of graffiti.

The audience, then, is being asked to experience the world as feminist ideology would have us believe women do. In conversation with the Man, Wayne says he can understand the latter wanting to go home. "I can understand that", he says. "I live in a room—and it isn't home. I live on earth—and it isn't home".

But the female doctor charged with looking after the Man uses hypnosis (also illegal in the new society), both to hasten the healing process and to perform an experiment—to change the Man's identity by imbuing him with a female spirit, specifically the character and memory of Katherine Mansfield. The doctor explains to Wayne: "I made him. Or what you think is him. You can give anybody a history that never happened and they'll believe it".

Giving the Man Mansfield's memory, though, also gives him a history. He is able to tell Wayne that what he thinks is graffiti was actually written by a man, John Keats. At the same time, it is the Man who is able to articulate Mansfield's artistic persona. "While I am writing I am engulfed. Possessed. Anyone who comes near me is my enemy. It takes the place of religion for me". However, the doctor finally balks at her experiment—an experiment to create a man "who could be an equal without being a danger". She faces the choice of stripping the Man of his new identity or letting him die. When she asks Wayne, he says "kill him" rather than destroy the identity Wayne has come to revere.

The Rivers of China is a feminist play. But De Groen is a sceptical feminist who does not allow her feminist, ideological explorations to detract from the aesthetic potential of the play, and so the play is, formally and temperamentally, an ironic work: ironic in its wit and scepticism. The new female society is a dystopia, after all. De Groen actually welcomes a society without the extremes either of patriarchy or matriarchy, and makes fun of the suppression of male literature. The play is also ironic in the way it juxtaposes scenes from the two narratives, successfully preventing the audience too readily accepting one version of reality as the "true" one.

Through its formal irony and through its fragmentary structure—its *bricollage*—the play attempts to create a genuinely feminist theatre in which the audience experiences the world through the female sensibility in two ways: firstly, in the sense that it is a history-less, male-constructed, non-identity, and secondly, in the more positive sense, that the world has a whole new potential when perceived through a liberated, female perspective. Katherine Mansfield and her art of the short story are held up by De Groen as exemplifying this ideal.

—Paul McGillick

A TASTE OF HONEY
by Shelagh Delaney.

First Publication: 1959.
First Production: 1958.

The play opens as Helen, a "semi-whore", and her teenage schoolgirl daughter, Josephine, are moving into a shabby flat in a slum area of Manchester. Soon Helen becomes engaged to her latest boyfriend Peter, a "brash car-salesman" who is ten years her junior. Left to fend for herself even before Helen is married, Jo invites her boyfriend Jimmy, a black naval rating, to stay with her over Christmas. The first act closes with Helen departing to get married, leaving Jo alone in the flat. In the second act Jo invites Geoff, a young homosexual art-student who has been thrown out by his landlady, to move in with her. When he discovers that Jo is pregnant and that her boyfriend has returned to sea, Geoff adopts the role of surrogate mother. He is however ejected rudely by Helen who, after Peter has left her for a "bit of crumpet", returns to her daughter's side.

A summary of the plot of *A Taste of Honey* conveys nothing of its contemporary impact and significance. It was written by a 19-year-old working-class girl from Lancashire, directed by Joan Littlewood, and opened at the Theatre Royal, Stratford East, in May 1958. A play written by one woman and directed by another was still a somewhat unusual circumstance even in the "new" British theatre of the 1950s. Although *A Taste of Honey* is basically realistic in approach and accorded with the current fashion for seedy locations and regional settings and accents, in production the fourth wall convention was abandoned and, during the first act, Helen occasionally addressed comments directly to the audience in the manner of a music-hall entertainer. In addition a live jazz-band played during the scene changes.

More significant than these stylistic devices was, however, the fact that the action of the play was seen solely from the viewpoint of women. Untypically for the theatre of the period the male characters are not the focus of the plot but are introduced when necessary to contribute to the play's exploration of the meaning of motherhood, a theme in itself uncharacteristic of a theatre dominated almost exclusively by male concerns. Centering upon this subject, the play constantly questions and re-evaluates social roles and assumptions. In the opening minutes of Act I Helen asserts that children owe a debt to their parents but later, when she is about to leave for a holiday with her boyfriend Peter, she absolves herself from the need to reciprocate by denying ever having "laid claim to being a proper mother". In one way or another each of the play's relationships is linked with motherhood and even Peter, with his one eye and his fondness for older women, is identified with Oedipus. Jo herself is set to become a mother in consequence of the Christmas spent alone with her boyfriend, but her initial response to pregnancy is that she wants to be neither a mother nor even a woman. She realises that, whatever Helen says to the contrary, mothers do have a responsibility for their children's upbringing, and contends that some women are so irresponsible that they should not be allowed to have any children at all. Indeed, underpinning this examination of motherhood is a belief, expressed repeatedly by Jo, in the sanctity of the individual, and a recognition that the role of mother is not one which all women necessarily find natural. In one of the play's characteristic reversals of role assumptions Geoffrey, in fact, proves to be far more supportive to Jo than was her biological mother, Helen.

Delaney's sympathetic portrayal of such social "outsiders" as gays or blacks differed markedly from their normally comic or patronising treatment by the contemporary British theatre. That is not to say however that homosexuality or race are explored in their own right. Indeed it is significant that, although Jo questions Geoff about what he does with other men, no reference is made to his lovers and he is kept away from any sexual activity during the action of the play. Jo's black lover is presented predominantly as a figure of fantasy—Prince Ossini—an escape from loneliness. "It was only a dream I had", Jo later admits to Geoff. Nevertheless, in contrast to the caricatured figure of Peter, both Geoff and Jimmy are presented as sensitive and caring human beings; a fact which, in itself, must be seen as a positive feature uncharacteristic of the period.

The play was well-received by both critics and the public and transferred in February 1959 to Wyndham's Theatre in London's West End. It was acknowledged as an unsentimental, honest, and vital expression of contemporary relationships: Kenneth Tynan applauded it in the Observer for its "smell of living" and called Shelagh Delaney, in retrospect rather prematurely, "a portent". The play offers no explicit message, and the absence of any wider reference to the world outside the flat serves to lead the audience's attention away from ideas and instead focuses it upon the interrelationship between the characters. The play's conclusion, although by no means a resolution of the problematic relationship between Jo and Helen (which one assumes will continue to be dominated by Helen's sexuality and their constant bickering), nevertheless does leave Jo with the understanding and confidence to carry on, and perhaps in time become a better mother than Helen. "For the first time in my life I feel really important", she tells her mother, "I feel as though I could take care of you, too!". The play has moved full circle from the uneasy relationship between the two women, through the ultimately unsatisfactory experiences with men, back to the unsentimental recognition that, however fraught it may occasionally be, there is some comfort in the shared bonds of blood and gender.

—D. Keith Peacock

THREE BIRDS ALIGHTING ON A FIELD
by Timberlake Wertenbaker.

First Publication: 1991.
First Production: 1991.

At the beginning of Timberlake Wertenbaker's play a blank, white canvas is auctioned for over one million pounds and an illuminated billboard with the words ART IS SEXY, ART IS MONEY, ART IS MONEY-SEXY, ART IS MONEY-SEXY-SOCIAL-CLIMBING-FANTASTIC in pink neon lights has a starting price of £30,000. This, however, proves to be the final fling of the booming 1980s art world; Cork Street is in decline and Jeremy, a cynical gallery owner, invites an American expert to help him find a new market. She believes that romantic English landscapes are the answer. Angry-in-exile is Stephen Ryle, a painter who was dropped by Jeremy because his work became unfashionable but who could be the gallery's salvation if he can be persuaded to return to the fold.

Biddy, the central character, is an upper class young woman who went to Benenden and has just embarked on her second marriage to an enormously rich Greek property dealer called Yoyo. He is desperate to enter London society and donates one million pounds to the Royal Opera House. He sees Biddy, in spite of her shyness and self-deprecation, as his entrée to all the right parties and threatens her with divorce unless she acquires an "interior life" that will, he imagines, make them both glamorous and desirable. Biddy is introduced to the rapacious world of Cork Street. She falls in love with Ryle's paintings and visits him in his studio in exile. He suspects that she has been sent by Jeremy. As her passion for art grows so does her self-confidence and her life acquires new meaning. Yoyo dies after a kidney transplant operation and Biddy falls in love with Ryle and goes to see him again. Biddy's portrait is painted by Ryle.

In the first version of the play Wertenbaker drew on the story of Philoctetes, comparing Ryle with the wounded warrior who was dumped on an island by Odysseus and then had to be lured back to take part in the Trojan War. But, however apt the parallel (and even that is dubious), the play couldn't take the sudden appearance of the characters draped in sheets and the scenes were wisely dropped for the later revival.

Although the transforming power of art was also a theme of *Our Country's Good*, *Three Birds Alighting on a Field* with its quick-witted, ebullient satire on 1980s values was something of a surprise and a change of direction for Wertenbaker. Coming out of the same Royal Court stable, it was in many ways a companion piece to Caryl Churchill's satire on the City *Serious Money*. Both plays were directed by Max Stafford-Clark and grew out of workshops in which the actors as well as the playwrights researched the subject matter. Wertenbaker's play covers a seething cross section of artistic and upper class society from the private doctor's clinic where Yoyo is given a Turkish kidney which his Greek body naturally rejects, to the lawn where he and Biddy picnic at Glyndebourne. But most frequently it focuses on Jeremy's Cork Street Gallery. More than any other art form, the visual arts are the playthings of the rich and so thrived in the 1980s. The art world is seen as a paradigm for the 1980s; monetary value is the only value considered worth discussing and presentation is all. A Romanian artist is harangued by Lady Lelouche because he cannot produce adequate slides of his country's works of art that he is in London to try and save: "I couldn't," exclaims Lelouche, "invite the Friends of the Tate to see some torn-out pages of a book." Paintings are always at the mercy of fashion and valued by how much people are prepared to pay for them. When an American couple try to return a painting by a once fashionable artist they discover that it is now worthless.

Fashion is created by the critics and Wertenbaker's most grotesque creation is a contemptuous, opinionated stylemonger who proclaims "the critic these days is the equal of the artist and without the critic to point out significance and deconstruct it, the artist's work is incomplete." That she is totally wrong is illustrated by Biddy's growing confidence as she learns to look for herself and comes to very different conclusions.

Biddy is the character we learn most about from two long and amusing monologues. In a daring move Wertenbaker creates a sympathetic Sloane Ranger who develops from being a figure of fun who watches *Brookside* because it is so exotic, to being a person who believes in the religious value of art and who becomes a companion to Ryle, an angry working class artist in the Lawrentian mode. Together they provide a strong moral contrast to the pseudo, post-modernist dedicated followers of fashion.

It is typical of Wertenbaker's optimism that she provides such an uplifting ending. Along the way, however, she takes in various aspects of 1980s society that jostle too uncomfortably together in one evening: the sale of kidneys from live donors; the collapse of Eastern European communism; the 1980s brand of feminism; homelessness; sponsorship; and English xenophobia. Had she pared down the themes and gone deeper she would have had a more substantial play; but as a witty and accurate examination of 1980s values it surely has few equals.

—Jane Edwardes

WEDDING BAND;
A Love/Hate Story in Black and White
by Alice Childress.

First Publication: 1974.
First Production: 1966.

Subtitled *A Love/Hate Story in Black and White*, *Wedding Band* is set in South Carolina during the summer of 1918. At the centre of the play is the love affair between a black woman, Julia Augustine, and a white man, Herman. State laws prohibit inter-racial marriages and social codes virtually prohibit any inter-racial relationships; yet the couple have survived ten years together. They imagine the freedom they might achieve by moving to New York City (where such laws do not prevail), but are prevented from leaving first by Herman's sense of familial responsibility to his mother and sister, and then, at the end of the play, by his death from influenza.

Wedding Band is not a typical Childress play, nor has it always been well received. Her choice of an inter-racial relationship makes it unlike her other works, which have only black protagonists, and the relationship itself has provoked censure from both black and white critics. The premiere performance of *Wedding Band* on the New York stage, as well as its later transmission on ABC television, broke a taboo in both media about representing inter-racial relationships, and this gave Childress's text an immediate notoriety. Black critics felt that *Wedding Band* should have concentrated on a black couple or that, at least, Julia should have rejected Herman. As *Wedding Band* demonstrates, however, Childress is more interested in staging the world which so many people experience than in offering an idealized portrayal of positive role models and their successes. White critics of the play felt that Herman should have left South Carolina, that he should have been strong enough to reject the claims of his mother and sister. Both types of criticism neglect Childress's ability to look with compassion at both black and white poor in the context of Julia and Herman's culturally unacceptable love. The play suggests the possibility, despite immense economic hardship, not only of survival, but of survival in loving relationships. With the death of Herman, however, it is evident that while the characters are, for the most part, survivors, they are always and especially vulnerable.

The play's opening set indicates the naturalism of Childress's dramatic method. The scene is three houses in a backyard, and Julia is the new tenant in the middle house. In this setting, we see the problems which dominate the everyday actions of working-class blacks and the pressures these place on familial and community relations. As well as being physically situated in the middle, Julia is also in the middle culturally. While she cannot even be acknowledged by her lover's racial group, she is also distanced from fellow blacks by that alliance. Her history is, as she says, one of constant moving in an attempt to avoid the apparently inevitable disapproval.

Through the presentation of the landlady and other tenants, as well as through Julia, Childress demonstrates the economic conditions and cultural values which inform and shape the experience of working-class blacks. Another tenant, Mattie, has an absent husband and her attempts to survive as a single parent are juxtaposed with Julia's economically easier, but socially impossible, situation with Herman. While both Julia and Mattie react to their circumstances with a persistent and determined dignity, events show that to be black and to be a woman is to be doubly disadvantaged. Yet Herman, white and male, is not portrayed as the play's villain.

Herman is trapped by his bakery store which he feels obliged to maintain in order to repay an earlier loan from his mother. While Herman's procrastinations might seem to be the direct cause of Julia's troubles, Childress points out that Herman's endeavours to fulfill class, race, and gender norms leave him as much a victim as Julia. At the end of Act I, Herman falls sick at Julia's home and the tension that having a white man stay in the black neighbourhood provokes is signalled by the act's stark closing line: the landlady makes the social unacceptability and, indeed, the risk of such an action all too apparent in her simple command to Julia: "Get him out of my yard".

In the second act, Herman's mother and sister arrive to take him back and much of the action centres on schemes to move him discreetly out of Julia's home. As the neighbours function as representatives of black, social values, so Herman's mother and sister provide stereotypic white responses. In many ways the intolerance shown to Julia and Herman's relationship by both communities stems from those people's sense of the difficulty in simply surviving, let alone with the extra burden of dealing with the claustrophobia of a society so rigidly divided on grounds of class, race, and gender.

The wedding band of the title that Herman gives to Julia (significantly to wear on a chain around her neck rather than on her finger) in celebration of their ten years "together" signifies survival despite racial prejudice. But what all the characters fight against is economic oppression. The black couple (Mattie and her absent husband), evidently as much "in love" as Julia and Herman, struggle endlessly and painfully like the latter to avoid destruction at the hands of class-determined economics. Moreover, Herman's mother describes her own life as putting up with a man who breathed stale whiskey in her face every night and enduring the birth of seven babies, five stillborn. For Annabelle, Herman's sister, the chance to marry for love depends on Herman's agreement to marry Celestine, his mother's choice.

Although based on a true story and on common circumstance, Julia and Herman's relationship is perhaps less than convincing. Nonetheless for the audience/reader who responds not only to the central couple but to all the characters Childress draws, *Wedding Band* underscores the dependence of everyone's individual happiness on prevailing social and political conditions.

—Susan Bennett

TITLE INDEX

The following list includes the titles of all stage, screen, radio, and television plays cited in the entries. The name in parenthesis directs the reader to the appropriate entry where fuller information is given. Titles appearing in **bold** are subjects of individual essays in the Works section. The date is that of first production or publication. These abbreviations are used:

s screenplay
r radio play
t television play

Abel's Sister (Wertenbaker), 1984
Abingdon Square (Fornés), 1984
Abortive (r Churchill), 1971
Above the Gods (Murdoch), 1986
Abundance (Henley), 1989
Acastos (Murdoch), 1986
Achilles (Sunde), 1991
Acts of Love (Yankowitz), 1973
Adam Was a Gardener (Page), 1991
Adaptation (May), 1969
Advances (Terry), 1980
After Birthday (Gems), 1973
After Dinner Joke (t Churchill), 1978
After Marcuse (t De Groen), 1986
After Nature, Art (Wymark), 1977
After-Life of Arthur Cravan (De Groen), 1973
Afternoon at the Seaside (Christie), 1962
Against the Wind (r Gee), 1988
Agnus Dei (r Page), 1980
Agrippina (Ridler), 1982
Aid Thy Neighbour (Wandor), 1978
AirWaves (t Hollingsworth), 1986
Akhnaton (Christie), 1973
Akhnaton and Nefertiti (Christie), 1979
Alarms (Yankowitz), 1987
All Them Women (Terry), 1974
All Things Nice (MacDonald), 1991
All You Deserve (Horsfield), 1983
Alli Alli Oh (Hollingsworth), 1977
Alli Alli Oh (r Hollingsworth), 1986
Alma Victoria (Hollingsworth), 1990
Am I Blue? (Henley), 1973
Amateur Means Lover (Smith), 1961
Ambiguity 2nd (Krauss), 1985
America Piece (Yankowitz), 1974
America Play (Parks), 1991
American King's English for Queens (Terry), 1978
American Wedding Ritual Monitored/ Transmitted by the Planet Jupiter (r Terry), 1972
Americans (Holden), 1981
Amiable Courtship of Miz Venus and Wild Bill (Gems), 1973
Amtrak (Terry), 1988
Ananse and the Dwarf Brigade (Sutherland), 1971
Anansegoro (Sutherland), 1964
And Baby Makes Seven (Vogel), 1986

And Out Goes You? (Pollock), 1975
And What of the Night? (Fornés), 1989
Anemone Me (s Parks), 1990
Angel Street (s Boland), 1940
Anne of the Thousand Days (s Boland), 1970
Annulla Allen (Mann), 1977
Annulla, An Autobiography (Mann), 1985
Annunciation (Fornés), 1967
Another Part of the Forest (Hellman), 1946
Anowa (Aidoo), 1970
Anti-Clock (s Arden), 1979
Antigone (Wertenbaker), 1992
Antiphon (Barnes), 1958
Anton, Himself (Sunde), 1988
Ants (r Churchill), 1962
Any Woman Can't (Wasserstein), 1973
Appearances (Howe), 1982
Apple in the Eye (Hollingsworth), 1983
Apple in the Eye (r Hollingsworth), 1977
Apple-Brown Betty (Vogel), 1979
Appointment with Death (Christie), 1945
Approaching Simone (Terry), 1970
Approaching Zanzibar (Howe), 1989
Arabian Nights (Boland), 1948
Arbor (Dunbar), 1980
Are You Sitting Comfortably? (Townsend), 1986
Armenian Childhood (Keatley), 1983
Armistice (r Page), 1983
Arrangements (r Horsfield), 1981
Arrow to the Sun (t Yankowitz), 1987
Ars Longa, Vita Brevis (D'Arcy), 1964
Art (Fornés), 1986
Art and Eros (Murdoch), 1980
Art of Dining (Howe), 1979
Arts and Leisure (Miller), 1985
As Husbands Go (Crothers), 1931
As I Was Saying to Mr. Dideron (r Hollingsworth), 1973
Ashes (r Townsend), 1991
Ask for the Moon (Gee), 1986
Asking for It (Renée), 1983
Attempted Rescue on Avenue B (Terry), 1979
Aunt Mary (Gems), 1982
Aurora (Fornés), 1974
Aurora Leigh (Wandor), 1979
Automatic Pilot (Ritter), 1980
Autumn Crocus (Smith), 1931
Autumn Garden (Hellman), 1951

Silk Room (Duffy), 1966
Silver Service (Lochhead), 1984
Silverstein & Co. (Miller), 1972
Singing Door (Lessing), 1973
Singing Ringing Tree (Keatley), 1991
Singles (t De Groen), 1986
Sink Songs (Wandor), 1975
Sinner's Place (Parks), 1984
Sins (t Rayson), 1993
Sirens (Cloud), 1992
Sisters Rosensweig (Wasserstein), 1992
Skag (t Norman), 1980
Skriker (Churchill), 1994
Skywriting (Drexler), 1968
Slaughterhouse Play (Yankowitz), 1971
Sleazing Towards Athens (Terry), 1977
Sleeping Beauty (Lavery), 1992
Sleepwalking (t Hollingsworth), 1986
Slip of a Girl (Chase), 1941
Sloth (t Rayson), 1992
Small Black Lambs Wandering in the Red
    Poppies (Krauss), 1982
Small Piece of Earth (r Lyssiotis), 1990
Smart Women/Brilliant Choices (Wasserstein),
    1988
Smith and Wesson (r Ritter)
Smoked, Choked, and Croaked (Pollock)
Snakes (Lavery), 1977
So Does the Nightingale (r Delaney), 1981
Softcops (Churchill), 1984
Softly, and Consider the Nearness (Drexler),
    1964
Soldier Who Became an Actor (D'Arcy), 1966
Solo, Old Thyme (Duffy), 1970
Solo Voyages (Kennedy), 1985
Song of a Maiden (Sofola), 1977
Song of the Seals (Hewett), 1983
Song of the Seals (s Hewett), 1984
Sore Points (Lavery), 1986
Sorority House (Chase), 1939
Sorrows of Gin (t Wasserstein), 1979
Sound Fields (Terry), 1992
Sound of Sand (r Sunde), 1963
South of the Border (t Pinnock), 1988
Southern Exposure (Akalaitis), 1979
Southwark Originals (Wymark), 1975
Spain/36 (Holden), 1986
Speak Now (Wymark), 1971
Spell #7 (Shange), 1979
Spellbound Jellybaby (Wymark), 1975
Spider's Web (Christie), 1954
Spies of the Air (s Boland), 1939
Spilt Milk (Wandor), 1972
Splendor (s Crothers), 1935
Split Seconds in the Death Of (r Pollock),
    1971
Splits (Ritter), 1978
Sport of My Mad Mother (Jellicoe), 1958
Springtime (Fornés), 1989
Standard Safety (Bovasso), 1974
Star Quality (Bolt), 1980
Starburn (Drexler), 1983

Star-child (Pollock), 1974
Starters (Wymark), 1975
Stay Where You Are (Wymark), 1969
Steaming (Dunn), 1981
Steeltown (Holden), 1984
Stephen (Shearer), 1980
Stick Wife (Cloud), 1987
Still Life (Mann), 1980
Still Life (Yankowitz), 1977
Stone Wedding (Sánchez-Scott), 1989
Stones (r Gee), 1974
Storm (Lessing), 1966
Story of an Hour (t Wandor), 1988
Strike Up the Banns (Wymark), 1988
String (Childress), 1969
String (t Childress), 1979
String Game (Owens), 1965
Strings (t Renée), 1986
Successful Life of Three (Fornés), 1965
Successful Strategies (Wertenbaker), 1983
Such Good Friends (s May), 1971
Sugar and Spice (Lavery), 1979
Sugar and Spite (Evaristi), 1978
Summer Wedding (r Wandor), 1991
Sun (Kennedy), 1969
Super Lover (Bovasso), 1975
Superscum (O'Malley), 1972
Superstition Throu' the Ages (Pollock), 1973
Surreal Landscape (r Hollingsworth), 1986
Susan and God (Crothers), 1937
Susan Peretz at the Manhattan Theatre Club
    (Terry), 1973
Susannah's Dreaming (Hewett), 1981
Susannah's Dreaming (r Hewett), 1980
Swallows (Wandor), 1974
Swan Song of Sir Henry (Vogel), 1974
Sweatproof Boy (De Groen), 1972
Sweet Land of Liberty (r Pollock), 1980
Sweet Nothings (t Lochhead), 1984
Sweet Potatoes (r Owens), 1977
Sweet Trap (Sofola), 1975
Swimming (Howe), 1991

Tabula Rasa (Yankowitz), 1972
Tahinta (Sutherland), 1968
Tale of Two Cities (Kesselman), 1992
Tales from Whitechapel (Wymark), 1972
Tales of the Lost Formicans (Congdon), 1988
Talk Him Down (t Bolt), 1975
Talk of the Devil (O'Malley), 1986
Talking in Tongues (Pinnock), 1991
Tangleflags (Bolt), 1972
Tango Palace (Fornés), 1963
Tartuffe (Lochhead), 1985
Taste of Honey (Delaney), 1958
Taste of Honey (s Delaney), 1961
Tatty Hollow Story (Hewett), 1976
Te Pouaka Karaehe (Renée), 1992
Tea in a China Cup (Reid), 1983
Technicians (Wymark), 1969
Teeth (Howe), 1991